AF699002

Project 5™ Power!: The Comprehensive Guide

Simon Cann

Course Technology PTR
A part of Cengage Learning

COURSE TECHNOLOGY
CENGAGE Learning™

Australia • Brazil • Japan • Korea • Mexico • Singapore • Spain • United Kingdom • United States

COURSE TECHNOLOGY
CENGAGE Learning™

Project5™ Power!: The Comprehensive Guide
Simon Cann

Publisher and General Manager, Course Technology PTR: Stacy L. Hiquet

Associate Director of Marketing: Sarah Panella

Manager of Editorial Services: Heather Talbot

Marketing Manager: Mark Hughes

Acquisitions Editor: Orren Merton

Project Editor/Copy Editor: Cathleen D. Small

Technical Reviewer: Jesse Jost

PTR Editorial Services Coordinator: Erin Johnson

Interior Layout Tech: ICC Macmillan Inc.

Cover Designer: Mike Tanamachi

Indexer: Larry Sweazy

Proofreader: Gene Redding

© 2008 Course Technology, a part of Cengage Learning.

ALL RIGHTS RESERVED. No part of this work covered by the copyright herein may be reproduced, transmitted, stored, or used in any form or by any means graphic, electronic, or mechanical, including but not limited to photocopying, recording, scanning, digitizing, taping, Web distribution, information networks, or information storage and retrieval systems, except as permitted under Section 107 or 108 of the 1976 United States Copyright Act, without the prior written permission of the publisher.

For product information and technology assistance, contact us at
Cengage Learning Customer & Sales Support, 1-800-354-9706

For permission to use material from this text or product, submit all requests online at **cengage.com/permissions**
Further permissions questions can be emailed to
permissionrequest@cengage.com

Project5 is a trademark of Twelve Tone Systems, Inc in the United States and/or other countries. All other trademarks are the property of their respective owners.

Library of Congress Control Number: 2007939368

ISBN-13: 978-1-59863-458-7

ISBN-10: 1-59863-458-5

Course Technology
25 Thomson Place
Boston, MA 02210
USA

Cengage Learning is a leading provider of customized learning solutions with office locations around the globe, including Singapore, the United Kingdom, Australia, Mexico, Brazil, and Japan. Locate your local office at:
international.cengage.com/region

Cengage Learning products are represented in Canada by Nelson Education, Ltd.

For your lifelong learning solutions, visit **courseptr.com**

Visit our corporate website at **cengage.com**

Printed in the United States of America
1 2 3 4 5 6 7 11 10 09 08

Acknowledgments

I would like to thank everyone involved in the production of this book. In particular, I would like to thank Cathleen Small, Orren Merton, and everyone else at Course Technology. In addition, I would like to thank Jesse Jost for his work as technical editor and Gene Redding for the proofreading.

About the Author

Simon Cann is a musician and writer based in London.

He is the author of many books, including *Cakewalk Synthesizers: From Presets to Power User, How to Make a Noise, Building a Successful 21st Century Music Career,* and *Sample This!* (with Klaus P. Rausch). In addition, he regularly works with a number of leading software developers on product development.

You can read more about Simon and his books at www.noisesculpture.com.

Contents

Chapter 2 Setting Up Your Hardware 51

Chapter 6 Using Synthesizers in Project5 191

Chapter 7 Working with Audio FX Units 275

Chapter 8
MIDI FX Units 311

Introduction

Welcome. And thank you for immense good taste in buying this book. I congratulate you further on your eminent common sense in reading it.

Before we get going, let me tell you a bit about the book and how it is laid out. The book is about Project5 from Cakewalk. (Obviously—you can read the cover, and you wouldn't be looking in the book if you didn't know what it was about.) You will see that the book is organized as short tutorials. These are intended to work as bite-sized chunks of information, but when taken as a whole, the book is a comprehensive guide to making music with Project5.

You do not need to read the tutorials in order: The intention is that each tutorial is as freestanding as possible without introducing repetition into the book. However, clearly there will be times when you need to understand a concept before you can build on the foundation. In these instances, I will cross-reference other tutorials. That being said, I recommend you check out Chapter 1 before you move on, because this chapter lays the foundations for the rest of the book.

You will also see that the tutorials don't just cover *how* to use Project5, but they also look at some of the *whys*. In particular, the tutorials aim to highlight some of the reasons why you might want to consider using a possible technique. As you probably know, with Project5 there are often many ways in which the same task can be achieved. Having an understanding of how you can use different techniques will help you to use the right tool at the right time.

The Recording Process

Before we go any further, I want to look at the recording process and the elements of creating music. Once we've got a firm grasp on those, we can look at what Project5 can do for you.

In the good old days (and I'm not quite sure when this was—sometime between the invention of electricity and now), recording was a comparatively simple process (see Figure I.1):

- You took a sound source (for instance, a band).
- You put a microphone in front of the sound source, and the musicians performed.

Figure I.1 Recording used to be a simple process.

- You recorded the performance onto tape.
- You took the recorded performance and pressed a record.

Recording then got more complicated. For instance:

- Mixing consoles allowed several sound sources to be captured and committed to tape—this also allowed individual performers (such as vocalists) to be heard more clearly.
- Multi-track recording allowed individual performances to be recorded. This meant that one person could record several performances, and mistakes could be fixed.
- Digital recording entered the arena. Digital offered the promise of noise-free recording and copying without compromise or degradation. Unfortunately, although digital initially made these promises, its early implementations left much to be desired, often giving quite "harsh" recordings.
- Machines started making music. Initially, there were simple sequencers and drum machines, but soon other instruments started to be replaced by machines.

And then computers came along, and everything changed. Before I talk about computers—and, in particular, computers that run Project5—let me just talk a bit more about the elements that are part of modern music.

What Is Audio?

As you have just read, audio used to be everything. However, these days it is quite possible to have a track that doesn't use any audio. So what is audio?

In short, audio is anything you record from a sound source. The most common source of audio recording today is the voice. However, there are many other audio sources you may record, such as a real instrument like a guitar, drums, or a piano.

You don't need an audio source to create music with Project5 (you can create audio using internal, software-based synthesizers); however, if audio is a part of your music, then you will need an interface between the outside world and your computer to convert the audio (which is an analog medium) into a digital form that Project5 can then manipulate.

There is another side to audio—the music you create in Project5 is in a digital form. You cannot "hear" this digital representation of your music. To listen to it, you must convert the digital source into analog form.

Most computers have digital-to-analog converters that will output audio much like an MP3 player will output audio. However, not all computers have converters that allow you to convert analog into digital, in which case you will need to get hold of one before you can record audio. I will talk further about converters in Tutorial 1: Getting Into and Out of Project5.

What Is MIDI?

MIDI—Musical Instrument Digital Interface—is a standard form by which musical instruments talk to one another. For instance, it allows a keyboard to tell a synthesizer which note is being played on the keyboard. Equally, MIDI could allow a hardware controller to tell a digital delay to increase its delay time.

The important issue about MIDI is that you can record this digital communication. By recording MIDI you can replay it and also manipulate it.

What Is a Sequencer?

At its most basic, a sequencer is a device to record and play back MIDI data. In addition, you can manually create MIDI data by entering it into a sequencer, and any stored MIDI data (whether recorded or manually input) can be edited.

Originally, sequencers were hardware devices, but they are now usually computer programs.

At its most basic, Project5 is a sequencer. However, it can do so much more than that.

What Is a DAW?

A DAW is a digital audio workstation—in other words, a computer that has been set up to make music. There is no prescription for what a DAW must (or must not) do; however, most DAWs will have the following features:

- A MIDI interface to connect with external MIDI hardware, such as a synthesizer or a keyboard. Clearly this is unnecessary if there is no hardware.
- An audio interface. The sophistication of this interface will depend on the recording and playback needs of the musician. There is no correlation between the cost of

the interface and the professionalism of a musician once you have reached a reasonable standard of interface—more sophisticated interfaces are only necessary if the musician uses a considerable amount of external gear.

- Lots of hard disk storage space. Often a DAW will have several dedicated hard disks. For instance, in my DAW there are three hard disks: one for the system files, one for my Project5 Project files, and a third to keep my samples on. You never know—if lots of people buy this book, I might buy myself another disk. . . .
- Software to create music, such as Project5.
- Processing power and memory. Music software puts much more strain on a computer than standard office software does, so you are likely to find that dedicated music-creating computers have more powerful CPUs and more memory.

A regular PC can be set up as a DAW, and a DAW can do other things, such as surf the Internet or run Microsoft Office. However, most serious musicians will dedicate a computer to DAW duties.

By the way, DAW is one of those phrases that gets used in different ways by different people: Some mean it to refer just to software, while others intend it to refer just to the hardware end of a recording setup. For clarity, in this book I always intend the term to refer to your whole setup (in other words, hardware and software).

The Recording Process and the Different Ways People Make Music

You've had the history lesson, so how do people make music today?

The simple answer is that there is no simple answer to that question. People make music in many different ways. The method they choose depends on a whole range of factors, including:

- The musicians who are involved. A DJ working on his or her own will create music in a very different way than a symphony orchestra working together (and a DJ working with a symphony orchestra will have yet another way of working).
- The style of music that is being created.
- The musical instruments and tools on hand.
- The creativity and skill of the musician(s).
- The desired end result.

One development in music creation that can't be overlooked is the use of loops. Whether or not you realize it, you probably hear loops in many pieces of music every day. A *loop* is a short piece of music or a short rhythmic pattern that can be deployed at will by the musician.

If you listen to a piece of classical music, you will often hear a short, repeated phrase. Sometimes the pitch of the phrase changes, and sometimes the tempo changes. These are just loops that were created before the technology we have today was available. Loops are, and always have been, a fundamental part of music.

It is only with the rise of sampling technology over the last 30 years that loops have come to be recognized as a separate musical phenomenon.

What Is Project5 and What Can Project5 Do for You?

Project5 is a piece of software that will help you create and arrange your music. It may be the only piece of software you need to create music. However, Project5 is flexible and will work with other software too.

Project5 is a highly sophisticated piece of software. It is not one of those things that you can describe in a word or two (or even in a nice marketing phrase). Rather than trying to understand what Project5 *is,* it might be easier to think about some of the things it can do for you.

- **Multi-track recording.** Project5 can record audio, either as individual Tracks or as several Tracks at one time. The only practical limit on the number of Tracks it can record is your hardware.
- **Audio editor.** Once you have your audio captured within Project5—whether this is audio you recorded, or it was created by your synthesizers—you can then edit this audio data. In addition, the program allows you to integrate an external audio editor (including the freeware editor, Audacity) to further extend the audio editing capabilities of Project5.
- **MIDI sequencing.** At the heart of Project5 is a powerful MIDI sequencer. This allows you to:
    - Record MIDI data.
    - Program MIDI data so you can write your music (and your musical directions) directly into Project5.
    - Edit MIDI data. You can edit the MIDI data manually, or you can use one of the MIDI FX units to complete the transformation in a more structured manner.

  With MIDI you can control the software synthesizers running inside Project5 and the external hardware synthesizers running outside of the program. You can then record the external synthesizers and edit that audio within Project5.
- **Arranging.** Once you have recorded your audio and MIDI, and you have your loops (which are mentioned in a moment) in place, then you can arrange your Track the way you want it and you can deploy your sounds in real time. You will also find that bringing various elements together can give you unparalleled power in

creating music. (For instance, if you combine one of the drum synthesizers with the included Patterns and the Groove Matrix, you will find you have a very powerful drum machine with onboard FX.)

- **Mixing.** Project5 can mix all of your sound sources—both audio that you have recorded and audio that you create—and output a finished mix.
- **Synthesizers.** Project5 includes a range of synthesizers that are designed for a number of different purposes. In addition to these, Project5 allows you to load any DXi- and VSTi-compatible synthesizers. As you will read, these synthesizers can then be controlled in many ways.
- **FX.** Project5 includes a wide range of FX units that allow you to treat your audio signals (including the output from your synthesizers) in a range of different manners. These allow you to make surgical changes, as well as perform out-and-out audio mangling changes. In addition, with the audio outputs, you can send your audio to external FX units and record the effected sound back into Project5.
- **Loops.** Project5 allows you to work with loops. It allows you to work with many formats of loops in many different tools. In particular:
    - You can work with audio loops in a range of different formats, including WAV/AIFF, SFZ, REX, and ACID. (Don't worry if these terms don't mean much to you—these are the main commercial formats in which loops are available.)
    - You can create and load your own loops as well as any loops you might acquire from elsewhere.
    - You can use MIDI loops (whether created by yourself or sourced elsewhere).

  All of the loops can be tempo-synchronized and beat-synchronized within Project5, meaning you can focus on creating the music, not on making your loop work within the software.
- **Content.** Project5 comes with a large amount of content, including many loops and Patterns that you can use to start making music immediately.
- **Freeze function.** A Freeze function allows you to free up CPU resources and keep working in Project5.
- **Metronome.** Project5 includes an audio metronome for people who like those things.

However, Project5 doesn't end there. There is also Project5.com, the Project5 website, which is supported by Cakewalk. The site has lots of resources and also lots of free stuff. You will find that it offers a range of other add-ons that you can purchase to improve your music making. As you will see in Tutorial 7: Using Other Synthesizers and Effects, it is a simple matter to load another synthesizer or effects unit into Project5.

Linear or Loop-Based: Introducing Clips

At this point you're probably scratching your head and saying, "Linear or loop? What are you talking about?" Let me explain.

In essence, music is linear. It has a beginning, a middle, and an end. Take a pop song: It will usually have an intro, a verse, a chorus, another verse, and another chorus; it will then go to the middle eight (or bridge) section, leading back into a chorus and the outro. This is an example of a linear piece.

However, within a linear structure there will be loops (in other words, repeating Patterns). These could be audio or MIDI loops. If you have a bunch of loops, at some point you'll want to use them in a Track. This is a simple task in Project5, which allows you to arrange a group of loops to create a linear Track (see Figure I.2).

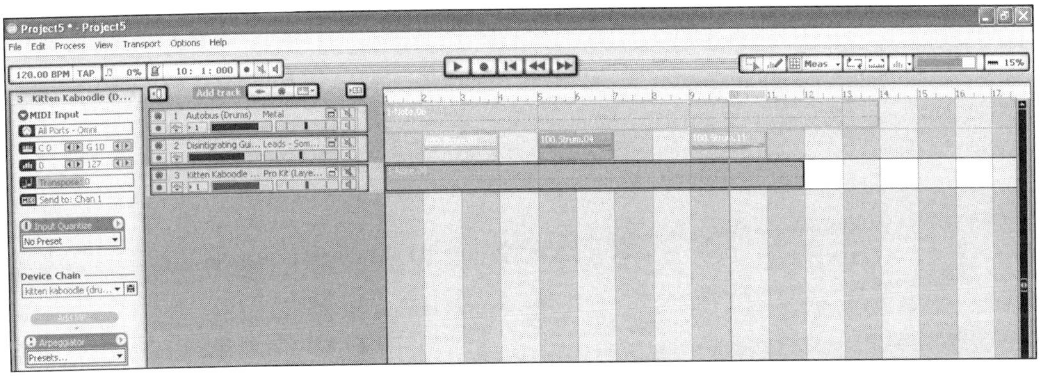

Figure I.2 With Project5 you can take loops and integrate them into the linear arrangement of a song.

The most basic element in Project5 is the Clip. *Clips* are short pieces of audio or MIDI data. They can be loops, they can be short linear phrases (for instance, a bass line in a chorus), or they can be a whole Track. Project5 doesn't care about the content; it just thinks about Clips.

As I will discuss in Chapter 3, "Working with Clips," Clips can be copied, edited, and arranged. For the moment, all you need to understand is that a Clip is the most fundamental element in Project5—you cannot avoid using a Clip in one way or another.

Who Should Use Project5 and Why?

So now that you understand some of what Project5 can do, who should be using it? There are a number of people:

- **Musicians (obviously).** Project5 is a great music production suite that comes with some cutting-edge software instruments and a range of tools that mean you can work in a way that suits you. If you're a musician (working in any style of music), then Project5 will help you make better music, quicker.

- **Writers.** Songwriters, TV and movie composers, and in fact anyone who writes to make a living (or who wants to earn money from writing) will find Project5's speed and straightforward workflow a benefit when writing.
- **DJs, beat creators, and producers.** Because Project5 does not have an *either* loops *or* linear structure, but instead allows you to bring both elements together, it is the ideal tool for DJs looking to push the sonic envelope.

I've already alluded to some of the reasons why you might use Project5, but let me bring these together:

- **Workflow.** Project5 lends itself to fast/modern production styles, offering you several ways to do the same thing. This means you will never be left saying, "I wish it worked *this* way."
- **Music focus.** The Project5 interface treats audio and MIDI in the same way, irrespective of how each element has been created and irrespective of whether the Clip is a loop or part of a linear Track.

Which Version of Project5 Are You Using?

There are two versions of Project5—the original boxed version (version 2.0) and the new downloadable version (version 2.5). Version 2.5 has updated functionality compared to version 2.0, and, as you would expect, it is the version featured in this book. If you purchased version 2.0, then you are entitled to a free upgrade to version 2.5. (For details, go to cakewalk.com.)

However, there is one significant difference between the two versions: Version 2.5 includes fewer synthesizers (although it does include one new synthesizer, Dimension LE). Table I.1 details the differences in the included synthesizers.

If you upgraded from version 2.0 to version 2.5, then you will have access to all of the 2.0 synthesizers (unless you didn't install them originally—in which case you can still install them from your original CD—or you have uninstalled them), as well as the 2.5 synthesizers. This book covers all of the synthesizers.

There is another version of the software, Project5 LE, which is included with some Edirol hardware. Project5 LE shares much of the functionality of Project5; the key difference is that a restricted set of synthesizers and effects units are included.

What Do You Need to Bring?

Clearly you need to provide a computer with an audio interface—and a MIDI interface too, if you want to control Project5 from external hardware or you want to control external hardware with Project5.

Table I.1 The Synthesizers Included with Project5

Synthesizer	Included with Project5 version 2.0	Included with Project5 version 2.5
Velocity	Yes	Yes
nPULSE	Yes	Yes
Cyclone	Yes	No
Roland GrooveSynth	Yes	No
PSYN II	Yes	No
DS864	Yes	No
Dimension	Yes	No
Dimension LE	No	Yes

Once your hardware is set up, you need two things: talent and inspiration. Once you've got those, read on.

Further Resources and Further Help

After you've read this book, if you still have any questions, there are lots of places to go for help and for further resources.

For help, the best place to go is the Cakewalk support forum at http://forum.cakewalk.com/tt.asp?forumid=6. Many knowledgeable people hang out at the forum and are ready to help try to answer questions.

Project5.com is the official Project5 website supported by Cakewalk. The site has many further resources (including lots of free stuff).

Finally, there is Project5 Wiki (http://p5.sonarama.com/p5/index.php). This is a wiki (in other words, a collection of information) about Project5. Sometimes it is very helpful; at other times, it may not answer your question.

1 Getting a Grip on Project5

The purpose of this first chapter is to introduce you to Project5 and show you what we've got here. While this chapter is quite chunky, it is intended to get you up and running as quickly as possible. You will see that there are many references to further tutorials that give a more detailed view of specific topics.

So let's now take a look around Project5 and see what we've got.

Tutorial 1: Getting Into and Out of Project5

As with all Windows-based software, getting into and out of Project5 is straightforward. However, as you would expect, quite a bit goes on when you open and close Project5.

Opening and Closing Project5

To open Project5, go to Start > Programs > Cakewalk > Project5 Version 2 > Project5 Version 2. Alternatively (if it wasn't done as part of the installation process), you can put a Project5 icon on your desktop. To do this, instead of left-clicking on the program name (having followed through from the Start menu), right-click and select Send To > Desktop from the pop-up menu.

Once Project5 is open, you can close it either by clicking on the red X in the top-right corner of the interface or by selecting File > Exit (Ctrl+Q). If you have an open unsaved project, you will be given the option to save it when you close Project5. I will look further at the options to save files in Tutorial 8: Working with Projects.

Scans Performed on Opening Project5

When you load Project5, it performs a number of scans and other checks; you can see this in action in Figure 1.1. One of these checks is to search for new VST effects and VSTi instruments. I will look at installing VST effects and VSTi instruments in Tutorial 7: Using Other Synthesizers and Effects.

You can enable (or disable) automatic scan by selecting Options > VST Plug-Ins and putting a check mark next to Scan for VST Plug-Ins on Startup (see Figure 1.2).

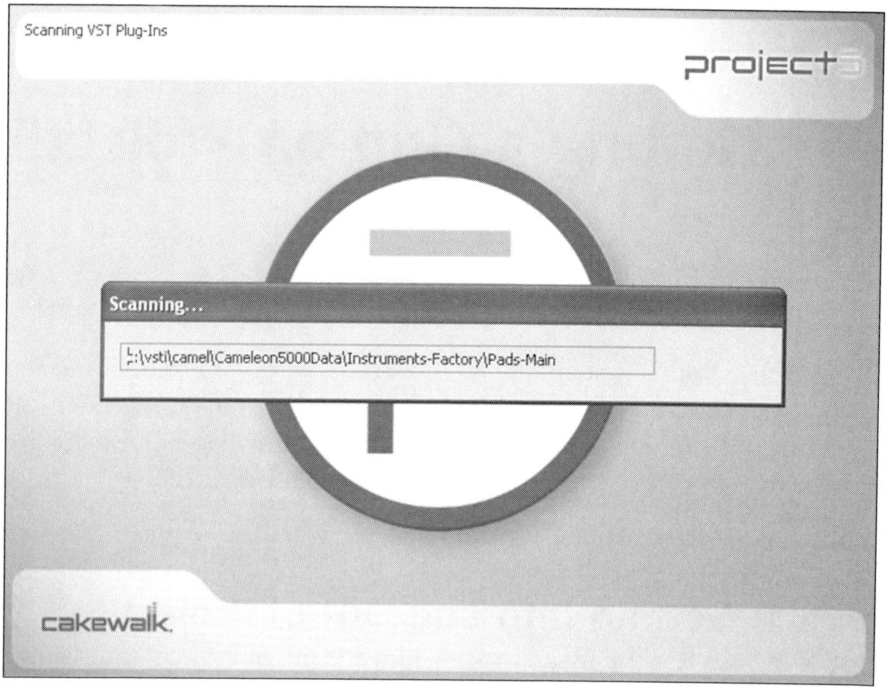

Figure 1.1 One of the startup scans in Project5. In this case you can see the VSTi Plug-Ins scan, which has found the Cameleon 5000 synthesizer from Camel Audio.

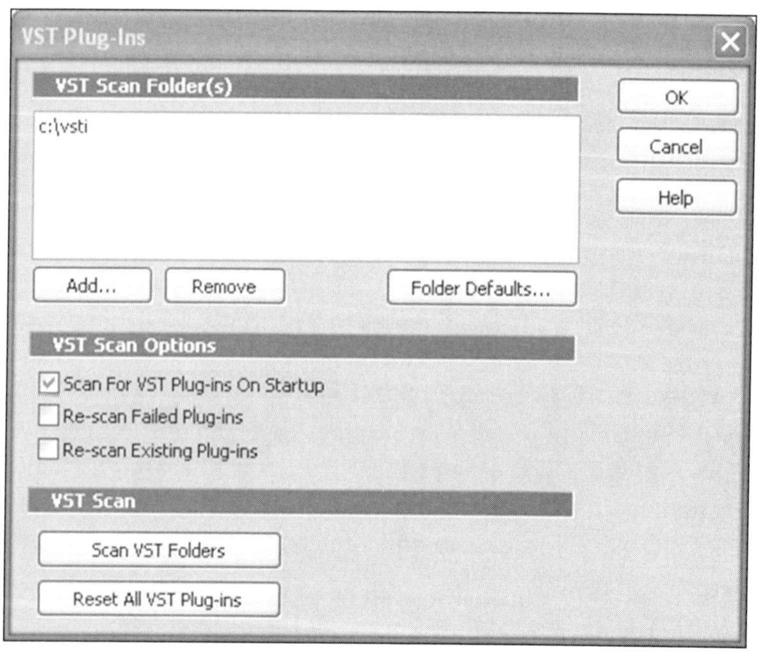

Figure 1.2 Selecting Scan for VST Plug-Ins on Startup.

The advantage of including this scan is that you can be assured that you will always have all of your VSTs and VSTis available to you. You can add new synthesizers or effects and know that they will automatically be available in Project5.

The disadvantage of including this scan is that it increases the time to load Project5. As I will mention in Tutorial 7, you can disable the automatic scan and then manually run it whenever you add a new VST or VSTi.

Checking the Software Version

You can check the version of Project5 that you are running by selecting Help > About Project5. As Figure 1.3 shows, this will display the version of the software that you are running and will also display your serial number (although this is obscured in the graphic).

I suggest you check the Cakewalk Project5 forum and/or the Cakewalk website to make sure you have the latest copy of the software.

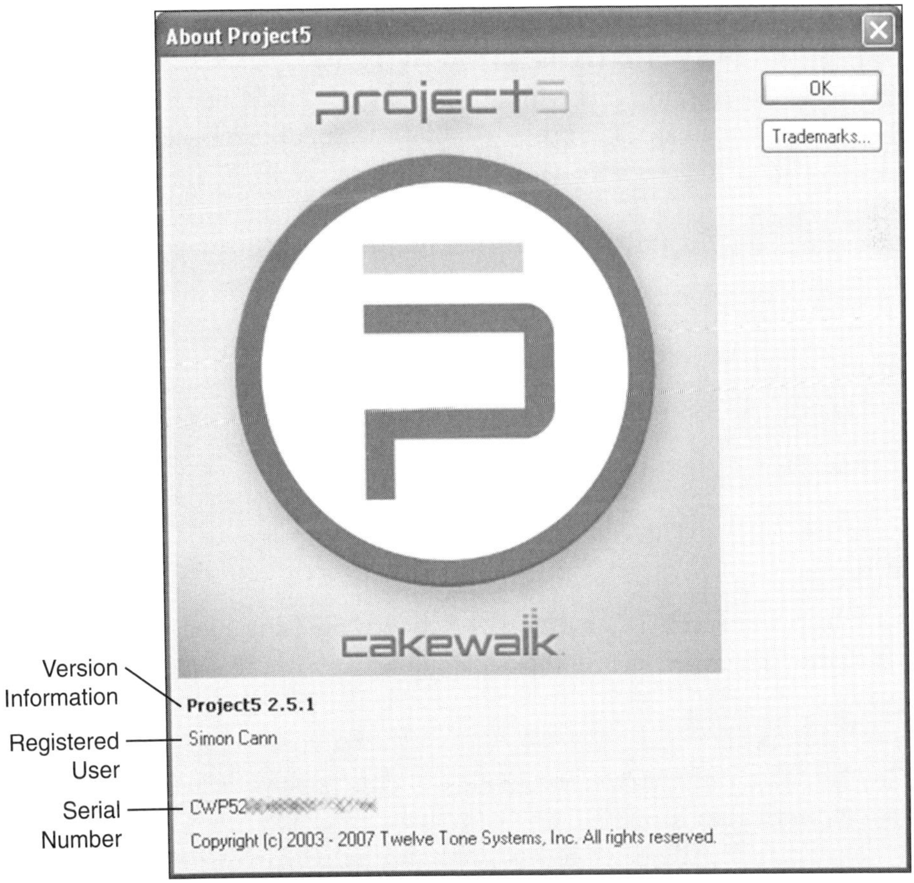

Figure 1.3 The About screen in Project5, which, among other things, shows the version, the serial number, and the registered user.

Conventional Windows Tools

If you're used to using Windows, you'll be quite at home with Project5 because it uses standard Windows keystrokes. In particular, you will find that:

- Ctrl+Z allows you to undo your last action.
- Ctrl+Shift+Z allows you to redo your last action.
- Ctrl+H brings up a list of your recent changes, from which you can undo recent changes.
- Ctrl+X allows you to cut (in particular, to cut a Clip).
- Ctrl+C allows you to copy.
- Ctrl+V allows you to paste.

As you would also expect, Delete deletes stuff.

Tutorial 2: Navigating through Project5

Figure 2.1 shows Project5. This is quite big and scary (and since the graphic has been squished to fit on the page, it's probably a bit too small), so once you've had a look at it, I'll move on to look at each element separately. I should point out that the Track/Bus Inspector changes depending on which Track/Bus Pane has been selected—I will discuss this further in Tutorial 6: Track/Bus Inspector.

Across the top of Project5 you will find:

- The left-hand Main Controls
- The Transport Controls
- The right-hand Main Controls

These are discussed in Tutorial 3: The Transport Controls and Tutorial 4: The Main Controls.

There's a lot to Project5. Let me give you a very brief introduction to some of the features that are described later in the book and tell you where you can read the details.

Groove Matrix

The Groove Matrix allows you to organize and arrange your loops and grooves (in both MIDI and audio formats). You can then trigger the loops and grooves in the Groove Matrix, either during a live performance or when you are recording. This is discussed further in Tutorial 22: Using the Groove Matrix.

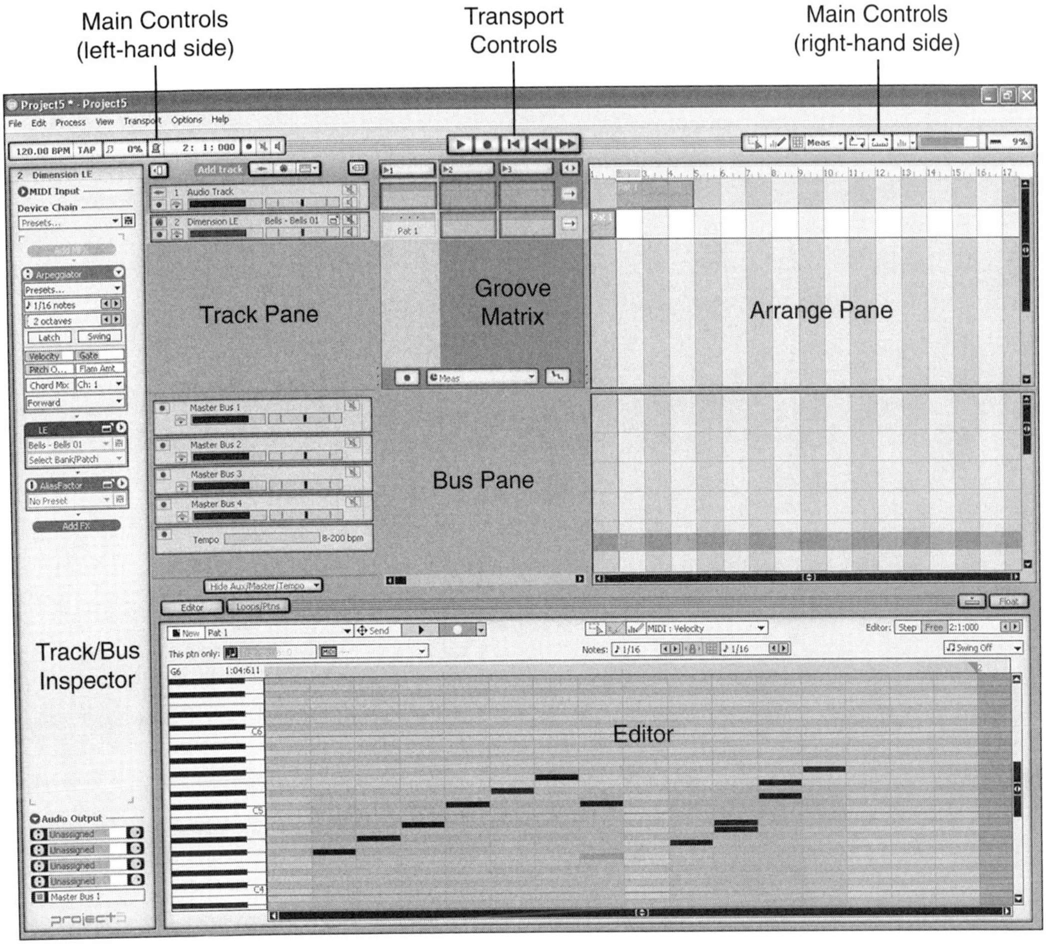

Figure 2.1 The Project5 interface.

Editors

There are three Editors in Project5:

- The MIDI Editor, which allows you to create and edit MIDI data—this Editor looks like a piano roll.
- The Audio Editor, which allows you to view audio data—as you will read later, you need to use an external audio editor (such as the freeware editor Audacity) if you want to edit audio data with a level of precision.
- The Loop Editor, which allows you to create and edit loops.

The Editors are discussed more fully in Chapter 3, "Working with Clips."

Piano Roll Views

If you look at the Editor Pane in either Figure 2.1 or Figure 2.3, you will see what is called a *piano roll view*. This is named after the image of the piano keyboard on the left-hand side of the pane. However, there is an alternate view that is more appropriate when you are programming drum parts.

If you look at Figure 2.2, you will see the Editor Pane with the drum view displayed. As you might be able to make out, instead of the piano keyboard, you have a list of drum names. This makes programming much easier.

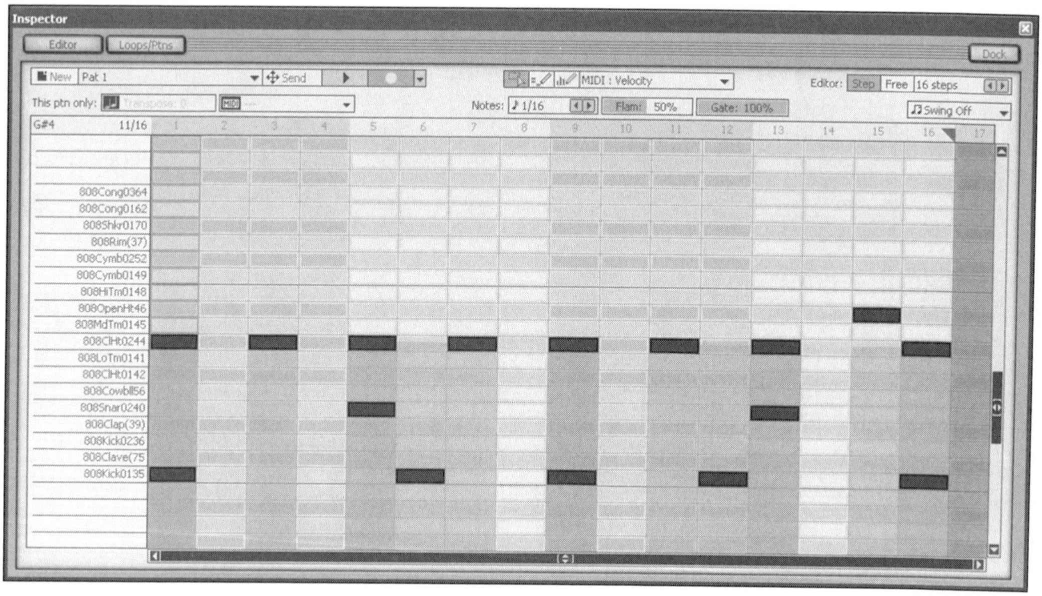

Figure 2.2 The drum view in the Editor Pane.

Loops/Pattern Browser

If you look at the top left of any of the Editors, you will see two buttons: Editors and Loops/Ptns. These buttons allow you to switch between the Editors views and the Loops/Pattern Browser.

The Loops/Pattern Browser works with both audio and MIDI data and is discussed in greater detail in Chapter 3.

Arrange Pane

The Arrange Pane allows you to arrange your Clips to create a linear track from the elements that you bring to the song. It is discussed in greater detail in Chapter 3.

Resizing the Panes

Within the Project5 view, you can resize the panes in order to focus more closely on the task at hand. As you mouse over the boundaries between two panes (marked as dotted lines on Figure 2.3), your cursor will show a doubled-headed arrow. You can click-drag these boundaries to resize the pane; the double-headed arrow indicates the direction the panes can be dragged.

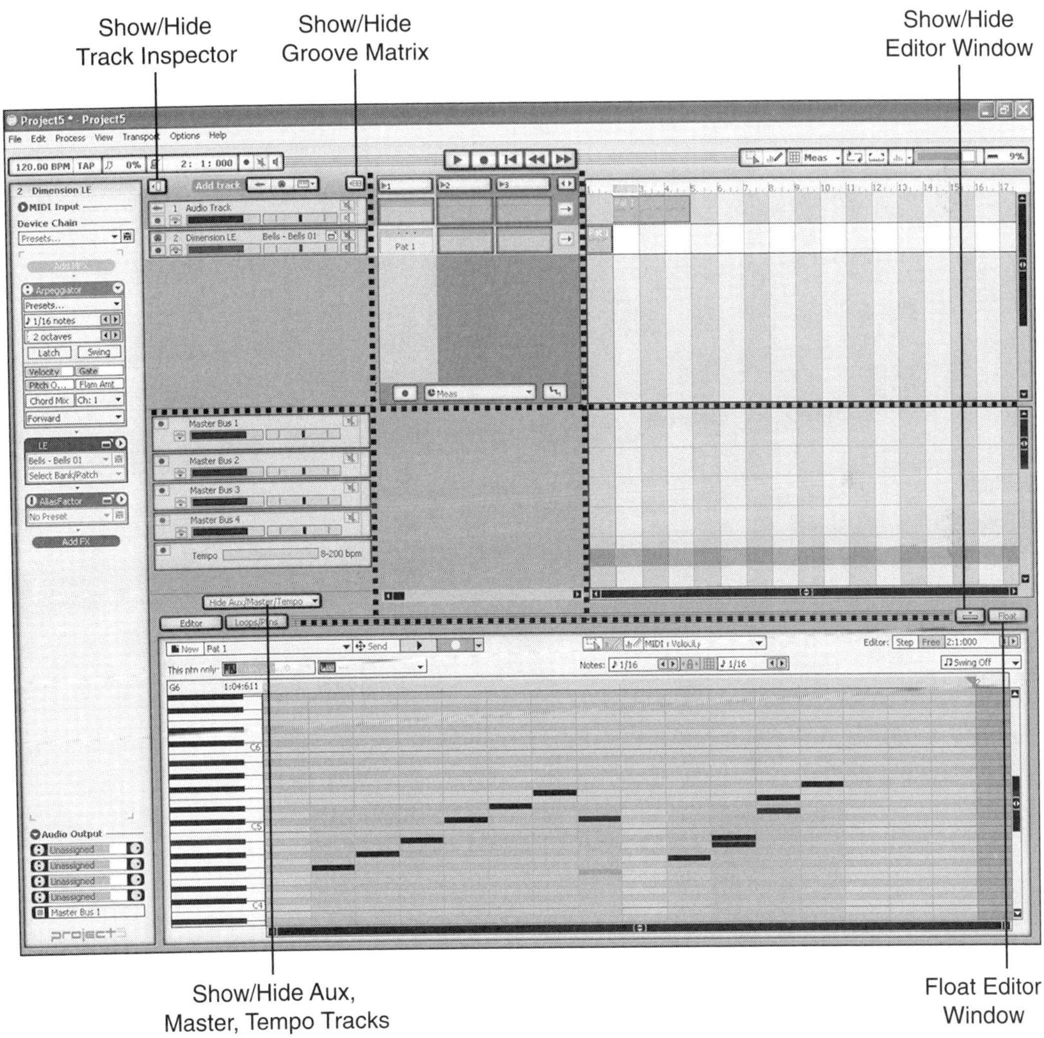

Figure 2.3 Project5's resizable panes. You can drag the dashed lines to resize the panes.

In addition, to clear more space, there are dedicated buttons to show or hide:

- The Track Inspector
- The Groove Matrix

- The Aux Busses, Master Busses, and the Tempo Track
- The Editor Pane

Lastly, you will also see that there is a Float Editor Window button. This floats/docks the Editor window, allowing you to place it in a convenient position on your screen. In my home setup, I use two monitors. I locate the Editor Pane on the second screen, as you can see in Figure 2.4.

Figure 2.4 Using Project5 in practice: the author's home setup. The Editor Pane is located on the left-hand monitor.

Tutorial 3: The Transport Controls

Figure 3.1 shows the Transport Controls.

There are five buttons in the Transport Controls section:

- The Play/Stop button makes Project5 play its current Project or stop playing. When the Track is playing, this button will show as a Stop button with a green background. The naming of this button is an act of sheer unrivaled genius.

  You can also stop and start playback by hitting the spacebar on your computer keyboard. When you stop playback, the Now Time marker will remain at that point. If you hit Play again, then playback will continue from the stop point.

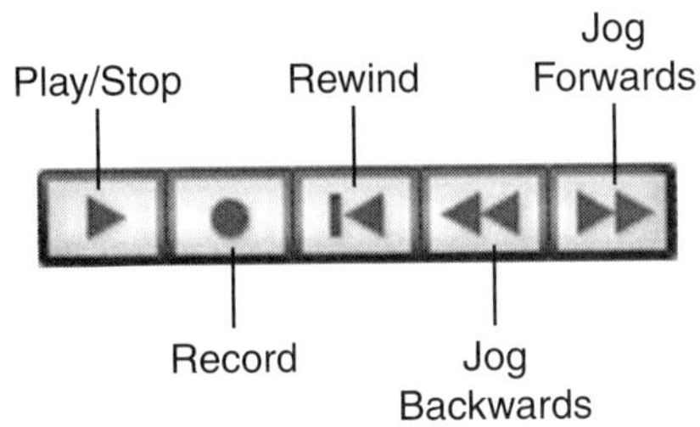

Figure 3.1 The Transport Controls.

- To record, click on the Record button, and playback will begin. You will then be able to record on any armed tracks. The record function only operates if you have armed one or more Tracks; this concept is discussed later in the book (in Tutorial 16: Creating a MIDI/Instrument Clip and Tutorial 19: Recording an Audio Clip). Instead of clicking the Record button, you can hit the R key on your keyboard.
- The Rewind button rewinds the Project to the beginning. Instead of clicking on the Rewind button, you can hit the W key on your keyboard. Project5 does not automatically rewind, so you will always need to rewind to play from the start of a song.
- The Jog Forwards and Jog Backwards buttons work during playback and will take you to the start of the next measure or the start of the current measure, as appropriate. Instead of using the Jog Forwards and Jog Backwards buttons, on your computer keyboard you can hit Ctrl+Page Up or Ctrl+Page Down, as appropriate.

These options are also available from the Transport menu.

In addition to playing the current project, you can play a single Clip—the Clip that is currently being edited in the Editor. You can do this by either:

- Hitting the Play button in the Editor.
- Selecting Transport > Pattern Preview. (The terms *Clip* and *Pattern* are interchangeable—for this book, I have stuck with the term *Clip* for consistency.)
- Pressing Shift+spacebar on your computer keyboard.

You can change the physical position of the Transport Controls by going to Options > Show Transport at Left (for Multiple Monitors). The idea here is that the Transport Controls will be moved to the left, so if you spread Project5 over two monitors, the controls will not drop down a hole in the middle.

Tutorial 4: The Main Controls

The Main Controls are split into two sections, which are located to the left and the right of the Transport Controls.

The Left-Hand Main Controls

Figure 4.1 shows the left-hand Main Controls.

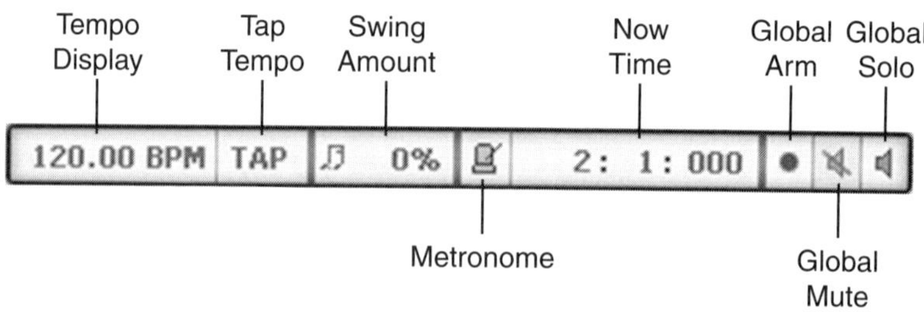

Figure 4.1 The left-hand Main Controls.

Tempo and Swing

You can set the tempo in a number of ways:

- Left-click and drag on the Tempo Display (up or down) to increase or decrease the tempo (in fairly coarse increments).
- Double-click on the Tempo Display and manually enter the tempo.
- Double-click on the Tempo Display and adjust the tempo with the fine adjustment controls (the plus and minus signs that appear to the right of the tempo).
- Left-click on the Tap Tempo button—you will need to click several times to establish a rhythm. If (like most human beings) you find it hard to click at a precise tempo, you can always hit the \ key on your keyboard rather than clicking with your mouse.

The Swing Amount Control allows you to introduce a shuffle into your music (so you can swing the off beats to get the groove you're after). You can set the Swing Amount in three ways:

- Left-click and drag on the Swing Amount Control to increase or decrease the Swing Amount.
- Double-click on the Swing Amount and manually enter the Swing Amount.
- Double-click on the Swing Amount and adjust the Swing Amount using the plus and minus adjusters to the right of the Swing Amount display.

Metronome

You can switch the audio metronome on or off by clicking on the Metronome button. Alternatively, hit the C key on your keyboard, or select Transport > Metronome On/Off. When the metronome is active, you will hear the metronome when your Project plays (obviously...), and the background to the Metronome button will change from gray to blue.

If you select Options > Metronome, the Metronome Properties page will appear (see Figure 4.2).

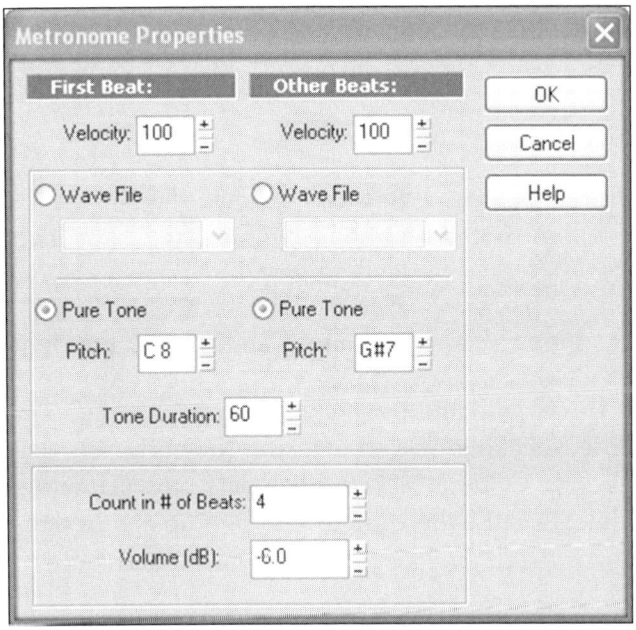

Figure 4.2 The Metronome Properties page.

From the Metronome Properties page you can:

- Set the velocity (that is, the loudness) of the first beat and the other beats.
- Select another WAV file as the metronome sound (again, for the first and the other beats).
- Set the pitch of the metronome notes and their duration.
- Set the volume of the metronome sound.

You can also set the metronome to count in before a song starts to record. This function does not work when you are simply playing a song; you must be recording. You also need to have the metronome switched on for the function to work!!

To switch on the count-in, either hit the O button on your keyboard or select Transport > Count-In On/Off. You can select the number of beats to count in from the Metronome Properties page.

Now Time

The Now Time display shows the current time of the song (and if the song has stopped, it shows the time at which it stopped, provided you haven't rewound the Project). The Now Time display can show the Now Time in two formats:

- Measures (Bars) : Beats : Ticks
- Hours : Minutes : Seconds

You can adjust each of the units in three ways:

- Left-click and drag. As you drag a unit's value, the Now Time indicator in the Arrange Pane will move to show the newly selected Now Time.
- Double-click and manually enter the values.
- Double-click and use the plus and minus adjusters to the right of the unit.

You can also set the Now Time by clicking on the Arrange Pane. You have the choice of whether left-clicking or right-clicking (or both) sets the Now Time. You can do this by selecting Options > Left Click Sets Now Time or Options > Right Click Sets Now Time. Because there are several pop-up menus that appear when you right-click on the Arrange Pane, you may want to deselect Right Click Sets Now Time.

Global Controls and Indicators

There are three further indicators in the left-hand Main Controls:

- The Global Arm button, which shows when at least one Track is armed
- The Global Mute button, which shows when at least one Track is muted
- The Global Solo button, which shows when at least one Track is soloed

When any of these buttons is lit up, you can switch off that function for all Tracks by clicking on the corresponding button.

The Right-Hand Main Controls

Figure 4.3 shows the right-hand Main Controls.

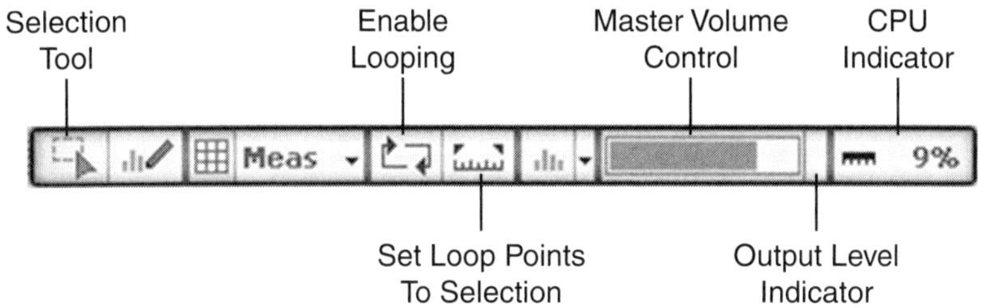

Figure 4.3 The right-hand Main Controls.

The right-hand Main Controls section does quite a lot; however, at this point I only want to look at four features. I will look at the other features in the context in which they are used.

Looping

The Enable Looping button switches on looping during playback. When engaged, the Project will loop between a loop start and a loop end point. If you start playing the song before the loop point, it will play normally up to the loop, but once it reaches the loop end point, the song will return to the loop start (and will then continue to cycle).

To set the loop start and loop end points to play a section:

- If you want to loop to start and end at the beginning of a Clip, select that Clip by left-clicking on it with the Selection Tool.
- If the intended loop section includes more than one Clip, you can do either of the following:
  - Drag around the Clips with the Selection Tool
  - Ctrl+left-click on the first and the last Clip

Once you have selected your Clip or Clips, you can then left-click on Set Loop Points to Selection Tool.

Master Volume

The Master Volume Control allows you to control the output volume of Project5. This Volume Control also controls the level of Master Bus 1 (which will be discussed in the next tutorial). The output level of Master Bus 1 is shown by the Output Level Indicator. If the peak output level is exceeded, then the top range of the output meter will show in red. These red indicators will remain until the meter is reset, which you can do by left-clicking on the meter.

CPU Indicator

The CPU Indicator shows how much of your CPU power is being used by Project5.

Resetting the MIDI Engine and the Audio Engine

From time to time you may need to reset the audio and MIDI engines—if you are experiencing any audio problems, the first step you should take is to reset the audio engine. To reset the audio engine and the MIDI engine, left-click on the CPU Indicator. It will take a moment or two, and then the engine will be reset.

Tutorial 5: Audio, MIDI, and Instrument Tracks

To get going with Project5 you'll need to load up a Track. The type of Track that you choose will depend on what you're trying to do:

- If you're recording audio or you want to work with an audio clip or loop, then you will need an Audio Track.
- If you want to play an external MIDI hardware synthesizer, then you will need to load a MIDI Track.
- If you want to play a software synthesizer that is installed on your DAW, then you will need to load an Instrument Track.

Adding Tracks: Loading Instruments, MIDI Tracks, and Audio Tracks

When you add a Track, its Inspector is automatically created. If you can't see the Inspector after you have added a Track, left-click on the Show/Hide Inspector button; see Figure 5.1.

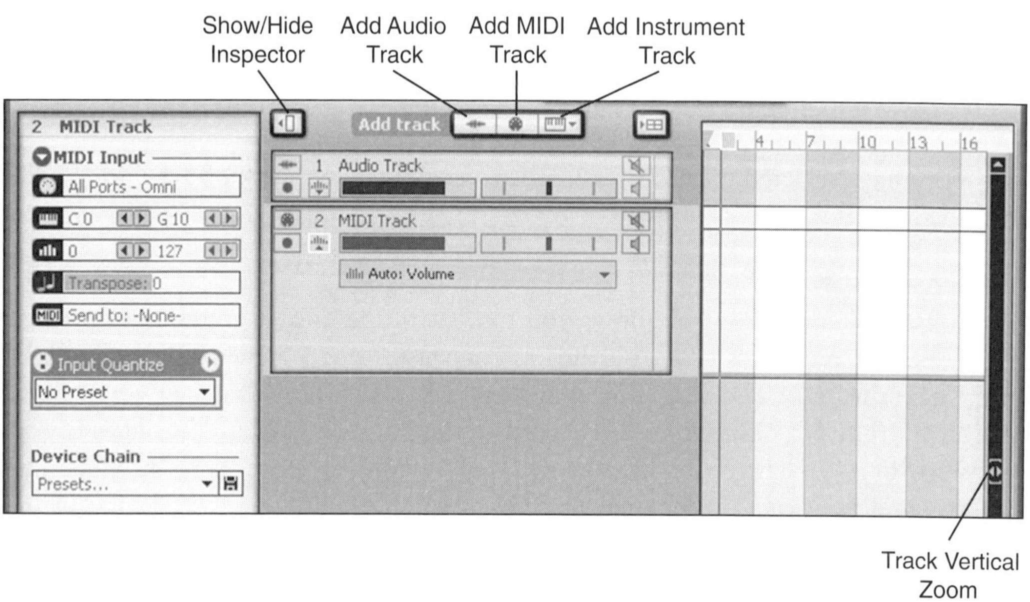

Figure 5.1 Working with the Track Pane in Project5.

Adding Tracks

There are two ways to directly load an Instrument Track, a MIDI Track, or an Audio Track:

- Right-click in the Track Pane and select the appropriate Insert option from the pop-up menu (from which you can navigate to the device to be loaded).
- Left-click on one of the Add Track buttons (which are shown in Figure 5.1).

When you click on the Add Audio Track or Add MIDI Track button, the Track will be added automatically. When you click on the Add Instrument Track button, a pop-up menu will appear (see Figure 5.2).

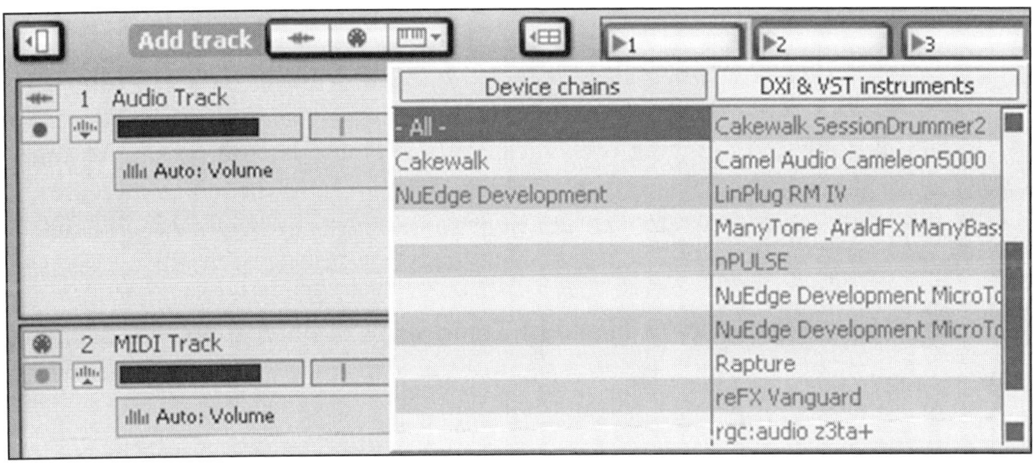

Figure 5.2 Selecting a DXi or VSTi.

There are two buttons at the top of the pop-up menu:

- Device Chains
- DXi & VST Instruments

This gives you the option of either loading the Instrument directly or loading an Instrument as part of a Device Chain. To load the Instrument directly, click on the DXi and VST Instruments button, and you will see two columns:

- In the left column is the categorization of the Instruments. (Often these are stored by the developer.)
- In the right column is a list of Instruments.

Click on the Instrument you want, and it will be loaded. You will see at the top of the Instruments column that the five most recently loaded Instruments are shown. (This is not displayed in Figure 5.2 because I have scrolled down the list of available Instruments.) If you want to load one of these five most recently loaded Instruments, just click on the name.

If the menu isn't big enough for you—as you can see in Figure 5.2, the menu looks a bit cramped—you can always left-click and drag the sides to increase its size.

In Tutorial 7, I will show you how you can arrange the synthesizers that show up in this menu.

Track Strip Height

You can adjust the height of a Track Strip in two ways:

- By left-clicking and dragging the bottom of the Track Strip (to adjust the height of one Strip).
- By left-clicking and dragging the Track Vertical Zoom button on the Arrange Pane scroll bar (which was shown in Figure 5.1). Drag to the left to increase the height of all Track Strips and to the right to decrease the height of all Track Strips.

You might want to increase the height of Track Strips in order to expose the automation assignment or to increase the height of the Clips in the Arrange Pane (which may make it easier to draw or edit automation).

Deleting Tracks

To delete a Track, right-click on it and select Delete from the pop-up menu.

Further Pop-Up Menu Options

You will see that there are other pop-up menu options, particularly if you right-click on an existing Track Strip. (For instance, there are Clone Instrument and Replace Instrument options.) The other options are described in Chapter 4, "Working with Tracks and Projects."

Adding and Deleting Busses

Project5 comes with one Main Bus for each hardware output that you have. You cannot have more, and you cannot have less.

You can have an unlimited number of Aux Busses, although each Track has a maximum of four Aux Bus Sends. To add an Aux Bus, right-click in the Bus Pane and select

Insert Aux Bus from the pop-up menu. Repeat the process to add further Aux Busses. To delete an Aux Bus, right-click on it and select Delete Aux Bus from the pop-up.

If you right-click on any of the Aux Busses or Main Busses, you will see a further option on the pop-up menu: Invert Phase. If you select this option, the phase of the audio signal will be inverted, as Figure 5.3 shows.

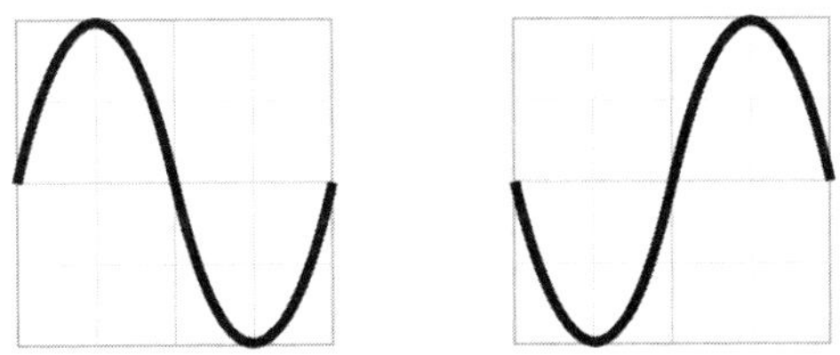

Figure 5.3 Two sine waves—one has its phase polarity inverted by reference to the other (and so one goes up when the other goes down).

If you have two audio signals that are exactly the same, except the phase polarity of one is inverted by reference to the other, and you add these two signals, then the two audio sources will be cancelled out. The purpose of changing the phase of a signal is to un-invert any audio signals that may be causing phase cancellation.

Device Chains

A Device Chain saves:

- A Track (whether, Audio, Instrument, or MIDI)
- The presets loaded in any Instrument (if it is an Instrument Track)
- The MIDI FX and audio FX loaded into the Track
- The Input Quantize and Track Arpeggiator settings (in the case of an Instrument Track or a MIDI Track)

You can then recall these settings as a combined preset. A Device Chain will not save Bus routings, and neither will it save Bus settings.

Project5 ships with a number of Device Chains. You can share your Chains with other Project5 users, although if your Chain includes synthesizers or FX units that the other user does not have installed on his or her system, then that user will not be able to load the shared Chain properly.

Loading a Device Chain

To load a Device Chain, left-click on the Add Instrument Track, and in the pop-up menu, click on the Device Chains button (see Figure 5.4).

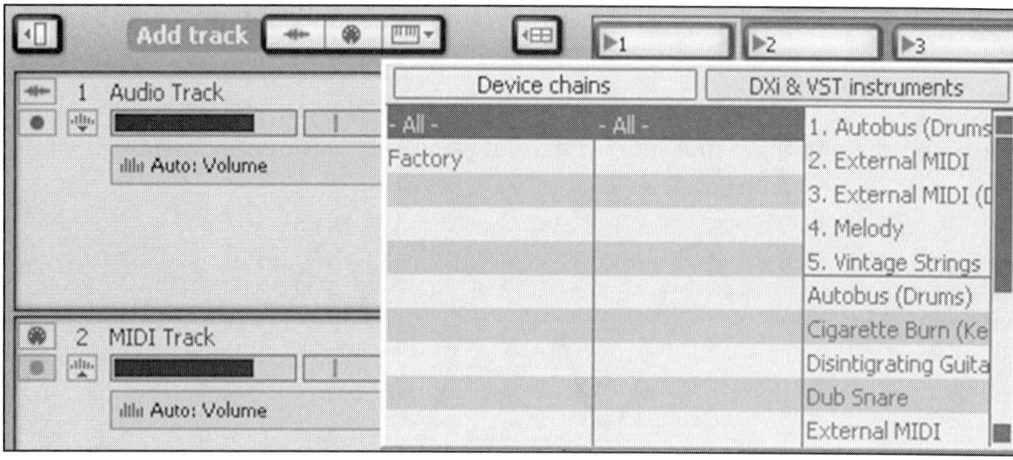

Figure 5.4 The Device Chains menu.

There are three columns in the Device Chains menu: The first two are categories (or categories and subcategories, if you prefer), and the third column contains the Chains. So the first category could be Synthesizer, the subcategory could be Bass, and the Chains column might contain a Chain called Dub Bass (to give an example).

To load a Device Chain, click on the name of the Chain, and the Track and associated FX and so on will be loaded. You will also see that the five most recently loaded Chains are listed at the top of the Chains column. If you want to load one of these, just click on the name.

Once the Device Chain has been selected, the pop-up menu will disappear.

Changing a Device Chain

Once you have loaded a Device Chain, it becomes a normal Track. You can replace any Track (and therefore any Device Chain) with a Device Chain. You can replace any type of Track with any type of Device Chain, so, for instance, you could change an Audio Track for a MIDI Track Device Chain.

We will look at the Inspectors in more detail in Tutorial 6. A short way down each Inspector is some text saying Device Chain. Under that is a drop-down menu selector with a floppy disk icon to the right of that. To change a Track with another Device Chain, left-click on the drop-down menu; this will give you another Device Chains menu (without the Instruments option that you see when you click on the Add Instrument Track button).

From this menu you can select another Device Chain. When you select a Device Chain, the menu will remain in place, allowing you to audition a number of Chains. When you have found the right one, click off the menu, and it will disappear.

Saving a Device Chain

There are two ways to save a Device Chain:

- Click on the floppy-disk icon next to the drop-down selector on the Inspector relating to the Track you want to save.
- Right-click on the Track you want to save and select Save as Device Chain from the pop-up menu.

Whichever option you choose, you will be given the option to save your Device Chain in the Device Chains folder. In that folder by default you will find two sub-folders: Factory (where the factory presets are stored) and User. You can use the User folder, or you can create a folder of your own.

You will remember that the Device Chains menu had three columns. The first folder (for instance, Factory) will show in the left column, and the Device Chain will show in the right column. You can further subcategorize your Device Chains by adding another layer of folders (for instance, Basses > Electric). This subcategorization will show in the Device Chains menu's center column.

Track Naming

You can name and rename a Track by double-clicking on the Track's name in the Track Pane (see Figure 5.5). You can rename an Aux Bus in the same way, but not a Master Bus.

The new Track/Aux Bus name will appear at the top of the corresponding Inspector. For Audio and Instrument Tracks' Inspectors, the name of a renamed Aux Bus will show in the Audio Output section with the word "Send" appended to it.

Open Instrument Interfaces

For Instrument Tracks there is an additional button (shown in Figure 5.5)—the Show Instrument Interface button. If you click on this, the Instrument's interface will be opened. You can also open the Instrument interface by double-clicking on any part of the Track Strip that doesn't have a control (such as the Track number).

Figure 5.5 A Track's name.

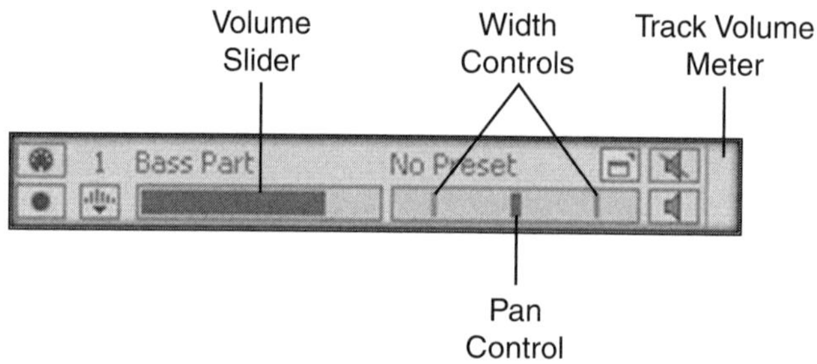

Figure 5.6 The Track Volume, Pan, and Width Controls.

Track Volume, Pan, and Width

From the Track Strip you can control a Track's volume, pan (in other words, its position in the stereo spectrum), and width (see Figure 5.6). For an explanation about the operation of the Width Control, see Tutorial 9: Signal Flow through Project5.

- To control the volume, left-click and drag the Volume Slider. If you double-click on the Volume Slider, it will be reset to the default level.
- To control the pan (or the balance between left and right channels in the case of stereo signals), left-click and drag the central Pan Slider. If you double-click on the Pan Slider, it will be reset to the center.
- To control the width, hold down the Ctrl key and then left-click and drag either of the Width Sliders. If you double-click on either Width Slider while holding down the Ctrl key, they will be set to the default value (90 degrees). You should note that while MIDI Tracks have a Width Control, it serves no function.

Mute and Solo Tracks and Busses

Each Track Strip has a Mute button and a Solo button; see Figure 5.7. Each Bus Strip only has a Mute button.

- When you left-click on a Track Bus Solo button, only that Track (plus any other Track that has been soloed) will be heard. The other Tracks will effectively be muted.
- When you left-click on a Track/Aux Bus Mute button, the output from that Track/Aux Bus will be muted. If you mute an Aux Bus, it is the audio output from that bus that is muted, so if the Track is sent elsewhere (such as to a Master Bus), it will still be heard.
- When any Track or Aux Bus is muted or soloed, the Global Mute and/or Global Solo buttons will be lit. If you click on either of these, all Mutes and/or Solos will be switched off.

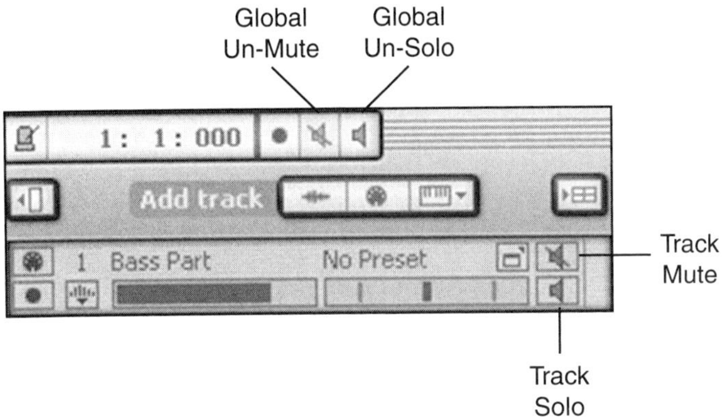

Figure 5.7 The Mute and Solo buttons in an Instrument Track Pane. The Global Un-Mute and Global Un-Solo buttons are also highlighted.

Tutorial 6: Track/Bus Inspector

When you create an Audio Track or a MIDI Track or you load an Instrument, a Track Strip is created. Associated with this new Track Strip will be a Track Inspector. The Busses also have associated Track Inspectors. This tutorial introduces you to the Track and Bus Inspectors. Although Track and Bus Strips are briefly mentioned here, their operation is not discussed in detail, but they will be discussed in later tutorials.

The Track/Bus Inspector changes depending on which Track or Bus you select by left-clicking on the corresponding Track in the Track Pane or Master Bus/Aux Bus in the Bus Pane. There are five Inspectors:

- An Audio Track Inspector
- A MIDI Track Inspector when Project5 is driving an external MIDI synthesizer (or other device)
- An Instrument Track Inspector when Project5 is playing a software synthesizer
- An Aux Bus Inspector when you have selected one of the Aux Busses
- A Master Bus Inspector when you have selected one of the Master Busses

If you think of the Inspectors as being a more detailed and expanded view of the Track or Bus, then you won't go far wrong; however, as you will see when we finally discuss the Track and Bus Panes, they do have specific utilitarian functions.

If the talk about Busses is getting rather confusing, don't worry: In essence, Busses are signal flows and will be explained later in the chapter, in Tutorial 9. For all of the Busses, the "signal" flows from the top of the Bus to the bottom—in other words, the processes at the top of the Inspector are undertaken before the processes at the bottom of the Inspector. The significance of this will become clearer as we look at the Inspectors.

As we look at the Busses, you will see that they are all very similar. You will also see that the Track Panes and Bus Panes all look very similar. This makes learning how to use the tools very quick.

Inserting Audio FX and MIDI FX

You can only insert an FX unit in an Inspector. To insert an FX unit, in the Inspector, click on:

- The Add MFX button to add a MIDI FX unit
- The Add FX button to add an audio FX unit

The FX unit will then be added for that Track/Inspector combination. To add further FX, repeat the process.

FX units apply to single tracks only—you cannot apply an FX unit to multiple tracks (unless you apply an FX unit to one of the Busses; see Tutorial 9 later in this chapter).

To change an FX unit for another, right-click on it and select Replace MFX or Replace Audio Effect, as appropriate, and then select the replacement unit.

To remove an FX unit, right-click on it and select Delete from the pop-up menu.

You can read more about the audio FX units in Chapter 7, "Working with Audio FX Units," and the MIDI FX units in Chapter 8, "MIDI FX Units."

Inspectors: Common Functionality

Before we start looking at the Inspectors, there are two pieces of common functionality that I want to mention. First, many of the modules in an Inspector share three buttons (or a subset of these three buttons). Take a look at Figure 6.1.

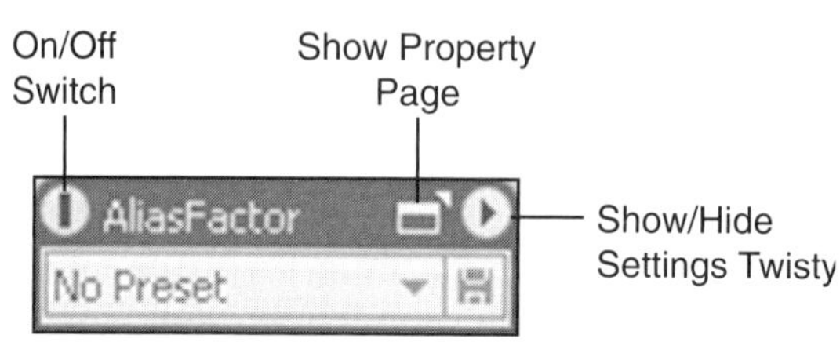

Figure 6.1 Many modules in the Inspectors share three common functionality buttons.

For Figure 6.1 you will see that I have selected Alias Factor, one of the audio FX units. However, similar buttons also apply to Instruments, MIDI FX, the Track Arpeggiator, Input Quantize, MIDI Input, and Audio Output.

To the left of a unit's name is a button: This is the function's On/Off button, which you can left-click on. When the button has a green background with a vertical black line, the unit is switched on. When the background is gray and there are two dots (like a colon), then the unit is switched off.

Immediately to the right of an Instrument or audio FX unit's name is a rectangle with an arrow at its top-right corner. If you hold your mouse over this box, a pop-up will appear, saying "Show Property Page." If you left-click on this button, it will open the Instrument or audio FX unit's interface.

For the Input Quantize and Track Arpeggiator functions, to the right of the unit, you will find a twisty arrowhead, which will open up a settings page. Here you can control the Input Quantize and Track Arpeggiator settings.

Controlling an Instrument or FX Unit

For instruments and audio FX units, the twisty arrowhead will open up the function's settings box (as I have done with Alias Factor in Figure 6.2). This view gives a reduced set of controls for the Instrument or FX unit so that you can tweak it without opening up the interface. The benefit of this tool is that it is fully configurable, so you can set four sliders to control your choice of functions in the Instrument or FX unit.

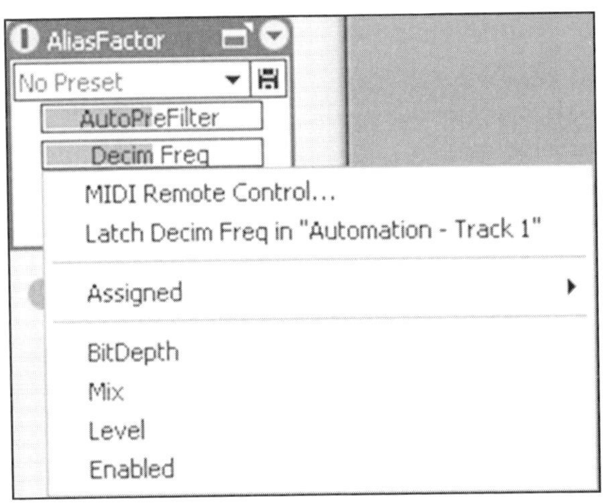

Figure 6.2 Assigning a slider control.

To assign a slider:

1. Choose the slider you wish to assign. (Any current assignment will be lost.)
2. Right-click on the slider, and a menu will appear. (Among other things, this menu has an item "Assigned," which shows how the slider is presently assigned.)
3. On the menu, select the appropriate new assignment.

MIDI Remote Control

MIDI Remote Control is what we did in the old days before ACT (*Advanced Controller Technology*), which is discussed in Tutorial 13: ACT (Active Controller Technology). It allows you to control the slider assignments with external MIDI hardware. Although this technology has been overtaken by ACT, you may still want to use it if you don't want to get ACT set up or if you like the simplicity of this approach. Equally, there are some other areas (for instance, triggering Cells in the Groove Matrix where there is a MIDI Remote Control option, but no ACT option).

Once you have assigned a slider to control an Instrument or audio FX unit, you can then assign the MIDI Remote Control settings to that slider. These settings will apply only for the Project in which they are set. The first step to set up MIDI Remote Control is to right-click on the slider you want to control and select MIDI Remote Control. This will access the MIDI Remote Control window, which looks much like Figure 6.3 (although this figure shows how the window looks after the assignment has been completed).

In the MIDI Remote Control window, you will see a list of Mapped Parameters on the left-hand side. In Figure 6.3 you will see that the parameter I am mapping is the Sampling Frequency (Decim Freq) in the Alias Factor audio FX unit. If you have more than one parameter mapped, you can click on each parameter to display its mapping settings. To cancel a set of mappings, click on the parameter in the Mapped Parameters list and hit the Delete button at the foot of the list.

To map your hardware to control a parameter, you have two options:

- Manually map the parameter by entering the data on the right-hand side—for this you will need to know the MIDI data that your hardware is outputting. To read more about the MIDI Input Source and MIDI Channel, check out Tutorial 11: Setting Up MIDI In and MIDI Out.
- Alternatively, use MIDI Learn.

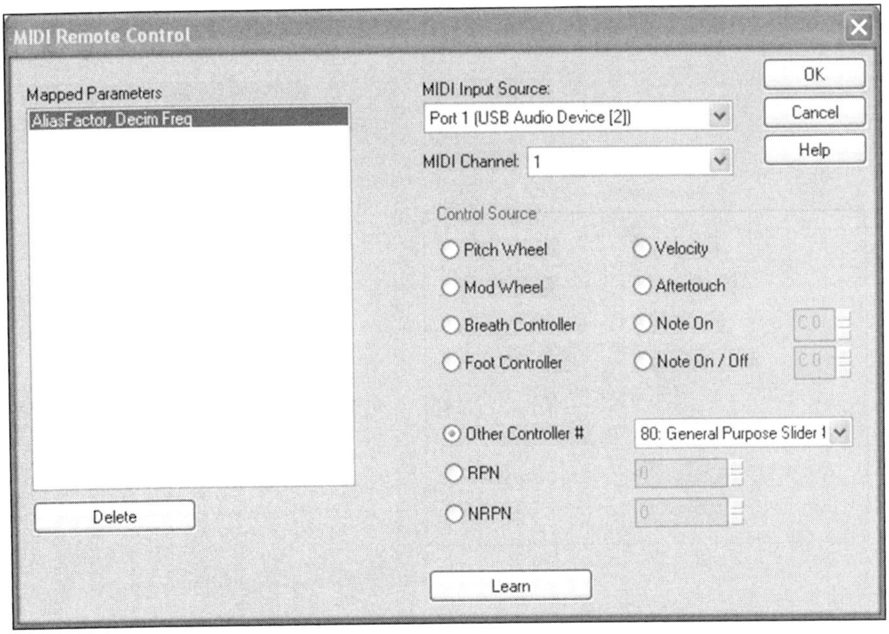

Figure 6.3 The MIDI Remote Control window.

The process to MIDI Learn is quite straightforward:

1. Left-click on the Learn button.
2. Move the controller on your MIDI hardware that you want to control the Instrument or FX unit.
3. Left-click on the Stop Learning button.

Audio Track Inspector

Figure 6.4 shows the Audio Track Inspector.

The Audio Input Selector selects the source from which audio is recorded. This selector is only relevant when you are recording audio and will be considered in greater detail in Chapter 3. Once audio has been recorded, the source for the Inspector is the recorded audio, and the Audio Input section has no further function for that Track.

You will note in Figure 6.4 that there is an Add MFX (Add MIDI FX) button and an Add Instrument button. You can add a MIDI FX unit, but it will have no effect in an Audio Track. If you invoke the Add Instrument function, it will convert this Audio Track into an Instrument Track.

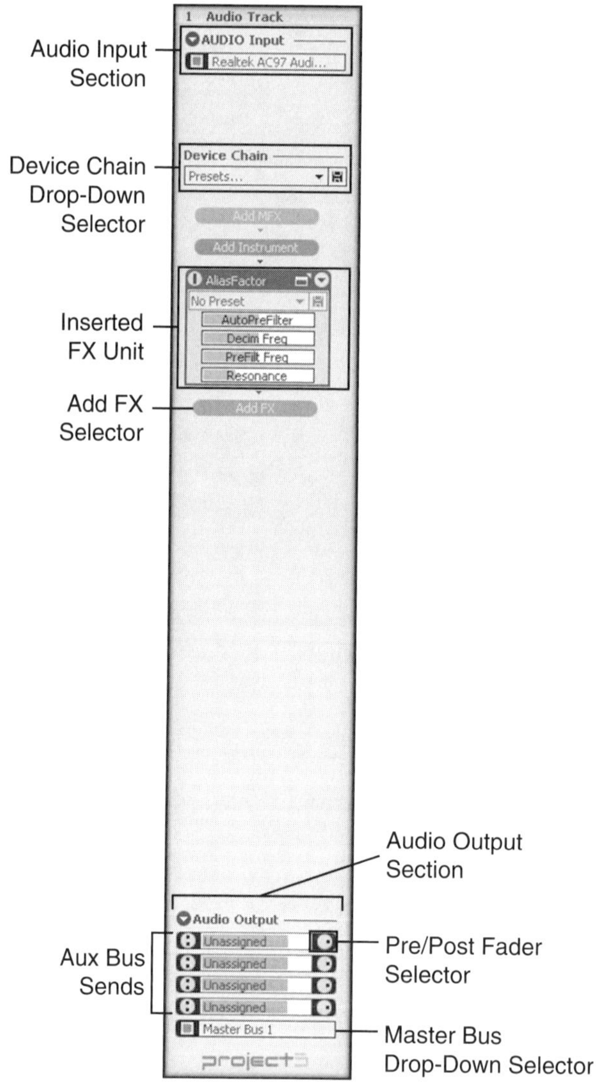

Figure 6.4 The Audio Track Inspector.

Remember, the signal flows from top to bottom. Therefore, in this Inspector, the audio first flows into the audio FX units. You can load one or more FX units by left-clicking on the Add FX Selector. The signal flows through the FX units from top to bottom—you can change the order of the FX units by dragging them (left-click on their name) to the desired order.

I will talk more about these FX units in Chapter 7.

At the bottom of the Audio Track Inspector is the Audio Output section. Here you can select:

- The extent to which the Track is sent to up to four assignable Aux Busses, and whether the signal is sent pre- or post-fader.
- The Master Bus to which the audio signal will be sent.

These features are explained in Tutorial 9 later in this chapter.

MIDI Track Inspector

Figure 6.5 shows the MIDI Track Inspector. This is used when you are driving an external piece of MIDI hardware (which could be a synthesizer or an FX unit, for instance). If you are exclusively using software synthesizers, then you will not need to use this Inspector. If you create a MIDI Track in error, intending instead to load a software instrument, then click on the Add Instrument button at the bottom and select the appropriate instrument, and you'll be good to go.

At the top of the MIDI Track Inspector, you'll find the MIDI Input section. This allows you to control the MIDI input so that you only record the data you want to record. You will also find the Input Quantize module, which allows you to compensate for some of the inconsistencies in live performance. I'll discuss the operation of both of these in Chapter 2, "Setting Up Your Hardware."

You will then find any inserted MIDI FX units, and you can add more by clicking on the Add MFX Selector. Unlike the audio FX units:

- There is no on/off switch for MIDI FX units; you have to turn off the MFX unit with the power button on its interface.
- There is no facility to assign sliders to control the MFX unit from the MIDI Track Inspector.

I'll discuss MIDI FX units in greater detail in Chapter 8.

After the MIDI FX units, the MIDI data flows to the Track Arpeggiator. The Track Arpeggiator is a very powerful and fun tool. Its operation is discussed in more detail in Chapter 4.

The last step in the MIDI Track Inspector is the MIDI Out Selector, where you can set:

- The MIDI Out Port
- The MIDI Out Channel

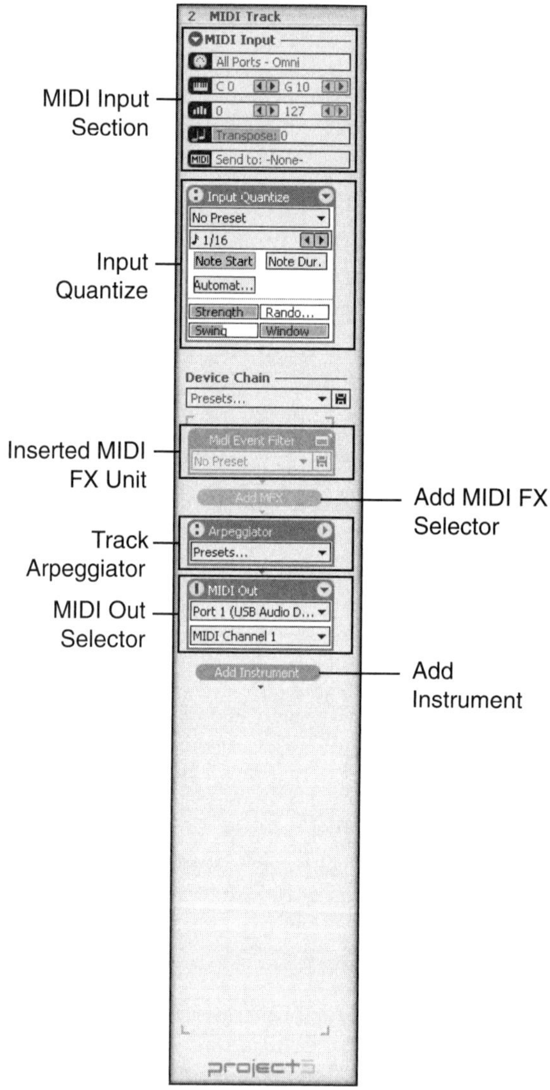

Figure 6.5 The MIDI Track Inspector.

These should correspond with hardware that you are using.

If you're intending to use external MIDI hardware, then I suggest you check out Chapter 2.

Instrument Track Inspector

The Instrument Track Inspector is essentially a cross between the MIDI Track Inspector and the Audio Track Inspector (as Figure 6.6 shows), so if you haven't read those earlier sections, I suggest you do so now.

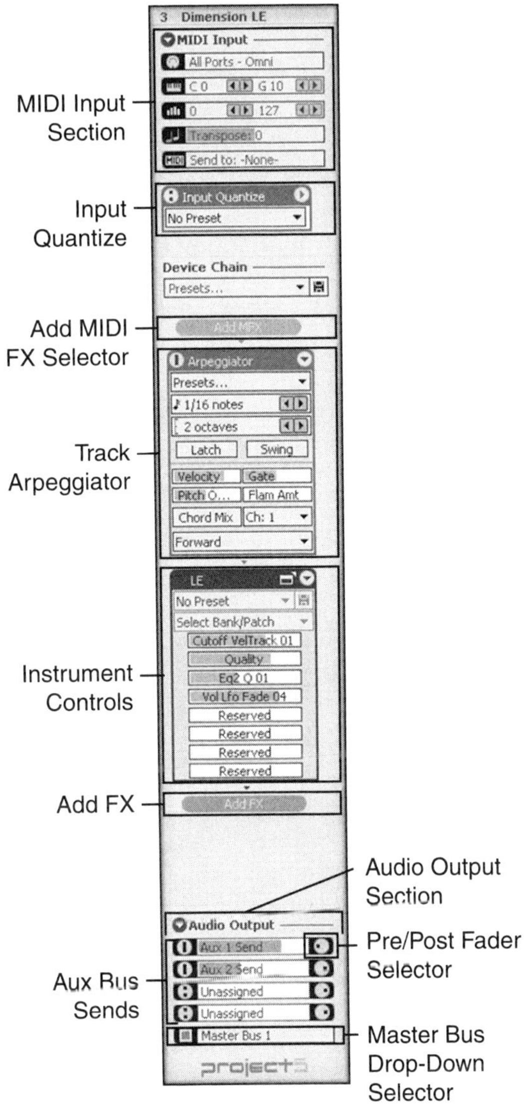

Figure 6.6 The Instrument Track Inspector.

Apart from the Instrument Controls, we have seen everything before. Before the Instrument Controls, you will find:

- The MIDI Input section
- The Input Quantize section
- MIDI FX slots
- The Track Arpeggiator

Figure 6.7 The Master Bus Inspector.

The Instrument Controls then give you control over the instrument. As noted in the earlier section, "Inspectors: Common Functionality," the sliders can be assigned to control the Instrument from the Instrument Track Inspector.

You will also note that you can select presets and banks/patches for your Instrument from the Instrument Controls. You don't have to select the sound from here; you can open up the Instrument and select the sound directly.

After the Instrument you can then add audio FX units.

Finally, the Instrument Track Inspector ends with the Audio Output section. The functionality this section offers will be discussed in greater detail in Tutorial 9 later in this chapter.

Master Bus Inspector

Master Busses are automatically created by Project5. You get one Master Bus for each physical hardware output that Project5 recognizes. The Master Bus Inspector is like a simplified Audio Track Inspector, as Figure 6.7 shows.

There are two controls in the Master Bus Inspector. First, there is the Add FX Control to apply audio FX to your master channel. Second, there is the Audio Output section, where you can determine the hardware output to which your Master Bus is sent. Check out Chapter 2 for further discussion about using this setting.

Aux Bus Inspector

The Aux Bus Inspector looks the same as the Master Bus Inspector with one difference: Instead of selecting the audio hardware output in the Audio Output section, in the Aux Bus Inspector you select the Master Bus to which the Aux Bus output is sent.

Tutorial 7: Using Other Synthesizers and Effects

Although Project5 ships with some great-sounding synthesizers and effects units, one of its greatest features is that it is an open system. This means you can use any synthesizer or effects unit with Project5 (provided the software is available in an appropriate format, and most software is). By comparison, software such as Reason by Propellerhead Software (www.propellerheads.se) is closed. This means that you can only use the synthesizers and effects that come with the program.

Software effects units and synthesizers are collectively known as *plug-ins* (or *plugs*), since you quite literally plug the software into your host (Project5). Indeed, plug-ins cannot be used without a host (although some synthesizers include a scaled-down host so you can run the synth in stand-alone mode outside of a host).

When you start looking, you will find that there are many plug-ins out there. Some are good. Some are bad. Some are free. Some cost. As you go through this book, I will make a few recommendations for plug-ins you should check out. You should also check out Project5.com and the Project5 forum, which both contain recommendations for further software.

If you are thinking about other synthesizers, then you should think about other Cakewalk synthesizers, especially Z3TA+ and Rapture. If you're going to check out these synths, then I also suggest you check out my book *Cakewalk Synthesizers:*

From Presets to Power User (Thomson Course Technology PTR, 2006), which tells you how to use the synthesizers.

Compatible Software

There are several software standards. The difference between them is technical and insignificant. In the 1980s the music instrument industry got together to agree upon MIDI, the *Musical Instrument Digital Interface* standard. Unfortunately, a similar standard has not been agreed upon for plug-ins.

Different standards are maintained for commercial reasons. The losers from the differing standards are the musicians:

- The differing standards mean that plug-in manufacturers have to create different versions of their plugs. The cost of maintaining these different versions has to be met somehow, so the manufacturers pass the cost on to their customers.
- Additionally, the differing standards simply create needless confusion. Most musicians want to make music and don't want to be computer technicians.

Project5 can run plugs in two formats: DX and VST. These are the most common formats, with VST being particularly prevalent. Historically, there were differences between the formats, but the differences are now irrelevant.

As you will see in a moment, the most apparent difference is that VST-format plugs need a wrapper to work in Project5, whereas DX-format plugs do not. This is not entirely correct. Both formats need "wrapping"; it's just that Project5 does the DX wrapping behind the scenes. By the way, a *wrapper* is simply a conduit through which Project5 and the plug-in communicate.

Unfortunately, all of the plug-ins use nasty abbreviations. You will find DX, DXi, VST, VSTi, and RTAS. Let me try to explain.

- DX and VST formats are used for effects.
- DXi and VSTi formats are used for instruments. However, some effects (mostly involving tempo synchronized features) can be created as DXi or VSTi plugs even though they are effects.
- Some DXi and VSTi instruments can be used as effects units (provided they have the necessary audio connections to allow this). For instance, Cakewalk's Z3TA+ synthesizer can be loaded as an effect. Check out your instrument's documentation to see whether this is allowed.
- RTAS-format effects and instruments do not work in Project5. This format relates to Pro Tools.

As you've already seen, loading an Instrument or an effect is simple. However, before you can load an Instrument or effect, you need to install the plug-in software on your computer and wrap the plug if necessary. After you have collected a number of plugs, you may also want to organize them. The remainder of this tutorial will address all of these issues.

Installing DX and DXi Plug-Ins

Often when you get a plug-in you will be given a choice of which format to install. For instance, take a look at Figure 7.1, which shows the options that were available to me when I installed Wave Arts' TrackPlug compressor/equalizer effect.

As you can see, I selected the DX version of the plug. As a general rule of thumb, if you have the choice between DX/DXi and VST/VSTi versions of a plug-in, I suggest you go for the DX/DXi version. However, there is no particular downside to going for the VST/VSTi version; you just don't need to worry about wrapping. Whatever you choose, only choose one format—otherwise, your plug-in will be available several times (which could get confusing).

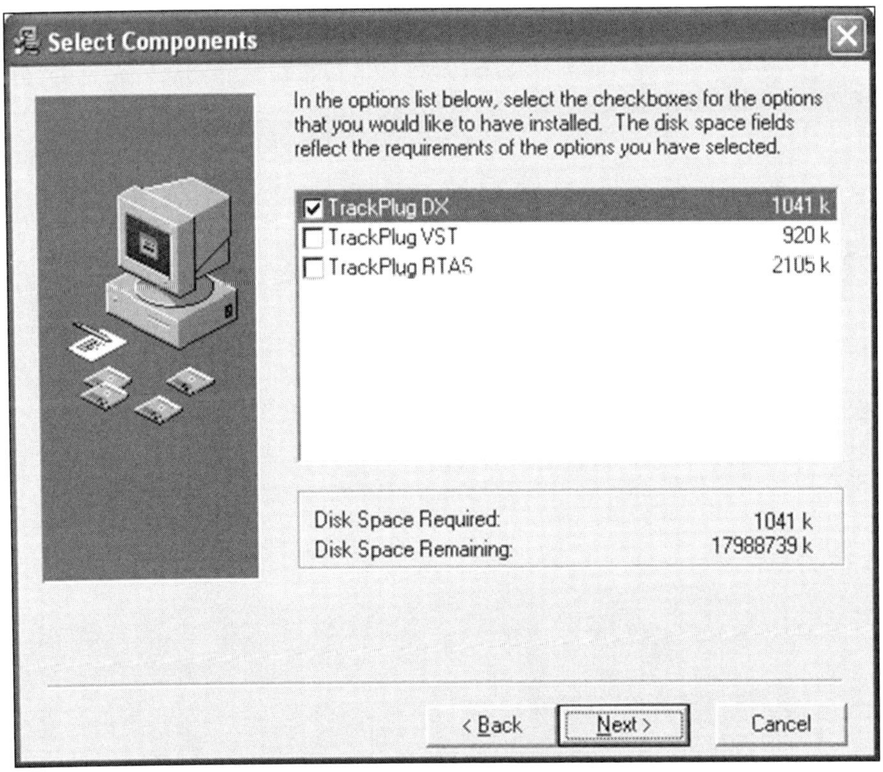

Figure 7.1 Installing the DX version of Wave Arts' TrackPlug.

The precise process for installing plugs differs between manufacturers, so I would strongly recommend that you check out the documentation that comes with your plug-in before installing it.

Once you have successfully installed a DX/DXi plug-in, it will be available the next time you load Project5. As you can see in Figure 7.2, TrackPlug is now available in my FX menu.

If you need proof that the newly installed plug-in works, take a look at Figure 7.3.

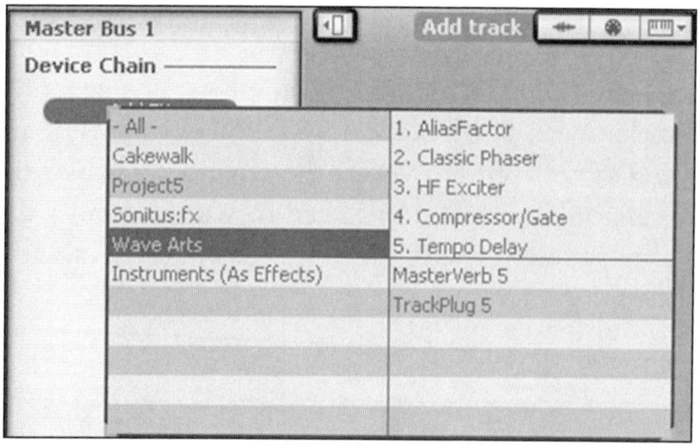

Figure 7.2 Once you have installed a DX/DXi plug-in, it will be available from the Add FX and Add Instrument Track menus.

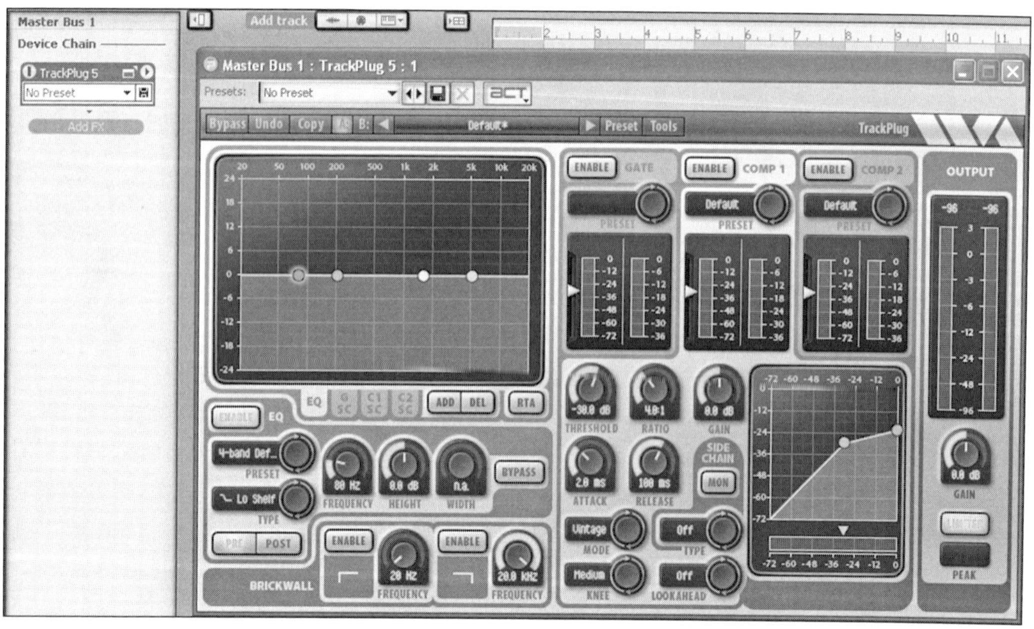

Figure 7.3 The newly installed Wave Arts TrackPlug DX plug-in in action.

Installing VST and VSTi Plug-Ins

As with the DX/DXi plugs, you should install the VST/VSTi software in accordance with the developer's instructions. When you install your VST/VSTi, you will be asked to confirm your VST folder. This is the place where the installer will locate your plug-in's software (which will be in the form of a .dll file). Project5 is likely to have set a default location during its installation, so unless you have a good reason to do otherwise, I suggest you stay with any default settings.

Wrapping a VST/VSTi Plug-In

Once the plug has been installed, it needs to be "wrapped" to work inside Project5. As you read in Tutorial 1: Getting Into and Out of Project5, under the section "Scans Performed on Opening Project5," this scanning process can be set to run automatically by selecting Options > VST Plug-Ins and putting a check mark next to Scan for VST Plug-Ins on Startup (see Figure 7.4).

As you can see from the VST Plug-Ins window, I have located all of my VST/VSTi plug-ins in the folder c:\vsti. Within that folder, I keep my plugs in separate folders—the scanner will look into subfolders without further intervention.

You can locate your plug-ins in several folders, however, you need to ensure that each separate folder is scanned. To tell the scanner to look in another folder, click on

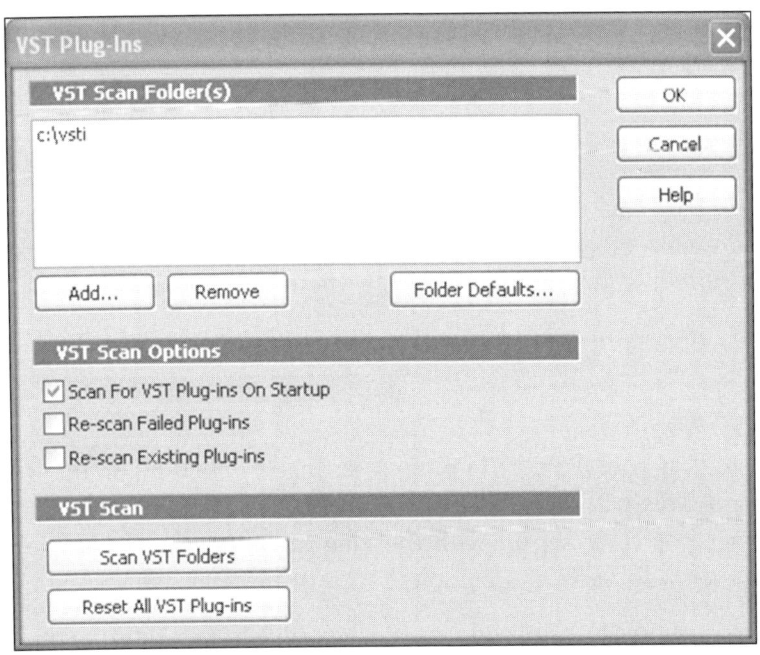

Figure 7.4 The VST Plug-Ins window.

the Add button and locate the new folder. To remove a folder from the scanning process, click on the folder in the list of scanned folders and hit the Remove button.

The third button under the list of VST Scan Folder(s) is the Folder Defaults button. This sets the default VST plug-in properties. The idea here is that you can set up separate VST folders where the VST will be treated in a different way. Unless you know what you're doing, I suggest you leave the defaults alone, since these settings are primarily intended for VST/VSTi plugs that may not operate in the normal manner. In any case, you can always change a plug-in's properties through the Plug-In Manager or from the VST/VSTi itself. (There is a VST drop-down menu option in the buttons across the top of each VST/VSTi—Plug-In Properties is the last option.)

VST Scan Options

As I've already mentioned, when the Scan for VST Plug-Ins on Startup option is checked, the scanner will check the VST Scan Folder(s) for new plug-ins whenever Project5 is loaded. This section then gives you two other options:

- Re-Scan Failed Plug-Ins will cause the scanner to check plug-ins that did not scan correctly and so are not functioning within Project5; any failed plug-ins will be rescanned whenever a scan is undertaken.
- Re-Scan Existing Plug-Ins causes all plug-ins to be scanned whenever a scan is run. This can slow the scanning process. You might want to use this option from time to time—for instance, if you have relocated a VST's .dll, then the plug will cease to work until it is rescanned.

Manual Scanning

If you deselect the Scan for VST Plug-Ins on Startup option, you can run a VST/VSTi scan at any time by clicking on the Scan VST Folders button. This will perform the same scan as would be performed if an automatic scan were undertaken and will rescan failed plug-is and existing plug-ins if these options have been selected.

You can also run a manual scan from the Plug-In Manager, which is discussed in a moment.

Reset All VST Plug-Ins

You can reset all of your VST/VSTi plug-in settings by clicking on the Reset All VST Plug-Ins button. This will delete all of your current VST/VSTi settings (including any manual settings you have set up with the Plug-In Manager). When you next run a scan, the scanner will perform a complete scan of the selected VST Scan Folder(s).

This "nuclear" option can be useful if you're having VST/VSTi problems, but because it deletes all of your current settings, I suggest you use it infrequently and with care.

Configuring Your Plug-Ins: The Plug-In Manager

We're now going to move on and look at the Plug-In Manager.

This is sometimes referred to as the *SONAR Plug-In Manager*. However, the Plug-In Manager is included with the Project5 installation, and it is a useful tool. That being said, because this tool was designed for SONAR, there are a few features that are apparently available, but which don't work for Project5. Accordingly, I will point to these, but I won't be detailing their use.

This is not the most interesting part of this tutorial, so if you're happy with the way your plug-ins work, you might want to skip ahead. You can always come back here and read this section if you've got a problem.

The Plug-In Manager is designed to manage all of your plug-ins, whether they be:

- VST/VSTi plug-ins
- DX/DXi plug-ins
- MIDI FX plug-ins
- DirectX Media Objects (DMO), which are Microsoft COM components that you are unlikely to use and so will not be mentioned further in this book
- Control surfaces, which may not seem like plug-ins, but the programs that relate to them are

For the Plug-In Manager to work, it must be installed. If it is installed, you can access it by going to Start > Program > Cakewalk > Project5 Version 2 > Plugin Manager. When the Plug-In Manager is loaded, it will look something like Figure 7.5.

Figure 7.5 shows (some of) the DirectX Audio Effects (DX). You can see in the list of Registered Plug-Ins (in the center column) that the Wave Arts TrackPlug effect that I installed earlier in this tutorial is listed (at the bottom of the list).

To the right of the plug-in you will see an area that is labeled in the figure as "Doesn't Function for Project5." This is quite a neat piece of functionality that allows you to arrange the groupings of your plug-ins and give them friendly names. Unfortunately, this only works with SONAR, not in Project5. However, as you will see, we can get a similar result without too much hard work.

You will also notice in Figure 7.5 that in addition to the Project5 effects that show up as registered plug-ins, there are a number of Sonitus:fx plug-ins. These are the plugs that come with SONAR, so unless you've got SONAR installed (or you have purchased these plug-ins), don't go looking for them.

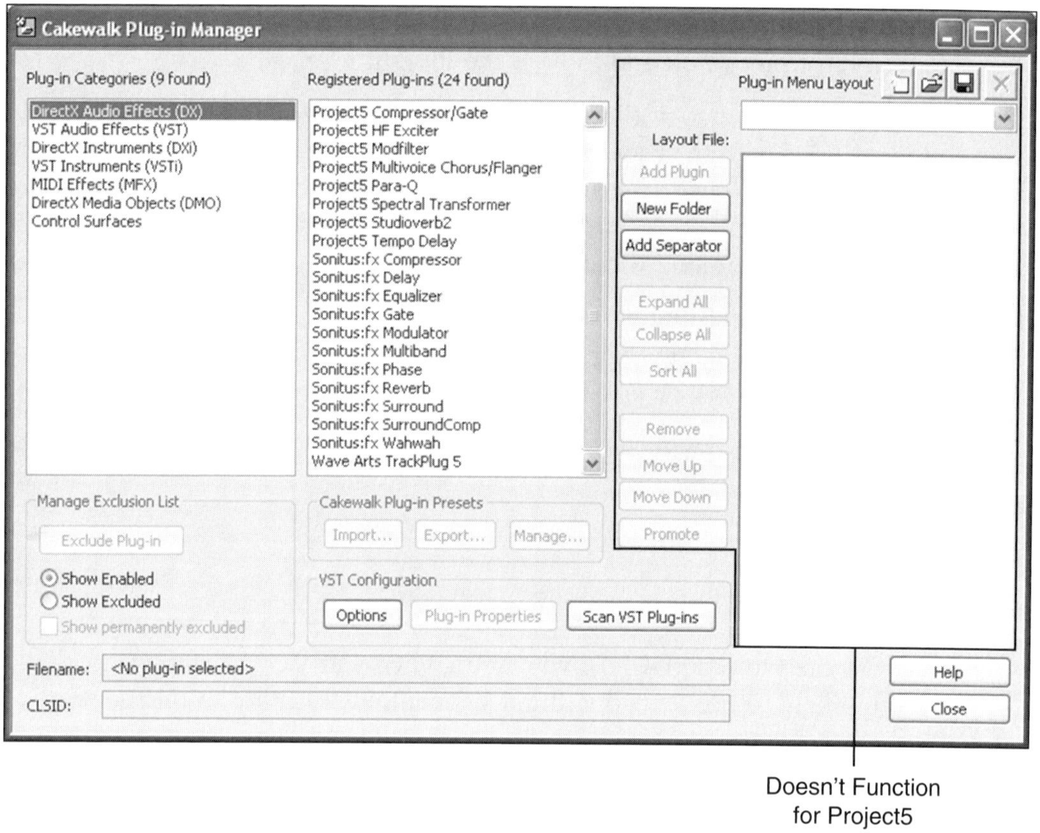

Figure 7.5 The Cakewalk Plug-In Manager.

As you click on the plug-in categories on the left-hand side, you will see the registered plug-ins within that category. If you click on a plug, at the bottom of the Manager you will see the filename (and file location) of the plug and either the class ID (CLSID), which identifies the component for DX plugs, or the vendor's name for VSTs.

Plug-In Inclusion and Exclusion

Under the Plug-in Categories list, you will see the Manage Exclusion List section. This allows you to exclude plug-ins, which you might want to do if a plug is misbehaving. You may find that if you have a troublesome plug, it is easier to exclude it, fix the problem, and then enable it again, rather than have it potentially crashing your system.

To exclude a plug, click on it and check that you have the right plug by looking at the Filename box, then click on the Exclude Plug-In button.

You will see that you have the option to show enabled plug-ins or to show excluded plug-ins. When the Show Excluded option is selected, you can re-enable a plug by clicking on it and then clicking the Enable Plug-In button.

Plug-In Naming and Organizing

If you double-click on a plug-in, a dialog box will appear, headed Set Plug-In Friendly Name (see Figure 7.6). You can use this function to set a more useful name for your plug-ins. It can be particularly helpful once you have a considerable number of similar plugs. Type in the new friendly name and click OK.

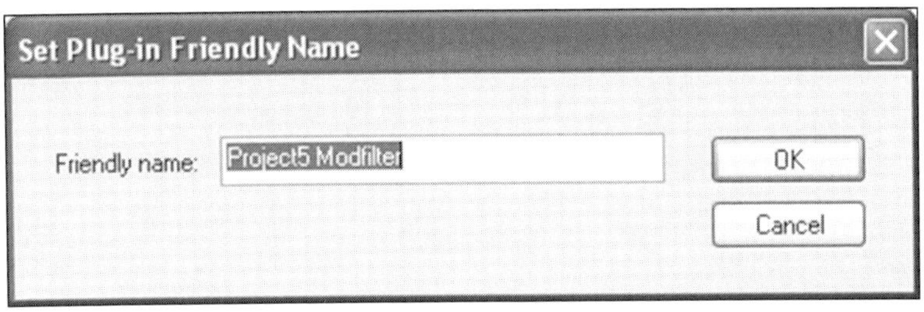

Figure 7.6 The Set Plug-In Friendly Name dialog box.

If you want to organize your plugs, you can do so by setting a friendly name. You will see that several plugs' names are prefixed Project5 (with a space between the prefix and the plug name). If you open the Add FX menu in Project5, you will see that all of the Project5 plugs are grouped together.

To group a bunch of plugs together, simply add your own prefix (followed by a space), and then add your own plug-in name. Using this function, you could (as an example) group all of your compressors together by adding a "Comp" prefix.

Plug-In Presets

In Chapter 7 I will talk about saving plug-in presets. The Plug-In Manager allows you to import, export, and manage your presets. As a first step to using this feature, click on the plug where the presets you want to manage are located.

- To import presets, left-click on the Import button. You might want to import presets if you are transferring them from another machine, or if a friend has shared his or her presets with you.
- Once you have located the preset library file (.spp) that you wish to import, right-click on the file name, and a list of presets in that library will appear in the Plug-Ins/Presets in Library box at the bottom of the dialog box. You can either import all of the presets by clicking on the Select All button or select specific

presets to import by Ctrl+left-clicking on the ones you wish to import. Once you have made your choice, click on the Open button, and the presets will be available to you next time you load Project5.

- To export presets, left-click on the Export button. You can then either Select All presets or select a number of presets (by Ctrl+left-clicking). Give the library of presets a name and hit the Save button.
- If you click on the Manage button, a Manage Presets dialog box will appear (see Figure 7.7). From this dialog box you can rename and delete presets.

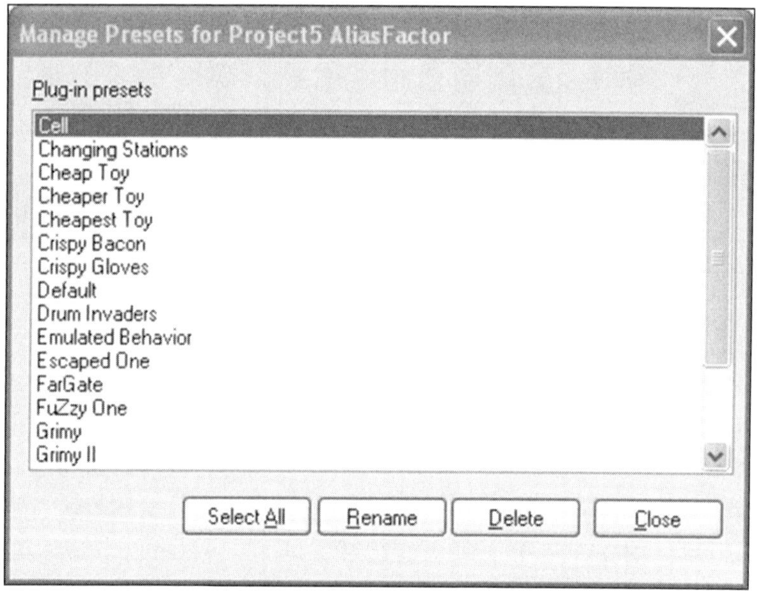

Figure 7.7 The Manage Presets dialog box.

VST Configuration

Under the preset management tools you will find the VST Configuration tools. These essentially mirror the tools that are available in Project5 that we discussed in the "Installing VST and VSTi Plug-Ins" section earlier in this tutorial.

- The Options button allows you to set the path (or paths) to be scanned and to determine whether the scanner will rescan failed plug-ins and existing plug-ins.
- Plug-In Properties opens a dialog box that allows you to change a plug-in's properties.
- Scan VST Plug-Ins triggers a manual scan of the selected VST folders.

Tutorial 8: Working with Projects

Once you start working with Project5, you'll want to know how to open and save files, and how to fit Project5 to your way of working. This may not be the most fascinating topic, but this tutorial includes some very important stuff.

Before we get going, let me explain the concept of a Project. A *Project* is a complete musical piece (or, if not complete, a work in progress). For instance, a song could be saved as a Project. If you are only dealing with one Track and one Clip, then you might work at the Clip level. However, when you start to deal with more than one Clip, then you will be working at the Project level.

Saving a Project

If you're familiar with Windows' standard saving procedures, then Project5 won't be too much of a stretch for you.

Save

To save a Project, select File > Save or hit Ctrl+S on your keyboard. The Save function will overwrite any existing file without asking for confirmation before it does this.

If you are saving a Project for the first time, then by clicking Save, you will invoke the Save As function.

Save As

You can invoke the Save As function by selecting File > Save As or by hitting Ctrl+Shift+S. The Save As function allows you to save new Projects and to save a copy of existing Projects under a new name.

When you invoke the Save As function, the Save As box will appear (see Figure 8.1).

When you save a Project, you save everything you are working on and all your settings, so you save all of your Clips and any audio files in the Project, plus the current settings for any Instruments or FX units.

By default this will locate your .p5p Project file (and any associated Audio Tracks) in the Cakewalk Projects folder. However, you can always navigate to a different folder. If you want to regularly use a different folder, then you could always include a shortcut in this default folder (alternatively, if you are so inclined, I'm sure a quick registry hack would sort you out).

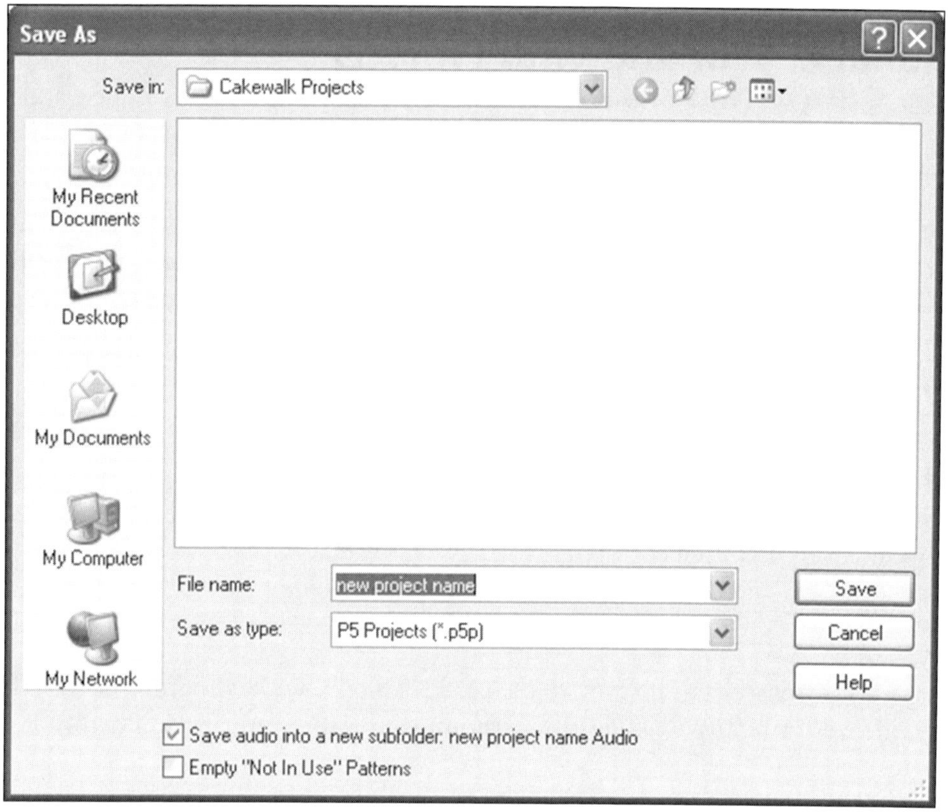

Figure 8.1 The Save As box.

There are two other options at the bottom of the Save As box, which you can select by checking them:

- Save Audio into a New Subfolder creates a subfolder with the same name as the Project. This ensures that all of your audio files are kept in one place, making them easier to manage and back up.
- Empty "Not in Use" Patterns will exclude Clips that are not in use from the Save function. The significance of this option will become more apparent during Chapter 3.

Song Information

If you want to save information about the song—for instance, a copyright notice and production notes—you can do by selecting File > Info, which opens the Song Information box (see Figure 8.2).

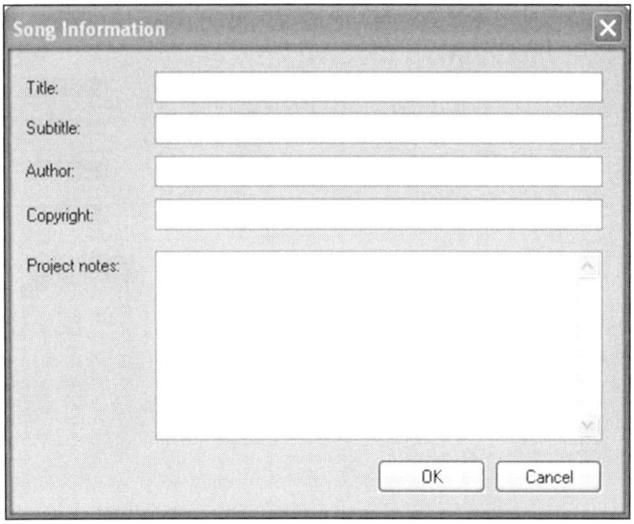

Figure 8.2 The Song Information box.

Save As Template

You can save a Project as a template by using the File > Save As Template command.

A template will save all of your settings, Song Information text, the Instruments and so on, and the layout. Setting up a template can save you a lot of time: When you next create a new Project, it will be based on any template you create.

Opening a Project

This isn't going to be the most difficult part of the tutorial.... There are three ways to open up a Project:

- Select File > Open (or hit Ctrl+O) and navigate to the Project you want to load.
- Select File and choose one of the recently opened Projects.
- In Windows Explorer, locate the Project and double-click on it.

Open Last Project

One option that Project5 gives you is to load up the last project you were working on when you start Project5. To set this option, go to Options > Open Last Project at Startup. When this option is selected, there is a check mark next to it. You can deselect the option (so Project5 doesn't load any Project when it starts up) by clicking on the option again (and the check mark will disappear).

Setting Up a New Project: Making Project5 Fit with Your Way of Working

When you open up Project5, it will load a blank Project based on the default template.

If you want to create a new Project while you are working with Project5, you have two options:

- File > New > Project (Ctrl+N) will create a blank Project so there will be no Instruments, Busses, or FX and so on, but the layout will be based on the default template.
- File > New > Project from Template (Ctrl+Shift+N) will create a new Project based on the default template.

Tutorial 9: Signal Flow through Project5

As you saw in Tutorial 5: Audio, MIDI, and Instrument Tracks, the audio signal in Project5's Tracks "flows" from the top of the Track Inspector to the bottom. When it gets to the bottom of the Inspector, it has to go somewhere. Before we look at the signal flow in Project5 between the Tracks and the final output, I want to talk a bit about some of the places and ways that the signal can flow.

Volume, Pan, and Width

Before the audio signal leaves a Track it must pass through the Volume, Pan, and Width Controls. These are located on the Track Panes. Their operation is fairly straightforward:

- The Volume Control controls the level of the Track.
- The Pan Control balances the Track in the stereo spectrum.
- The Width Control works as if someone comes into your studio and moves your loudspeakers.
  - When the Width Control is set to 90°, the stereo field behaves as you would expect.
  - When the Width Control is below 90°, it is as if the speakers are moved closer together. Set the Width Control to 0°, and the stereo field behaves as if both speakers have been moved to the center of the audio field. (In other words, you will hear a mono output.)
  - When the Width Control is set above 90°, it is as if a little person has jumped out of the computer and moved your speakers outward to give a wider stereo field.

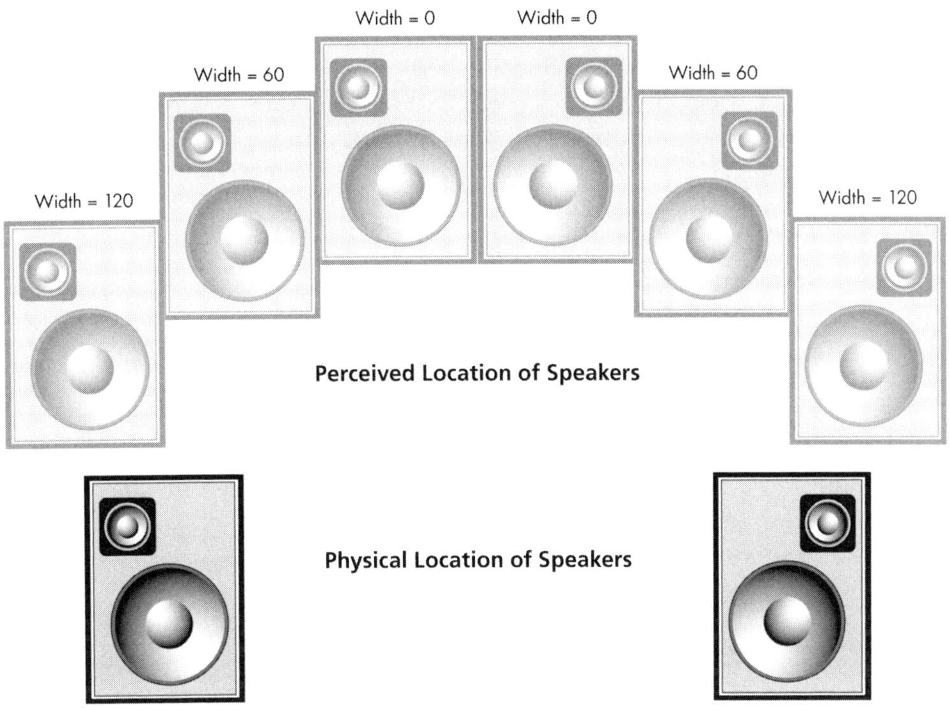

Figure 9.1 The Width Control in operation.

Figure 9.1 illustrates the operation of the Width Control in practice.

Each of the Aux Busses and the Master Busses also has a Volume, Pan, and Width Control.

Audio Busses

A *Bus* is a channel through which audio is sent. At the end of each Track's audio chain, the signal has to be sent somewhere, and that somewhere is along an Audio Bus. Project5 has two main types of Audio Busses:

- Master Busses
- Aux Busses

Master Busses

Master Busses are the mechanism by which Project5 is connected to the hardware outputs of your DAW. Every Track and every Aux Bus is connected to a Master Bus. Project5 will create a Master Bus for each hardware output that it recognizes.

Project5 can therefore provide many Master Busses, so it is capable of outputting many separate audio signals. Although this sounds great, remember that you can only mix to stereo (in other words, two channels) within Project5. If you want to hear more than two channels of audio, then you'll have to hear it directly from Project5 (or ReWire Project5 into a host, such as SONAR, that is capable of mixing a greater number of audio outputs—ReWire is discussed further in Tutorial 27: Using Project5 with Other Hosts).

In practice, for most of your audio work, one Master Bus is likely to be sufficient.

To assign an Instrument Track or an Audio Track to a Master Bus, click on the selector at the bottom of the Inspector. (It will show the currently selected Master Bus.) From the pop-up menu (see Figure 9.2), select the new Master Bus.

Figure 9.2 Selecting the Master Bus to which the Track's audio output is routed.

Aux Busses

An *Aux Bus*, or *Auxiliary Bus*, is a separate audio channel, outside of the link from the Tracks to the Master Bus. You don't have to use Aux Busses, but they can be very handy. Project5 allows a large number of Aux Busses—the number you can set up depends on the power of your DAW. However, each Track has a maximum of four Aux Bus Sends.

The one main purpose for an Aux Bus is to provide a conduit where several audio sources can share the same FX unit (easing workflow, as you've only got one FX unit to adjust, and saving your CPU). So for instance, you may put a reverb on an Aux Bus and then send your vocals, your guitar, and some of the drums to the Aux Bus to add some reverb to all of the signals. Aux Busses are very much like Audio Tracks, so you can load more than one audio FX unit into an Aux Bus.

There is a secondary purpose for an Aux Bus: to create a sub-mix. A *sub-mix* is where you mix several parts together and then send the mixed parts to the Master Bus, but you don't send the unmixed parts to the Master Bus. The sub-mix allows you to more easily control the level of the sub-mix (because you control just one fader, not a group of individual faders). So for instance, you could sub-mix together some vocal parts, add some FX to the sub-mix, and then send the sub-mix to the Master Bus.

The output from an Aux Bus is sent directly to a Master Bus, and you can select the Master Bus to which the Aux Bus is sent. In Project5 you cannot send the output from one Aux Bus to another.

Before you can send a Track's signal to an Aux Bus, you must insert the Aux Bus. Once you have done that, you can then assign one of your Track Sends to the Aux Bus. You do this by right-clicking on the Send and selecting the Aux Bus from the pop-up menu (see Figure 9.3).

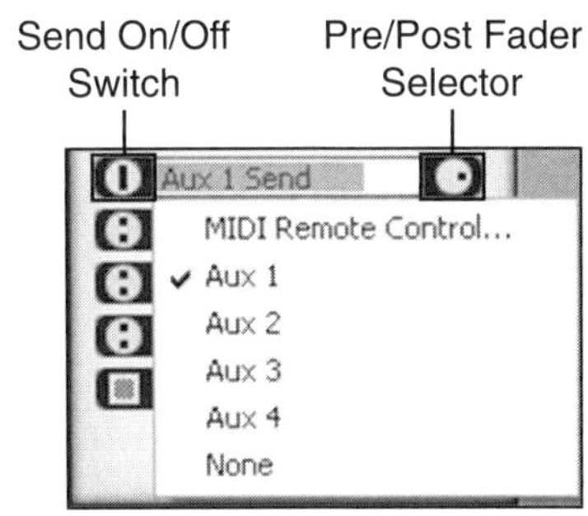

Figure 9.3 Assigning an Aux Bus and selecting pre-fader or post-fader Send.

Once you have assigned your Aux Send, you can decide whether the Send should be pre-fader or post-fader. This option can be selected with the Pre/Post Fader Selector. When the dot in the selector is to the left, the Send is pre-fader, and when the dot is to the right, the Send is post-fader.

Lastly, you can switch off an Aux Send with the Send On/Off switch.

Pre-Fader Sends

When a signal is sent pre-fader, a feed from the audio signal is taken after it has passed through all of the FX processing in the Track Inspector, and before it passes through the Volume, Pan, and Width Controls (see Figure 9.4).

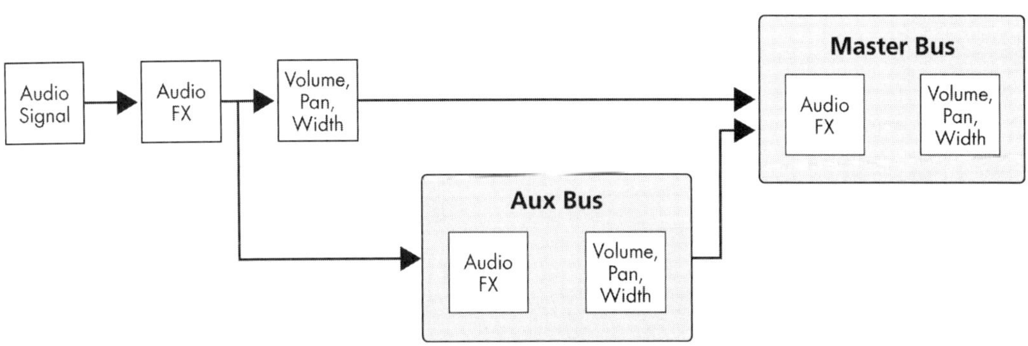

Figure 9.4 The pre-fade Send to an Aux Bus.

By taking a pre-fade Aux Send, the signal is not affected by the Volume, Pan, and Width Controls. The level of the Aux Send is controlled solely by the Aux Send slider, even if you set the volume of the Track to zero.

You are most likely to send a signal pre-fader if:

- The signal in the Aux Bus is being processed by a level-dependent device—for instance, a compressor—and changes to the level will have a material effect on the tone or the operation of the FX unit.
- You want to create a sub-mix.

Post-Fader Sends

When a signal is sent post-fader, a feed from the audio signal is taken at the end of Track's audio chain, after it has passed through the Volume, Pan, and Width Controls (see Figure 9.5). This means the level of the post-fader send is controlled by the Aux Send Slider and by the Volume Control of the Track.

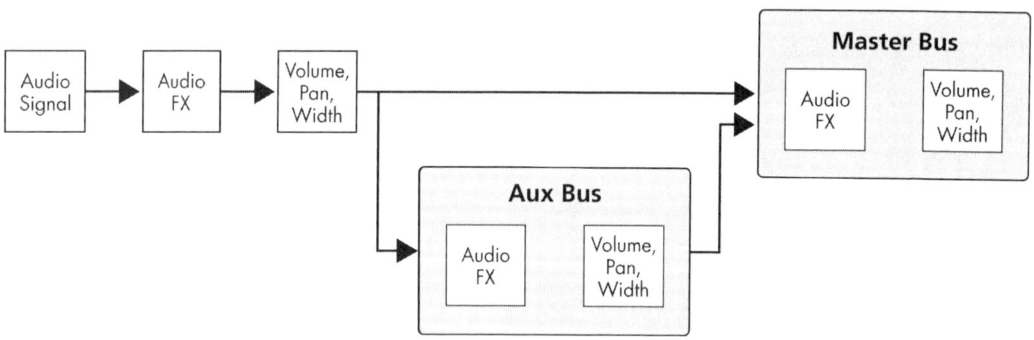

Figure 9.5 The post-fade Send to an Aux Bus.

When sending audio signals to FX units, post-fader signals are usually employed so that the amount of the effect varies with the level of the volume, ensuring that the proportion between wet and dry signals remains the same.

Looking at the Signal Flow

So now that you've got an idea of the components of signal flow and the principles, let's have a look at how the signal flows through Project5. Figure 9.6 shows the signal flow.

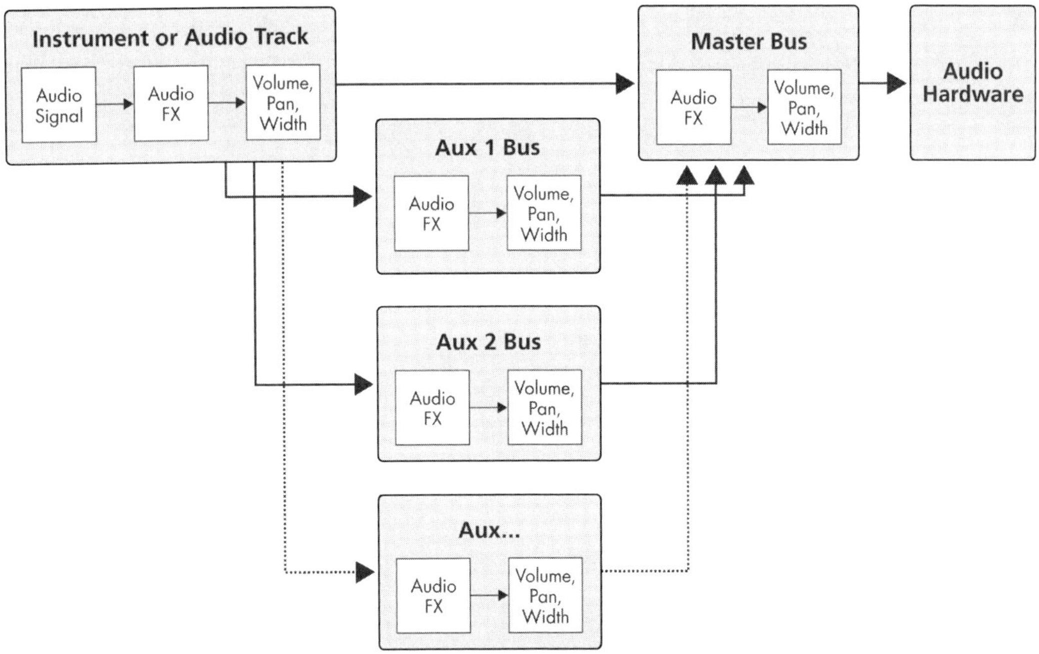

Figure 9.6 The signal flow in Project5.

You will remember that there are at least two possible outputs from each Instrument or Audio Track:

- Each Track must be sent to one of the Master Busses. This routing occurs after the Volume/Pan/Width block. Each Master Bus is then directly connected to one hardware audio output.
- Each Track can additionally have up to four Aux Bus Sends. These Sends can each be set up on either a pre-fader or a post-fader basis. Each Aux Bus must then be sent to one of the Master Busses.

In addition, the Aux Busses and the Master Busses all have:

- Capability of loading audio FX units
- A Volume/Pan/Width block

Audio In: What Gets Recorded?

If you are recording audio, you may listen to the signal with audio FX. For instance, if you are recording a singer, the singer may find it more natural and easier to sing if you add some reverb.

With Project5, the dry signal is always recorded, so you can add as many FX as you want (and your latency and CPU can stand). Figure 9.7 shows the signal flow for recorded audio.

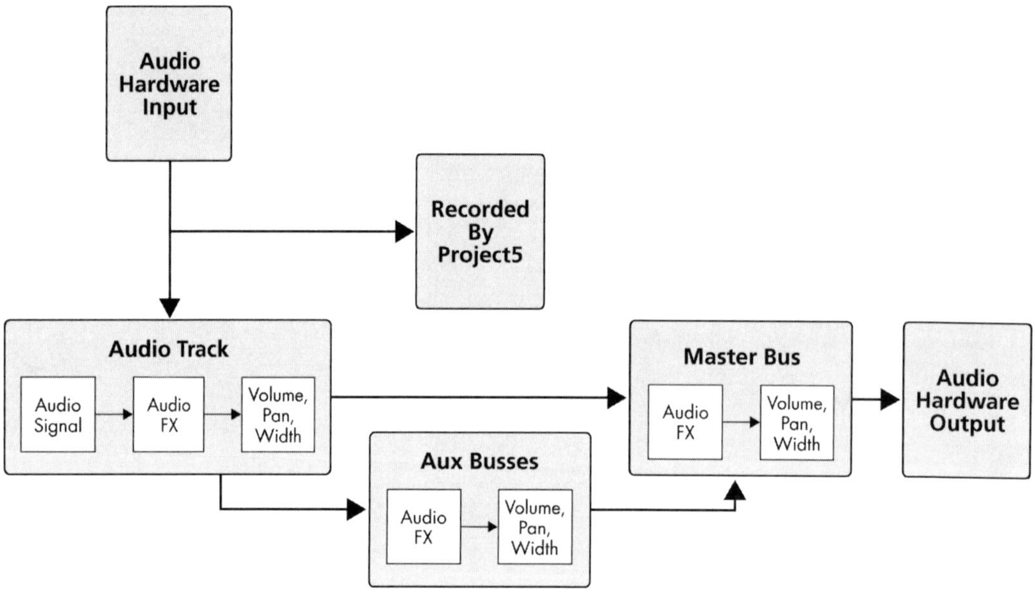

Figure 9.7 The signal flow for recorded audio in Project5.

2 Setting Up Your Hardware

This chapter is about setting up Project5 to work with your hardware. More accurately, it is about the interface between your hardware and Project5 and how to set that up and optimize it to fit with your way of working.

Before you set up your computer to run Project5, you need to set up your MIDI and audio hardware. You can do this at the same time that you install Project5, but then if you have a problem you may find difficulty in establishing whether the problem is with the hardware or the software.

Before you install new hardware, read the manufacturer's instructions. In fact, read them twice and follow them to the letter. Before you install the hardware, you might also want to check out any support sites or forums to see whether there is any problem you should be aware of (although I hope you will have made this check before you purchased the hardware).

Ninety-nine times out of a hundred, problems with audio come down to a simple issue: the drivers supplied with the hardware. The other one percent of the time can usually be attributed to rogue plug-ins (particularly cracked software and dodgy freeware) that don't fully correspond with published standards.

If you are looking to purchase some new hardware, then I cannot recommend strongly enough that you buy your gear from a reputable manufacturer with a history of producing professional-quality audio gear (even if you are not a professional music maker). Do check out any support sites or forums before you buy, and if the gear looks to be cheap, then there is probably a reason for that (and it won't be a good audio reason).

Once you have your new piece of hardware installed and running perfectly, then leave it alone. If the manufacturer updates the drivers, by all means download these new drivers. However, *do not* install these new drivers as a matter of routine. If your machine is working well without the driver, what purpose will a new driver serve? The best you can hope for when you install a new driver on a machine that is functioning perfectly is that you maintain the same level of performance.

However, if you are experiencing problems, then check the release notes that come with the new driver. If these don't suggest that the new driver will solve your problems, then think hard before you install the new software. If the driver's notes suggest that the new software will sort out your problems, then proceed with caution. As before, once you have a machine that is running as you would hope, then leave it alone—there's no promise that a new driver will solve your problems.

Tutorial 10: Setting Up Audio In and Audio Out

To get up and running with Project5, you need an audio interface that can output audio. Anything after that is a luxury (or superfluous, depending on your point of view). However, since Project5 can only address one audio interface at a time, when you get an audio interface, make sure that it has sufficient flexibility for any project you may work with.

Audio interfaces come in a wide range of different shapes and sizes, from simple stereo-in and stereo-out setups to huge multi-format interfaces that can cope with many streams of audio (perhaps more than 50). Figure 10.1 shows the interfaces that I use. I have an older setup, and instead of using a FireWire or USB converter, I have a PCI card in my computer. The card I use is an RME Hammerfall card (which I don't think is manufactured anymore). This is a digital card that doesn't actually convert the digital data into audio, but instead, it passes digital audio data into the computer.

For me the conversion is undertaken by two units:

- A TL Audio 5051 Mono Valve Processor
- A Behringer Ultragain Pro-8 Digital ADA8000

Figure 10.1 shows my setup.

I use the TL Audio interface for vocals. As its name suggests, it is a valve (tube) unit that has a warm sound. The interface combines a pre-amplifier for the vocal microphone with a compressor, EQ, noise gate, and analog-to-digital conversion. This gives me convenience and high quality in one package. I put an analog microphone in one end and take a digital signal at the other end. I can also take a direct analog feed from the unit so the vocalist can hear his own vocals—the reason for this will become clear in the section about latency, later in this tutorial.

The Behringer is an 8-input/8-output digital converter, with 8 pre-amps. I rarely use the inputs (as I prefer the sound of the valve unit). However, I do use the output

Figure 10.1 The audio interfaces in the author's home setup.

from this unit more frequently. (If nothing else, this is my only digital-to-analog converter.) These outputs are set up as four (stereo) pairs. This means I can output four different stereo signals from Project5 and treat them in different ways. So for instance, if I wanted to run Project5 into an external FX unit, I could.

Alternatively (and more likely within the way I work), I can create a different submix for a singer. (Singers often prefer to work with a simpler backing track to make their pitching easier.) You may notice in the picture that there are two mixers and some hardware effects—the second mixer and the effects units are to give a dedicated mix for the singer.

The number of inputs or outputs on an interface is not an indicator of quality, although depending on the purpose you will put your interface to, you may need more or fewer inputs. As you can see, my more expensive converter only works in mono and then only converts from analog to digital. The indicators of quality are:

- Bit depth
- Sample rate
- Quality of the converters

The first two items are comparatively easy to assess: The bit depth and the range of sample rates that an audio interface can cope with will be included in the audio interface's marketing material (and are probably indicated on the face of the unit). The quality of the converters is much harder to assess. Unless you can get several interfaces together and test them side by side, or you have access to put one through its paces, then you are likely to have to rely on reviews and reputation.

Before we go any further, let me lead you through a very quick and dirty digital audio crash course. The purpose of this introduction is to give you enough information to understand what Project5 is doing and to make the right selections so you get the best possible audio results. This introduction is not intended to make you an expert about all digital audio matters!

Bit Depth and Sample Rate

Audio waveforms are stored in a digital format inside Project5. Once the audio is in a digital format, there are two key factors you need to think about:

- Bit depth
- Sample rate

The bit depth determines how many different levels of loudness a digital waveform can have. The minimum standard for audio creation is 16 bit, with 24 bit being the norm. Sixteen bit means there are 65,536 (2^16) possible levels of loudness for a waveform. Twenty-four bit gives 16,777,216 (2^24) possible values for a wave.

The second factor determining the quality of digital waveforms is the sampling rate, which is the number of slices a waveform is cut into. A sampling rate of 44.1 kHz would mean that the waveform is cut up into 44,100 snapshots of the wave each second. This is the rate used for audio CDs and is the default value for high-quality audio.

In Chapter 7, "Working with Audio FX Units," I will look at using Alias Factor, which is an audio FX unit that allows you to creatively play with the bit depth and sample rate to dirty up the sound.

As you can see in Figure 10.2, digital audio is not perfect, but it is pretty good. A higher sampling rate and a higher bit rate will give greater resolution—from the listener's perspective, greater resolution means better sonic fidelity.

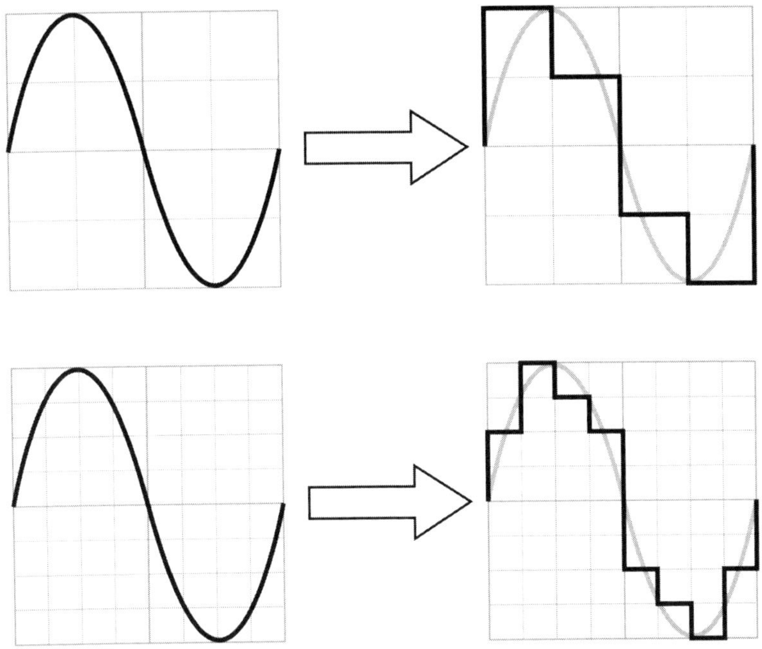

Figure 10.2 The imperfection of digital audio. A higher bit rate and an increased sample rate can give a better digital representation of the sound.

Apart from the most basic models, most audio interfaces can convert to and from both 16- and 24-bit digital formats and can cope with a wide range of sample frequencies. At the moment there are no mass-market digital interfaces with a bit rate above 24 bit.

However, internally Project5 works at 32 bit for all audio (both recorded audio and audio created by the Instruments). Irrespective of their bit depth, all digital sounds have a finite dynamic range. If you add two signals together and the internal dynamic range is exceeded, this would lead to digital distortion (a bad thing).

To prevent distortion, one option would be to reduce the levels of both of the signals; however, this would lead to rounding errors and would degrade the sound quality. Project5 takes the alternative approach and works internally at 32 bit but reduces the bit rate of the output signal (to the default project bit rate). This avoids rounding errors as a signal passes through Project5.

Unless you have a good reason not to, I would suggest you always work at 24 bit because it will give you the highest audio fidelity. Although it is a great benefit that Project5 works internally at 32 bit, you cannot improve the fidelity of recorded audio by converting it from 16 bit to 24 bit.

Also, when you record digital, you often need to reduce your input level to ensure there is no digital distortion—unlike analog, overloading the input doesn't give "warmth," but instead leads to a very harsh form of distortion that cannot be removed. When you reduce the level at 16 bit, it will have a much more detrimental effect than a similar reduction at 24 bit will have.

As far as sample rates go, I tend to stick with 44,100 Hz, since that is the CD standard. Any variation that will require the sample rate to be converted may introduce unwanted side-effects on the material when it is converted for CD output. Some people also favor 88,200 Hz because it converts (comparatively) smoothly to 44,100 Hz. You *can* mix different bit rates together within a Project, but you cannot mix different sampling rates.

Monitoring and Latency

When you start working with digital audio, you will hear the word *latency* a lot. Latency means delay: the delay between the input of audio into your computer and when you hear it come out of your speakers. In the world of music and audio, latency is therefore a bad thing. However, in the world of digital audio, latency cannot be avoided.

Latency arises in many places in the audio chain. It is the unfortunate combination of several latency-inducing devices that can lead to problems. Let me give some examples of where latency can arise.

Audio Conversion

The most noticeable form of latency arises when analog audio is converted to digital, and vice versa.When analog audio is converted into digital, the analog signal passes through an analog-to-digital converter (often called an *ADC*). The ADC cuts the audio into slices and takes a snapshot of each slice. The number of slices is determined by the sampling rate, and, as mentioned in the last section, the most common sampling rate is 44,100 Hz. The ADC outputs digital data, which is then recorded by Project5.

There are two phases to the sampling process:

1. Taking the snapshots
2. Passing the digitized data

ADCs work by taking the snapshots and then passing a bundle of data representing several snapshots to the recording device (see Figure 10.3). Because a number of snapshots are passed at once, there is an inherent delay in the processing of the

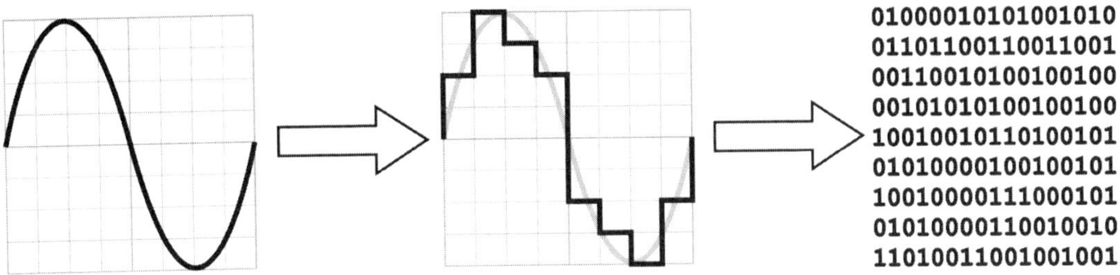

Figure 10.3 The operation of an analog-to-digital converter. First it converts the analog signal into digital format, and then it passes the data to Project5 to record.

data—the first snapshot is not passed until the last snapshot in the bundle is also passed. This delay is the input latency.

The keen-minded among you will have already figured a straightforward solution: Pass the snapshot immediately, or if you can't pass the data immediately, pass fewer snapshots more frequently. This is the root of finding a workable solution. However, the more frequently that data is passed, the more CPU intensive the process becomes. Accordingly, a balance has to be struck between reducing the CPU hit and the delay caused by waiting for the converted data to be passed.

When audio leaves a computer, there is a similar issue. The data is passed to a digital-to-audio converter (called a *DAC*), which then outputs an analog signal. A DAC will deal with bundles of data, which are then converted to analog audio. The size of the bundle that is converted will determine the latency, and the number of bundles will have CPU implications.

As well as the CPU hit, the other main factor that determines the latency is the audio driver (which may also have an effect on the CPU consumption). I will look at these drivers in the next section.

You will have seen Project5's CPU meter. If you are using a modest amount of CPU in your project, then you might feel happier decreasing the latency and so increasing the CPU hit. However, when you start working with large projects, you may find that you run up against your system's limitations, so you have to increase the latency to drop the CPU hit.

Dealing with Latency

If you are simply recording an audio source, then input latency is unlikely to be an issue because it won't matter when the digital data is recorded. Equally, if you are listening to the output audio that has already been created, there will not be a problem because Project5 can adjust its timing to take account of latency. There are two places where latency is a particular issue:

- When the musician is playing an Instrument in Project5
- When the musician's audio output is being recorded, and the musician is listening to the track that is being recorded (for instance, if a singer is listening to his or her performance)

The difficulty when a musician is trying to play (and perhaps record) an Instrument part in Project5 is that the output of the synthesizer has to pass through a DAC, which introduces latency. Since this is a live performance, Project5 cannot compensate for the latency, although it can compensate when the recorded performance is played back.

When a musician's audio output is recorded and the musician is listening to the recorded signal (perhaps so that some processing can be added), then the audio signal must pass through an ADC and then back through a DAC before the musician can hear the signal. This double conversion will lead to a delay that is particularly noticeable for singers.

There are two common solutions for these issues.

When a musician is playing a software Instrument, then the latency should be reduced as far as possible. This will ensure that as the keyboard (or other MIDI controller) is struck, the note is heard immediately without delay. If there is a delay between when the musician triggers the note and when the musician hears the note, then the musician's playing will be (adversely) affected. I will look at freezing tracks and other ways to reduce the CPU hit in Chapter 4, "Working with Tracks and Projects."

For musicians (such as singers) who are recording an audio source, the most practical solution is to split the audio signal: One part is then fed into the ADC, and the other is fed to the musician's audio monitor. This is the solution I have adopted in my setup since it means there is no audio delay for the musician. Alternatively, there are several audio interfaces that provide hardware monitoring for this purpose.

Internal Processing FX Units

In addition to the conversion process, latency is also added as the audio signal passes through Project5. Perhaps the most obvious place where latency is added is in the audio FX units, where the intensive nature of the processing can add a delay. This is one reason why you may not want to use FX units within Project5 while you are recording audio.

However, on replay, the latency inherent in Project5 and introduced by the audio FX units is not an issue because Project5 will automatically compensate for the latency.

Audio Driver Standards: ASIO, WDM, and DirectSound

There are three audio driver standards that Project5 can work with:

- ASIO (Audio Stream Input/Output)
- WDM (Windows Driver Model)
- DirectSound

DirectSound is an older Microsoft standard that isn't really cut out for music—typically, this will give less than optimum latency. For low-latency sound, you need to choose ASIO or WDM drivers, but what's the difference between the two?

The difference between ASIO and WDM is comparatively irrelevant since they can both produce high-quality, low-latency results. What matters is which standard your audio card supports. If your card supports one standard, then the matter is decided for you. If your card supports both standards, then you can try each and see which works best for you. You may, for instance, find that one standard gives you a glitchy result with audio problems. Equally, you may find that one standard gives you much lower latency than the other does.

As long as you are using a reputable brand of audio interface, you have a computer with a reasonable amount of power, and you are working with ASIO or WDM, then you are likely to be able to achieve acceptable results. If you want spectacular results (with typically means latency under 1.5ms), then you may be able to achieve this on a regular PC. However, if you really want the best results, then you need a dedicated audio PC (which doesn't run Office programs, virus programs, or any of the other junk that is likely to slow your PC's performance).

Audio Options in Project5

Now that we've looked at the various factors involved with digital audio, we can move on and look at what this means in Project5. There is one key menu in Project5, the Audio Options menu, which controls how Project5 interacts with its audio hardware. Take a look at Figure 10.4 to see the menu.

Audio Device and I/O Selection

The first section is Audio Device and I/O Selection. From the Device drop-down menu, you can select your audio card. Although you may only have one device,

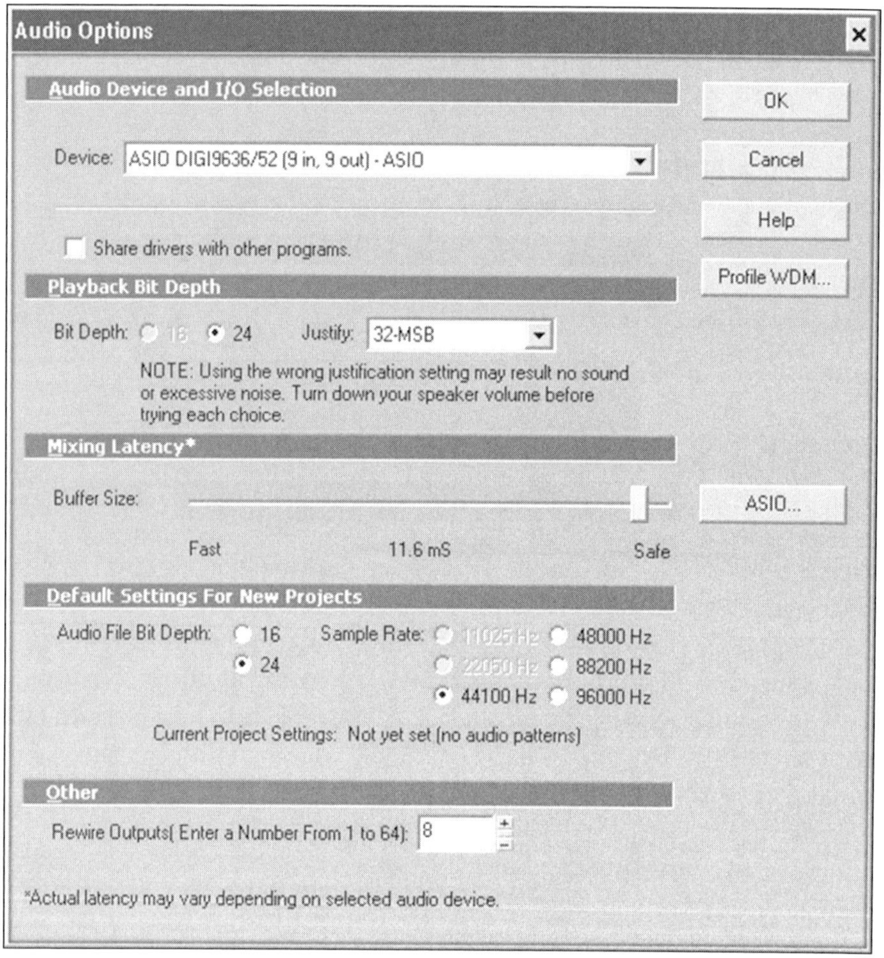

Figure 10.4 In the Audio Options menu, you can set how Project5 interacts with your audio hardware.

you may see several devices listed: Typically, each set of drivers is listed as a separate device, so as you can see in Figure 10.4, the device I have selected is the ASIO version of my audio card.

You can only select one device. You will remember from my setup earlier that I have three "devices": the RME card (shown in the figure as ASIO DIGI9636/52 (9 in, 9 out) – ASIO), plus the TL Audio and Behringer converter units. Project5 doesn't care about the converter units (in the same way that it doesn't care about my choice of loudspeakers). Its only concern is the RME card. Since the RME card has nine stereo inputs and outputs, by choosing this interface I can ensure that Project5 will create nine Master Busses.

As I mentioned earlier, if you have a choice between ASIO and WDM, then the best way to find out which works best on your system is to try both drivers. If you really start to stress your system (load up lots of software synths being processed through many audio FX units, and start replaying a track), then you may find that one set of drivers performs better under pressure than the others. When performing this test, you might also want to adjust the Buffer Size Slider (which is mentioned in a moment under the "Mixing Latency" heading).

When you first loaded Project5, it profiled your WDM drivers. You can manually force the profiling by hitting the Profile WDM button.

The final option you will notice in this top section is the Share Drivers with Other Programs check box. You might run other programs at the same time as Project5 if, for instance, you use an external editor (which I will discuss in Chapter 3, "Working with Clips"). You might want to uncheck this option if you are having problems with your audio (particularly if you are trying to troubleshoot); otherwise, it probably does no harm to select this option.

Playback Bit Depth

Depending on your audio hardware, you may or may not get a choice about the Playback Bit Depth option. If you have a choice, I recommend you go for 24 bit—you will get larger audio files, but the audio fidelity will be increased.

You will notice that there is a Justify setting—here you get the choice of 32-LSB and 32-MSB. Check your audio hardware documentation to find the correct setting, or if you're too lazy to read the documentation, turn your volume down and try the choices, as the Note on the Audio Options box suggests.

Mixing Latency

In the Mixing Latency section, the Buffer Size Slider allows you to strike the balance between the CPU hit and the latency. If you read the earlier text under the "Audio Conversion" heading, this slider allows you to control the size of the bundle of data that is passed from the ADC to Project5.

Take some time to find the balance between CPU consumption and latency. However, do remember that you can always change the latency while you are working on a Project. If you find that your CPU is getting overloaded, then increase the latency (move the slider from Fast toward Safe), and you are likely to find your system runs more smoothly.

If you are using the ASIO version of your hardware, an ASIO button will appear to the right of the slider. This button allows you to open your ASIO hardware control panel.

Under the slider you will see a latency figure is given. If you take this as an indicative figure to illustrate relative levels of latency, and not as an absolute scientific measure, then you won't be disappointed. As I mentioned before, there are many factors that affect latency, and this indicator does not take account of them all.

Default Settings for New Projects

The Default Settings for New Projects section does what its name suggests: It sets defaults. Unless you have a good reason to do otherwise, I recommend you stick with 24 bit and 44,100 Hz.

You may notice (as is the case in Figure 10.4) that some of your sample rate options are grayed out. This is an indication that your hardware does not support those sample rates.

Other

The Other section allows you to set the number of (stereo) ReWire Outputs. ReWire is discussed further in Chapter 4.

Tutorial 11: Setting Up MIDI In and MIDI Out

You don't need to use MIDI ins and MIDI outs to get a lot out of Project5; however, they might help.

There are two main uses for MIDI in Project5:

- To hook up a piece of hardware to control Project5—particularly if you are then using ACT (*Active Controller Technology*, which is discussed in Tutorial 12: MIDI Input Controls) and you want to attach an external hardware controller or if you want to use a MIDI keyboard or MIDI drum pads to play a synthesizer in Project5
- To control external MIDI hardware, such as a hardware synthesizer

Like audio hardware, MIDI hardware comes in many shapes and sizes. Figure 11.1 shows the MIDI interface I use: an Edirol UM-880. (It is the third unit down, under the mixer.)

I chose this interface several years ago when I used more hardware synthesizers and fewer software synthesizers than I now do. It is an eight-input/eight-output unit, and I still find having the flexibility that the unit offers useful. There is no downside to having spare MIDI input and output ports available to call upon.

Figure 11.1 The MIDI interface in the author's home setup.

Setting Up Your MIDI Device

Once your MIDI hardware has been successfully connected to your computer, it is quite straightforward to set up the device in Project5. Select Options > MIDI Devices, and a window will appear like that shown in Figure 11.2.

On the left of the window you will see two boxes:

- Available MIDI Input Devices
- Available MIDI Output Devices

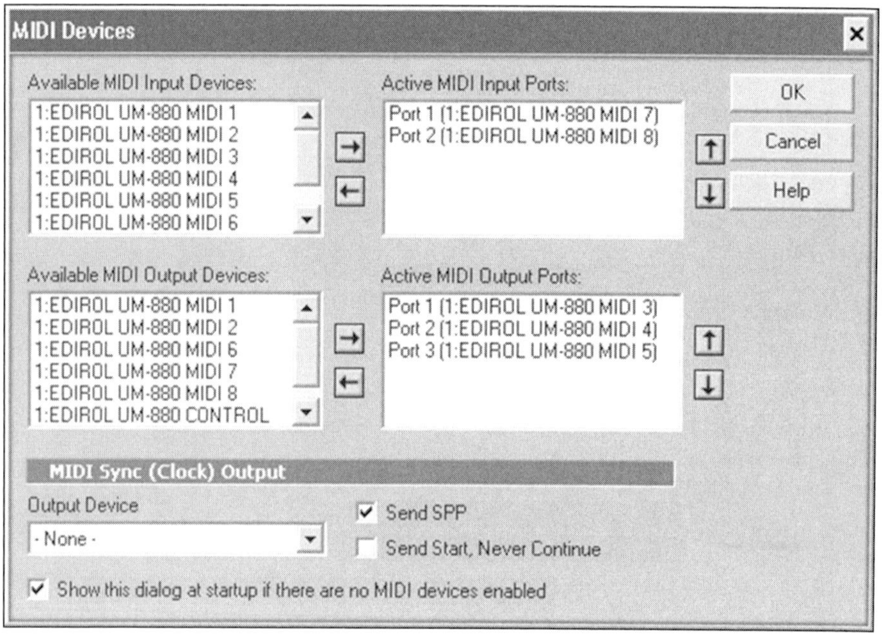

Figure 11.2 The MIDI Devices window in Project5.

Next to these two lists you will see two further lists:

- Active MIDI Input Ports
- Active MIDI Output Ports

To activate an input or output device, left-click on its name, and then left-click on the right arrow between the Devices and Ports lists. The device will then be listed under the Active Ports list.

To deactivate an input or output device, left-click on its name, and then left-click on the left arrow between the Devices and the Ports lists. The device will then be listed under the Devices list.

Clearly you need to make a port active in order to send or receive MIDI data through that port. However, you may want to make some of your ports inactive so that your MIDI Port Selector only lists the ports that are linked to some hardware. That way you won't accidentally select an unused port.

To the right of the Active Ports lists you can see up and down arrows. If you want to change the order of the active Ports, left-click on the Port that you wish to reorder and move it up or down the list as appropriate. The benefit of reordering the Ports is that it changes the order of the Ports in the drop-down selector list.

MIDI Sync Output

There will be times when you want to synchronize Project5 with an external piece of gear—for instance, you might want to synchronize it with a drum machine to record a part into Project5, or you may want to synchronize with an external recorder to transfer a part (or several parts) into Project5.

Masters and Slaves

Project5 will synchronize with external equipment; however, in this case Project5 must act as the synchronization master, so the other pieces of gear will follow Project5's lead (making Project5 the sync master and the other piece of gear the sync slave). The only way that Project5 can work as the sync slave is if it is ReWired into a ReWire host (such as SONAR). SONAR can work as a sync slave, and that slavery could then be applied to Project5 too.

ReWire is discussed in greater detail in Chapter 4.

Sync Options

At the bottom of the MIDI Devices window you will see the MIDI Sync (Clock) Output section. If you're not going to synchronize Project5 to another device, you can safely ignore this section. If you are going to synchronize Project5, there are three aspects for you to attend to:

- Output Device. From the Output Device drop-down, choose the MIDI Port to which the device to be synchronized is attached.
- Send SPP. If the MIDI device you are going to enslave requires Song Position Pointer (SPP) information, then check this box. This is likely to be the case if the device you are enslaving needs its time location to correspond with Project5's (for instance, if it is a drum machine that will replay a complete song).
- Send Start, Never Continue. If you just want the slave device to be tempo synchronized to Project5, then check the Send Start, Never Continue option.

Sharing MIDI Devices

While Project5 is good about sharing its audio resources, it's less happy about sharing MIDI. If another piece of software is using your MIDI ports when you load Project5, it won't be able to access them. If you check the Show This Dialog at Startup If There Are No MIDI Devices Enabled option at the bottom of the MIDI Devices window, you will be alerted if Project5 cannot access its MIDI ports.

Tutorial 12: MIDI Input Controls

Once you've got your MIDI input and output sorted out, you can start to manage your MIDI data as it flows into Project5. Of course, you can just let the data flow. However, when you start splitting, layering, and dealing with multi-timbral instruments, then you need to think about your MIDI input controls.

For anyone who may not be used to MIDI, let me give you two details about MIDI that may aid your understanding of this tutorial:

- For each MIDI port (in other words, each MIDI input or output), MIDI data can be sent on up to 16 channels. This means you can get 16 separate parts sent down one MIDI cable, so for instance, you could send your bass part on channel 1, your violin part on channel 2, your trumpet part on channel 4, and your piano on channel 13.
- Instead of sending data on a single channel, you can send it on all channels. This is called *Omni mode*.

Most keyboards and other MIDI-generating hardware devices send MIDI Omni data by default. However, you can also usually set a keyboard only to send data on a specific channel. More sophisticated keyboards also allow you to send the MIDI output from different regions of the keyboard on different MIDI channels.

Whatever MIDI data Project5 receives, it can handle it, provided you know your way around the MIDI Input section.

MIDI Input

The MIDI Input section appears at the top of the MIDI Track Inspector and the Instrument Inspector (see Figure 12.1).

Think of the MIDI Input section as being like a gatekeeper: There's lots of MIDI data flowing in, and this section lets you filter it so you only get the information you want.

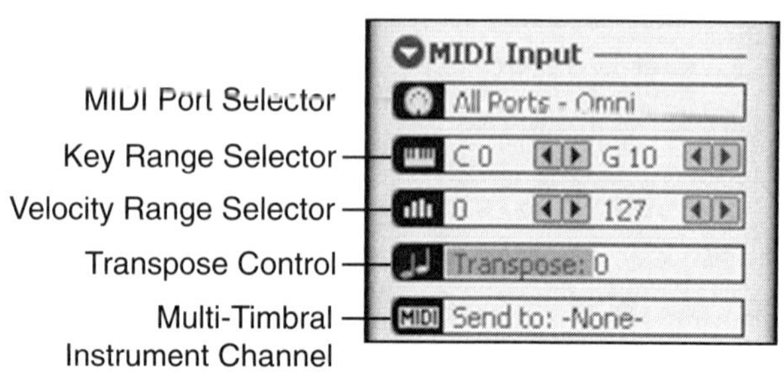

Figure 12.1 The MIDI Input section.

The first control in the MIDI Input section is the MIDI Port Selector drop-down. By default, this selects All Ports – Omni—in other words, all channels from all of the MIDI ports that you have activated. (Refer back to Tutorial 11 if you can't remember the details about activating MIDI ports.)

If you don't want all MIDI channels from all MIDI input devices to communicate with this track, then from the drop-down you can instead select:

- Omni data for only one MIDI Port
- One MIDI channel's data for all MIDI Ports
- One MIDI channel's data for only one MIDI Port

This ensures you can receive only the Port and MIDI channel data that you want to receive.

The Key Range Selector allows you to narrow the range over which notes can be received. By default the lowest note you can receive is C0, and the highest is G10; this corresponds to a full piano keyboard and more. You can select a narrower range by adjusting the top and bottom of the key range.

In the Key Range Selector there are three ways to adjust the lower and upper keys of the key range:

- Left-click on the nudge up/nudge down arrowheads to the right of the range indicator.
- Left-click and drag on the range indicator.
- Double-click on the range indicator and manually enter the correct value. (You will notice that when you double-click in this manner, you also get plus and minus nudge buttons.)

In MIDI-speak, *velocity* means how hard you hit an instrument. The force with which you strike a real instrument affects the tone and the volume. With a synthesizer, this varying force, velocity, is given 128 degrees of loudness. The effect of different levels of velocity is dependent on how the synthesizer that is being controlled by varying velocity has been programmed to react.

Conventionally, you would expect a synthesizer to react to the full velocity range (0 to 127). However, with the Velocity Range Selector you can set a synthesizer to react only to a narrow band of velocity. For instance, you could allow your synthesizer to only react to quiet playing by setting the Velocity range to 0 to 35. You can adjust the Velocity Range Selector in the same three ways that you adjust the Key Range Selector.

The Transpose Control transposes the incoming MIDI data over the range plus or minus 128 semitones. You can adjust the Transpose Control by:

- Left-clicking and dragging
- Double-clicking and directly entering the appropriate value
- Double-clicking and then left-clicking on the plus and minus nudge buttons

The Multi-Timbral Instrument Channel Selector selects the MIDI channel that is sent to a multi-timbral instrument. This will make a lot more sense after you have read the "Multi-Timbral Synthesizers" section in a moment.

Splits and Layers

It's probably easiest to illustrate how to use splits and layers with an example. Before we get going, let me explain the terms:

- A *layer* occurs when two instruments respond to the same part. (Two instruments will be triggered by the same note.)
- A *split* occurs when one instrument is playable over part of a keyboard, and another is playable over another part of the keyboard, with neither part overlapping.

For this example, I am going to take a piano, which I am going to layer with a bass guitar over the lower keys and a string part over the higher keys.

To start off, load up three instances of Dimension LE (which will create three Instrument Tracks):

- In the first instance, load the Ballad Piano program (which can be found in the 10 – Electric Pianos folder).
- In the second instance, load the Simple Fingered 1 program (which is in the 03 – Real Basses folder).
- In the third instance, load the Symphony S4WsTriNgs program (which is in the 02 – Pads folder).

So far, we have set up three layers rather than two layers, one of which has a split. You will notice that the layers have happened because this is a new Project, and each

Instrument Track has defaulted to Omni mode. To ensure that these layers all respond to the same MIDI input data, I could select a MIDI channel that would be common to all three layers; however, I'm not going to (because it is unnecessary for this example).

To change the bass and string layers into a split, I need to make a tweak to Key Range Selector in their respective Instrument Inspectors, as follows:

- For the bass part, keep the lower Key Range Selector at C0 and set the upper key to B4.
- For the strings part, set the lower Key Range Selector to C5 and leave the upper at G10.

As a final tweak, try transposing the string part by −12 semitones.

You can now play the three Instruments together, and you will hear the bass part in the lower ranges and the string part in the higher ranges. The piano part covers the whole keyboard range.

As a side note, if you are using Dimension (or Dimension Pro) rather than Dimension LE, you can set up your splits and layers by setting the key ranges within Dimension (or Dimension Pro). The advantage of setting up the split and layer by using Project5's MIDI Input section is that you can change your Instruments and retain the split/layer. In addition, by using Project5, you can channel and filter the incoming MIDI data.

Multi-Timbral Synthesizers

Most synthesizers are mono-timbral: They respond to one MIDI input source. However, some synthesizers can behave like several synthesizers strapped together. Each separate "synthesizer" can respond to a different MIDI source. These are called *multi-timbral* synthesizers.

One example of a multi-timbral synthesizer is Dimension (which came with Project5 version 2.0). Dimension Pro and Rapture are two other multi-timbral synthesizers; Dimension LE is mono-timbral.

Dimension has four Elements. Each of these four Elements can be separately addressed by a different MIDI channel. This means that, for example, you could:

- Load a violin into Element 1.
- Load a viola into Element 2.

- Load a cello into Element 3.
- Load a string bass into Element 4.

Each Element could then have its own separate MIDI part, and the stereo output of Dimension would then output a full string orchestra.

Some synthesizers (not Dimension nor Rapture, but VELOCITY and nPULSE are two examples) have multi-outputs, which allows you to adjust each output separately, so you can give each output its own EQ or effects settings. The combination of a multi-timbral instrument with multiple outputs allows considerable control for the musician or producer. Setting up multi-output instruments will be discussed in Chapter 4.

The Multi-Timbral Instrument Channel Selector determines the MIDI channel that is sent to an Instrument. This allows you to address one of a multi-timbral Instrument's channels.

You can't control a multi-timbral Instrument with Omni data. If the MIDI data that is coming into Project5 is not addressed to the correct channels (often called *Multi mode*), you will need to use some ingenuity to split the data. Once the MIDI data has been recorded in Project5, you can change the MIDI channel output by a MIDI Clip (so that it can address the appropriate channel with a multi-timbral Instrument). If you have set the MIDI channel at the Clip level (and this will be discussed in Chapter 3), then any setting in the Multi-Timbral Instrument Channel Selector will override the setting in the Clip, so in this case you should set the selector to Send to: -None-.

Don't worry if this sounds horribly complicated. In practice, when you're working with a multi-timbral instrument, it's much easier to see what's going on!!

How Does the MIDI Input Section Affect Data inside Project5?

The MIDI Input section is largely intended to deal with incoming MIDI data. However, it does have some effect on MIDI data once it is inside Project5. As I have already mentioned, when you are playing back a MIDI Clip, the Clip's MIDI channel is overridden by the Multi-Timbral Instrument Channel Selector. The Clip's pitch is also directly controlled by the Transpose Control. However, if you record MIDI input data, the effect of the Transpose is not recorded (so if you record and play back MIDI data with the Transpose Control switched on, the data is not transposed twice).

On playback, the MIDI Input Port Selector, the Key Range Selector, and the Velocity Range Selector all have no effect.

MIDI Input Override

The MIDI Input section doesn't have an on/off switch. However, you can override the section on a track-by-track basis (in both MIDI and Instrument Track Panes). When the MIDI Input section is overridden, incoming MIDI Omni data will pass directly to the overridden channel (even if No Port has been selected in the Inspector).

To override the MIDI Input section, click on the MIDI Routing Override button; see Figure 12.2. This will show with a light blue background when it is active.

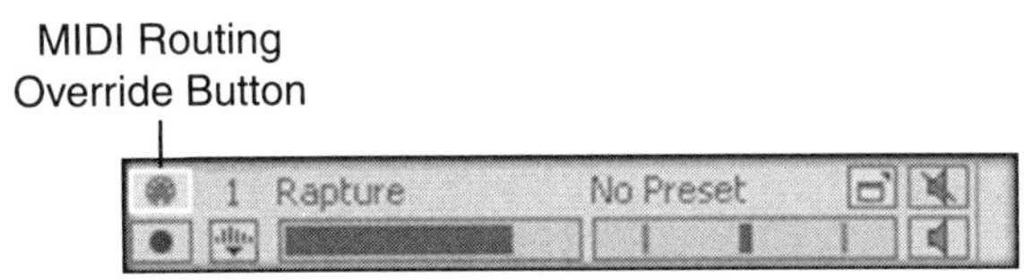

Figure 12.2 The MIDI Routing Override button.

As an alternative to the MIDI Routing Override button, you can select Options > MIDI Override Follows Current Track. In this case, the currently selected Track will have its MIDI Input section overridden as if the MIDI Routing Override button had been pressed (and the button's background will turn light blue when its Track is selected). By selecting this option, you may speed your workflow when auditioning Instruments.

Input Quantize

Input Quantize is a new feature that was added with version 2.5. It appears in the MIDI Track Inspector and the Instrument Track Inspector.

Quantization is a tool intended to remove (or reduce) timing errors introduced when you record a MIDI performance. It allows you to set a timing grid (for instance, sixteenth notes—all notes are then snapped to the nearest sixteenth note). This snapping can be applied to:

- The note's starting time, so you can tighten a beat.
- The note's duration, so the length of each note can be consistent.
- The note's automation—if you quantize a note's start time, but not its automation, you can get unwanted results.

Input Quantize is a destructive tool (in other words, it makes permanent changes) that applies quantization to incoming MIDI data as it is recorded. It doesn't affect the live performance; however, when MIDI data that has been through the Input

Quantize filter is replayed, it will be quantized. If you record MIDI data without Input Quantize, and you subsequently want to quantize that data, then you should use the Quantize MIDI FX unit, which is discussed in Chapter 8, "MIDI FX Units," (because the Input Quantize function has no effect on recorded data).

Although Input Quantize is a destructive editing tool, immediately after you have recorded a Track with Input Quantize selected, you can undo the quantize effect by selecting Edit > Undo Input Quantize.

After that introduction, let's have a look at the Input Quantize unit, which is shown in Figure 12.3.

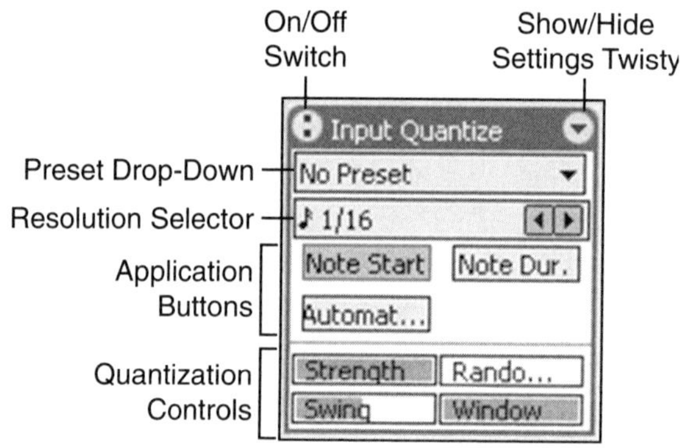

Figure 12.3 The Input Quantize unit in Project5.

I hope that by now I don't need to explain the On/Off switch or the Show/Hide Settings twisty.

The Preset drop-down menu gives you three options:

- Open Preset. This allows you to navigate to an Input Quantize preset and load it.
- Save Preset. This allows you to save the current Input Quantize settings as a preset.
- Load Preset. Any presets saved in the Project5v2_5/Input Quantize Presets folder will be directly accessible from this option. Any presets not saved in this folder can be accessed by using the Open Preset option, discussed a moment ago.

The Resolution Selector allows you to define the grid to which notes will be quantized. You can select the value by left-clicking on:

- The current value—a drop-down menu will appear, from which you can select the resolution.
- The nudge up/nudge down buttons to the right of the Resolution display.

The three Application buttons determine what the quantization is applied to:

- **Note Start.** The Note Start button applies quantization to the start of the note (in other words, its timing).
- **Note Dur.** The Note Duration button applies quantization to the length of the note, so its duration will snap to the quantization amount.
- **Automat.** The Automation button applies quantization to automation data as well as note data.

Finally, the four Quantization Controls determine how the quantization is applied:

- **Strength.** The Strength Control determines how close to the quantization grid a note is snapped. When this is set to 0% there is no snapping, and when it is set to 100% the note snaps precisely to the timing set by the grid.
- **Random.** The Random Control adds an element of random timing to a note. This may seem an odd feature in a quantization section. However, you can use it to add some humanization once the quantization has sorted the timing problems.
- **Swing.** The Swing Control shifts the off beats to give a Track an element of shuffle.
- **Window.** The Window Control sets the area over which the Input Quantize looks for notes to quantize. With higher settings, all notes will be quantized. At lower settings, only those notes that are slightly mistimed will be quantized (and *badly* wrong notes will be ignored).

Tutorial 13: ACT (Active Controller Technology)

If you're used to the idea of MIDI Learn or you've got your head around MIDI Remote Control (which was discussed in Tutorial 5: Audio, MIDI, and Instrument Tracks), then ACT (*Active Controller Technology*) may seem unnecessary to you. It may also seem a bit complicated. However, once you start using it in practice, you may start to question how you ever lived without it.

Let me try and put into words why ACT is a step forward and why you should be interested.

With MIDI Learn or MIDI Remote Control, your hardware controller is permanently linked to a destination (typically, a parameter on an Instrument or a Track) that you want to control. The advantage of this arrangement is that when you turn a knob you will always know what it does. The disadvantage of this arrangement is that when you run out of hardware knobs you have to go back to using a mouse.

However, with ACT, the mapping from MIDI hardware to the destination is applied on a tool-by-tool basis, so you can have all of your hardware controls available for each Instrument, Track, or other destination. This means that the same knob can, for instance, control the cutoff frequency on a synthesizer, the volume on a Track, and the wet/dry control on an FX unit. With ACT, Project5 will know which Instrument, FX unit, and so on has focus and will direct the messages from the hardware controller to that destination.

If there is a downside to this arrangement, it is that you have to spend a few extra moments setting it up. However, you're really not doing much more than you would if you were to set up the MIDI Learn routings properly, so this isn't such a big problem.

ACT: How It Works

There are two stages to setting up ACT:

- First, each of the controls on the MIDI hardware controller must be linked to Project5's ACT MIDI Controller. In essence, this is a one-time MIDI Learn exercise.
- Second, the controls on the MIDI hardware controller must be linked to the parameters to be controlled on the Instrument, Track, FX unit, or other device to be controlled. This second step must be performed for each destination that you want to control.

The reason for the double linking—and part of the complication of ACT—is that the ACT MIDI Controller in Project5 works something like a routing box, sending MIDI messages from the hardware controller to the appropriate Instrument or other device, when that device has focus. Although using ACT Learn may feel similar to using MIDI Learn (in other words, it may feel as if you are linking your hardware directly to the Instrument, FX unit, and so on), in practice you are actually linking the Cell in the ACT MIDI Controller to the destination—it just happens that the Cell is controlled by the hardware.

I will look at each stage separately. However, before we do that, you need to load up a control surface.

Setting Up the Control Surface

To use a MIDI hardware Controller, you need to tell Project5 what you are using and where the MIDI data will come from. If you select Options > Controller/Surfaces > Options, the Controllers/Surfaces window will appear. This will look like Figure 13.1 (except that the table will be completely blank until you have assigned a Controller).

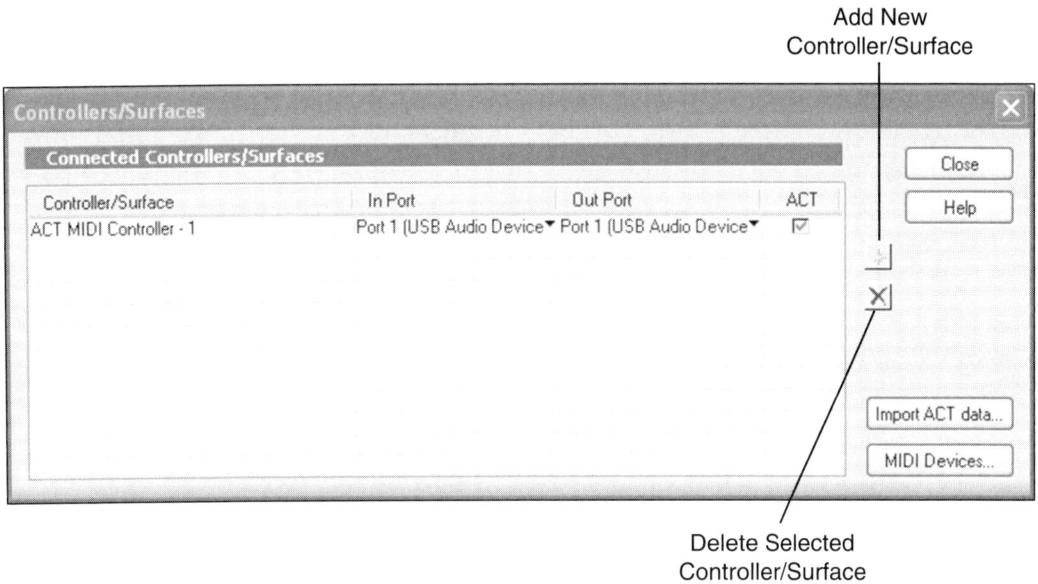

Figure 13.1 The Controllers/Surfaces window with a Controller loaded.

From the Controllers/Surfaces window, click on the Add New Controller/Surface button, and the Controller/Surface Settings window will appear (see Figure 13.2).

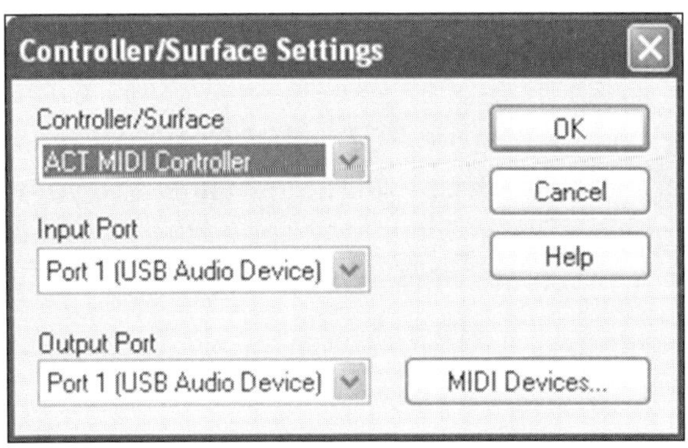

Figure 13.2 The Controller/Surface Settings window.

In the Controller/Surface Settings window, there are three drop-down menus:

- From the Controller/Surface drop-down, select the hardware surface you are using. If your surface isn't listed, then select ACT MIDI Controller.
- From the Input Port drop-down, select the MIDI Input Port where your hardware controller's MIDI data will be received.

- From the Output Port drop-down, select the MIDI Output Port that is attached to your MIDI hardware device. You will need to send MIDI data to your hardware if it supports parameter feedback. (You might use this if you have a motorized fader or LCD display—the position of the controllers on your hardware can be moved to the appropriate position on the device to which they are pointing.)

Once you've made your selections in the Controller/Surface Settings window, the new controller will show in the Controllers/Surfaces window. From this window you can change the Input Port and the Output Port for the new controller, but you can't change the controller. If you've selected the wrong controller, select the Controller/Surface and hit the Delete Selected Controller/Surface button.

For the new controller, there should be a check mark in the ACT column. If there isn't, then add one (assuming you want the controller to work with ACT).

You've now added your hardware, so you're ready to take the next step and link the hardware to the ACT MIDI Controller.

Before we move on, there are two further buttons on the Controllers/Surfaces window. These options are quite self-explanatory:

- **Import ACT Data.** This allows you to import an existing ACT data file, which contains ACT parameter mappings.
- **MIDI Devices.** This is also present on the Controller/Surface Settings window; it opens the MIDI Devices window and allows you to change your active MIDI Ports.

Linking Your Hardware to the ACT MIDI Controller

Once your controller has been set up, you need to link it to your hardware. This is a one-time MIDI Learn exercise. While it may not be the most interesting thing to do, once you have done it you never need repeat the exercise.

As a first step, call up the ACT MIDI Controller window, which should look much like Figure 13.3.

If you are using one of the more popular hardware surfaces, there may already be a preset you can use. Check out the presets from the Presets drop-down menu at the top left of the window. If there isn't a preset, or there is a preset but it doesn't quite meet your needs, then you'll have to create your own settings. This is where MIDI Learn comes in. By the way, on the subject of presets, you can save your own ACT presets—preset management is discussed further in Tutorial 42: Preset Management Tools.

You will see that there are 32 cells arranged as four rows of eight cells. The top two rows are designed for continuous controllers (by default the top row is labeled for

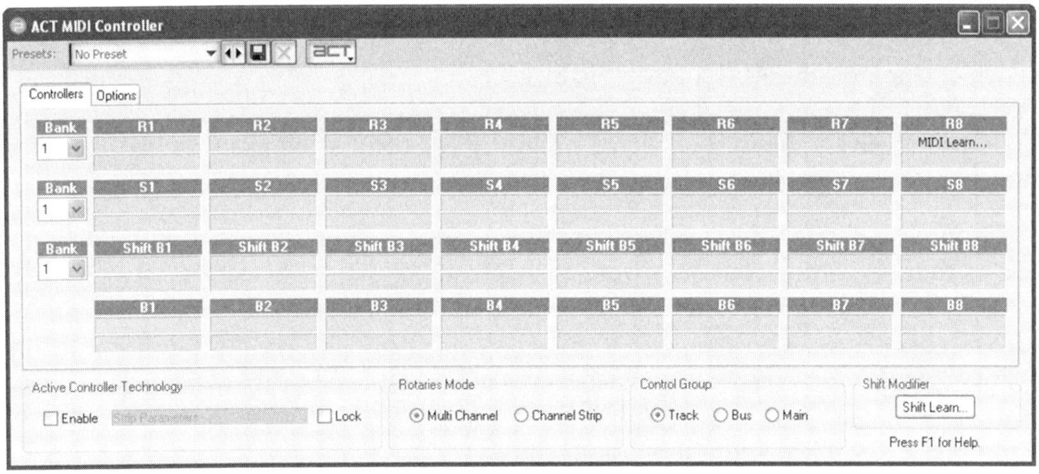

Figure 13.3 The ACT MIDI Controller window.

rotary controls, and the second row is labeled for sliders), and the bottom two rows are for buttons and Shifted button presses. Project5 doesn't care about the source of the MIDI data (it can't see whether you're using a rotary control or a slider); however, the top row does behave differently to the second row, depending on the Rotaries Mode selection, which is discussed in the "Fine-Tuning the Operation of the ACT MIDI Controller" section.

The aim in creating your own settings is to assign the controls on your hardware to the cells in the ACT MIDI Controller. To do this:

1. Click on the blue-colored part of a Cell. In the middle row you will see the message MIDI Learn (as you can see in the top-right Cell in Figure 13.3).
2. Move the control you want to assign to the Cell.

Repeat this task for each hardware control.

ACT in Practice

Now that you've set up your hardware and you've linked it to the ACT MIDI Controller, you can start using ACT. Say you want to now control a synthesizer—and for this example, let's say you want to control the synthesizer's cutoff frequency:

1. Click on the ACT button on your synthesizer—its background will turn from gray to blue.
2. Move the hardware control you want to assign to your synthesizer's cutoff frequency.

3. Move your synthesizer's cutoff frequency knob (with your mouse).
4. Click on the ACT button again.

You will receive a message saying, "1 Parameters and 1 Controls were touched. Do you want to keep these assignments?" Click OK, and the assignment is made.

All you now have to do is repeat the process for the other controls on the synthesizers that you want your hardware to control. As the confirmation message suggests, you can assign more than one control at one time, so you could set up all of your assignments in one go. Also, you don't need to click the ACT button on the target device—it just makes life easier that way (and ensures the correct device has focus). You can click any ACT button or select Options > Controller/Surfaces > ACT Learn to enter ACT Learn mode.

Once you have switched out of ACT Learn mode you will find that you can control your target whenever that target has focus, so for instance, if you are using a synthesizer, you need to open the synthesizer's interface and click on it to give it focus.

The ACT assignments will be remembered the next time you open Project5. However, when you first move a knob you may think that the ACT isn't working. If you are in Absolute Value mode (which will be explained in the "Cells" section in a moment), your hardware controller needs to pass through the current value of the assigned control before it latches. In other words, you might need to twist your knob through its full range before you take over control.

Cells

Once you have set up your ACT assignments, your Cells will look like Figure 13.4.

Each Cell has three rows:

- The top row shows the Cell's name.
- The middle row shows the parameter the hardware controller related to the Cell controls.
- The bottom row shows the current value of the hardware control.

To change a Cell's name, left-click on its name. A pop-up will appear (see Figure 13.5) where you can insert a new name.

You can change how the hardware control behaves in the Cell MIDI Properties window, which you can access by Ctrl-clicking on a Cell (see Figure 13.6).

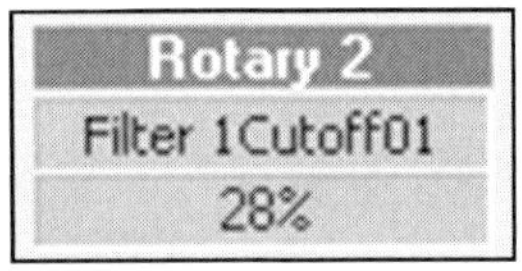

Figure 13.4 An active Cell in the ACT MIDI Controller.

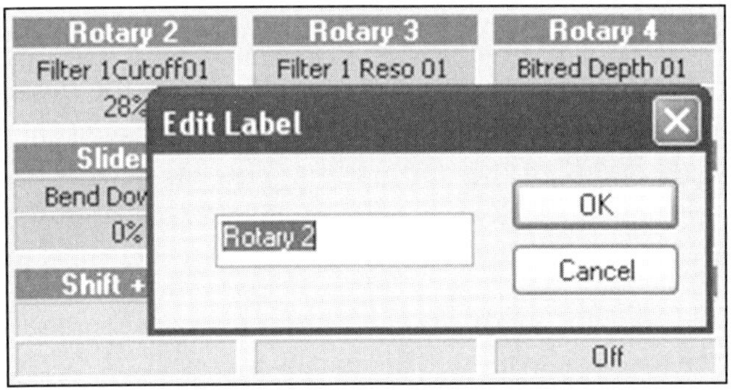

Figure 13.5 Changing a Cell's name in the ACT MIDI Controller.

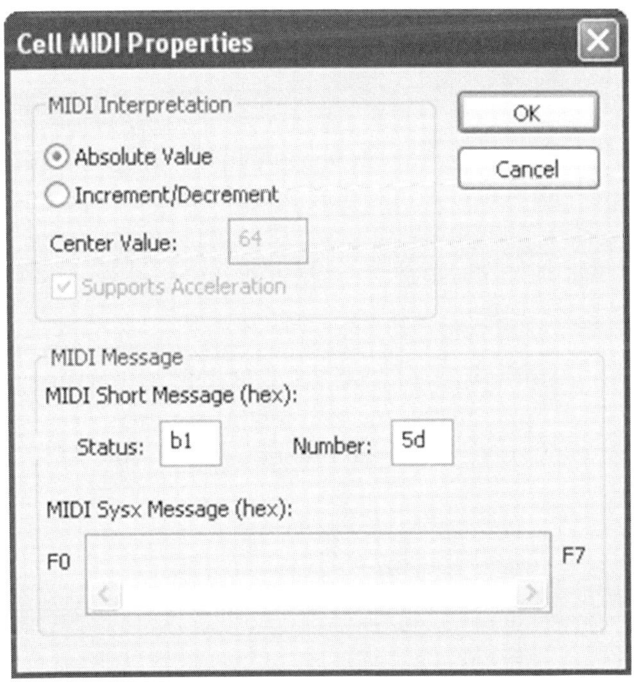

Figure 13.6 The Cell MIDI Properties window.

From the Cell MIDI Properties window, you can control how your hardware affects its target. In the MIDI Interpretation section, you can determine whether your hardware controller transmits an absolute value or increment/decrement information:

- If an absolute value is transmitted, then the position of the knob will correspond directly to the position of the control on the destination. When you are adjusting the hardware, until it corresponds with the current value at the destination, it will have no effect (and so it may seem that ACT isn't working).
- With Increment/Decrement mode, the control affects the destination (nearly) immediately; however, there will be a disconnect between the position of the hardware and the value of the destination. You can set the center value from which the increment or decrement will be calculated. You will find that this mode is ideally suited to controllers with infinitely spinning rotary encoders.
- In Increment/Decrement mode you can also check the Supports Acceleration check box. In this case as you turn the hardware faster, the destination is affected to a greater extent.

If MIDI Learn doesn't hook up your hardware as you hoped, then you can always enter the MIDI hex values in the MIDI Message section of the Cell MIDI Properties box. Check in your hardware's documentation to find this information.

MIDI Unlearn

From the Cell MIDI Properties window you can unassign any MIDI Learn assignments on a Cell-by-Cell basis. To do this, insert 00 into both the Status and Number fields. If you want to remove all MIDI Learn assignments, then in the ACT MIDI Controller window, click on the Options tab and hit the Clear MIDI Learn button.

Fine-Tuning the Operation of the ACT MIDI Controller

Once you've got ACT up and running, you might want to tweak its operation. Take a look at Figure 13.7, which shows the bottom of the ACT MIDI Controller window.

Let's have a look.

Figure 13.7 The bottom of the ACT MIDI Controller window.

Active Controller Technology

In the center of the Active Controller Technology section is the focus display field; this confirms the destination that has focus which is being controlled by ACT.

To the left of this is a check box to enable ACT for the device. If this is not checked, then ACT will not apply to that Instrument (or other destination).

To the right of the focus display field is a Lock check box. When this is checked, ACT will apply exclusively to the selected instrument (or other destination), irrespective of which destination has focus.

Rotaries Mode

The Rotaries Mode section gives you two modes:

- Multi Channel
- Channel Strip

The Rotaries modes apply when you select a Track Strip (whether an Instrument Track, a MIDI Track, or an Audio Track). If you select Multi Channel mode, then a rotary controller will be allocated for each Track Strip to control the panning, and a slider will be allocated for each Track Strip to control its level. If you select Channel Strip, then the rotaries only control the selected Track.

You can switch between the two Rotaries modes; you may even want to assign a button to switch between the two. Rotaries mode is an assignable parameter in the ACT MIDI Controller window—you can assign it to a button as a controllable parameter on the Options page.

Control Group

The Control Group section determines whether the hardware will control:

- Tracks
- Aux Busses
- Main Busses

In the same way that you can switch between the Rotaries modes, you can assign a button on your hardware to switch between the Control Groups. If you assign a button to switch between these three options (use the Next Group and Previous Group options), you will be able to switch between the three choices without clicking on a Track, Bus, or Main with your mouse.

Shift Modifier

In the Shift Modifier section is one button: Shift Learn. You can use this button to MIDI Learn another Shift key on your hardware controller. The Shift function allows you to assign a second parameter to a button (much the same way that the Shift key on your computer keyboard allows you to access different characters).

Banks

You can control only as many Track controls as you have hardware controls. However, you are not limited to 16 continuous controllers and 16 switches. Next to the rotaries, sliders, and shifted switches, you will see a Bank drop-down menu. There are four Banks to choose from. These Banks extend the range of destinations to which you can assign your hardware controls. As long as you have done the MIDI Learn business for Bank 1, you can assign your controls for Bank 2 through 4 without needing to think about MIDI Learn.

You can switch between the banks by assigning a button to switch banks.

3 Working with Clips

Clips are short pieces of audio or MIDI data and are the most basic element in Project5. They can be loops, they can be short linear phrases (for instance, a bass line in a chorus), or they can be a whole Track. Project5 doesn't care about the content, it just thinks about Clips. A Clip is the fundamental element from which a song or performance is constructed.

From a workflow perspective, both Audio and MIDI/Instrument Clips are treated identically, so you don't need to think about what the underlying data is. Instead, you can think in terms of your song/Project.

Tutorial 14: Importing Clips

Project5 comes with a fair chunk of content, including a lot of MIDI and Audio Clips. In addition, you are likely to have your own audio and MIDI files that you want to bring into Project5 to use in a Project. There are several ways to get Clips into Project5 so they can be arranged to form part of a song or edited.

Importing MIDI and WAV Files

One way to import a MIDI file or a WAV file (in WAV format) is to select File > Import and navigate to the MIDI or WAV file.

See. It's not that hard.

Using the Loops/Pattern Browser

Instead of importing MIDI and WAV files, you might want to use the Loops/Pattern Browser. This has several advantages over the Import function—perhaps the most obvious is the facility to preview Clips before you open them.

We're going to look at the Clip Editor later in this chapter, so don't worry about the fact that I haven't yet explained how it works. If you look at the Editor Pane, you will see two buttons:

- Editor, which gets you into the Clip Editor
- Loops/Ptns, which takes you to the Loops/Pattern Browser (see Figure 14.1)

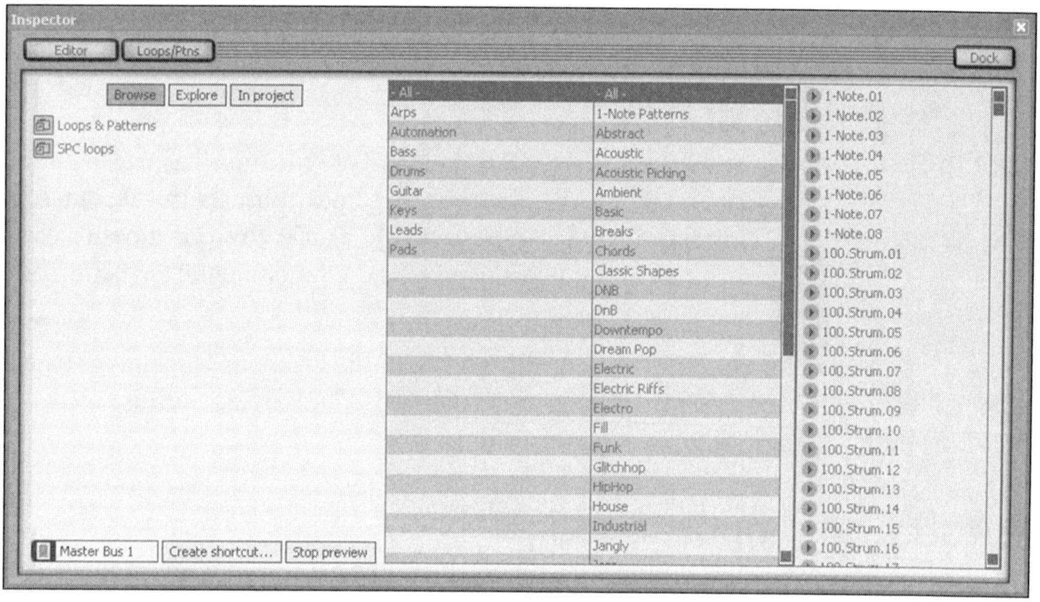

Figure 14.1 The Loops/Pattern Browser with Browse view selected.

At the top left of the Loops/Pattern Browser, you will see three buttons:

- Browse
- Explore
- In Project

These give you three different ways to access your data.

Browse View

The Browse view (which was shown in Figure 14.1) allows you to see your files but takes advantage of the folder structure to organize your Clips.

You can see that the Browse view is arranged as three columns. The first shows the main folders, the second shows the subfolders within those main folders, and the third allows you to see the Clips within the subfolders. This arrangement means you can organize and categorize your Clips so you can get to what you are looking for immediately. To reorganize your columns, all you need to do is reorganize and re-categorize the underlying folders using Windows Explorer.

To the left of each of your Clips, you will see a Play button. Click on this, and the Clip will preview. To stop the preview you can either click on the Play button again or click on the Stop Preview button at the bottom of the Browse view.

If you are previewing a MIDI Clip, you will need an Instrument loaded or the MIDI Track set up so that the sounds of the Clip can be heard. If you are previewing an Audio Clip, it must be sent to a Master Bus that is attached to a hardware output. You can select the Master Bus by clicking on the Master Bus drop-down selector in the bottom-left corner of the Browse view.

Explore View

The Explore view (see Figure 14.2) allows you to navigate a Windows Explorer–type view. Whereas the Browse view is fast, its content is limited to the selected main folder. With the Explore view, you can look for Clips anywhere on your computer.

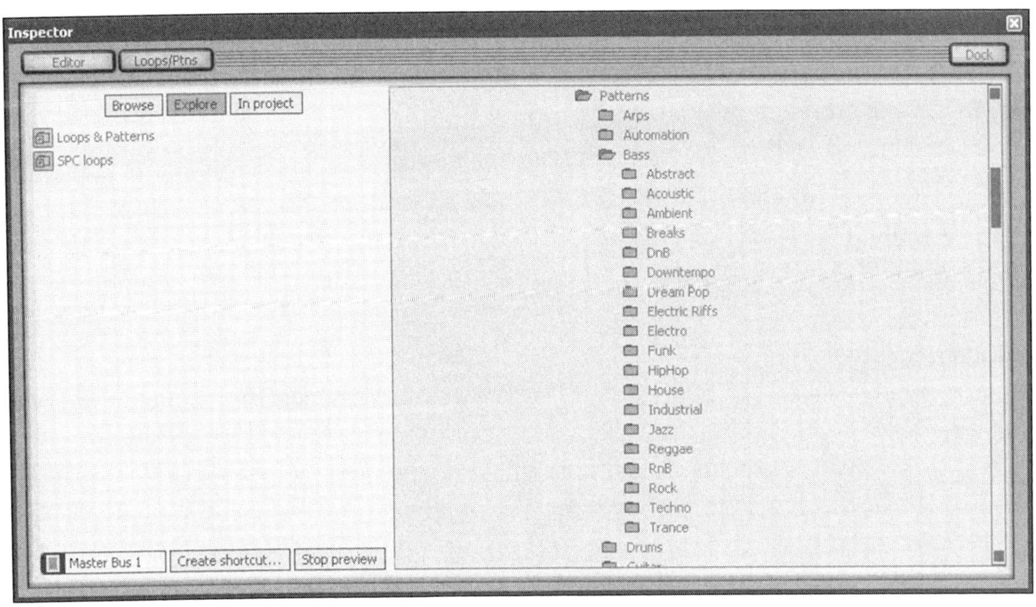

Figure 14.2 The Explore view.

In Project View

The In Project view (see Figure 14.3) allows you to see all of the Clips that have been loaded in the current Project.

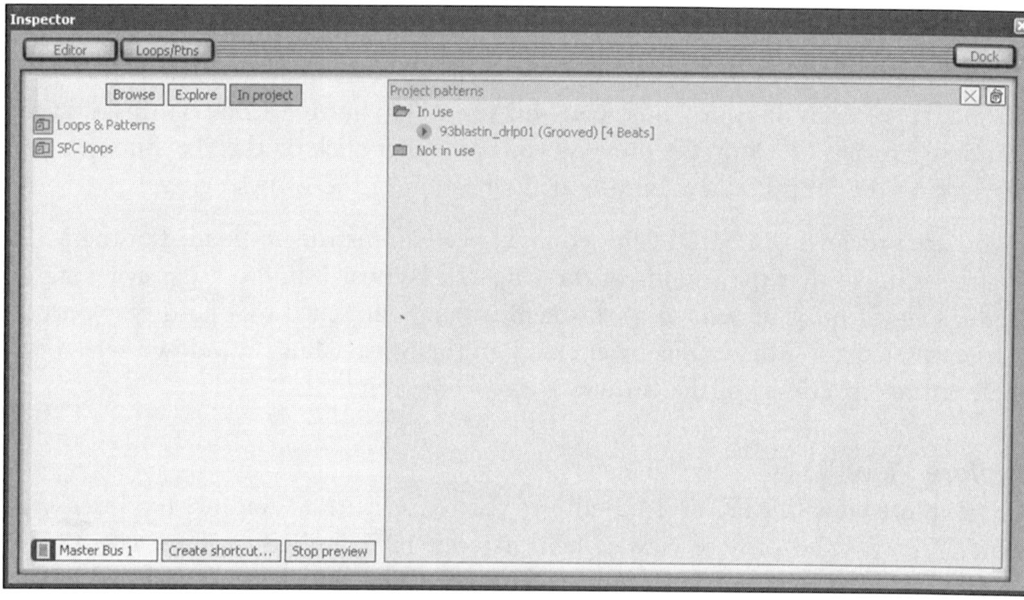

Figure 14.3 The In Project view.

As you can see from Figure 14.3, the view further categorizes Clips (Project Patterns) as In Use or Not in Use. The Not in Use folder shows Clips that were used in the Arrange Pane and then deleted, and Clips that were created in the Pattern Editor but never sent to a Track.

At the top right of the view there is a trashcan and an X. The X allows you to remove individual Patterns from the In Use/Not in Use list (click on the Clip and then hit the X), and the trashcan allows you to delete all of the unused Clips.

Shortcuts

By now you've probably figured that the Browse view is neat but limited, and the Explore view is detailed but cumbersome. If this is the case, you'll be pleased to hear that you can create shortcuts. A shortcut will take you directly to a specified folder. In the Browse view this will let you see your files organized in folders and subfolders, and in the Explore view this will take you to the appropriate folder on the directory tree.

To set up a shortcut:

1. In the Explore view, navigate to the folder to which you want to make a shortcut.
2. Click on the Create Shortcut button.
3. Give the shortcut a name (or go with the default).

The shortcut will show up in the list on the left-hand side of the Browse view.

To delete a shortcut, right-click on it and select Delete from the menu. As you will see, you can also use this menu to rename a shortcut.

Getting Clips from the Browser into Project5

So now you know how to find Clips, and you can preview them. But how do you get them into Project5?

Simple: drag and drop. You can drag and drop from any of the three Browser views. In the next tutorial I will talk about how to arrange the Clips further.

Tutorial 15: Arranging and Working with Clips

Fundamentally, it is not that difficult to arrange Clips in Project5: You drag them to the place you want them to be in the Arrange Pane. All you have to do is left-click on a Clip, drag it, and then let go of the mouse button when the Clip is where you want it to be.

Thankfully, there is a bit more to arranging Clips; otherwise, this would be a *really* short tutorial.

Bring to Front

In the Track Pane you can have several Clips at the same place. This could mean you can see the top Clip, but not the Clips underneath.

If you have two or more Clips stacked in this manner, when you right-click on the top Clip, one of the options on the pop-up menu will be Bring to Front. From this option, a submenu will appear, listing the Clips behind the top Clip (see Figure 15.1). If you want to bring one of the back Clips to the front, select it from this menu. You can also arrange multiple Clips in Track Layers, as Tutorial 23: Advanced Track Pane Features will discuss.

Snap to Grid

When you are moving Clips around, while you want them in a different place, most of the time you will want to retain their beat relationship with the Project. In other words, you will probably want to keep your beats on the beat after you have moved them. This is where Snap to Grid can help. Snap to Grid will ensure that after dragging, your Clip will start on the beat.

To engage Snap to Grid, left-click on the Snap to Grid button (see Figure 15.2). While Snap to Grid is active, the background to the Snap to Grid button will turn

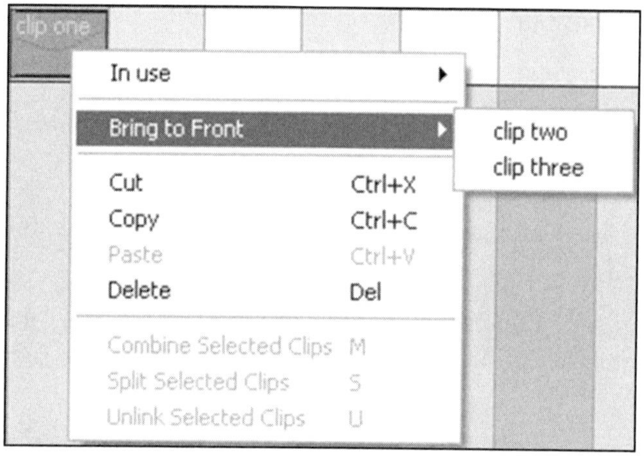

Figure 15.1 Accessing the Bring to Front submenu.

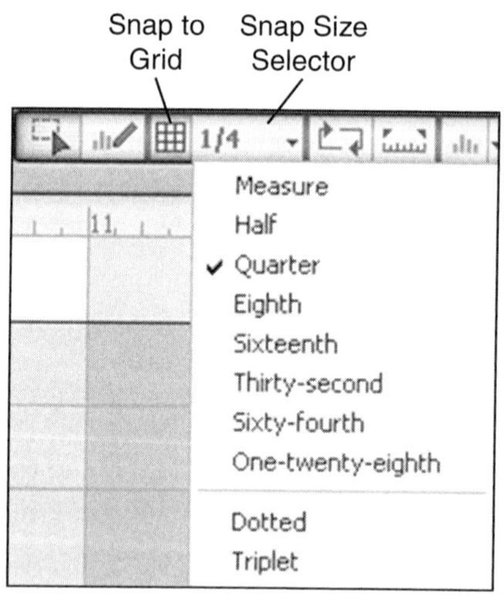

Figure 15.2 The Snap to Grid button, and the Snap Size Selector drop-down menu.

blue. Left-click on the button again to disengage the Snap to Grid function (whereupon the button's background will revert to gray).

If you click on the Snap Size Selector, a drop-down menu will appear. From this you can select the grid size. Once selected, the grid size will display on the button.

Take care when you select the grid size that you snap the Clip to. For instance, if you have a Clip that starts a beat before a measure (on the fourth beat of the previous measure), you wouldn't want to have the grid set to Measure because the Clip start would snap to the start of the measure (when you want the Clip to start a beat before the measure). For this example, the Quarter grid size may be more appropriate.

Copying Clips

The process to copy Clips is straightforward: Hold down the Ctrl key and, in the Arrange Pane, drag and drop the Clip you want to copy. The copied Clip will snap to the grid if the Snap to Grid function is engaged.

You can:

1. Right-click on a Clip.
2. Select Copy from the drop-down menu.
3. Right-click on the Arrange Pane where you want to place the Clip.
4. Select Paste from the drop-down menu.

Or, you could alternatively:

1. Select a Clip (by clicking on it).
2. Select Edit > Copy.
3. Click at the desired location.
4. Select Edit > Paste.

As you would also expect, you can cut and delete, as well as copy, in a similar manner.

Linked Clips

When you copy a Clip, it is linked to the Clip from which it was copied. When you edit one linked Clip, all of the other linked Clips are changed too. Linked Clips are recognizable by their shared color.

Unlinking Clips

You might want to copy a Clip and then edit the copy but leave the original intact. To do this, you need to unlink the Clips after you have copied the Clip.

To unlink a Clip—or several Clips, if you have selected more than one Clip—right-click on the Clip and select Unlink Selected Clips from the right-click pop-up menu. Alternatively, select the Clip or Clips and hit the U key on your computer keyboard.

Once the Clip or Clips have been unlinked, they will each show as a different color.

You can also copy an unlinked Clip by Ctrl+Alt-dragging the Clip.

Slip Editing and Slip Copying

Later tutorials in this chapter will look at how to edit a Clip's data. Slip Editing provides a fast way to hide the start and end of a Clip without affecting the underlying data. When you hide the data in this way, it will not be heard, but it is still available if you want to reverse the Slip Edit. With Slip Editing you can also extend a Clip and copy its contents. (This is called *Slip Copying* or *Rolling Out.*)

Slip Editing

When you hold your mouse over the left or right edge of a Clip, the pointer will change to a two-headed left/right arrow (with something that's meant to look like a Clip next to it). See Figure 15.3.

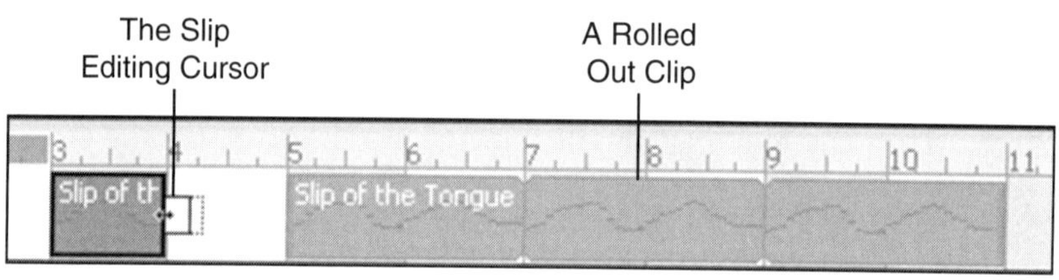

Figure 15.3 The Slip Editing cursor and a rolled-out Clip.

When the Slip Edit cursor appears, you can drag the left or right edge of the Clip (into the Clip) to hide the underlying data. If Snap to Grid is switched on, then the Slip Edits will snap to the selected grid size.

You can reverse any Slip Edits by Slip Editing the Clip again.

Rolling Out

Instead of Slip Editing to hide data by dragging the edge of a Clip into the Clip, you can drag the edge of the Clip outward. This is called *Rolling Out*. When you start Rolling Out, the Clip is copied, so as you can see, this is a really fast way to repeat a Clip.

Figure 15.3 also shows a rolled-out Clip. As you can see, the corners of a rolled-out Clip are cut off at the point that the Clip starts to repeat. (Look at the 7 and 9 measure markers.)

Rolled-out Clips are linked Clips, so if you edit the underlying data of one Clip, the change will be propagated through the whole of the rolled-out Clip.

Before you can Roll Out an Audio Clip, Groove-Clip Looping needs to be switched on. This is discussed further in Tutorial 21: Creating and Working with Groove Clips.

Combining and Splitting Clips

You may want to join two or more Clips together or split a Clip into two or more parts.

Splitting Clips

If you want to split a Clip, right-click at the place where you want the split to occur (remembering that the Snap to Grid function will have an effect if it is switched on) and select Split Selected Clip from the drop-down menu. Alternatively, select the Clip to be split by clicking at the point where you want the split to occur and hit the S key on your keyboard, or select Edit > Split Clip.

When you split a Clip, Project5 undertakes two tasks:

- First, it creates a linked copy of the Clip.
- Second, it Slip Edits the two Clips so that they meet (without overlapping) at the split point.

You can now edit the Clips further (and tweak the split point), but these Clips will remain linked unless you unlink them.

Combining Clips

You can combine one or more Clips of the same type. So, for instance, you can combine two Audio Clips, or you could combine two MIDI Clips and an Instrument Clip (which is just a MIDI Clip). The Clips to be combined must be in the same Track, so unless you've loaded an Audio Clip onto a MIDI Track, you're unlikely to have problems here.

To combine two or more Clips:

1. Select the Clips to be combined, either by dragging around all of them or by Ctrl-clicking on them—the selected Clips will be slightly grayed out.
2. Right-click on one of the Clips and select Combine Selected Clips from the drop-down menu. Alternatively, once you have selected the Clips, you can hit the M key or select Edit > Combine Selected Clips.

Combining Clips makes a destructive edit. If you combine two (or more) Clips that have been Slip Edited, then any data that is hidden by the Slip Edit will be discarded before the Clips are combined. After combining, you will not be able to access that discarded data (except by undoing the Combine command).

Tutorial 16: Creating a MIDI/Instrument Clip

Now that you know how to arrange your Clips, let's look at how to create MIDI and Instrument Clips. There is no difference between MIDI Clips and Instrument Clips—they are both just MIDI Clips—so for the remainder of this book, unless otherwise specified, if I refer to a MIDI Clip you can assume I'm also referring to an Instrument Clip.

There are a number of ways to create a MIDI Clip, but before you get going, you first need to create a MIDI Track or an Instrument Track. If you don't, then when you create a Clip it won't play back. Once you've loaded up your MIDI Track or Instrument, we'll get going.

Recording a MIDI Clip

The most straightforward way to create a MIDI Clip is to record it. There are two ways to do this:

- In the Track Pane/Arrange Pane
- In the Clip Editor

There are advantages to both options—which you choose will depend on what you are trying to achieve.

In the Track Pane/Arrange Pane, you will create a single linear Clip. It will start when you start recording, and it will end when you stop recording.

In the Clip Editor, you will create a looped piece. The length of the loop is set in the Clip Editor. This allows you record a Clip one Element at a time. Although this may be useful when you are recording melodic phrases, this way of working is particularly useful when you are creating a rhythm pattern.

Both options will be affected by the MIDI Input Quantize section settings.

Recording in the Track Pane/Arrange Pane

To record in the Track Pane/Arrange Pane:

1. Click on the (Track) Arm button on the MIDI Track Pane or the Instrument Track Pane (see Figure 16.1).
2. Hit the Record button in the Transport Controls.
3. Perform the part.

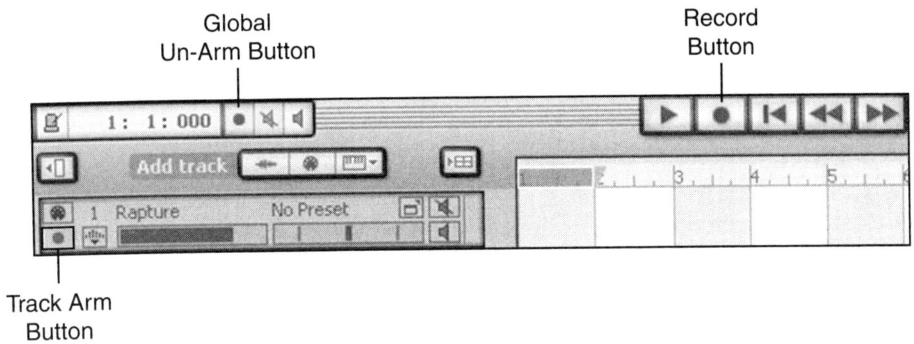

Figure 16.1 The Arm and Record buttons to record a MIDI/Instrument Clip.

4. Click on the Stop button in the Transport Controls when you have finished recording.
5. Disarm the Track Pane by clicking on the Arm button or the Global Un-Arm button.

Having recorded the new MIDI Clip, you will see that it is now visible in the Arrange Pane and automatically shows up in the Editor's piano roll view, much like Figure 16.2.

Recording in the Clip Editor

To record in the Clip Editor:

1. Select the length of the Clip with the Clip Length Selector. You can:
   - Use the up/down nudge buttons on the right of the selector to increase or decrease the length in beats.
   - Double-click on the current display to manually enter the length (and then adjust the tick value with the plus and minus buttons).
   - Alternatively, click and drag the Clip Length end marker.
2. Click on the Clip Editor Record button.
3. Perform the part.
4. Click on the Clip Play/Stop button (to the left of the Clip Editor Record button).

Inputting Data Directly and Editing

You can enter MIDI data directly in the Clip Editor. Once the MIDI data has been entered (whether by recording, direct entry, or Step Recording, which is discussed in the next section), it can be edited in the Clip Editor.

You can enter data directly (that is, with a mouse) in Free mode or Step mode (which is described in the next section). The difference between Free mode and Step mode is that in Step mode, each note has a fixed length and is snapped to the grid. By contrast, in the Free mode, each note can have its own length and does not have to snap to the grid.

To input data directly in Free mode, dial up the length of your Clip in the Clip Length Selector (refer back to Figure 16.2 if you can't remember where this is) or drag the Clip Length end marker and then engage the Notes Tool (see Figure 16.3). You can now enter your notes directly into the piano roll by left-clicking.

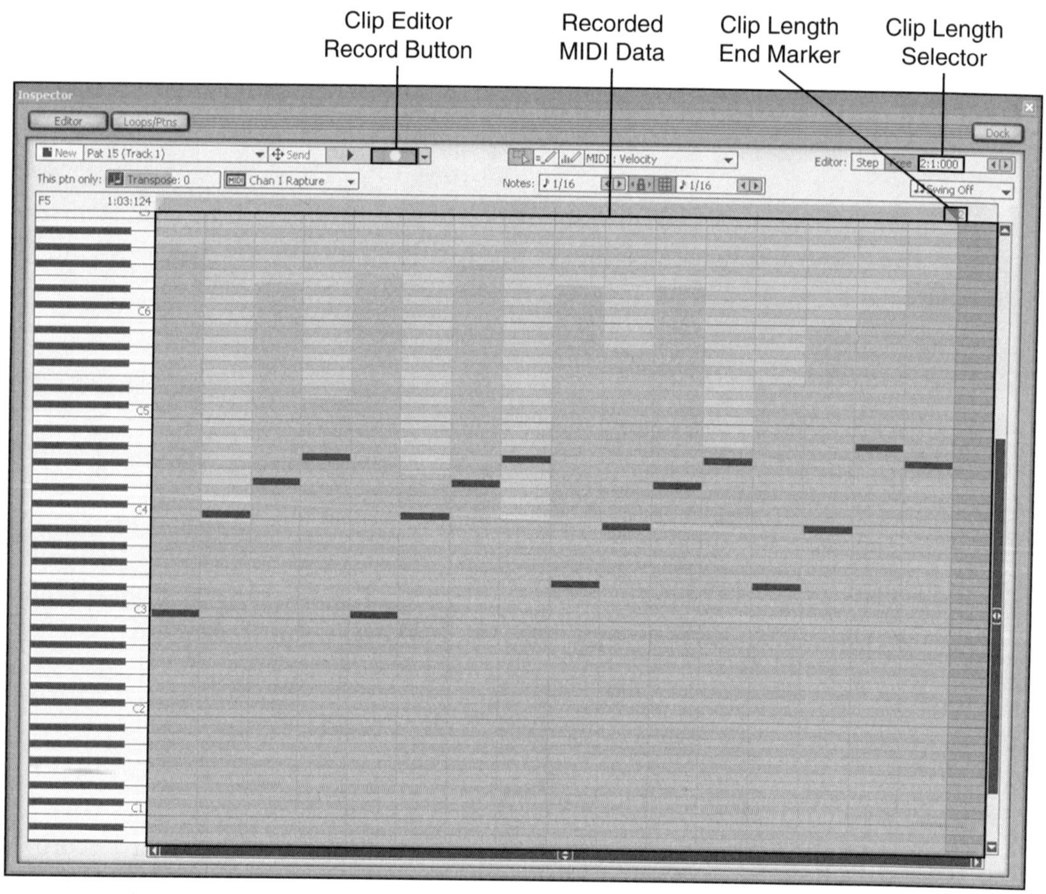

Figure 16.2 Recorded data showing up in the MIDI Clip piano roll view.

As Figure 16.3 shows, you have a range of tools to speed up your data entry and editing.

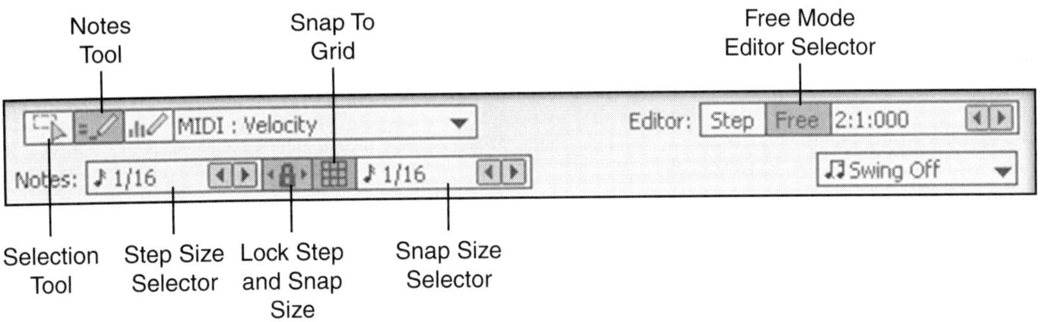

Figure 16.3 The main note entry tools.

Pencil Tool

When you select the Notes Tool and you hold your cursor over the piano roll, it will look like a pencil (see Figure 16.4).

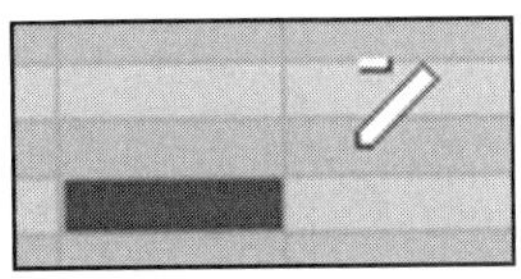

Figure 16.4 The Pencil Tool to manually insert and edit notes.

Using the Pencil Tool, you can insert notes (left-click where you want to insert a note) and move existing notes (left-click on the note and drag and drop it to the correct pitch/time).

Edit a Note's Length

If you hold your Pencil Tool over the beginning or the end of a note, it will change into a double-arrowed cursor (see Figure 16.5). You can now click and drag to extend the note or shorten it.

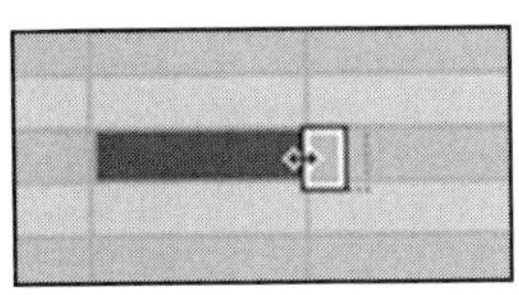

Figure 16.5 If you hold the cursor over the start or end of a note, you can drag to change its start time and/or length.

Velocity Tool

If you hold the Pencil Tool over the top of a note, it will change into the Velocity Tool (see Figure 16.6). Under the note you will see a light-blue bar (it looks gray in

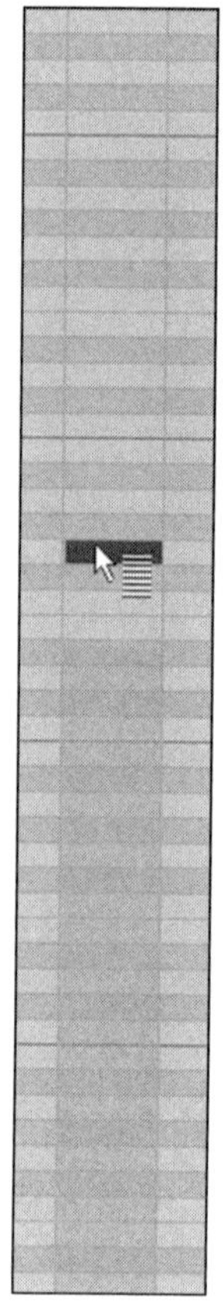

Figure 16.6 The Velocity Tool.

the figure)—this represents the velocity level of that note. When the Velocity Tool is visible, left-click and drag up or down to increase or decrease the note's velocity. As you will read in Tutorial 18: Automating a Clip, you can also draw in velocity data with the Automation Tool.

Fraser Tool

When the Pencil Tool is active, if you right-click, the Eraser Tool will appear (see Figure 16.7). Using the Eraser Tool, you can erase any note.

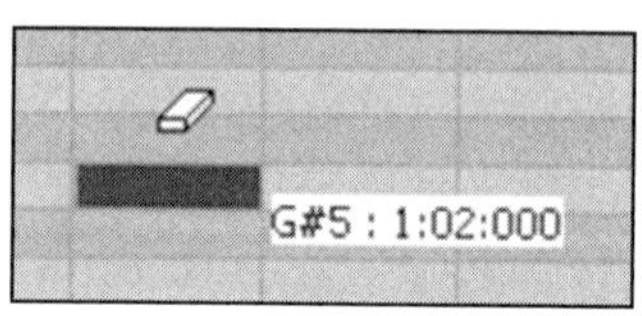

Figure 16.7 The Eraser Tool.

Selection Tool

The Selection Tool allows you to select several notes by dragging around them or Ctrl+left-clicking on them. You may want to select several notes to apply one of the transformations described in Tutorial 17: Processes for Handling MIDI Data.

Getting Snappy

There is a range of Step Size and Snap tools that apply to notes inserted and edited in the Clip Editor.

- The Step Size Selector determines the length of the note inserted with the Pencil Tool.
- The Lock Step and Snap Size button sets the Step Size Selector and the snap grid (Snap Size Selector) to the same value. When this feature is engaged, the background behind the padlock turns blue.
- Snap to Grid switches on the Snap to Grid function for the Clip Editor. This works independently of the Snap to Grid function in the Arrange Pane.
- The Snap Size Selector selects the snap grid division.

Step Recording

Step Recording allows you to enter notes from your MIDI keyboard (or other MIDI input device). As you enter each note, you step to the next entry automatically. This makes Step Recording a great way to enter arpeggios and bass lines. However, you can also enter chords if you want. Because you are using your MIDI controller to enter notes, this means that each note will receive input velocity messages too.

Step Recording in Step Mode

You can Step Record in Free mode—and I will explain how to do this later—but it makes far more sense to Step Record in Step mode, which you can access by clicking on the Step Mode Selector (see Figure 16.8).

Once you are in Step mode, the first thing to do is set the number of steps (using the Step Count Selector) and the duration of each step (using the Step Duration Selector). You can alternatively set these values by selecting Options > Default Step Count for Step Sequencer and Options > Default Step Size for Step Sequencer, as appropriate.

The number of steps is unrelated to a measure. So, for instance, if you select eight steps and set the duration of each step to half notes, then the Pattern you create in the Step Sequencer will last for four measures.

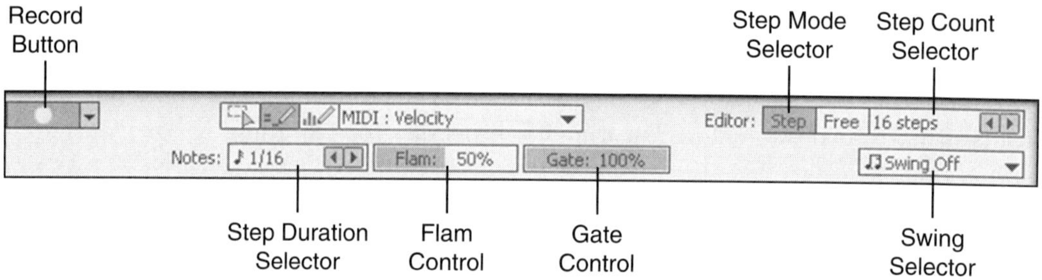

Figure 16.8 The main Step Mode Controls.

Once you've set the step duration and the number of steps, you're ready to start Step Recording:

1. Click on the Record button.
2. Enter the notes on your MIDI keyboard. You will notice that you jump forward to the next step each time your release a note.
3. Hit the Tab key when you want to jump forward without entering a note (in other words, when you want to enter a rest).
4. Click on the Record button when you have finished entering your notes.

You can now edit your notes with the Pencil Tool. If you switch to Free mode, you can shift the timing of individual notes away from the regimented grid of Step mode.

You are not restricted to adding single notes—you can add chords in Step mode. When you do this, hold down at least two notes of the chord at one time. It is not necessary to hold down all of the notes together. The chord will be entered when you release the final note; all of the notes you have hit will then be entered.

Flam

A *flam* is a ghost note added just before the main note. Most often this technique is used by drummers. You can convert a conventional note into a flam by double-clicking on the note with the Pencil Tool. Flammed notes show with a vertical marker in the middle of the note (see Figure 16.9).

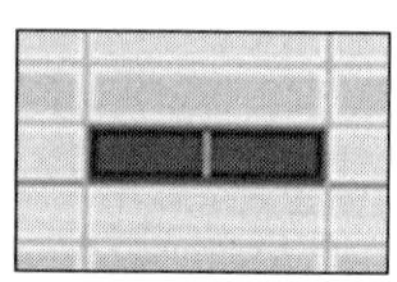

Figure 16.9 A flammed note.

The Flam Control controls the behavior of flammed notes. The value determines how long after the ghost note the main note sounds.

Gate

The Gate Control determines the duration of each step as a percentage of its possible length. So, for instance, if you have set your Step Duration Selector to quarter notes and the Gate Control to 50 percent, each note will only be heard for the duration of an eighth note.

Swing

The Swing Selector drop-down turns the Swing function on and off for the Clip. This selector is also visible in Free mode.

The amount of the swing is determined by the Swing Amount Control in the left-hand Main Controls. (Check back to Tutorial 4: The Main Controls for details.)

Clip Editor Utility Functions

To the top left of the Clip Editor, you will find a few utilities to help you (see Figure 16.10).

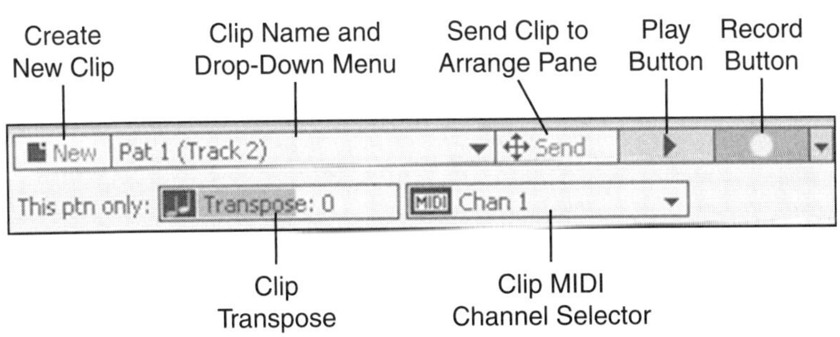

Figure 16.10 The Clip Editor utilities.

New Clips

To create a new Clip, click on the Create New Clip button. A new Clip will be created, into which you can record data, manually enter data, or Step Record data. The new Clip will be located on the currently selected Track at the Now Time.

Clip Name

New Clips are given a default name (Pat 1, Pat 2, Pat 3, and so on). To rename a Clip, double-click on its name and insert the new name. The new name will show in the Clip Name box and on all instances of the Clip in the Arrange Pane.

Clip Transpose

The Clip Transpose Control transposes the Clip (and only the Clip that is being edited) over a range of plus or minus 128 semitones.

To transpose a Clip you can:

- Left-click and drag the Transpose Control.
- Double-click on the Transpose Control and manually enter the transpose amount.
- Double-click on the Transpose Control and adjust the transpose amount with the plus and minus nudge buttons.

Clip MIDI Channel

The Clip MIDI Channel drop-down allows you to select the MIDI Channel for the currently selected Clip. By selecting different MIDI Channels for a number of different Clips, you can address the different channel of a multi-timbral instrument from a single Track.

Record Modes

To the right of the Record button you will see a down arrow, which opens the Record Modes drop-down menu (see Figure 16.11).

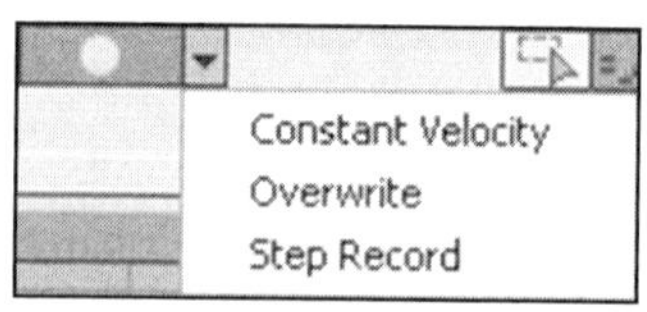

Figure 16.11 The Record Modes drop-down menu.

There are three record modes, and you can select one, two, or all three modes.

- **Constant Velocity.** When Constant Velocity mode is selected, all MIDI input velocity data (when you record a Clip or use Step mode) will be set to the same velocity level.
- **Overwrite.** In Overwrite mode, the existing Pattern is deleted. Also in this mode, if you try to record a Pattern while the Clip loops, at the start of each loop the existing Pattern will be deleted.
- **Step Record.** This mode switches on the Step Record function in Free mode. When you are in Step mode, this option is not available on the drop-down (since you are already in Step Record mode).

Clip Drop-Down Menu

If you click on the arrowhead to the right of the Clip's name, a drop-down menu that looks like Figure 16.12 will appear. Before we go any further, let me remind you that the terms *Clip* and *Pattern* are interchangeable: For consistency in this book, I have largely stuck with the term *Clip*.

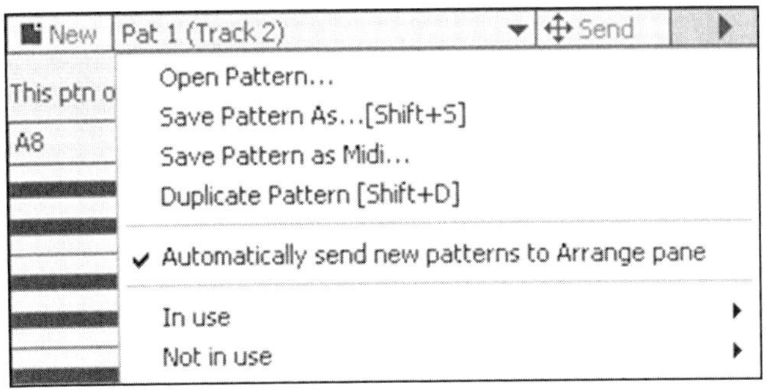

Figure 16.12 The Clip drop-down menu.

Let's look at the first four options:

- **Open Pattern.** Allows you to open a saved Pattern (including the Patterns that come with Project5).
- **Save Pattern As.** Allows you to save a Pattern so you can reload it later. You can also save a Pattern by hitting Shift+S on your keyboard.
- **Save Pattern as MIDI.** Allows you to save a Pattern as a MIDI file so you can load it into other software or synthesizers (for instance, Cakewalk's Z3TA+ synthesizer allows you to load MIDI files as arpeggiator Patterns).
- **Duplicate Pattern.** Allows you to duplicate a Pattern so you can edit the duplicate without affecting the original. You can also duplicate a Pattern by hitting Shift+D on your keyboard.

Interaction between the Clips Editor and the Track Pane

Once you've created a Clip, you're going to want to send it to the Arrange Pane. You're also likely to want to call up Clips to edit them.

Transferring Clips to the Arrange Pane

There are several ways that Clips get from the Clip Editor to the Arrange Pane.

- From the Clip drop-down menu (which was shown in Figure 16.12), if you have selected Automatically Send New Patterns to Arrange Pane, then whenever you create a new Clip it will show in the Arrange Pane automatically. It will be located on the currently selected Track at the Now Time.

- You can also send a Clip to the Arrange Pane at any time (irrespective of whether the Automatically Send New Patterns to Arrange Pane option has been checked) by clicking on the Send button. Again, the Clip will be located on the currently selected Track at the Now Time. The timing of the sent Clip will not take account of any Snap to Grid settings, so if you stop playback halfway through a measure and send a Clip, then the Clip will be placed halfway through a measure.
- You can also drag and drop from the Send button to the Arrange Pane or the Groove Matrix (which is discussed in Tutorial 22: Using the Groove Matrix). When dragging to the Arrange Pane, the Clip will be located on the Track and at the time you select when you drop it. When you drag and drop a Clip, its position will be affected by any Snap to Grid settings in the Arrange Pane.

If you send the same Clip several times or drag and drop the same Clip several times, each of the Clips will be linked.

Opening Clips in the Clip Editor

There are several ways you can open a Clip in the Clip Editor:

- In the Arrange Pane, double-click on a Clip.
- Use an option from the Clips drop-down menu. In the Clips drop-down menu, there are two options: In Use and Not in Use. Each of these opens up submenus of the Clips in use and not in use, respectively. All you have to do is select the Clip you want to edit from the submenu.

Tutorial 17: Processes for Handling MIDI Data

Project5 comes with a range of specialized processes for handling MIDI data. These processes can be applied:

- To one or more Clips in the Arrange Pane
- To one or more notes in the Clip Editor

The benefit of these tools is that they have all been designed with a specific purpose and make quick work out of transforming your MIDI data.

To perform the transformation, use the Selection Tool in the Arrange Pane or the Clip Editor to select the Clip or notes that you want to transform, and then call up the process. All of the processes can be found under the Process menu. If the options on the menu are grayed out, then you have no MIDI data selected.

Some of the functions performed by these processes can also be undertaken by the MIDI FX units (which are discussed in Chapter 8, "MIDI FX Units"). You are likely to want to use these processes rather than the MIDI FX units if you want to make a permanent change.

Quantize

Quantize is a "snap to grid after the event" process. As you would expect, it functions like the Input Quantize Tool and has many similar controls. As you can see in Figure 17.1, there are three main sections in the Quantize process.

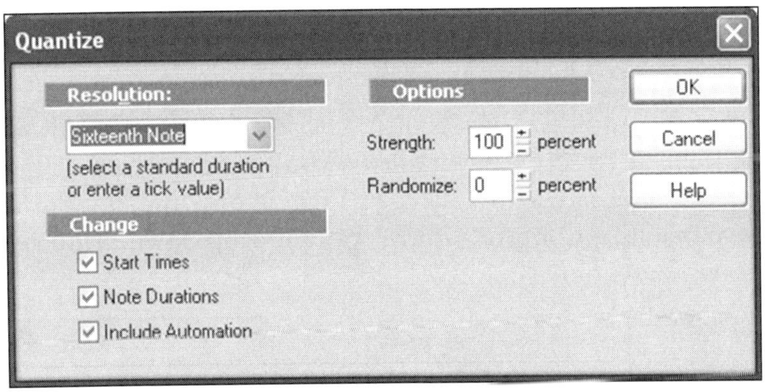

Figure 17.1 The Quantize process.

In the Resolution section, you can select the grid to which notes are quantized.

In the Change section, you can determine how the Quantize process applies by selecting one or more of the three check boxes.

- **Start Time.** When you quantize start time, you snap a note's start time to the grid selected in the Resolution section.
- **Note Durations.** When Note Durations is selected, the length of the note is quantized to the nearest multiple of the Resolution value.
- **Include Automation.** Include Automation allows you to determine whether any automation data is also quantized. Automation is discussed in Tutorial 18: Automating a Clip.

In the Options section, you can adjust the settings either by clicking on the plus and minus nudge buttons or by doubling-clicking and directly entering a value. The Options section gives you two controls:

- **Strength.** The Strength Control determines how close to the quantization grid a note is snapped. When this is set to 0% there is no snapping, and when it is set to 100% the note snaps precisely to the timing set by the grid.
- **Randomize.** The Randomize Control adds an element of random timing to a note. This allows you to add some humanization once the quantization has sorted the timing problems.

Groove Quantize

Groove Quantize works very much like the Quantize process. However, instead of snapping to a timing grid, it snaps notes to a groove. This allows you to quantize while keeping a more natural musical feel.

As you can see in Figure 17.2, there are many similarities between the Quantize process and the Groove Quantize process.

The Groove File drop-down allows you to choose a Groove File. Alternatively, the button to the right of the drop-down allows you to browse to a new Groove File. Once the Groove File has been selected, you can choose the Pattern to which you want to groove-quantize from the Groove Pattern drop-down menu.

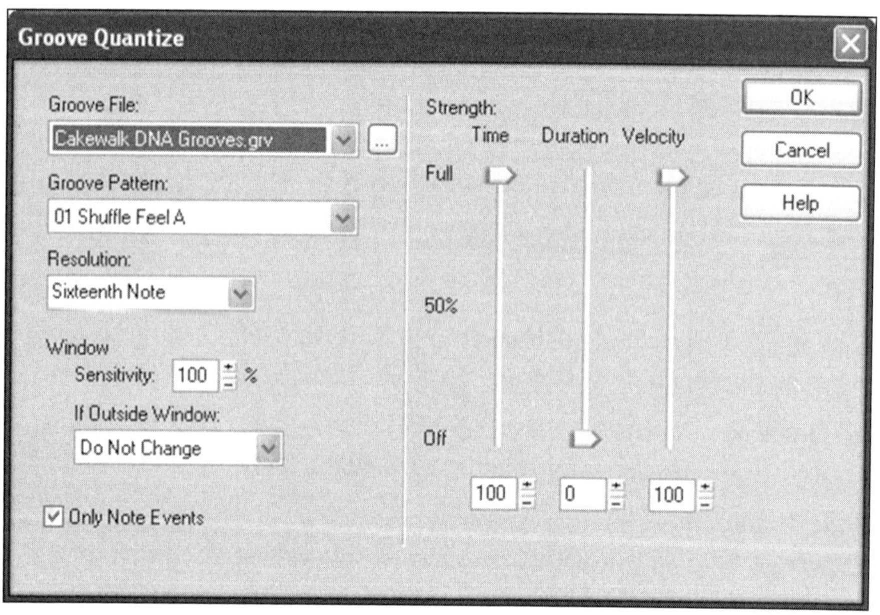

Figure 17.2 The Groove Quantize process.

The Resolution drop-down allows you to control the precision of the quantization in relation to the groove.

The Window Control sets the area over which the Groove Quantize process looks for notes to quantize. With higher settings, all notes will be quantized. At lower settings, only those notes that are slightly mistimed will be groove-quantized. From the If Outside Window drop-down, you can then select how the notes that fall outside the window are dealt with.

- **Do Not Change.** If you select Do Not Change, notes outside of the window will be ignored.
- **Quantize to Resolution.** When the Quantize to Resolution option is selected, notes outside of the window will be quantized to the Resolution setting.
- **Move to Nearest.** When Move to Nearest is selected, notes outside of the window will be moved to their nearest groove event.
- **Scale Time.** With Scale Time selected, notes outside of the window will be equally spaced.

When the Only Note Events box is checked, only notes will be groove-quantized. If you want to groove-quantize controller data and so on, then uncheck this box.

On the right-hand side of the Groove Quantize process, there are three Strength sliders:

- **Time.** The Time Slider determines how much note starts are groove-quantized.
- **Duration.** The Duration Slider determines the extent to which note durations are groove-quantized.
- **Velocity.** The Velocity Slider determines the extent to which note velocities are changed to reflect the groove pattern's velocities.

Transpose

The Transpose process (see Figure 17.3) will increase or decrease the pitch of the selected notes or Clips by the Amount setting.

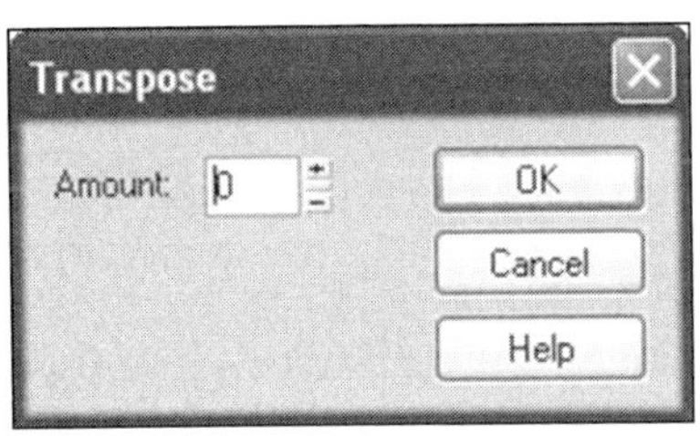

Figure 17.3 The Transpose process.

Slide

The Slide process (see Figure 17.4) moves the selected notes or Clips. Positive changes delay a note, while negative changes move the note in front of the beat.

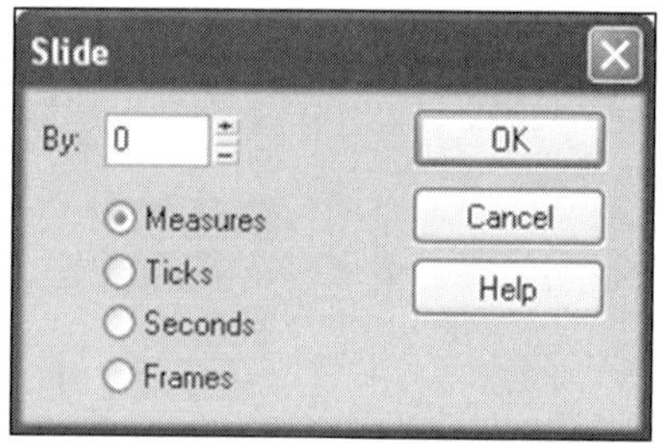

Figure 17.4 The Slide process.

With the Slide process, you can choose to move notes by:

- Measures
- Ticks (there are 960 ticks per beat)
- Seconds
- Frames (which may be useful if you are working with video)

Length

The Length process (see Figure 17.5) is intended to change the duration of a single note or a group of notes.

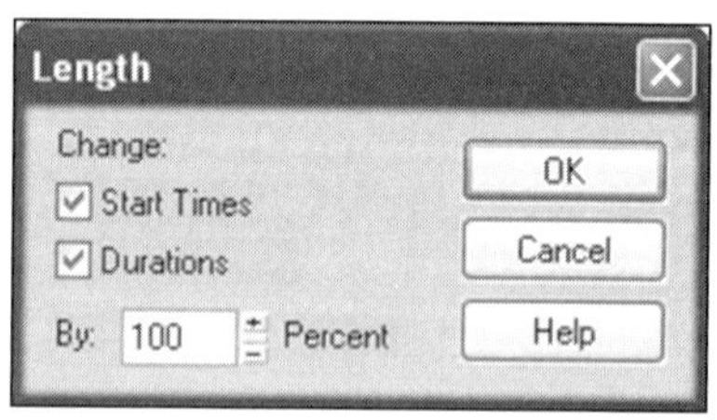

Figure 17.5 The Length process.

The By Control allows you to determine the length of the transformed note as a percentage of the original note. Values greater than 100% will result in a note's length being increased.

There are two check-box options in the Change section:

- **Start Times.** The Start Time option determines whether a note's start time is changed as part of a transformation. You will often want to select this option if you are transforming a group of notes. Suppose you have a measure of eight eighth notes and you want to halve their duration. If you simply select 50%, then you will have eight eighth notes, each lasting for the time of a sixteenth note. However, if you also select the Start Time option, you will get eight sixteenth notes (which last for half a measure).

- **Durations.** The Durations option determines whether the length of a note is changed.

Scale Velocity

The Scale Velocity process (see Figure 17.6) changes the velocities of a group of selected notes.

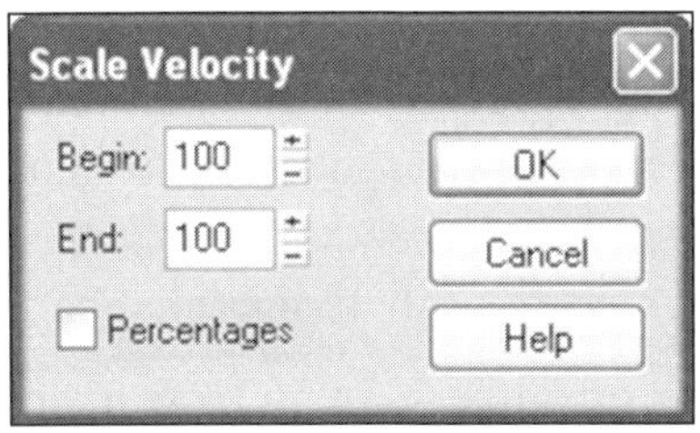

Figure 17.6 The Scale Velocity process.

The Begin value and the End value set the velocity of the first and last selected notes (in the range of 0 to 127). The values of the notes in between the Begin and End values are scaled to create a crescendo or a decrescendo.

If you check the Percentages box, then the scaling is applied as a percentage of the existing velocity.

Retrograde

Retrograde is a simple process—so simple that it doesn't need an interface. It works by reversing the order of the notes in a selection.

You can also invoke the transformation by hitting Ctrl+R on your keyboard.

Tutorial 18: Automating a Clip

Once you've got your Project up and running, you're likely to want to add some automation. Once you start using automation, you're likely to find you use it a lot. It will be that added ingredient that makes a good track a great song.

You will find that you can use automation in a lot of areas—for instance, with Clips, with Tracks, with FX, and on Busses. With automation (see Figure 18.1), you can

Figure 18.1 Automation in action.

move knobs on your synthesizer (or whatever it is you want to automate) either with ACT or by using a mouse, and Project5 will record that change. Alternatively, you can draw in the automation.

There are three tutorials in this book that cover automation: this tutorial; Tutorial 21, which looks at automation in Groove Clips (as well as looking at Groove Clips), and Tutorial 25: Automation, which looks at Track automation. You need to read all three tutorials to understand the full range of automation functions that are available in Project5. This first tutorial is intended as an introduction to automation, so it won't have all of the detail that the others include.

This tutorial looks at adding automation to an Instrument (MIDI) Clip. Similar principles (and more) apply with Groove Clips. As you will see, automation cannot be applied at the Clip level to audio files, which are not Groove Clips.

Before we get going, please remember the fundamental difference between Clips and Tracks: Clips are (generally) short pieces, and Tracks are, by comparison, long pieces. Track automation can occur over the whole length of a Track. By contrast, Clip automation can only occur over the length of the Clip. If you repeat the Clip three times, then the automation will repeat three times. If you want the automation to begin when the Clip first begins and end after the third repeat, then you need to use Track automation.

Clip Automation: What Can You Automate?

With Clip automation, you can automate most things. For instance, you could automate:

- The Clip's level, panning, or Aux Send level
- Any control on any Instrument
- Any control on any audio FX unit
- The Track Arpeggiator

Automation is essentially a two-step process:

- Select the automation target (for instance, a synthesizer's cutoff frequency).
- Draw the automation.

Unlike Track automation, you cannot record Clip automation, so you have to draw it in.

Drawing Clip Automation

Clip automation is best illustrated with an example.

Suppose you have a Clip that is playing Dimension LE, and you want to control the filter cutoff with automation. The first step is to select the automation target in the Clip. This is done from the Automation Assignment drop-down menu (see Figure 18.2).

This is quite a confusing menu with lots of options that I will explain in greater detail in Tutorial 25. It is particularly confusing for Dimension LE, which has a multitude of parameters to automate (as Figure 18.2 indicates). I'm lucky and know where to look. As you can see, if you select DXi > DX Automation > Filter Type 04 – Eq1 On/Off 04 > Cutoff 01, then the automation will control the cutoff frequency for Element 1's filter.

As a side note, there is a benefit to this level of complexity. You will read in Chapter 7, "Working with Audio FX Units," that Dimension LE is essentially Dimension Pro with a different interface. The different interface is simplified for ease of use, but this has the secondary effect of giving access to a reduced number of parameters. With automation you can immediately access all of these restricted parameters.

Back to automation… Now that the automation assignment has been made, click on the Automation Tool and draw in your automation (see Figure 18.3).

Try it. It's much easier to do in practice than it is to try to understand from reading on the page.

There are two things to note when you draw automation:

- Automation adheres to the Snap to Grid parameters, so you might want to switch this function off while you are drawing your automation, unless you like jerky changes.
- If you want to draw a straight line (which will override any Snap to Grid settings), hold down the Shift key when you draw in the automation. This is what I did when I drew Figure 18.3. As you can see, the automation snaps to the finest grid, resulting in much smoother changes.

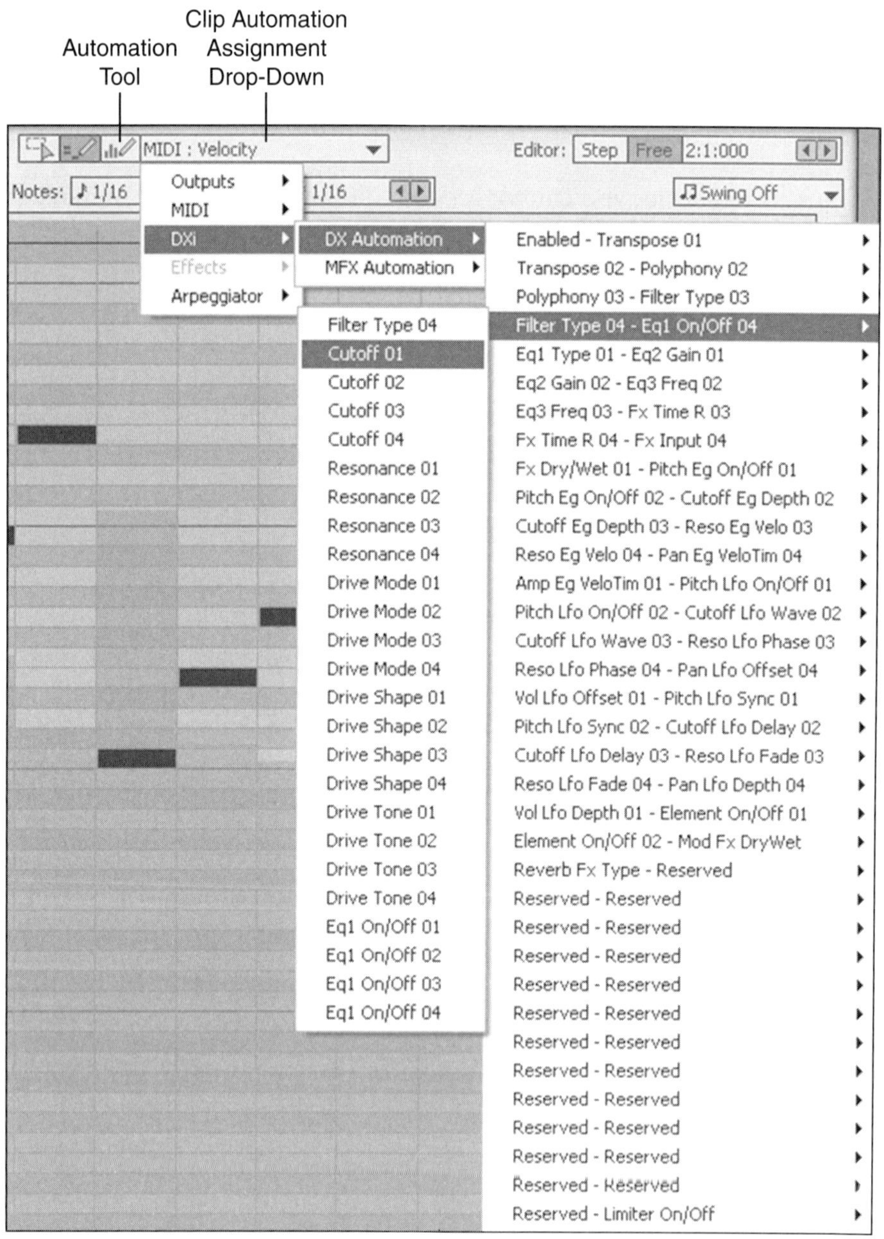

Figure 18.2 The Clip Automation Assignment drop-down menu.

What Now?

As I mentioned at the start of this tutorial, there are many other features of Clip automation. To save duplication, I have included these in Tutorial 25. I suggest you skip ahead to that tutorial if you want some hardcore automation in your life.

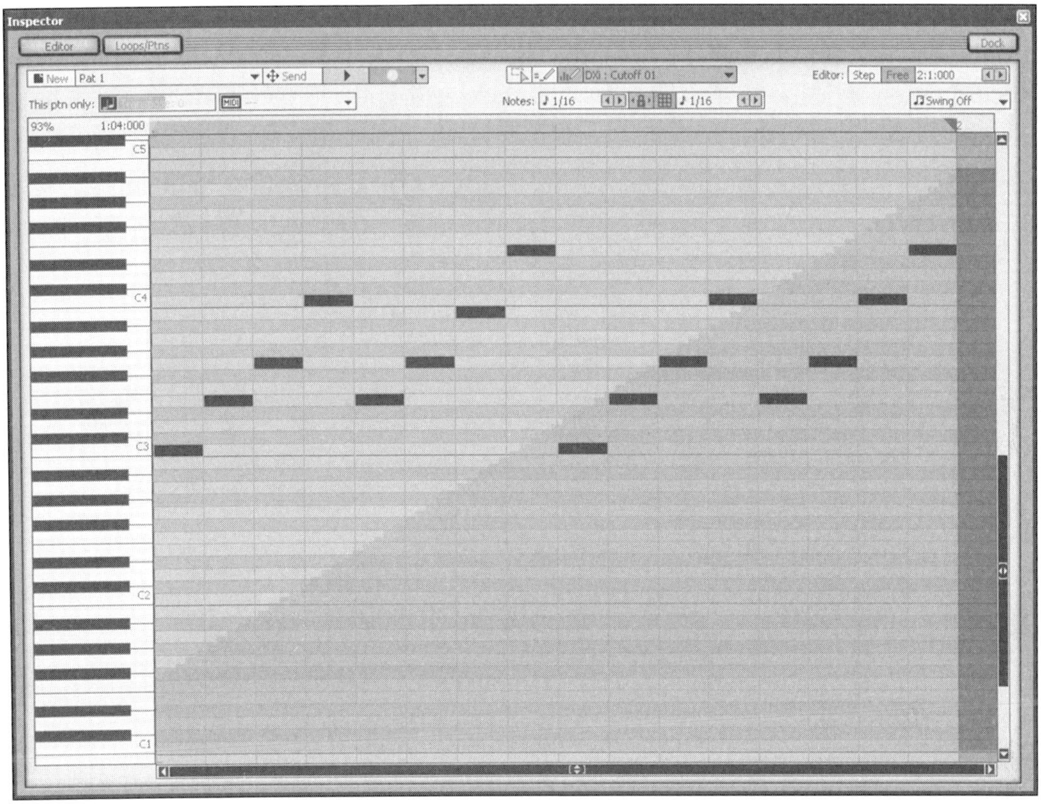

Figure 18.3 The drawn-in automation (which will show in blue on your screen). Note that the Automation Assignment drop-down shows the parameter that is being automated.

Tutorial 19: Recording an Audio Clip

As you've already seen, you can import audio Clips into Project5 either by importing them from the File menu or by dragging them from the Clip Browser. There is another way to get audio into Project5: Record it directly. Before you can record audio, you will need an audio interface connected and properly set up, so if you haven't done so already, I suggest you check out Tutorial 10: Setting Up Audio In and Audio Out.

Depending on the limitations of your hardware, you can record one or several Audio Tracks at once. You can record in mono or stereo. The principles set out in this tutorial apply irrespective of whether you are recording one mono track or several stereo tracks.

Setting Up an Audio Track for Recording

Before you can record audio, you need to insert an Audio Track in the Track Pane. You can do this by clicking on the Add New Audio Track button or by right-clicking on the Track Pane and selecting Insert Audio Track from the pop-up menu. At this point you may find it useful to rename the Audio Track Pane to note what you are recording—you can do this by double-clicking on the Track's name (which by default is Audio Track).

When you insert an Audio Track, the Audio Track Inspector will appear (see Figure 19.1).

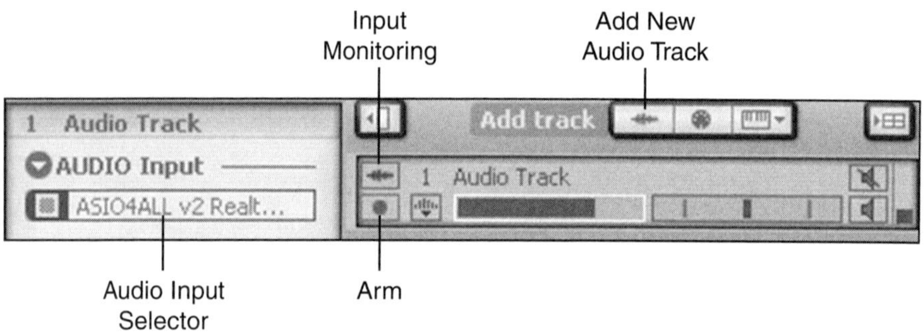

Figure 19.1 An Audio Track and the Audio Input section of the corresponding Audio Track Inspector.

In the Audio Input section of the Audio Track Inspector, select the appropriate audio input from the Audio Input Selector drop-down menu. The appropriate audio input is the one to which your sound source is attached.

Setting Levels

The next step is to set the input level. The level you should be looking for is as high as possible but without exceeding the maximum input level. If you're unsure about the maximum level, then back it off a bit—more than anything in this world, the one thing you want to avoid is digital distortion. Once you overload your input, you will get digital distortion. Digital distortion cannot be removed. The best you can do is work around it, but that is likely to affect your audio detrimentally.

The input level is set by your soundcard, so you'll need to refer to your interface's documentation to sort this level.

Input Monitoring

You can listen to the performance that is being recorded by clicking on the Input Monitoring button. If you can hear an echo or a slight delay, this is due to latency.

For this reason, I would suggest you avoid Input Monitoring if you can (check out Tutorial 10 to see my personal solution to this issue).

Recording

When you're ready to record, hit the Arm button (on your Track) and then punch the Record button (or push the R key on your keyboard). This will record a Clip in the Arrange Pane. To end recording, hit the spacebar or the Stop button. To stop recording but allow the song to continue, hit the R key on your keyboard or click on the Record button.

When recording ends, the Clip that you have just recorded will be visible in the Clip Editor.

Recording Multiple Audio Tracks

If you are recording multiple Audio Tracks in one take, repeat the process set out here to set up the individual Tracks. However, each separate Track should be fed from a separate audio input.

Tutorial 20: Editing an Audio Clip

From Project5's perspective, audio comes in two forms: plain old audio and Groove Clips. *Groove Clips* are simply pieces of audio that also include timing information so you can link the audio to the tempo of your Track and do clever things. Groove Clips will be discussed in detail in the next tutorial.

For this tutorial, I want to look at non–Groove Clip audio. This might be a vocal part, or it could be an instrumental part. Equally, it could be a rhythm part that you will subsequently turn into a Groove Clip.

You can get Audio Clips into Project5 in three main ways:

- Import the audio (File > Import).
- Record the audio (refer to Tutorial 19).
- Load the audio through the Loops/Pattern Browser.

Audio Clip Editor

If you look at an Audio Clip in the Clip Editor (see Figure 20.1), you will see that, unlike the MIDI Clip Editor and the Groove Clip Editor, you don't have a range of tools. In fact, for audio, the Clip Editor isn't an editor as such, but rather it is a viewer.

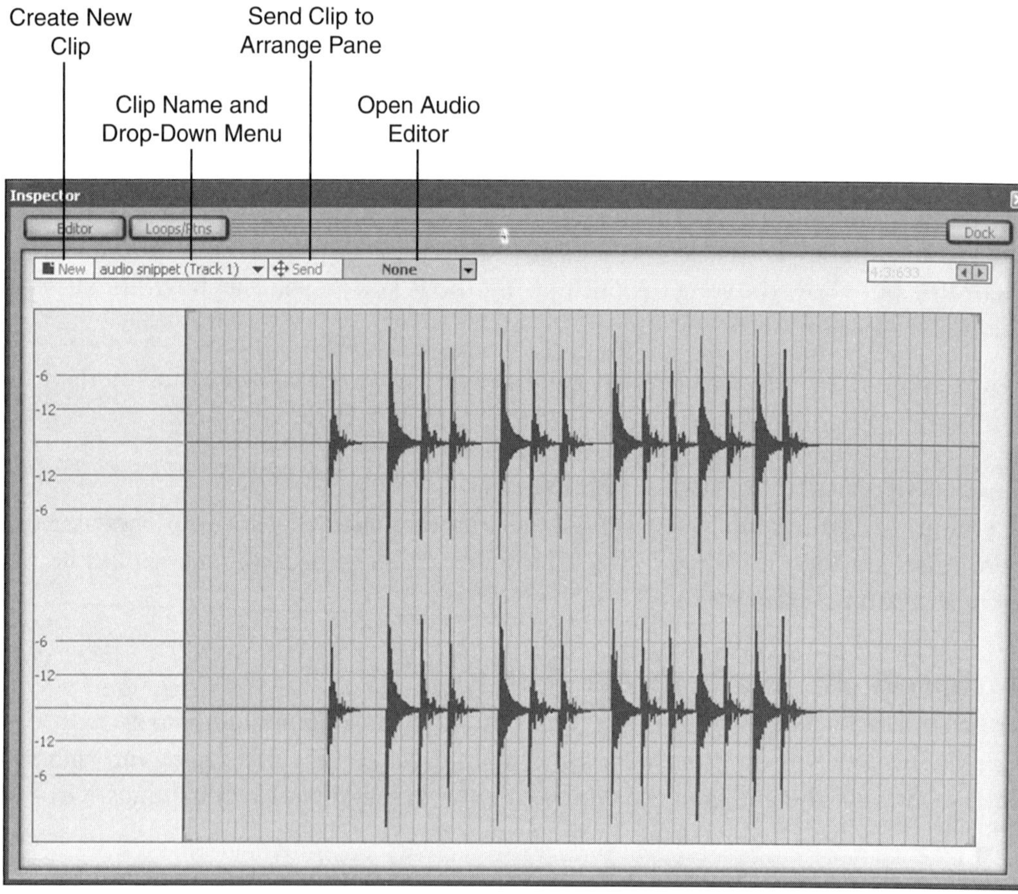

Figure 20.1 The Audio Clip Editor.

The Audio Clip Editor shares three buttons with the MIDI Clip Editor (and the Groove Clip Editor):

- The Create New Clip button
- The Clip Name and Drop-Down menu
- The Send Clip to Arrange Pane button

These three buttons work in exactly the same manner as they do in the MIDI Clip Editor—look back to Tutorial 16: Creating a MIDI/Instrument Clip for further details. The fourth button, Open Audio Editor, is only found in the Audio Clip Editor. This allows you to open (and edit) an audio track in an external audio editor (such as the well-respected freeware editor, Audacity, which is available from audacity.sourceforge.net). In a moment, I will look at the Open Audio Editor function and how to set up an external audio editor to work with Project5.

The option to use an external audio editor is only available for Audio Clips. If you have a Groove Clip, you will need to switch off Groove-Clip Looping before you can open such a Clip from the Audio Clip Editor.

Audio Editing Tools within Project5

Although the Audio Clip Editor may look restrictive, you can still perform most of your audio editing tasks in Project5 in the Arrange Pane.

In particular, you can:

- Copy, cut, paste, and delete Clips
- Slip Edit the Clip to hide the start and end of the Clip (although you can't Roll Out a non–Groove Clip piece of audio)
- Combine two or more Clips to create a new Clip
- Split a Clip

Refer to Tutorial 15: Arranging and Working with Clips for details on how to perform these tasks.

In addition, with Track automation you can you can perform a range of transformations to your audio. Track automation is discussed in Tutorial 25.

Setting Up an External Audio Editor

There are a number of reasons why you might want to open an Audio Clip in an external audio editor. For instance, you might want to trim the start and end of the Clip but find that the Slip Edit is rather imprecise. Equally, you may want to remove a click or pop in your Audio Clip: Audacity (like many audio editors) can work at the sample level and will allow you to redraw your audio wave to remove clicks and pops.

Project5 allows you to call on up to two external audio editors. However, before you can call up an audio editor, you need to install it. Once your audio editor is installed, click on the down arrow to the right of the Open Audio Editor button and select Properties from the drop-down menu. This will bring up the Configure Audio Editor (see Figure 20.2).

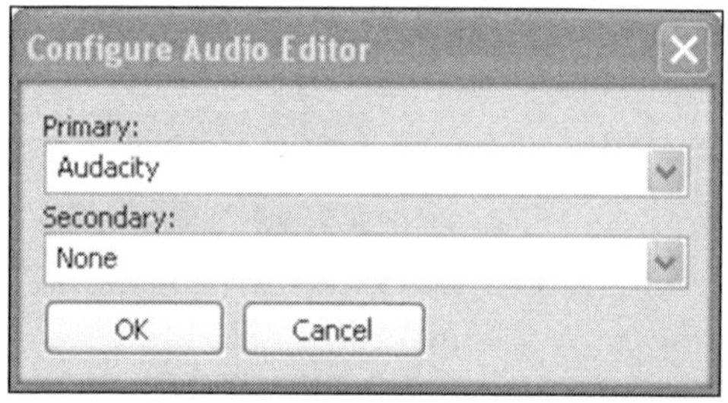

Figure 20.2 The Configure Audio Editor.

The Configure Audio Editor has two drop-down menus from which you can select your primary audio editor and your secondary audio editor. Click on these drop-downs and select the appropriate editors. Some audio editors (such as Audacity) don't automatically show up in the drop-downs—I'll look at these in a moment.

Once you have selected your audio editors, the name of the primary editor will show on the Open Audio Editor button. When you have an Audio Clip in the Clip Editor, click on the Open Audio Editor button, and the Audio Clip will automatically be opened in your primary audio editor.

To open a Clip in your secondary audio editor (if one has been selected), click on the down arrow to the right of the Open Audio Editor button, and select the secondary audio editor from the drop-down menu.

Setting Up Audacity to Work with Project5

If an audio editor that is installed on your system does not show up in the Configure Audio Editor window, you need to make a slight tweak to your registry. This is not for the faint-hearted, nor the stupid, so please proceed with caution. Please also ensure you have a copy of your registry backed up before you undertake these changes.

I hope it also goes without saying that if you ******* everything up, then don't come running to me. This is tricky stuff, and you're on your own.

Close Project5 and then follow this procedure.

1. Select Start > Run.
2. In the Run window, type REGEDIT and click OK.
3. Click the plus sign next to HKEY_LOCAL_MACHINE.
4. Click the plus sign next to Software.
5. Click the plus sign next to Cakewalk Music Software.

6. Click the plus sign next to Tools Menu.
7. Right-click on the Tools menu and select New > Key. A new folder will be created, which can be named with the name of your audio editor (for instance, Audacity). You can always rename this folder by clicking on it and selecting Rename from the pop-up menu.
8. Right-click the new folder again and choose New > String Value. A new String Value entry will appear. Enter the string value name (shown in Table 20.1). Then double-click on the newly created string value and enter the data value shown in Table 20.1.

Table 20.1 Registry Key Values to Set Up an External Audio Editor in Project5

String Value	Data Value
ExePath	The full path and name of your audio editor's executable file—for instance, c:\program files \audacity\audacity.exe
Type	WaveEditor
MenuText	The name of your wave editor—for instance, Audacity
HelpFilePath (this is optional)	The full path and name of your audio editor's online help file
StatusBarText (this is optional)	The text that will show in the status bar when the audio is highlighted in the Tools menu

Once you have inserted these values, close the Registry Editor and restart Project5. You should now be able to select your audio editor in the Configure Audio Editor window.

Getting Your Audio Back into Project5

After you have got your audio into your external audio editor and you have finished editing it, you need to get the audio back into Project5.

To do this, save the audio file as a WAV file in your audio editor—use the same bit depth and sample rate that you are using for your Project in Project5. Then import the newly saved audio file back into Project5.

The old audio file can be deleted from the Arrange Pane and, if you want, deleted from the Clips Not in Use list too.

Tutorial 21: Creating and Working with Groove Clips

Groove Clips are one of the ways that Project5 handles loops.

Groove Clips are audio files with beat and tempo information. These files can be synchronized to the tempo of a Project in Project5. If the tempo of the Project changes, then the Groove Clips will work with the new tempo, staying on the beat.

Different Loop Formats

Loops come in different forms—the most common formats include WAV, REX, and ACIDized. Project5 can handle these different forms of loops, but different types of loops require different considerations. There are two main ways that loops can be dealt with:

- Slicing
- Compressing/stretching

Slicing Tools

The first widely used slicing tool was ReCycle from Propellerhead (www.propellerheads.se). There are other similar tools, but ReCycle was the original and is still perhaps the best known.

ReCycle introduced several innovations.

- First, it introduced slicing—this is where a loop is taken and is cut up so that each beat forms a separate slice. One of the key features of the tool is the ability to sense where each transient comes and therefore where the slices should be made.
- Second, ReCycle allows the resulting slices to then be exported and loaded into a sampler—a separate MIDI file is also exported, which can be loaded into a sequencer. The MIDI file then triggers the sample slices in the sampler in the correct order and at the appropriate time to replay the loop flawlessly.

As a side note, you may hear people talk about REX files, and I will mention REX files later: .rex and .rex2 are ReCycle-format files.

Because the beats are broken up into separate slices, each slice can be played back without pitch adjustment. When sliced loops are speeded up, the slices overlap. Normally this isn't a problem since the end tail of a previous sample will be masked by the transient of the new sample. However, when loops are slowed down, gaps appear between the samples (since the samples aren't stretched)—this can lead to an unnatural stuttering effect.

Compression/Stretching/Warping Tools

So if there are problems with slicing, then the alternatives must be better? Well, no. Just different. This is where we come across ACIDized loops. ACID from Sony Creative Software (www.sonycreativesoftware.com/default.asp) was the original program to widely employ this method of loop control. ACIDized loops are WAV audio files that contain tempo, beat, and pitch information, which is then used to stretch/compress the loop to match the project tempo.

Generally the ACID-style tools will add some form of Beat Markers, much like the slicing points. When a loop is stretched or compressed, these markers are used like quantize points—this means that the important transient information can be kept on the beat, and the less important decay information can be pushed and pulled around, but because the waves are stretched when they are slowed down, there will be no stuttering gaps. The tempo range over which a loop can be pulled without hearing unwanted artifacts is limited.

Groove Clips are essentially ACIDized WAV files.

You will find that ACIDized WAV files can also be loaded into Cyclone, and (as mentioned earlier) REX files can be loaded into Dimension LE. Both of these tools are mentioned in Chapter 7. The advantage of Cyclone and Dimension LE over the Groove Clip Editor is that you can mess with the order of the individual slices.

Loading a Groove Clip

You can load a Groove Clip in exactly the same way that you load a normal audio file (by importing it, or from the Clip Browser). The difference you will notice when a Groove Clip is loaded is that the Clip Editor will look somewhat different (see Figure 21.1). In particular, you will be able to see the Beat Markers.

You don't need to figure out whether you are loading a plain Audio Clip or a Groove Clip: Project5 will make that decision based on whether there is embedded tempo and beat information in the Clip. Both types of Clips can be loaded into an Audio Track, and both types of Clips can be present in the same Audio Track.

In the Groove Clip Editor, you will see some familiar controls:

- The Create New Clip button
- The Clip Name and Drop-Down menu

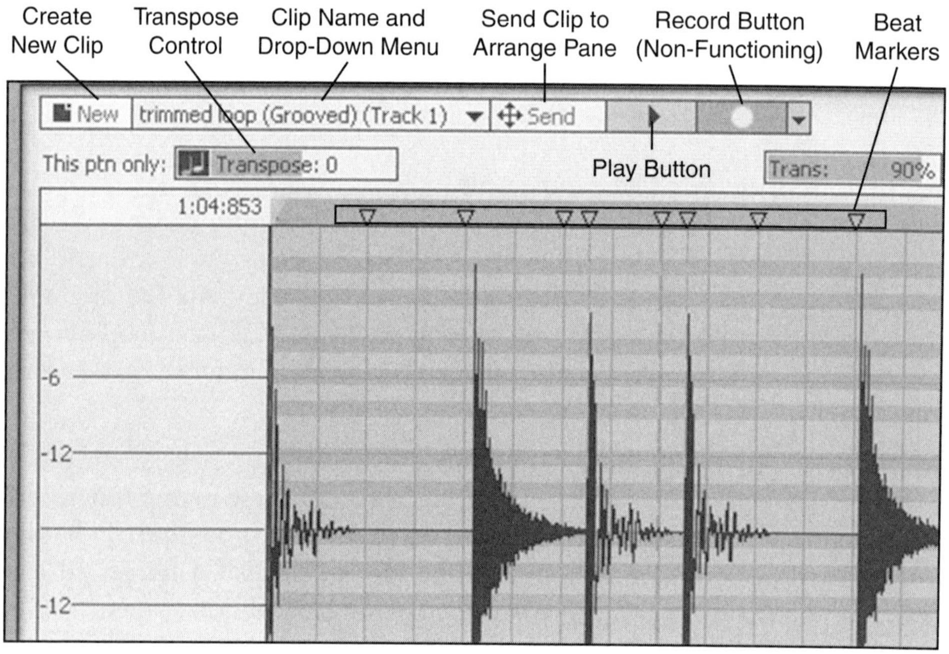

Figure 21.1 The Groove Clip Editor.

- The Send Clip to Arrange Pane button
- The Play button
- The Record button
- The Transpose Control

On the whole these work as you would expect (check the earlier tutorials in this chapter). However, the Record button does not operate in the Groove Clip Editor. (If you want to record a Groove Clip, then record an Audio Clip and convert it.)

Creating a Groove Clip

If you have a regular Audio Clip, you can convert it into a Groove Clip. To do this, go to the Arrange Pane, select the Clip, and then either:

- Hit Ctrl+L on your keyboard
- Right-click and select Groove-Clip Looping

You now have a Groove Clip.

Repeat the process to convert a Groove Clip to a regular Audio Clip (which you might want to do if you want to open your Groove Clip in an external audio editor).

Fine-Tuning a Groove Clip

When you convert a regular Audio Clip to a Groove Clip, Project5 will make its best guess about the length of the Clip and the number of beats based on the length of the Audio Clip. Generally, if the Clip you convert to a Groove Clip is of a similar tempo to the Project, then Project5 will make a fairly good guess.

However, Project5 doesn't always get things right, and you might want to tweak the Groove Clip a bit further. You can, of course, tweak Groove Clips that you imported into Project5—your editing is not restricted only to those Groove Clips that you created.

To start editing, you're going to need to use the Groove Clip Editor tools (see Figure 21.2).

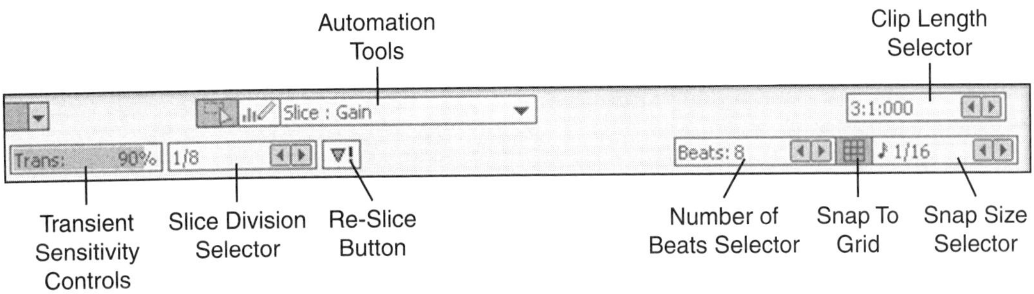

Figure 21.2 The Groove Clip Editor tools.

Getting the Basics Right

The first task before you tweak your Groove Clip is to make sure the number of beats and the length of the Clip are correctly set. For these you need to know the number of beats in the Clip—if you don't know, you can always listen! You can set the beats and length with:

- The Number of Beats Selector
- The Clip Length Selector

You can switch the Snap to Grid function on and off with the Snap to Grid button and set the grid size with the Snap Size Selector drop-down. The Snap to Grid function applies when Beat Markers (which are discussed in a moment) are dragged, and also if the Clip length is edited by dragging the Clip Length end marker. The Snap to Grid function does not apply to the underlying audio: If the underlying audio is "wrong," then you need to take more drastic action, such as cutting up the slices and loading them into VELOCITY or one of the Dimensions and playing back the slices at the "right" time.

Transients and Slices

Groove Clips work by adding Beat Markers to indicate the transients. As the tempo of a Track is changed, the audio between the Beat Markers is adjusted to give tempo-synched delivery of the audio at the next Beat Marker. The slices of audio in between these markers are then pushed and pulled around to fit the new tempo. Through this process, the transients (which are crucial to the rhythm) are maintained, but the less important decay parts of each beat are pushed and pulled.

The successful reproduction of the Groove Clip at differing tempos is dependent on the transients being correctly identified. There are several tools in the Groove Clip Editor to help you identify the transients and add Beat Markers.

- **Transient Sensitivity Control.** The Transient Sensitivity Control adjusts the sensitivity of the transient detector. At higher settings, the transient detector becomes more sensitive and so recognizes more transients. You will notice as you drag this selector that the number of Beat Markers increases or decreases.
- **Slice Division Selector.** The Slice Division Selector adds Beat Markers as a division of the beat.
- **Re-Slice button.** The Re-Slice button restores all Beat Markers (according to the current Transient Sensitivity Control and Slice Division Selector) that may have been moved or deleted.

Manual Editing of Beat Markers

You can manually drag Beat Markers to the correct position. Any dragging will be constrained by Snap to Grid if this function has been switched on. You can also delete individual Beat Markers by right-clicking on them.

Automating a Groove Clip

Like Instrument and MIDI Clips, you can automate Groove Clips, and you have largely the same automation options (although you can't automate any synthesizer functions unless you have a synthesizer inserted as an audio effect, in which case the automatable controls will show up under the Effects submenu from the Automation drop-down menu).

Slice Automation

There are three Groove Clip–exclusive automations. These can be applied on a per-slice basis: If you increase the number of Beat Markers, you will increase the number of slices that can be automated.

You can automate each slice's:

- Gain
- Pitch
- Pan

You access these options from the Automation drop-down menu under the Slice Envelopes option. Once you have selected the envelope you want to edit, click on the Automation Tool and draw in your automation on a per-slice basis.

The only difference from MIDI/Instrument Clip automation is that you can't hold down the Shift key to draw a straight line—you have to do it all by hand.

Tutorial 22: Using the Groove Matrix

The Groove Matrix is the heart of Project5. It is the place where you can bring all of your Clips—whether MIDI, Audio, or Groove Clips—together in one place to form the basic elements of a song and then deploy them. It is the live link between your Clips and the Arrange Pane.

Groove Matrix Basics

Click on Show/Hide Groove Matrix to open the Groove Matrix (see Figure 22.1).

Arrangement of the Groove Matrix

You will see the Matrix has Cells arranged in columns and rows.

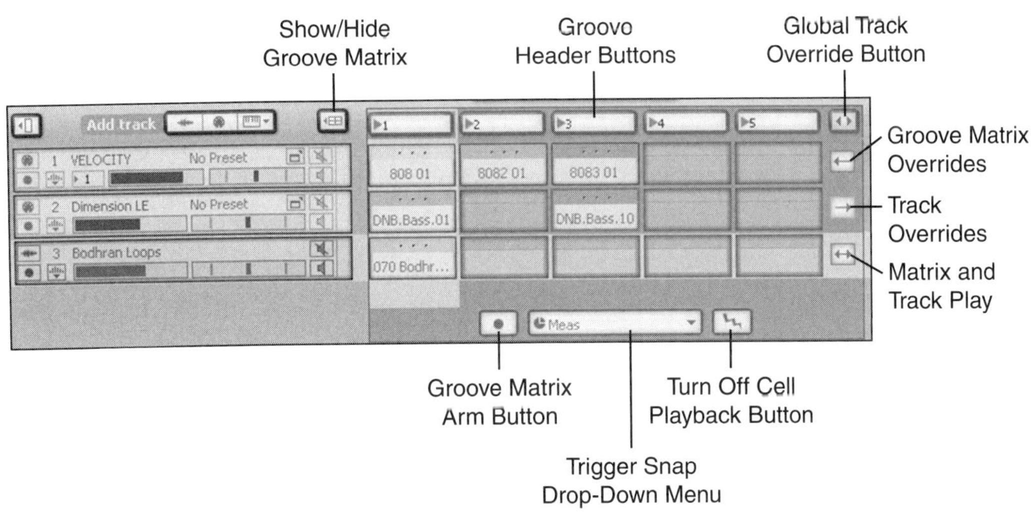

Figure 22.1 The Groove Matrix.

- The rows correspond to Tracks. Only one Cell in a Groove Matrix row can be active at any one time. If you trigger a second Cell in a row, then it will replace the first.
- You can have as many columns as you want, so you have as many Clips on call as the Project requires.

Loading Up the Cells

You can load Cells with Clips, much like you load the Arrange Pane, by dragging from the Clip Editor. In addition, you can drag Clips from the Arrange Pane (which will copy the Clip), or you can paste a Clip. As in the Arrange Pane, if you put a MIDI Clip in an Audio Track Cell, then the Clip won't play.

To delete a Clip from a Cell, left-click on the colored bar of the Cell and then hit the Delete key or select Edit > Delete.

Playing Cells in the Groove Matrix

To play a Cell:

- Left-click on the Cell (on the gray panel showing the Clip's name). If Project5 is not in Play mode, then it will start playing.
- Left-click on one of the Groove Header buttons, and all of the Cells in that column will be triggered.
- Trigger a Cell using MIDI Remote Control.

To stop playback:

- Hit the spacebar. This will stop the Project.
- Left-click on the Turn Off Cell Playback button. This will stop the playback of all Cells but will allow the Project to continue playing.
- Left-click or Ctrl+left-click on a Cell (depending on which Trigger mode has been selected—see the "Trigger Mode" section later in this tutorial). This will stop the playback of the clicked Cell only. The other Cells and the Project will continue to play.

Groove Matrix or Arrange Pane?

There will be times when you want to play the Clip in the Groove Matrix. There will be other times when you want to ignore the Matrix and listen to whatever is loaded in the Arrange Pane. And, there will be other times when you want to play both.

This is where you need the Override buttons, which are located to the right of the Groove Matrix (refer to Figure 22.1).

You can make your selection by left-clicking on the buttons. The arrows will point to the source. You can also left-click on the Global Track Override button. This switches between an all-Tracks override and Groove Matrix overrides.

Groove Headers

At the top of each column are the Groove Header buttons, which you can click on to trigger all of the Cells in a column. If you right-click on a Groove Header button, a pop-up menu will appear (see Figure 22.2).

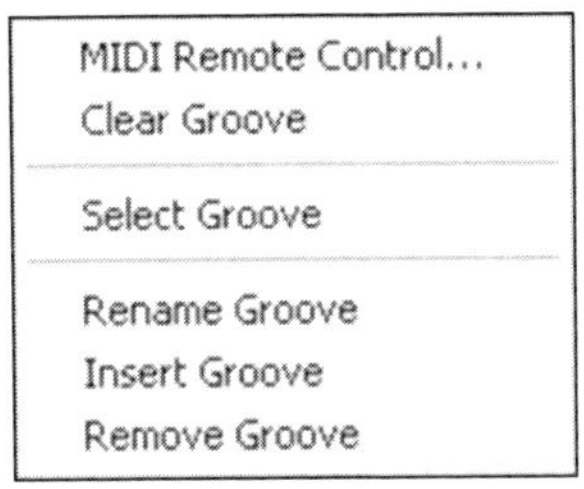

Figure 22.2 The Groove Header button pop-up menu.

From this menu you can select:

- **MIDI Remote Control.** You can use MIDI Remote Control to trigger a column of Cells. You can also set MIDI Remote Control to trigger individual Cells (by right-clicking on the appropriate Cell and selecting the option from the pop-up menu). See Tutorial 5 for further details about setting up MIDI Remote Control.
- **Clear Groove.** The Clear Groove command will delete any Clips in the selected column (leaving blank Cells).
- **Select Groove.** The Select Groove command will select all of the Cells in the current column.
- **Rename Groove.** The Rename Groove command allows you to name the Groove Header button.
- **Insert Groove.** Insert Groove inserts a blank column of Cells and moves the existing Cells to the right.
- **Remove Groove.** Remove Groove deletes all of the Cells in a column (and moves the Cells located on the right to the left to fill the hole).

More Advanced Control over Cell Playback

Project5 gives you a lot of flexibility over the playback of individual Cells.

Trigger Snap Controls

With the Trigger Snap drop-down menu (see Figure 22.3), you can choose when one Cell stops playing and when the next one starts. Project5 will then seamlessly transition between the two Cells (and all you will hear is a perfect groove).

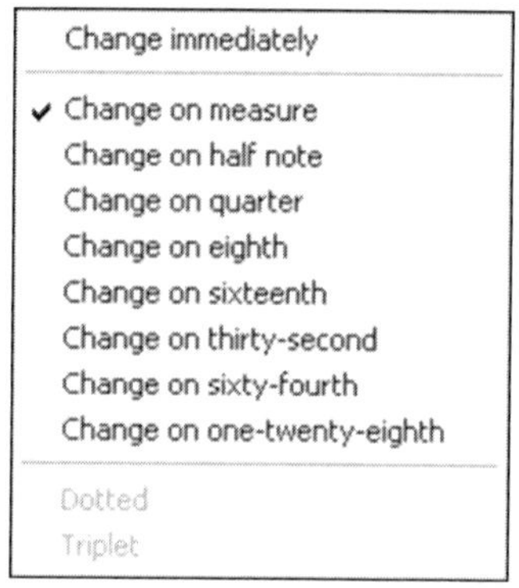

Figure 22.3 The Trigger Snap drop-down menu.

So for instance, you could select Change Immediately, and the transition from the first Cell to the second Cell would happen when you left-click on the second Cell (or when you trigger it by MIDI Remote Control). Alternatively, you could select Change on Measure, and the change would occur at the start of the next measure.

Play from When?

If you right-click on a loaded Cell, a pop-up menu will appear (see Figure 22.4).

There are two options in the middle of this menu that affect how a Cell plays when it is triggered. In both cases, the Cell begins to play at the next Trigger Snap point after being triggered.

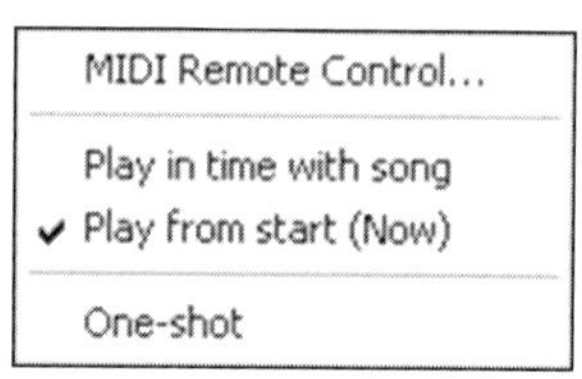

Figure 22.4 The loaded Cell pop-up menu.

- **Play in Time with Song.** When the Play in Time with Song option is selected, the Cell will begin playing with the beats of the Cell synchronized to the beat of the song. So if the next Trigger Snap point after you trigger the Cell is the third beat of a measure, then the Cell will start playing at that point on the third beat of its measure.
- **Play from Start (Now).** When the Play from Start (Now) option is selected, then the Cell will start to play from the beginning of its Pattern, irrespective of which beat the song is playing. In other words, the Clip will be tempo-synchronized, but it will not be beat-synchronized.

When the Play in Time with Song option is selected for a Cell, a small clock icon will show on the left of the Cell.

Loop and One-Shot

Usually you will want your Groove Matrix Cell contents to play continuously as a loop. However, there are times when you may not want this. In these instances you can select One-Shot mode, and when triggered, the Cell will play once.

Trigger Mode

If you right-click on an empty Cell, a pop-up menu will appear (see Figure 22.5).

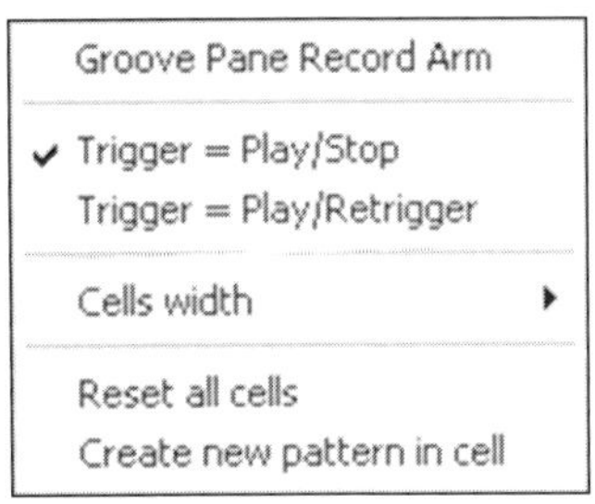

Figure 22.5 The Groove Matrix empty Cell pop-up menu.

This has some useful options:

- **Groove Pane Record Arm.** This function arms the Groove Matrix for recording. This is discussed in the next section.
- **Trigger = Play/Stop.** When Trigger = Play/Stop has been selected, you can start or stop a Cell by left-clicking on it.
- **Trigger = Play/Retrigger.** When Trigger = Play/Retrigger has been selected, you can start a Cell by clicking on it. If you click again you will retrigger the Cell. If you want to stop playback of an individual Cell when this mode is selected, then Ctrl+left-click on it.

- **Cells Width.** The Cells Width option allows you to select the visible width of all Cells. There are three choices: small, normal (as shown in the figures), and large.
- **Reset All Cells.** The Reset All Cells option resets all of the Cells. This means that when the Project next starts to play, none of the Groove Matrix Cells will play (unless they are reselected).
- **Create New Pattern in Cell.** The Create New Pattern in Cell option does what you would expect: It creates a new Pattern (in other words, a new Clip). This will only create a MIDI/Instrument Clip (even if you invoke the option in an Audio Track row).

Recording the Groove Matrix Output

The Groove Matrix is great for trying things out; however, at some point you're likely to want to stop play and finalize your Project. At this point, you can record your Groove Matrix output. This will result in the Groove Matrix output being recorded in the Arrange Pane. If you made a mistake, then you can always reorganize the Arrange Pane.

The process to record the Groove Matrix output is straightforward:

1. Left-click on the Groove Matrix Arm button.
2. Left-click on the Record button (or hit R on your keyboard).
3. Trigger the Cells in the Groove Matrix.
4. When you have finished recording, press the spacebar or left-click on the Stop button.
5. Disarm the Groove Matrix.

4 Working with Tracks and Projects

So far we have focused on working with Clips. I now want to move on and look at how you can work with Tracks and Projects.

With a Track you can arrange a series of Clips and so move from a loop-based approach to a linear performance within a song structure. Check back to Tutorial 15 in Chapter 3 to refresh your memory about arranging your Clips within a Track.

Your Tracks are automatically grouped together in a Project. As well as working at a Track level, you can also work at the Project level—for instance, as I will discuss later in this chapter in Tutorial 29: Mixing and Mastering in Project5, you could apply mastering FX to a whole Project to get a professional-sounding result.

Although we're going to be working at the Track and Project levels, don't forget Clips. Your Tracks are just groups of Clips, even if there is only one Clip in the Track and that Clip lasts for the whole song. Whatever you do with your Track, you will not affect the underlying data in your Clip, so you can be quite bold with your Tracks, safe in the knowledge that if you don't like what you've done, you can always go back to your original Clip and start again.

So let's move on and start the Track and Project tutorials.

Tutorial 23: Advanced Track Pane Features

As you know from Tutorials 5 and 6, for each Track and Bus Pane there is a corresponding Inspector. I now want to have a look at the features of the Track Pane that we haven't looked at already, and especially some of the right-click menu features. If you haven't already checked out Chapter 3, you might find this tutorial much easier if you do so first.

A Brief Recap

Take a look at Figure 23.1, and you'll see the pop-up menu that appears when you right-click on a Track Pane. Figure 23.1 is an Instrument Track Pane, but the menus for Audio and MIDI Track Panes are very similar.

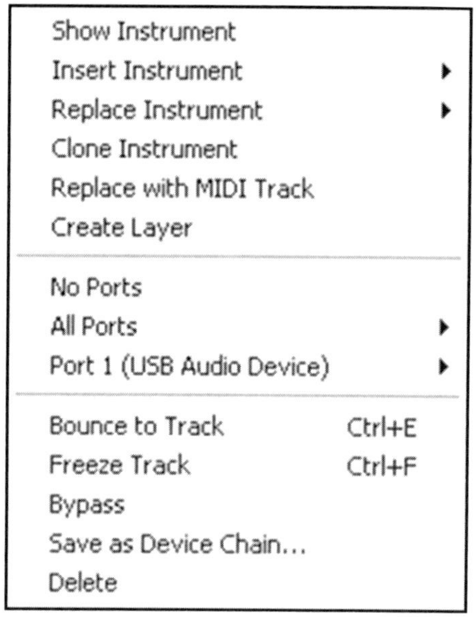

Figure 23.1 The Instrument Track Pane right-click pop-up menu.

Let me briefly recap the features of this menu that have already been covered and point you to the tutorials where the remaining issues are discussed.

- **Show Instrument.** Show Instrument opens the current Instrument's interface. This option only appears on the right-click menu of Instrument Tracks.
- **Insert Instrument.** Insert Instrument creates a new Instrument Track with the Instrument you select from the submenu.
- **Replace Instrument.** Replace Instrument removes the current instrument (in the case of an Instrument Track), but keeps the current Track settings (as far as possible) and inserts the new Instrument selected from the submenu. If you use this option with an Audio or MIDI Track, the data is left, but the Track will become an Instrument Track.

  When you replace an Instrument, the name of your Track doesn't change (so if you create the Track using Dimension LE and replace that Instrument with VELOCITY, then the name of the Track will remain as Dimension LE until/unless you change it).
- **Clone Instrument.** Clone Instrument creates a new Track with the same Instrument loaded (in the case of an Instrument Track) as the current Track. Track and Inspector settings (for instance, volume or pan settings) are not duplicated.

- **Replace with MIDI Track.** Replace with MIDI Track replaces the current Audio or Instrument Track with a MIDI Track.
- **Create Layer.** Create Layer is addressed later in this tutorial, in the "Track Layers" section.
- **No Ports/All Ports/Port *x*.** The three ports menu options replicate the controls available in the Inspector's MIDI Input section.
- **Bounce to Track/Freeze Track/Bypass.** These three features are discussed in Tutorial 28: Freezing and Other Ways to Save Your CPU.
- **Save As Device Chain.** Save As Device Chain saves the current Track and its settings as a Device Chain. (Check back to Tutorial 5 for further details.)
- **Delete.** Delete deletes the current Track and its settings.

Track Layers

You can create a Track Layer by right-clicking on the Track Pane and selecting Create Layer. You can remove a Track Layer by right-clicking on its Track Pane and selecting Delete from the pop-up menu. As Figure 23.2 shows, a Track Pane with a Track Layer added looks rather like a doubled Track Pane (or a tripled Track Pane if two Track Layers are added).

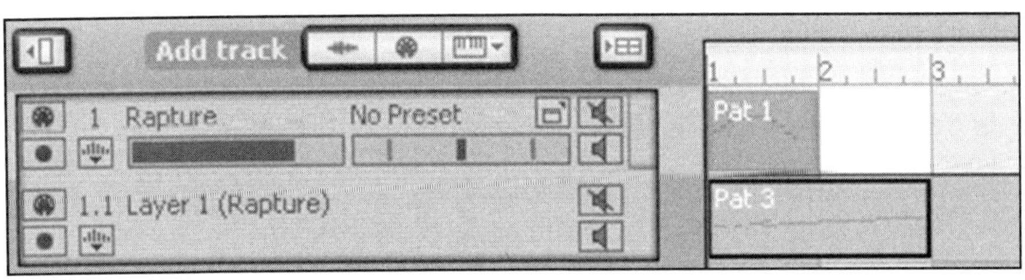

Figure 23.2 An Instrument Track Pane with a Track Layer added.

Great, But What Do Track Layers Do?

At its most basic, the Track Layers function allows you to open up your Tracks so you can keep your Clips in separate, but related, lanes. With the separate lanes you can:

- Put different MIDI Clips on different lanes. By organizing your Clips in this manner, you can get away from having Clips hidden by overlapping Clips.
- Set different MIDI Input settings and record multi-timbral parts that are related but kept separate.

- Show more than one automation control at one time.
- Apply different MIDI FX to different parts of a Track.

In short, Track Layers are an organizational device, but they are a very useful tool, and there is no limit to the number of Track Layers you can call up. Let's look at how Track Layers can be used for day-to-day applications.

What's Covered and What's Not?

Before you start using Track Layers, you need to understand what is controllable at the Track Layer level and what is managed at the Track level. The following features are defined at the Track level.

- Volume, pan, and width are all defined at the Track level, so, for instance, you can only have one volume setting irrespective of how many Track Layers you have for a Track.
- The Track Arpeggiator, which is discussed in the next tutorial, applies to all Track Layers. (In other words, it works at the Track level.)
- Audio FX apply at the Track level, as you are still dealing with only one Instrument.

The following features can be controlled at the Track Layer level:

- Arm, mute, and solo are controllable at the Track Layer level, so you can solo a single Track Layer to hear what it sounds like on its own.
- MIDI Input controls work at the Track Layer level, so if you are recording several channels of MIDI data, you can keep the data separate but on linked Track Layers.
- Input Quantize applies at the Track Layer level, so you can quantize one MIDI channel but not another.
- MIDI FX apply to individual Track Layers. You can't automate MIDI FX; however, you can set up a number of Track Layers, each with different MIDI FX settings, and drag your Clips to the different lanes. This way, you can apply different MIDI FX (or simply no MIDI FX) to your Tracks at different times.

Multi-Timbral Instruments

Multi-timbral instruments can create more than one sound, and those different sounds can be addressed by different MIDI channels. If you are dealing with a multi-timbral Instrument, simply setting up Track Layers does not mean you will address each separate element within your synthesizer. In order to work with a multi-timbral instrument, you need to do one of the following.

- Set the channel of each MIDI Clip at the Clip level. (Refer back to Chapter 3 for details.) Once you have set your Clips with different MIDI channels, you may find them easier to organize if you keep each channel on a separate Track Layer.
- Create separate Track Layers and address each separate Layer to a different MIDI Send To channel. This has the advantage of being straightforward, and you can easily add new Clips that are directed to the correct MIDI channel. However, you may still end up with overlapping Clips.

Multi-Output Instruments

Multi-output Instruments are Instruments that have more than one stereo output. Each separate output can then be treated in a different manner. VELOCITY is a multi-output instrument that has five stereo outputs. This gives you the flexibility to send different drums to different outputs. So, for example, you could send the kick drum to one output and the snare drum to another. The kick drum could then be processed by a compressor, and the snare could have a large amount of reverb added.

Although they are closely related, multi-timbral and multi-output instruments are not the same thing. However, it is possible to have a multi-timbral, multi-output instrument.

Loading a Multi-Output Instrument

When you open a multi-output Instrument, Project5 will automatically create a Track Strip for each output. These Track Strips will be stacked one on top of another. The only way to differentiate between the Track Strips is to look at the Active Output Selector (see Figure 23.3).

You can have different settings (for instance, volume, pan, solo/mute status) on each output Track Pane. In addition, each output Track Pane has its own Inspector, so you can insert a different set of audio FX units for each output. However, there is only one MIDI lane in the Arrange Pane for all of the output Track Panes (unless you add new Track Layers, in which case these new Layers are common to all output Track Panes).

Switching between Output Track Panes

You can switch between output Track Panes (and their corresponding Inspectors will change too) by left-clicking and dragging on the Active Output Selector. Alternatively, right-click on the output Track Pane and, from the pop-up menu, select Active Output and choose the appropriate output.

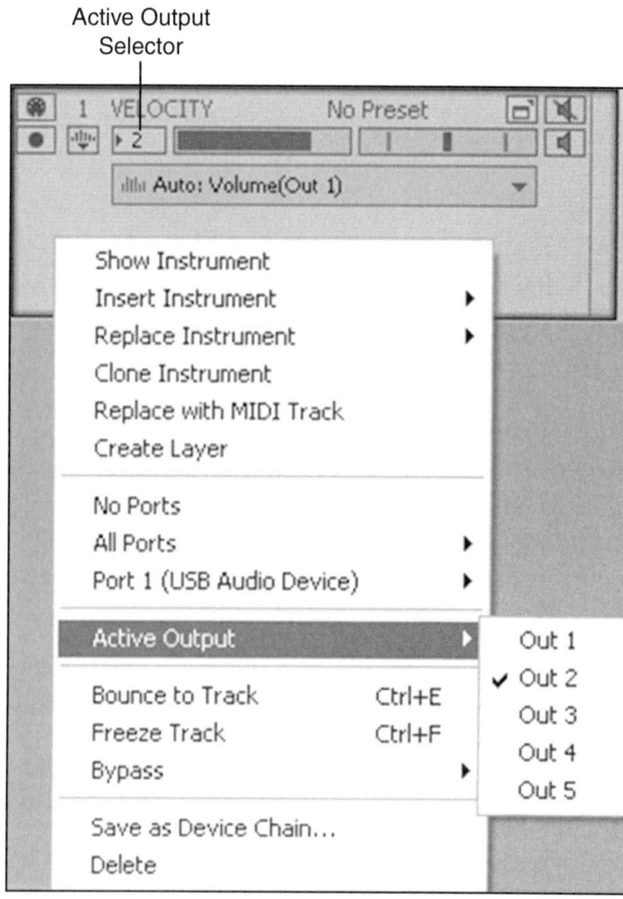

Figure 23.3 The Active Output Selector on a multi-output Instrument Track Pane.

Setting Up Multi-Output Instruments

A multi-output arrangement, and the routing of sounds to outputs, is set up in the individual Instrument, so the process will vary from Instrument to Instrument. This is usually a straightforward process—for instance, with VELOCITY you can set the audio output for each Cell by dragging the Audio Output Selector up or down (see Figure 23.4).

As you can see from Figure 23.4, the kit that has been loaded into VELOCITY has been set up so that:

- The main percussion pieces (clave, claps, cowbell, shaker, and congas) are directed to Audio Output 1 (the main output).
- The two kick drums are directed to Audio Output 2.

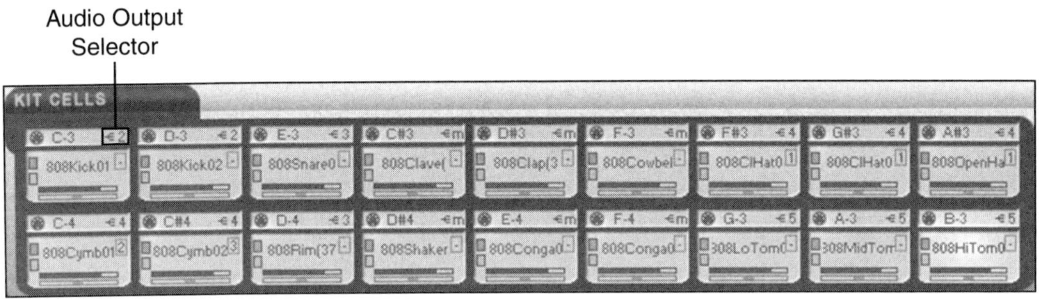

Figure 23.4 Selecting the audio output for each Cell in VELOCITY.

- The snare and rim shot are directed to Audio Output 3.
- The hats and cymbals are directed to Audio Output 4.
- The toms are directed to Audio Output 5.

This allows similar pieces to be processed and mixed together. The levels and panning of the individual kit pieces can still be controlled by the settings in VELOCITY.

For more details about VELOCITY, check out Tutorial 41: Introducing VELOCITY.

Disabling Outputs

You may not want to work with all of the outputs that your Instrument offers you. In this case you can disable the unused outputs and save on your CPU hit. To do this, right-click on the multi-output Instrument Track Pane and, from the pop-up menu, select Bypass. This will call up a menu that looks like Figure 23.5.

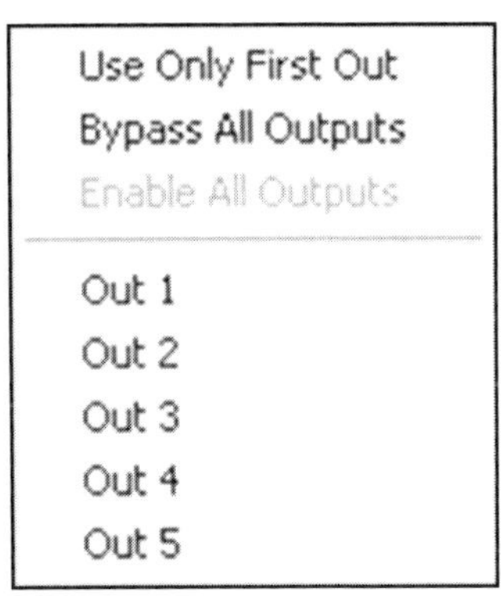

Figure 23.5 The multi-output Bypass menu.

When the Instrument is working in full multi-output mode and all of the outputs are active, Enable All Outputs will be grayed out on the menu.

You can choose to disable individual outputs by clicking on them. The disabled outputs will then show with a check mark against them.

If you select Use Only First Out, then that option will be grayed out, and there will be a check mark against all outputs except Out 1.

If you select Bypass All Outputs, then that option will be grayed out, and there will be a check mark against all outputs. In addition, the Track Pane and the Track in the Arrange Pane will be grayed out.

When you try to select an Instrument Output Pane where that output has been bypassed, the Active Output Selector for the bypassed layer will have a gray background instead of its customary blue.

By default, when you load an Instrument, all outputs except the first are bypassed in order to preserve CPU.

Tutorial 24: Using the Track Arpeggiator

An arpeggiator takes the notes of a chord and plays them individually in a preset order, thereby converting a plain chord into a rhythmic pattern. The Track Arpeggiator converts a Track's chords into arpeggios.

As you will see in Chapter 8, "MIDI FX Units," this is not the only arpeggiator in Project5—there is also the MIDI FX Arpeggiator. However, there are several advantages of the Track Arpeggiator. Perhaps the two most obvious advantages are its immediacy and the fact that it can be automated. In addition, the Track Arpeggiator can work as a Pattern player, which the MFX Arpeggiator cannot do.

One other difference between the Track Arpeggiator and the MFX Arpeggiator is that the Track Arpeggiator applies to the whole Track, including Track Layers. By contrast, the MFX Arpeggiator applies to Track Layers, so you might need to insert several instances if you have several layers.

Finding Your Way around the Track Arpeggiator

Figure 24.1 shows the Track Arpeggiator, which can be found in each MIDI Track Inspector and Instrument Track Inspector.

The Track Arpeggiator's controls are all visible on its face.

- **Beat Division.** The Beat Division Selector allows you to set the arpeggio speed as a division of the beat. You can set the speed from the drop-down menu that

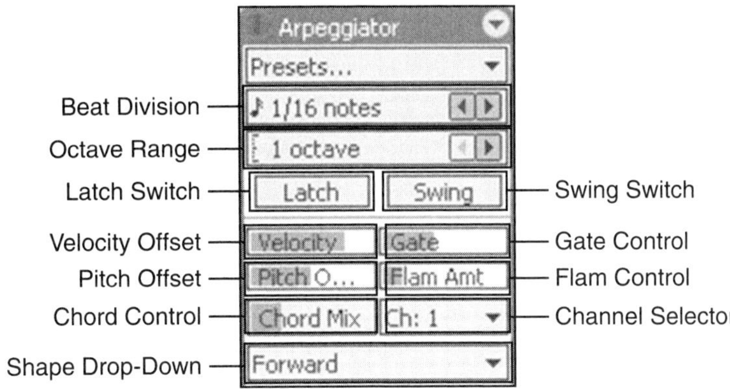

Figure 24.1 The Track Arpeggiator.

appears when you click on the current beat division, or by clicking on the nudge up/down buttons to the right of the beat division.

- **Octave Range.** The Octave Range Selector sets the range over which the arpeggio will play. When set to one octave, only the played notes will be arpeggiated. You can set the octave range from the drop-down menu that appears when you click on the current octave range, or by clicking on the nudge up/down buttons to the right of the octave range.
- **Latch.** When Latch is engaged, the background of the button turns blue, and any played notes will be held. This only affects notes played from MIDI/Instrument Clips and not incoming MIDI data.
- **Swing.** The Swing Control swings the beat of the arpeggio according to the swing amount set in the left-hand Main Control.
- **Velocity Offset.** The Velocity Offset Control adjusts the velocity of the MIDI data received by the arpeggiator when it is sent to the Instrument. When it is set to 100, there is no adjustment. Above that level, the output velocity is increased, and below that level, the output velocity is decreased.
- **Gate.** The Gate Control adjusts the duration of the arpeggiated notes to give a more staccato or legato feel to the arpeggio.
- **Pitch Offset.** The Pitch Offset Control adjusts the pitch of the arpeggio, increasing it or decreasing it in semitone steps over a range of plus or minus two octaves.
- **Flam Control.** The Flam Control introduces a flam on the arpeggiated notes, and then controls the timing of the flam. When it is set to zero, there is no flamming.

- **Chord Mix.** The Chord Mix introduces the un-arpeggiated chord from which the arpeggio is constructed.
- **Channel Selector.** The Channel Selector drop-down allows you to choose the channel on which the arpeggio is played. While the Track Arpeggiator will apply to all Track Layers, by selecting a specific MIDI channel, you can ensure that only one element in a multi-timbral Instrument receives the arpeggiated data.
- **Shape.** The Shape drop-down menu allows you to choose the arpeggio's pattern—for instance, forward (up), backward (down), and so on.

Pattern Player

As well as functioning as an arpeggiator, the Track Arpeggiator also works as a Pattern player. If you're familiar with Cakewalk's Z3TA+ synthesizer, then you will be familiar with this feature. If you're not, then let me explain.

When a Pattern is loaded, as you strike a key the Pattern will be played rather than an arpeggio. The root note of the Pattern will be the key you strike. Where arpeggios work best with chords, these Patterns work best with single notes—you will find that you get some fairly crazy results when you try to play chord Patterns.

Opening and Saving Presets

You can open and save presets from the Preset drop-down menu. When you open a preset, you will see there are two files types:

- **Arpeggiator files (.arp files).** These give arpeggiator Patterns (in other words, a played chord will be split into an arpeggio). By default, these files are stored in the Shapes folder.
- **Pattern files (.ptn files).** These play Patterns. By default, these files are stored in the Rhythms folder.

Sometimes it's not always clear whether you have loaded an arpeggio or a Pattern. If you try playing a chord, it will usually become obvious quite quickly. Also, you will find that when a Pattern is loaded, the Octave Range Control has no effect.

There is a third option on the drop-down menu, Load Preset. This opens up a submenu of your Arpeggiator folder, allowing you to find the Shape or Pattern you are looking for.

Creating Patterns

You can create a Pattern in the Instrument or MIDI Clip Editor. This can be any sort of Pattern. You can then save the Pattern as a Pattern file (.ptn), which can then be loaded into the Clip Editor; review Tutorial 16: Creating a MIDI/Instrument Clip for further details. You can also load these Patterns (along with a large number of preset Patterns that are included with Project5) into the Track Arpeggiator. While you can browse to the Patterns from the Open Preset command, if you move the Pattern to your Arpeggio folder, you will find it quicker to locate.

While Z3TA+ can import MIDI files and use them as Patterns, with Project5 you have to go through a two-stage process and import the MIDI file, and then resave it as a Pattern.

Tutorial 25: Automation

I've already mentioned automation in the context of Clips in Tutorial 18: Automating a Clip. This was covered in Chapter 3. I now want to move on and look at how to automate tracks and busses.

But Why Automate a Track? What Can You Do with Track Automation?

Functionally, Track automation is very much like Clip automation. However, there is a fundamental difference that goes to the root of thinking about Clips and linear Tracks. When you automate a Clip, the same automation gets repeated each time that Clip plays, and the automation only affects that specific Clip. However, when you automate a Track, the automation can change as the Clip plays. So, for instance, if you have a synthesizer riff, you could automate the filter over the course of the verse. Also, with Track Layers it is much easier to see what is going on if you are automating two targets (see Figure 25.1).

With both Clip and Track automation, you can automate anything that's automatable. That sounds a bit circuitous, so let me elaborate. If any feature of a Track or a Track's instrumentation—that is to say, a synthesizer or FX unit function, a Track

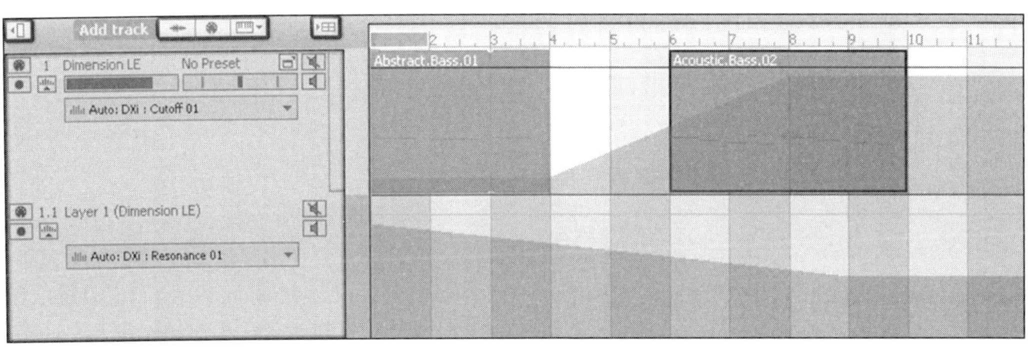

Figure 25.1 With Track automation you can easily see what is going on if you use Track Layers. The automation is also not restricted to the length of your Clip.

function such as volume, a MIDI function, or the Track Arpeggiator—*can* be automated, then it can be automated through Track automation. So, for instance, you could automate:

- The cutoff frequency of the filter in a synthesizer.
- The switching on and switching off of the Track Arpeggiator.
- A control on an FX unit, such as the feedback in the Tempo Delay Stereo Echo, which could be adjusted to increase the number of repeats. Alternatively, you could apply an echo to just one word in a vocal.
- The volume of the Track or the level of a Track that is sent to an FX unit on an Aux Bus.

In addition, with Track automation, you can automate any of the Busses (both Aux Busses and Master Busses) and any audio FX unit on those Busses. The automation principles apply regardless of whether you are automating an Instrument, an Audio Track, a Master Bus, or an Aux Bus.

One advantage that Track automation has over Clip automation is that the automation can happen when there isn't a Clip. Although intuitively you won't care about automation when there is no Clip, in practice you might. For instance, to give two examples, after a Clip ends you may still hear the release stage of a synthesizer's envelope playing, or some echo may remain after a Clip ends. Either of these sources of sound could be automated.

Before we get going, a word of caution. You can have too much automation! If you automate a parameter at the Clip level and try to automate the very same parameter at the Track level, then the two automations will conflict. All you will then get is confusion. So for this tutorial, I will only automate at the Track level.

How Automation Works

Automation in Project5 is straightforward:

1. You assign an automation lane to control a specified function (for instance, the cutoff frequency in a synthesizer's filter).
2. You then draw the automation in the lane.

Figure 25.2 shows these steps in practice.

Once you've set up the automation, as you would expect, you can edit the data. In theory, automation can lack a certain relevance, so let's look at an example of automation in practice.

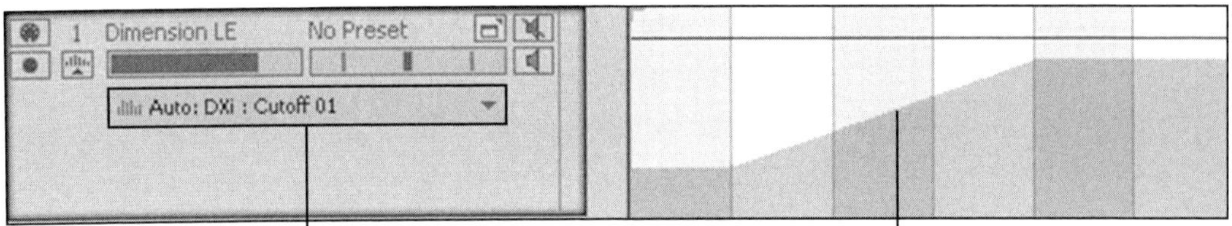

Figure 25.2 To set up Track automation in Project5, assign the automation lane and draw in the automation.

Preparing to Automate

For this example, I'm going to automate an FX unit that is loaded into a synthesizer Track. In this case, I am using Dimension LE and Alias Factor, so go ahead and load these two:

1. For Dimension LE, right-click on the Track Pane and select Insert Instrument > Dimension LE. I've then loaded the Ballad Bass program in the Synth Basses folder of the Program Browser.
2. Once Dimension LE has been loaded, click on Add FX in the Track Inspector and choose Project5 > Alias Factor.

Alias Factor works to add some dirty digital mangling and is quite a noticeable effect. As you will hear, the effect of changing its parameters can be readily heard.

Once this combination has been loaded, I need a Pattern to play. For this example I have chosen Bass > Electric Riffs > Bassline.02 in the Loops/Pattern Browser and dragged it to the Track. I then Slip Edited this Clip so that it plays for a while—I extended its length to 16 bars, but feel free to change its length to whatever suits you.

Before you automate anything, open up Alias Factor. For a more detailed explanation of what this FX unit does, check out Tutorial 43: Introducing Alias Factor in Chapter 7, "Working with Audio FX Units." The control I am going to automate is the Sampling Frequency Control. Now that we've dragged in the bass line, if you start the song playing and move the Sampling Frequency Control, you'll hear the effect of the unit.

You will notice that for this bass sound, the range over which the Sampling Frequency Control has some really noticeable effect (and lets the sound through) is quite narrow—from approximately 545 Hz to 7 kHz. It does have effect outside of that range; however, to get maximum effect, we will aim to automate within that limited area.

To set up the automation, first look at the right-hand toolbar (see Figure 25.3).

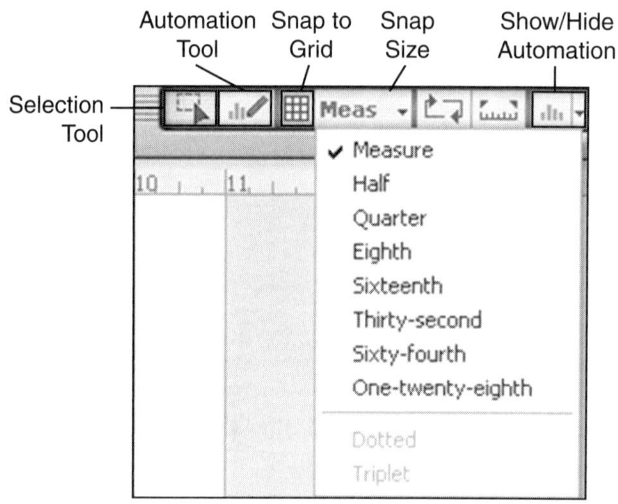

Figure 25.3 The automation controls in the right-hand Main Controls toolbar. You will notice that the Snap Size drop-down menu is displayed, from which you can select the Snap to Grid resolution for your automation.

In the toolbar you will see:

- **Selection Tool.** You don't need this to draw your automation, but you may need it when you come to edit the automation. When the Selection Tool is active, this button will turn blue.
- **Automation Tool.** Click on this when you're ready to draw your automation. When this tool is active, the Automation Tool button will turn blue.
- **Snap to Grid.** You can determine the precision of your automation with this option. When Snap to Grid is engaged, the timing of the automation that you draw will be synchronized to the time division you select in the Snap Size drop-down menu, and the button will turn blue. Click on this button again, and the Snap to Grid function will be switched off, at which time the button will revert to its conventional gray color.

  This feature may help you fit your automation to the timing, but where each automation event is snapped to the grid, it may make noticeable step changes in your automation.

- **Snap Size.** The Snap Size drop-down menu, as shown in Figure 25.3, sets the resolution when Snap to Grid is engaged. You can have a resolution from a whole measure (in other words, the automation setting changes once every measure) to a 128th note. (In other words, you could potentially have 128 automation levels in one measure.) The selected snap size is shown on the toolbar button.
- **Show/Hide Automation.** This button reveals or hides the automation lane. When automation is revealed, this button turns blue. There is a drop-down menu to the right of this button that gives you two options:
  - Show/Hide Automation for All Tracks
  - Show/Hide Automation for Selected Strip

There is also a button to reveal or hide the automation lane on each Track Pane. (Figure 25.4 highlights that button.) When Show/Hide Automation for Selected Strip is selected, the Show/Hide Automation button in the individual Track Pane is disabled. So that I have the flexibility to reveal or hide the automation on a Track-by-Track basis, I always select Show/Hide Automation for All Tracks. However, that is just *my* way of working.

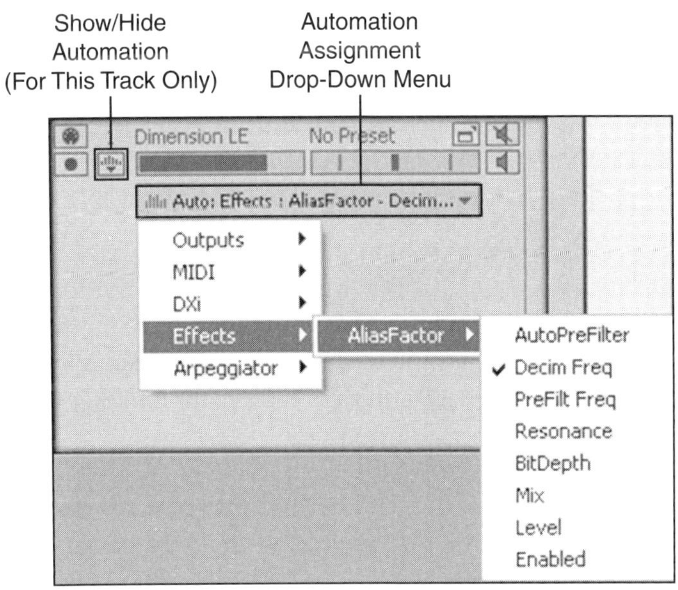

Figure 25.4 Assigning the control to be automated.

When automation is visible, the appearance of the Selection Tool will change. Instead of simply being a pointing arrowhead, it will become a pointing arrowhead with a little squiggle showing to the top left of the arrow. The squiggle is intended to represent the automation graph. The Automation Tool (which is a pencil with a squiggle to its top left) will not show unless automation is visible.

To start automating a Track:

1. Select the Automation Tool.
2. Turn on Snap to Grid and select the appropriate snap size if this is a feature that you want. For me, due to the stepping that this feature introduces, I usually switch off Snap to Grid.
3. Show automation by turning on the Show/Hide Automation button.

As a final step, because you're going to be drawing in the automation, I suggest you increase the height of the Track in the Track Pane window. You can do this by dragging the bottom of the Track Pane.

Assigning Automation

You're now ready to draw in your automation, but you need to decide what you're going to automate and assign this control. As I said earlier in this tutorial, for this example I am going to automate the sampling frequency in Alias Factor. To do this:

1. In the Track Pane, there is a drop-down menu (by default it says Auto: Volume). From this menu you select the automation destination, so click it, and you will see a drop-down menu like the one shown in Figure 25.4. The options are quite daunting, but I will explain them in a moment.
2. In this case, select Effects > Alias Factor > Decim Freq. I can see you're shaking your head and saying, "But we're automating sampling frequency!" True, we are. However, Alias Factor exposes its Sampling Frequency Control to the automation parameters with the label Decim Freq. Unfortunately, you have to live with these oddities. Check out Chapter 7 for an audio-FX-unit-by-audio-FX-unit translation.

If you accidentally select the wrong control to automate, go back and reselect the correct control from the menu before you draw the automation. You can reassign the control after you've drawn the automation, but the process is slightly more complicated, as you will read in the "Assigning Automation to a Different Control" section later in this tutorial.

That's it. You're ready to start drawing your automation. If you don't want to read about the drop-down menu options, go straight to the "Drawing Automation" section.

As I said, the options under the drop-down menu seem quite daunting. Let me try to explain your choices:

- **Outputs.** Under the Outputs option, you can adjust the main levels of a Track—in particular, its volume, panning, and Send levels to the busses.
- **MIDI.** MIDI allows you to send MIDI Control Codes (MIDI CCs) to a synthesizer (both software synthesizers running within Project5 and any external hardware units that you may have hooked up).
- **DXi.** Under the DXi option, you can access the controls that a synthesizer exposes for automation. Sometimes there is a frightening array of options, and the labeling used by some synthesizers can be quite confusing. If you're not sure what you're automating, the best thing to do is to try something and see what it does. If you don't get the desired result, you can always change the assigned parameter.
- **Effects.** If you have any audio effects loaded for the selected Track, these will be listed here, together with a list of the exposed parameters that can be automated. If you have no effects loaded, then this option will be grayed out. The effects that come with Project5 are discussed in greater detail in Chapter 7.
- **Track Arpeggiator.** These options allow you to turn the Track Arpeggiator on and off and control its settings. For further information about the Track Arpeggiator, check out Tutorial 24: Using the Track Arpeggiator, earlier in this chapter.

If you automate an external MIDI synthesizer, you will get three options: MIDI, Effects, and Arpeggiator. If you automate an Audio Track (including an Aux Bus and a Master Bus), you will only get two options: Outputs and Effects.

Drawing Automation

Now that you have assigned the parameters to be automated, you just need to draw your automation. This is straightforward. With the Automation Tool selected, your cursor will show as a pencil when you hold the cursor over the automation lane, and you can draw the automation in the appropriate lane, as Figure 25.5 shows. The automation will snap to any Snap to Grid settings you have selected.

In the automation lane you will be able to see any Clips in the current Track. However, while the Automation Tool is selected, you won't be able to move or edit these Clips in the main part of the lane. Instead, you can tweak your Clips in the very narrow Track lane on top of the automation lane.

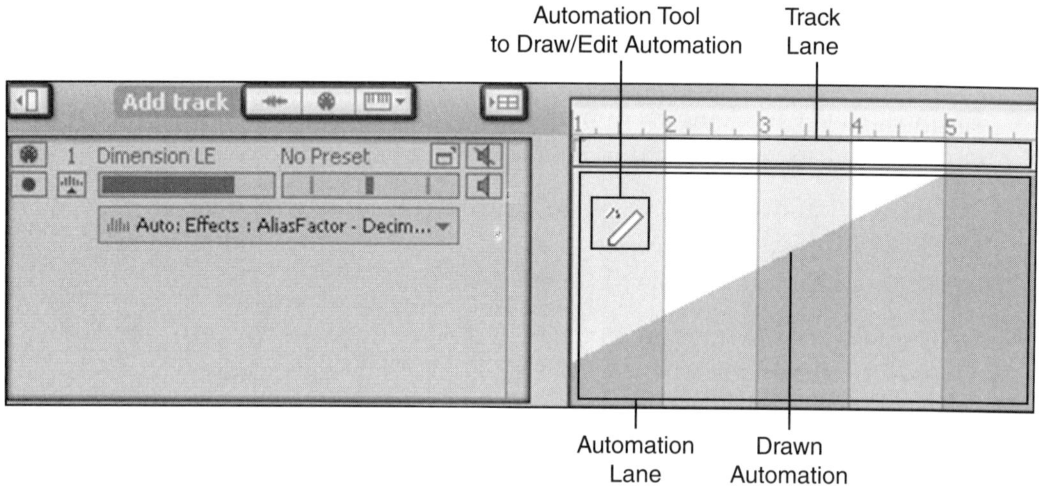

Figure 25.5 Drawing the automation.

If you want to draw a smooth transition (and override any Snap to Grid settings), then hold down the Shift key when you draw the automation.

Recording Automation

Instead of drawing an automation curve, you can record parameter changes. To do this:

1. Arm the Track you intend to automate by clicking on the Track Arm button (see Figure 25.6). You will see that the Arm button turns red.
2. Hit the Record button (which should be flashing red).
3. Move the parameter (or parameters) you want to automate as the song plays. You can move the parameter on the instrument/FX unit's interface either by clicking and dragging with a mouse or by using MIDI Learn or ACT.
4. When you have recorded the automation, disarm the Track (unless you want to record further automation) by clicking on either the Track Arm button or the Global Un-Arm button.

You can use this technique to automate any parameters, whether they are Track parameters or a control on a synthesizer or FX unit. One clear advantage of this option is that you don't have to assign the automated control to a controller lane—the assignment will be done automatically.

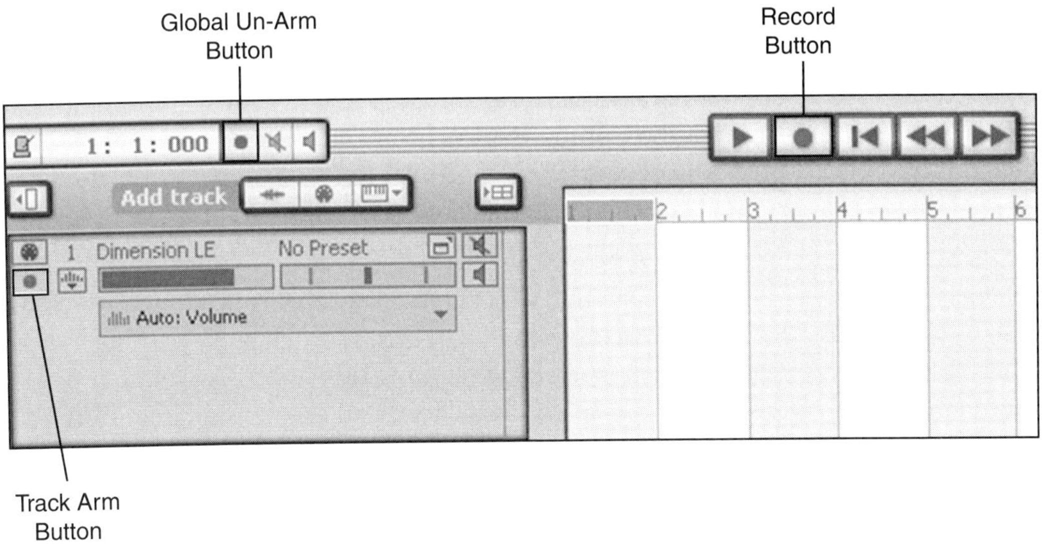

Figure 25.6 The controls to record Track automation.

Editing Automation

Once you have created your automation, you can edit it.

Here you have several options. The first and most obvious way is to redraw the automation. To do this, take the Automation Tool pencil and redraw the automation until you get the control you like. Alternatively, you can re-record the automation.

You can, of course, cut and paste automation. With the Selection Tool engaged, select the automation and then right-click and select Copy or Cut. Then right-click and select Paste at the appropriate place. As you would expect, Ctrl+C, Ctrl+X, and Ctrl+V work as normal.

When you copy and paste, or cut and paste, you will copy or cut one automation event (that is, one automation step). So, for instance, if you have a volume increase of 24 steps over 6 measures, you can only copy one step at a time. However, if you have several steps all at the same level, then these will all be copied.

You can also copy a step by holding down the Ctrl key when you drag an automation step.

Automating a Second Parameter

So what happens if you want to automate a second parameter? It's easy; just repeat the process!!

The difficulty with this approach is that you can only see one automation lane at a time. To switch between two (or more automations), in the Track Pane drop-down menu where you select the parameter to be automated, you will see an additional menu item—In Use—against the feature that has been automated. For instance, now that we have automated Alias Factor, if you select Effects > Alias Factor from the drop-down menu, you will see this In Use option showing the parameter that has been automated.

There is a much easier way to keep your second (and any other) automation separate and so visible: Create another Track Layer. To do this, right-click on the Track Pane and select Create Layer. This will give you something that looks like another Track (see Figure 25.7), except that there isn't a heavy horizontal separating line. With this layer you can create your next automation the way we did earlier on.

Figure 25.7 Creating a second layer allows the automation for two parameters to be visible at the same time.

Assigning Automation to a Different Control

So what happens if you've drawn in your automation and it's perfect in every way apart from one—you've assigned the automation to control the wrong function?

Easy! Just reassign the automation in the following manner:

1. Make sure the automation is showing. (Click on one of the Show/Hide Automation buttons.)
2. Engage the Selection Tool.

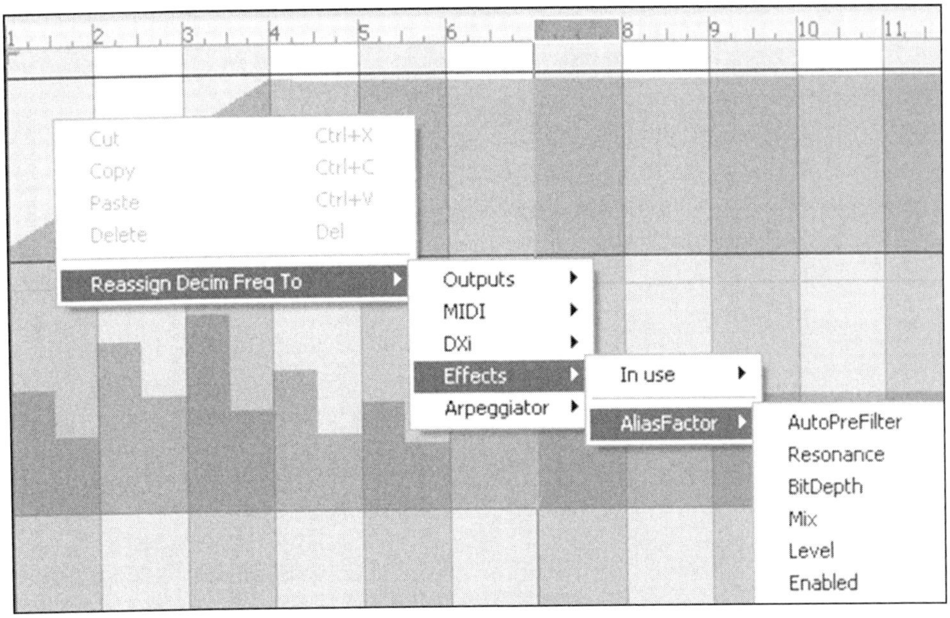

Figure 25.8 Reassigning an automation control in Project5. Note that you can also see the In Use option from the Effects menu.

3. Right-click on the automation, and a pop-up menu will appear (see Figure 25.8).
4. The last option on the pop-up shows Reassign [the control] To, and then there is a submenu that is very similar to the menu when you selected the feature to automate. Simply select the correct function that you want to automate.

You now have a control that was automated but is now disconnected. You may need to tweak this to get it to its right level in the same way that you set any other control.

Deleting Automation

Alternatively, instead of reassigning automation, you may want to delete the automation completely. There are two ways you can do this, and for both you need to ensure that the automation is visible by clicking the Show/Hide Automation option.

- With the Automation Tool selected, right-click. As you right-click, you will see the icon turn from a pencil into an eraser, which can rub out the automation.
- With the Selection Tool chosen, right-click on the automation to be deleted and select Delete from the pop-up menu.

As when you reassign a control, after you have deleted the automation you may need to tweak the previously automated control to set it at the right level now that it will not be automated.

Latch Control

Before leaving this tutorial, let me briefly cover one other easy way to add automation into a Track: with the Latch Control. You can use this control in several ways, but let me illustrate with the Track Volume Control (although you can set the Latch Control to control other functions, such as an Instrument's slider setting). Set the latch as follows:

1. At a point where you want to set the Track's volume level, set that level.
2. Once you have set the level, right-click on the Volume Control and select Latch Volume.

When you replay the Project, at the point where the latch was introduced, the Volume Control will jump to the latch level that you set.

Tutorial 26: Tempo and Time Signatures

Project5 allows you to set—and change during the course of a performance—the tempo and the time signature of a piece.

Time Signatures

You can set the base time signature in Project5 by selecting Edit > Change Time Signature. From the pop-up window (see Figure 26.1), you can dial in the correct time signature.

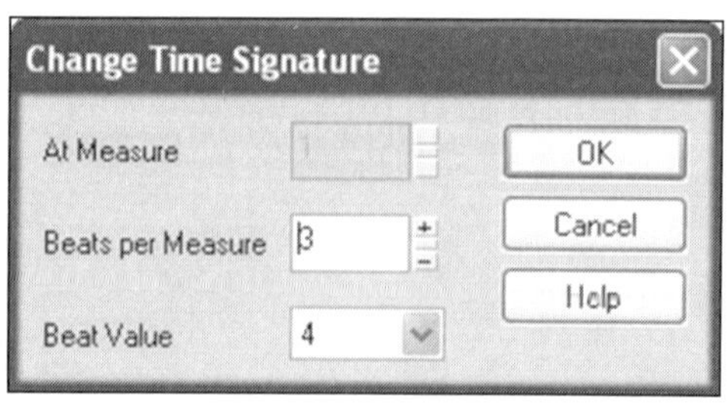

Figure 26.1 The Change Time Signature window in Project5, which sets the base time signature for a Project.

You can change the time signature at any point in the Project by selecting Edit > Insert Time Signature. This pop-up window (see Figure 26.2) allows you to select a new time signature and define the measure from which this change will take effect.

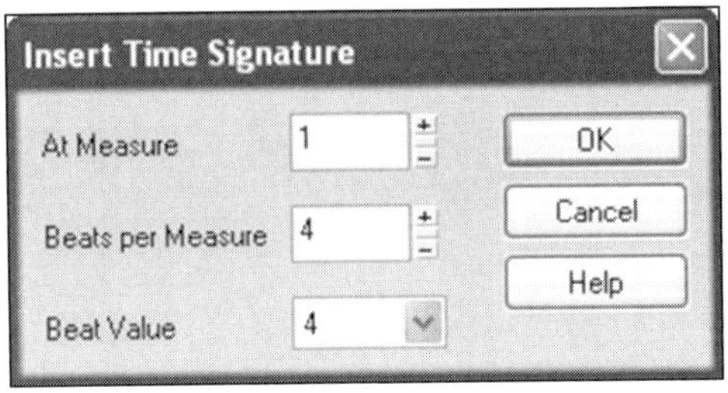

Figure 26.2 The Insert Time Signature window, which allows you to change a time signature during the course of a piece.

You can delete a time signature change by selecting Edit > Delete Time Signature.

You can also select Insert Time Signature, Change Time Signature, or Delete Time Signature by right-clicking on the time ruler above the Arrange Pane and selecting the appropriate option from the pop-up menu.

Setting the Tempo

As noted in Tutorial 4, you can set the tempo in a number of ways:

- Left-click and drag on the Tempo Display (up or down) to increase or decrease the tempo (in fairly coarse increments).
- Double-click on the Tempo Display and manually enter the tempo.
- Double-click on the Tempo Display and adjust the tempo with the fine adjustment controls (the plus and minus signs that appear to the right of the tempo).
- Left-click on the Tap Tempo button—you will need to click several times to establish a rhythm. If, like most human beings, you find it hard to click at a precise tempo, you can always hit the \ key on your keyboard rather than clicking with your mouse.

Tempo Map

Once you have set your tempo, you can change the tempo of your piece. The change can be a one-off step—for instance, changing from 90bpm to 120bpm—or a progressive increase or decrease over a number of measures.

To change the tempo, you need to use the Tempo Map. This is accessed by clicking on the Show Aux/Master/Tempo button at the bottom of the Track Pane. The Tempo Map is at the bottom of the Master Busses and any Aux Busses. Before you start editing, I suggest you increase the height of the Tempo Map, as I have done in Figure 26.3, by clicking and dragging the bottom of the Tempo Track strip.

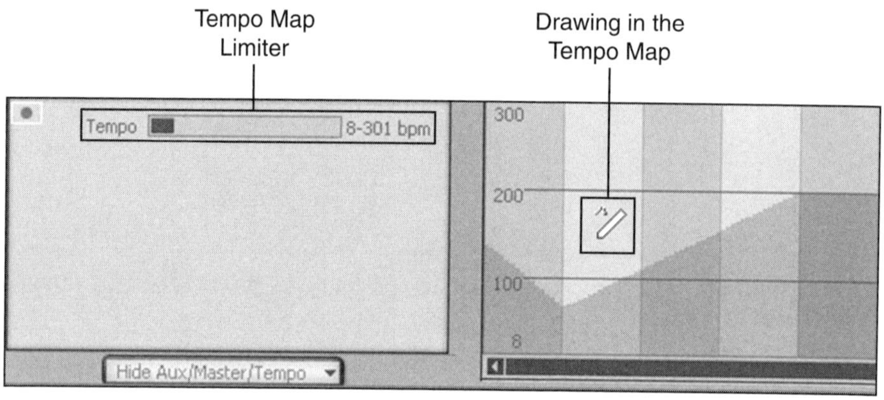

Figure 26.3 The Tempo Track and Tempo Map.

Before you start messing with your tempo, it is sensible to set your Tempo Map Limiter. This sets the maximum tempo that your Track can reach. By default this is set to 200bpm. It is unlikely that you would want your Track to exceed this tempo, but if you do, drag the Tempo Map Limiter to the maximum setting.

Once you have set the Tempo Map Limiter, select the Automation Tool in the right-hand Main Controls and draw the Tempo Map. Drawing the tempo is very much like drawing automation. For instance:

- If the Snap to Grid function is engaged, then tempo changes will snap.
- If you want to draw straight lines (in other words, smooth tempo changes), hold down the Shift key and draw the tempo change.

Tutorial 27: Using Project5 with Other Hosts

ReWire is a protocol that allows two pieces of audio software to work together and share audio data, as if you had hooked up two pieces of audio hardware, but without the signal degradation. This means that you could, for instance, run SONAR and Project5 together using the respective strengths of each piece of software, but combining their audio outputs, and all with complete timing accuracy.

The main reason for using two pieces of software ReWired together is to take advantage of their respective strengths and different workflow features. For instance, you may like Project5's way of working but prefer how SONAR handles audio recording. By using ReWire, you can synchronize the two and take a direct audio feed from one to the other without the need to mix down, and export and import the audio. This way, you benefit from the strengths of both, and there is no degradation in the audio signal.

ReWire can support real-time streaming of up to:

- 256 individual audio channels from one application to the other
- 4,080 MIDI channels (255 MIDI buses with 16 channels per bus)

So, as you can see, you can transfer a lot of audio data with ReWire.

ReWire Host and Client

There are two elements to a ReWire setup:

- The Host
- The Client

Project5 can work either as Host or Client (see Figure 27.1).

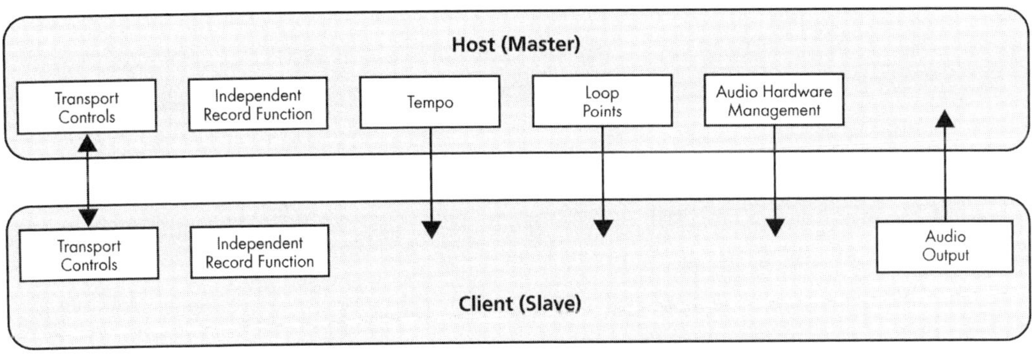

Figure 27.1 The Host and Client in a ReWire setup.

For any one Project, you can have a maximum of one Host and one Client. You can set a different Host and a different Client for each Project that you work on.

Common Functions

In both the ReWire Host and the ReWire Client, the Transport Controls will have the same effect, so you can start and stop playback and rewind and fast forward from either piece of software.

Both the Host and the Client will retain the facility to record audio independently. Therefore, you can choose to record incoming audio to either (or both) pieces of software.

Role of the Host

The ReWire Host is the Master in a Master/Servant relationship with the ReWire Client. As the Master, the Host sets:

- The tempo
- The loop points

Any changes to these two aspects made in the Client will be overridden.

Role of the Client

The Host is also responsible for the management of the audio hardware, so any audio settings in your Client will be ignored. However, the audio output from the Client will be directly fed into the Host.

What Can I ReWire?

I will look at the mechanics of ReWiring in a moment. Before we get there, a word of caution: ReWire only works with ReWire-compatible software, so if your other software isn't ReWire compatible, then you won't be able to ReWire it into (or from) Project5.

You will also find that some software can only act as either a ReWire Client or a ReWire Host, and not as both in the same way that Project5 can. For example, SONAR can only work as a ReWire Host.

You don't need to do anything special to set up a piece of software as a ReWire Host or Client, other than install it on the same computer on which you are running Project5. All of the ReWire stuff will be loaded as part of the installation process.

Project5 Acting as ReWire Client

There are two aspects to running Project5 as a ReWire Client:

- Setting up Project5 to offer maximum flexibility as a Client
- ReWiring Project5 into the Host

Setting Up Project5 as a Client

When you are running Project5 as a ReWire Client, there is one thing to do before you open it as a Client, and that is set the number of audio outputs. You can do this from the Audio Options window (see Figure 27.2), which you reach by selecting Options > Audio.

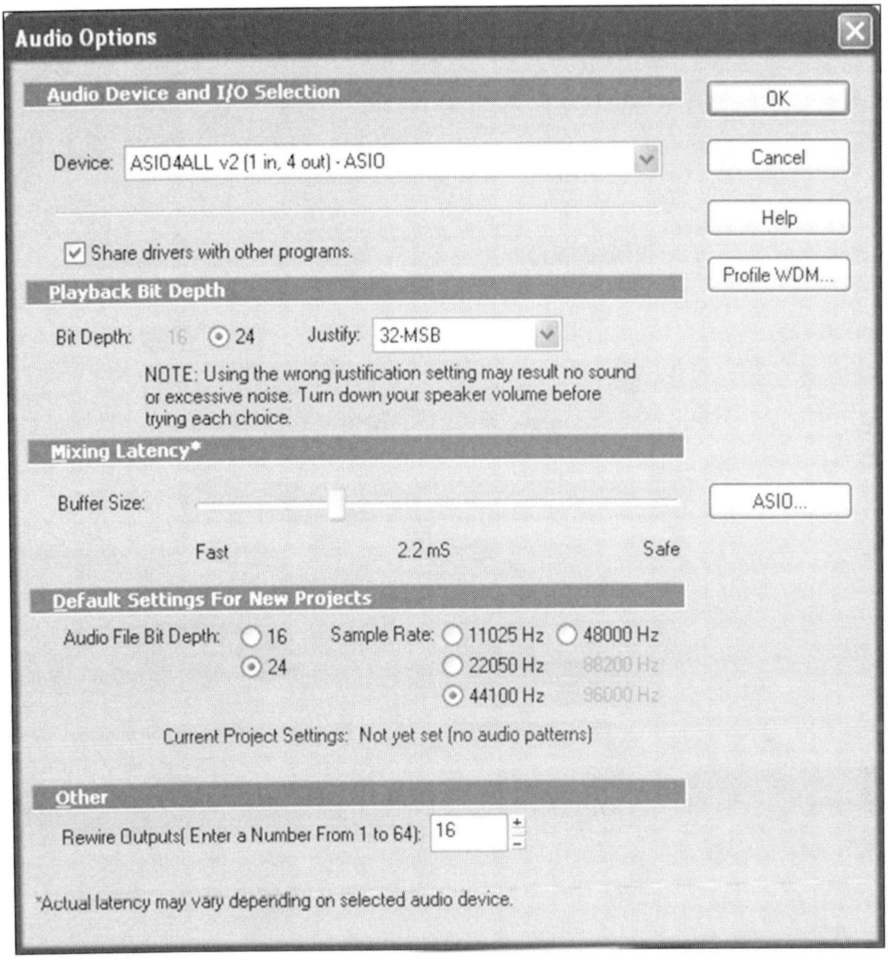

Figure 27.2 The Audio Options window, from which you can select the number of ReWire outputs.

You need to set the number of ReWire outputs before you open Project5 as a Client. When you open Project5 as a Client, you will find that this option has been grayed out.

Because you are ReWiring internally, it doesn't matter how many hardware outputs you have—you can assign up to 64 stereo channels of audio from Project5.

Project5 exposes its outputs to the ReWire Host, including Master Busses, Aux Busses, and Tracks. For example, if you have one Master Bus and four Aux Busses, the ReWire Host application will list Project5's Master Output first, followed by the four Aux Busses, then the Tracks. So if you have enabled 64 ReWire Outputs, Master is 1, the Auxes are 2–5, and the Tracks 6–64.

Once you have set your ReWire outputs, you don't need to assign Tracks to Busses until Project5 has been ReWired. However, when you start using the Busses, you will find that you can send direct feeds and sub-mixes to your Aux Busses. Where you might use an Aux Bus for an FX unit, there is no need if Project5 is ReWired, because you can add the FX unit within your Host.

ReWiring Project5 into the Host

How you load Project5 as a ReWire Client will depend on your Host. However, most Hosts are fairly straightforward, and you will need to open your ReWire Host and load the song you are working on before you open your ReWire Client.

If you want to open Project5 as a ReWire Client in SONAR, go to SONAR's Synth Rack and, from the Insert Soft Synths and ReWire Devices drop-down, select ReWire Devices > Project5 Version 2 (see Figure 27.3).

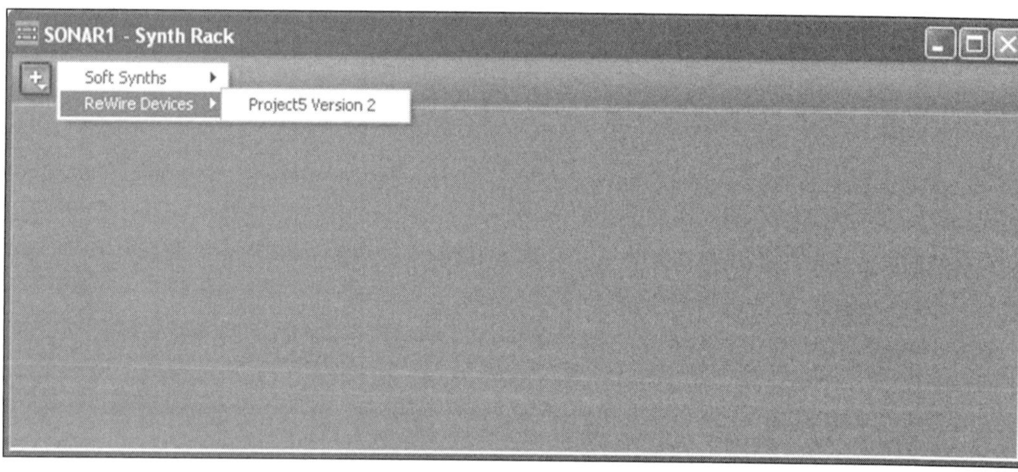

Figure 27.3 Opening Project5 as a ReWire Client in SONAR 7.

After you have selected Project5, the Insert Soft Synth Options window will appear (see Figure 27.4).

If you are simply taking a stereo feed from Project5, then select First Synth Audio Output. However, if you want to take advantage of multiple audio outputs from Project5, then select All Synth Audio Outputs: Stereo. You can select the Mono option, but since Project5 doesn't have any mono outputs, this may cause you a lot of routing hassles.

Project5 should now be cheerfully sitting in your Synth Rack (see Figure 27.5). If you click on the Properties button, Project5 will open. You can load a Project into Project5, and it will play in sync with your song in SONAR.

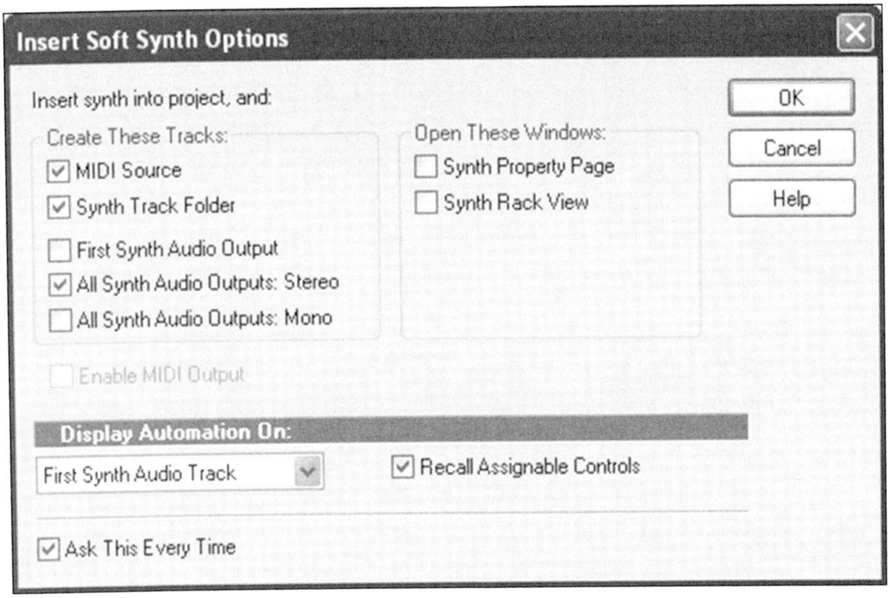

Figure 27.4 The Insert Soft Synth Options window in SONAR 7.

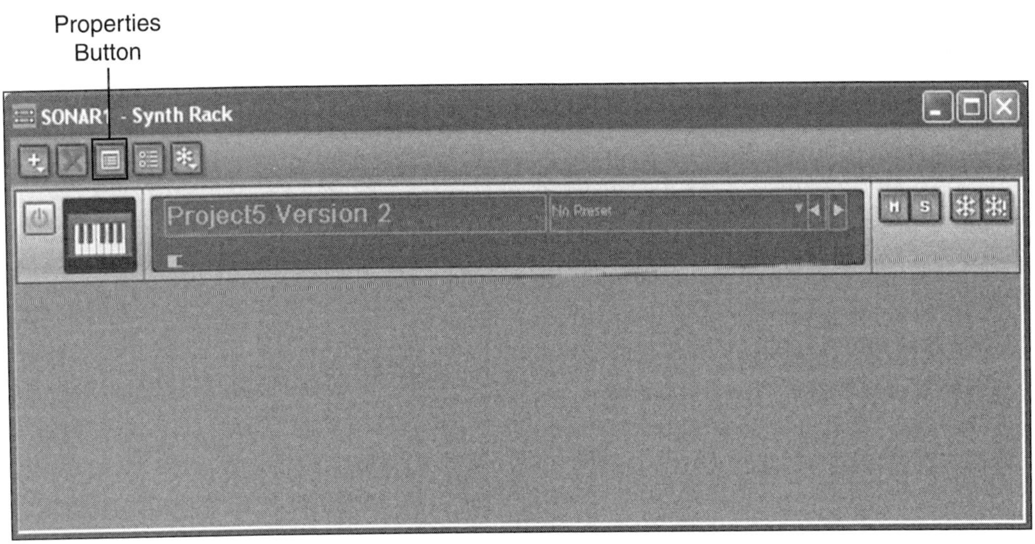

Figure 27.5 Project5 loaded into the SONAR 7 Synth Rack.

Exiting the Host

To come out of the ReWire Host:

1. Save the song you are working on with Project5 ReWired.
2. Exit Project5.
3. Exit the ReWire Host.

More about ReWiring in SONAR

For further details about using Project5 as a ReWire Client in SONAR, check out *SONAR 7 Power!: The Comprehensive Guide* (Course Technology PTR, 2007) by Scott Garrigus.

Project5 Acting as ReWire Host

Project5 can also act as a ReWire Host, so you could then load Cakewalk's Kinetic, Ableton Live, or Propellerhead's Reason, to give three examples, as a ReWire Client.

Loading a ReWire Client is straightforward: Go to the Add New Instrument Track menu and select DXi and VST Instruments. Your ReWire Client will be available from that list. Select it, and your Track will be created, looking like a regular Instrument Track.

If your ReWire Client has multiple outputs, then the Track will operate in the same manner as when a multiple output synthesizer is loaded. (Check back to Tutorial 23 for details.) When you click on the Show Instrument button, then your Client will open.

As when Project5 is working as a Client, do ensure you save your Project and close your ReWire Client before you exit Project5.

Tutorial 28: Freezing and Other Ways to Save Your CPU

Each Track, each Instrument, and each FX unit will use some of your system resources. Added to which, simply opening Project5 will use an element of your resources. If you want to use plug-ins, which give you a lot of feedback (in other words, plug-ins with great graphics and lots of flashing lights), then they will use even more of your CPU.

Unless you are using the most powerful computer known to mankind, or all of your Tracks are highly simplistic, then at some point you are likely to see your CPU meter indicating that you have a problem. When this happens you have three choices:

- Get a new, more powerful, computer. However, there's a sort of Parkinson's Law that means as your computer gets more powerful, your projects will get more CPU heavy, thereby nullifying the effect of any enhanced CPU power.
- Increase the latency of your Project. Check back to Tutorial 10 for a discussion about some of the issues involved.
- Freeze tracks and free up some resources. These options are discussed in this tutorial.

Of course, you can adopt a combination of approaches.

Tracking Down the CPU Hogs

It is important to point out that just because a plug-in makes high demands on the CPU, that isn't necessarily a bad thing. If the plug-in sounds good and is doing some highly complex calculations, then high CPU consumption may be justifiable. Most plug-in coders will tell you it is easy to make a CPU-lite plug-in—you just drop the quality!

In addition, don't try to compare apparently similar plug-ins—even apparently similar plugs made by the same manufacturer. Just because two things sound superficially similar and appear to have a similar workflow (as divined from the interface), that doesn't mean that the underlying engineering can in any way be compared. Added to this, although two plugs may sound similar in one given situation, that doesn't mean they will sound similar in *all* situations.

Different plugs will also use differing amounts of CPU in different situations. For instance:

- Some plugs will consume huge amounts of CPU while no signal is being passed. This is not a fault, but a matter of design.
- Other plugs will use large amounts of CPU while processing signals. As well as the processing using CPU, the visual feedback (meters and so on) will also use CPU.
- Other plugs will use differing amounts of CPU depending on which features have been selected. For instance, some synthesizers will use more CPU if you use more powerful filters.
- If input monitoring is enabled for a Track, then all plug-ins on that Track will be processing full-time.

From your perspective, you don't need to know why a plug uses a lot of processing power; however, you do need to understand when a plug will use power and how much. You can get a rudimentary idea about how much of your CPU's power is devoted to each plug by looking at the CPU meter.

To get an idea of how much CPU is being consumed, open a new Project and look at the CPU meter. Assuming you have nothing loaded, you should see a CPU load of around one or two percent. Now open a Project that has a number of plugs loaded, and you will see your CPU meter rise. When you play back the Track, the meter will rise still further.

You can now do some detective work to find out which plugs are munching your CPU.

As a first step, bypass every Audio Track and every Instrument Track. You do this by right-clicking on the Track Pane and selecting Bypass from the drop-down menu. This should reduce your CPU overhead considerably. There are two reasons to bypass the Tracks in this way. First, you will switch everything off with one action, and second, you can't switch off Instruments from the Inspector.

Unfortunately, you can't bypass Aux Busses or Master Busses in this manner, so to reduce the load of any plugs on these Busses, go to each Bus Inspector and switch off the FX units individually. Switch off your plug on the Track Inspector, not on the plug, since a bypassed plug may still process data (and therefore use some CPU overhead).

You will now have switched off all of your CPU-consuming sources, so your CPU meter should be showing at a level that is close to the level it showed for an empty Project. If it isn't, then you haven't switched something off. You can now start to find which plugs eat your CPU.

Un-bypass your Instrument and Audio Tracks one by one. (To do this, right-click and select Bypass, which will have a check mark next to it.) As you un-bypass your Track, you may see the CPU meter increase. Then start playback of that single Track and check out what happens to the CPU meter. If you are using an Instrument and Audio FX, you might want to switch out the FX so you can get an idea of how much CPU each FX unit consumes.

By switching each element in and out of your audio chain and comparing the at-rest state to the playing state, you will be able to develop an idea of how much CPU each of your plugs consumes. You may also be able to figure out what features within each plug will affect its consumption. With this knowledge, you will be able to identify which plugs you should get rid of first when you need to free up resources.

Freeing Up Resources: Freezing Tracks

Although hitting the Bypass option frees up CPU resources, it also has a downside, namely that you lose the sound of the Audio Track or Instrument that has been bypassed. Freezing allows you to gain the benefit of freeing up your CPU resource but allows you to keep your sound intact.

What Does Freezing Do?

You can freeze Audio Tracks and Instrument Tracks. When you freeze a Track, the Track is converted into processed audio. So, for instance, if you take an Instrument Track, the MIDI file is played through the Instrument, the Instrument's output is routed through any audio FX, and the end signal is then recorded as an Audio

Track. The Instrument and FX are then bypassed. When you freeze a Track, you freeze just that Track—you don't freeze any Aux Bus that the Track is sent to, for instance, so these will still continue to use the CPU.

The freezing process leaves you with an Audio Track that uses far less CPU than an Instrument Track or an Audio Track with audio FX processing. You can choose to freeze one Track or several Tracks. If you want, you could freeze all of your Tracks.

Freezing is an internal processing of the signal. When you freeze a Track, it is very much like mixing down a single Track. Since the whole of the CPU's resources are available for the freezing process, freezing is a much quicker process than playing the Track.

Once you have frozen a Track you cannot edit it, so, for instance, you can't change a MIDI Pattern. However, you could unfreeze it, make the change, and then refreeze the Track. Also, frozen Track parameters can't be changed (with a few exceptions). However, any automation will be included as part of the freezing process, so you will be able to hear its effect.

Once a Track is frozen, the only parameters that can then be edited or automated are:

- Volume
- Pan
- Width
- Aux Sends
- Phase Invert
- Main Bus output selection

To Freeze a Track

When a Track's MIDI data stops, you may still hear sound. This may come from the synthesizer notes that have not fully decayed or from reverb or echo tails that are still sounding.

When you freeze a Track, you will probably want to make allowance for any possible tails. You can do this by setting the Freeze Tail Duration (which is the period of time after the Track stops that will be captured by the freeze). To set the tail length, go to Options > Freeze Tail Duration. This will open a window much like the one shown in Figure 28.1.

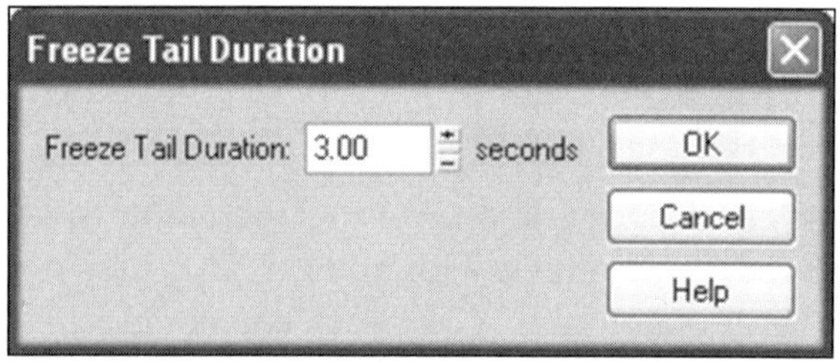

Figure 28.1 The Freeze Tail Duration window.

By default, the Freeze Tail Duration option is set to 3 seconds. I suggest you leave it at this setting unless you have a good reason to change it (for instance, if you like long echoes).

Once you have set your freeze Tail Duration, to freeze a Track, right-click on the Track and select Freeze (or hit Ctrl+F on your keyboard). Repeat this process for every Track you want to freeze.

To Unfreeze a Track

When you come to mix down your Project, you can leave a frozen Track frozen, and the frozen Track will be included in the mix. Alternatively, you can unfreeze your Track and have the original data mixed. Of course, you may also want to unfreeze a Track (or several Tracks) in order to edit them.

The process to unfreeze a frozen Track is straightforward: Right-click on the Track and select Unfreeze (or hit Ctrl+F on your keyboard). Repeat for all Tracks you want to unfreeze.

Freeing Up Resources: Bouncing Tracks

Bouncing is very similar to freezing, but there are two key differences:

- A new Audio Track is created—the bounced Track is mixed to that Track.
- The bounced Track is still active. To save CPU resources, once a Track has been bounced, it should be bypassed.

The Bounce process does not include a Track's:

- Volume
- Pan
- Width
- Effects processing through an Aux Bus or one of the Master Busses

However, in the destination Track, Project5 copies those setting from the source Track.

To Bounce a Track

To bounce a Track, right-click on it and select Bounce from the drop-down menu or hit Ctrl+E on your keyboard. You can now bypass the source Track.

To Un-Bounce a Track

There is no process to un-bounce. However, to reverse the process, you can delete the destination Track and un-bypass the source.

Tutorial 29: Mixing and Mastering in Project5

Project5 gets away from the old analog notion of having a mixer to mix down your tracks. Instead, you can set your levels, panning, and width in the Track and Bus Panes and then use automation to control these parameters over time.

However, there is slightly more to the process of mixing and mastering, and Project5 comes with a range of tools to help with the process. In addition, there are other plug-ins that have been designed to help you achieve a professional-sounding "radio ready" mix.

What Is Mixing? What Is Mastering?

Before we go any further, I think it is worth taking a moment or two to talk about what we mean when we talk about mixing and mastering, and what these two processes involve.

Mixing

Mixing is the process by which you take all of your Tracks and blend them into a single Audio Track.

At its most basic, mixing involves getting the levels of each respective part right. At its most complicated, mixing is a performance.

Although each mix will vary, and the process you will follow will vary, there are likely to be several aspects that you will have to consider in every mix:

- First, there is the need to get the respective levels right. You need to do this so that each part can be heard, and to get the right "sound" for the song.
- Beyond getting the levels right, each Element will either need its own space or to work perfectly with another part. This will usually involve using some EQ

(which is discussed in more detail in Chapter 7) to sculpt an area in the sonic spectrum for each instrument.

- To keep each part's volume within an acceptable level (in relation to the other parts), and perhaps to give the part some more presence or a bit of punch, you may find yourself calling up a compressor (or several). These, too, are discussed in greater detail in Chapter 7.
- Mixing is a time for looking and listening to the whole Track. As part of this process, you might want to think some more about whether each part works in the context of the completed Track. If it doesn't, the mix stage is your last opportunity to cut anything that doesn't work. Equally, the mix is your last opportunity to add some creative gloss to the Track. Often this creative gloss is enhanced with the use of some effects to augment the Track. As you've probably figured by now, effects are considered in Chapter 7.
- The last main consideration during the mix stage is the dynamics of the overall song. If you get it wrong, you can take a punchy and upbeat song and leave it flat. This is the point when you should look at the song's structure and make sure your mix and arrangement support the song. For instance, does the verse build into the chorus? After an uplifting chorus, does the next verse gently take the song down a notch or two (giving you room to build into the next chorus)?

Mastering

Mastering is the process of adding that final polish to a Track. It is the process of taking a mixed Track and making it sound better. In this context, *better* is a subjective term usually encompassing terms such as *tighter*, *brighter*, *punchier*, and so on.

Historically, mastering engineers were needed to ensure that mixed tracks transferred properly onto vinyl. Vinyl is a physical medium with inherent limitations. For instance, if the groove is cut to be too shallow, then the record would be physically quieter. (Often this was the case with compilation albums in which the maximum amount of material was squashed onto a disc.) Conversely, if the groove was too deep, this could limit the amount of material that could be included. There were other issues to consider: One of the most significant was the effect of stereo—an unbalanced low-frequency sound (such as a bass guitar or kick drum panned to one side of the stereo spectrum) could easily cause a record to skip.

With CD and digital distribution, the role of the mastering engineer has changed. The role is now twofold:

- First, getting the sound brighter/punchier and so on
- Second, getting the sound as loud as humanly possible

With digital audio, *loud* is an absolute, not a comparative, term. Once you hit the digital peak, that's it—you cannot get any louder. However, if you listen to the radio or TV, you will hear that the adverts sound subjectively louder. I will look at some techniques for getting this subjective loudness later in this tutorial.

Mastering engineers are also called upon to make sure that all of the tracks on a CD have a cohesive feel. However, in a world where everyone wants to be loud and tracks are sold individually at iTunes, this role is often a secondary consideration.

Dithering

Often songs will be produced and mixed at 24 bit. If you have read the earlier chapters, you will see that I recommend you work at 24 bit. However, CDs use 16-bit audio.

There is a simple way to get from 24 bit to 16 bit: Throw away 8 bits. This is called *truncating*. As you might expect, the results from this process may not be perfect, and you may hear some unwanted audio artifacts. So how do you deal with these artifacts? You add some dithering.

In highly simplistic terms, dithering is noise that is added to cover digital artifacts. This might sound bad, but from a digital audio perspective, it is actually good. Rather than try (and fail) to explain the science and the application of dithering, check out the further reading under the next heading.

Further Reading

I'm going to say these phrases several times before the end of this book, so get used to them now! You could write a whole book about mixing. You could write a whole book about mastering. Luckily, some other guys have done just this. If you're serious about mixing and mastering, then I recommend you check out these books:

- Owsinski, Bobby. *The Mixing Engineer's Handbook*. Thomson Course Technology PTR, 2006.
- Gibson, David. *The Art of Mixing*. Thomson Course Technology PTR, 2005.
- Gallagher, Mitch. *Mastering Music at Home*. Thomson Course Technology PTR, 2007.

There are also two guides that I suggest you check out. These have been produced by iZotope, the people behind Ozone (which I will be mentioning later in this tutorial). They have produced two guides that are well worth getting hold of (and they're free). These guides are:

- Mastering with Ozone
- Ozone Dithering Guide

You can download these guides from www.izotope.com/products/audio/ozone/guides.html.

How to Mix in Project5

In this section (and the upcoming section, "Mastering in Project5"), I'm going to mention tools such as compressors and EQ. If you want to read more about these tools before I talk about how you can use them for mixing and mastering, then skip forward to Chapter 7 before you read these next sections.

In one way, you cannot *not* mix a Project in Project5. You will always hear the result of all of the un-bypassed Tracks being fed to your audio outputs, so in one way you will always be mixing your Project as you write and produce it. This can help to make Project5 a highly streamlined way of working. However, it can also mean that you can end up with a sonic "lump" rather than a well-crafted mixed song.

Different people advocate different styles of mixing. For instance, some people suggest that to mix a song, you need to set the level of each part to zero and build. Others will suggest that you start with certain parts and cut out the rubbish. I'm pretty agnostic about which school of thought is correct; however, I am a firm believer that you should actively mix rather than just letting it happen. If you are going to actively mix a song, then you need to listen to it—in particular, you will need to listen to the individual elements and hear what works and what conflicts—and you will probably then want to make some changes.

What Are the Elements? What Might Conflict?

The elements of any song will be specific to that song. However, most songs have one or more of the following elements:

- Drums—these will include kick and snare drums, which will carry the main rhythm, and there could be many rhythm parts using conventional and unconventional percussion instruments.
- Bass, whether acoustic, electric, or synthetic.

- Melody.
- Harmony (both vocal and instrumental harmonies).
- Pads, which may be in the form of sustained pads (for instance, a string, synthesizer, or organ part).

For the purpose of this tutorial, I am going to assume you are making what might loosely fall within the definition of "popular" music. For most pieces that fall into this categorization, there are two key elements:

- The rhythm
- The melody (which is usually delivered through the vocal part)

Everything else is gravy.

Elements of a song are likely to conflict when one obscures another. For instance, if a bass guitar obscures a kick drum, you could find that the rhythm of the song is diminished by this conflict. Alternatively, if a pad muffles the lead vocal, then you might have another conflict that you need to fix.

Conflict Resolution

This sort of conflict doesn't need a United Nations peacekeeping force—it just needs a bit of work on your part.

Before you start fixing conflicts, listen to each individual Track, regardless of whether they are conflicting. The aim of this exercise is to pick up anything that shouldn't be there. It can be very disheartening if you have worked to sort a conflict, only to find there's still a problem with the source material. By the way, don't try to mix a Project by listening to each Track and perfecting each one on its own. The aim of mixing is to make all of the Tracks works together, not to have a "perfect" Track that doesn't work in a mix.

There are several things you can do to address conflicts, but it depends on the nature of the issue you face. The two main tools at your disposal are compression and EQ, which are discussed in the next two sections.

Compression in a Mix

You might use compression for two reasons: creative and surgical. For this tutorial, I am looking at some of the surgical uses for compression.

As you know, compression is effectively an automatic volume control. The surgical use for compression in a mix is to keep the level of a Track reasonably constant. This means that playing inconsistencies can be ironed out, and you won't have a Track being too dominant in one part and then too quiet in another.

This sort of compression is subtle and will need a low ratio, perhaps 2:1 or lower. As an alternative, you can automate the level of your Track; however, if you are looking to rein in individual notes, then a compressor will be a much better tool.

EQ in a Mix

Like compression, EQ can be used creatively (for instance, to brighten a part) and surgically.

EQ is often used surgically to sculpt a sound to ensure that it doesn't conflict with another. For instance, if you have a string-pad sound that is muffling the lead vocal, then you might want to apply some surgical EQ to the pad. In this case you could cut the pad sound (you can use the Para-Q plug for this) at around the frequency range of the vocal.

There's a good chance you won't know the frequency of the vocal (and it will vary—that is the nature of melody), so you won't be able to set the EQ from its dial. This isn't a bad thing. In fact, it's quite good: It means you need to use your ears and listen to the context in which the sounds are playing. In this case, set your EQ to an extreme setting—for instance, set the gain to −12 dB and set a wide bandwidth. Then adjust the Frequency Control until the pad is cut so that you can hear the vocal part.

At this point you will probably have changed the pad part too much, but don't worry—you will also be close to finding the right EQ settings. From here you can gradually narrow the bandwidth and reduce the EQ gain cut. As you do this, tweak the Frequency Control to make sure you are cutting the right frequency. You will find that you need to balance the three controls to get the right amount of cut so that the vocal sits well in its backing Track.

You could alternatively boost your vocal instead of cutting the pad. However, that would cause a frequency hump (in other words, you would have a lot of sound at one frequency) and would not actually resolve the conflict. This approach will also cause problems at the mastering stage.

In many instances, rather than EQ at the mixing stage, it is better to go to the source and fix the problem there. In Project5 many of your sound sources will be synthesizers. If you can program and edit sounds in your synths, you will find that you can far more easily create a well-balanced mix without relying on EQ. I will look at synthesizer programming in more detail in Chapter 6, "Using Synthesizers in Project5."

Sub-Mix Strategies

One way to deal with separate parts is by sub-mixing. This is the process of mixing each element to its own separate Bus. So, for instance, you could mix the kick drum and bass parts to one Bus, the vocals to another, the pads to a third Bus, and so on. With the sub-mixes you then have the opportunity to look for, and resolve, conflicts:

- Within each sub-mix, so you can make sure the kick drum and bass work together
- Between each Bus, so you can ensure the vocal sub-mix is not obscured by the pad sub-mix

Although you can perform these tasks without using sub-mixes, you will often find it easier and faster to work this way.

To create a sub-mix you need to use Aux Busses. Route your Track to an Aux Bus and set the Send to pre-fader, and then turn down the Track's Volume fader. You will now find that you can create a sub-mix on the Aux Bus. The sub-mix can then form part of the mix.

Figure 29.1 show how sub-mixing could be used in practice to avoid conflicts. Here you will see that there are three main parts:

- All of the vocal parts are sub-mixed to one Bus.

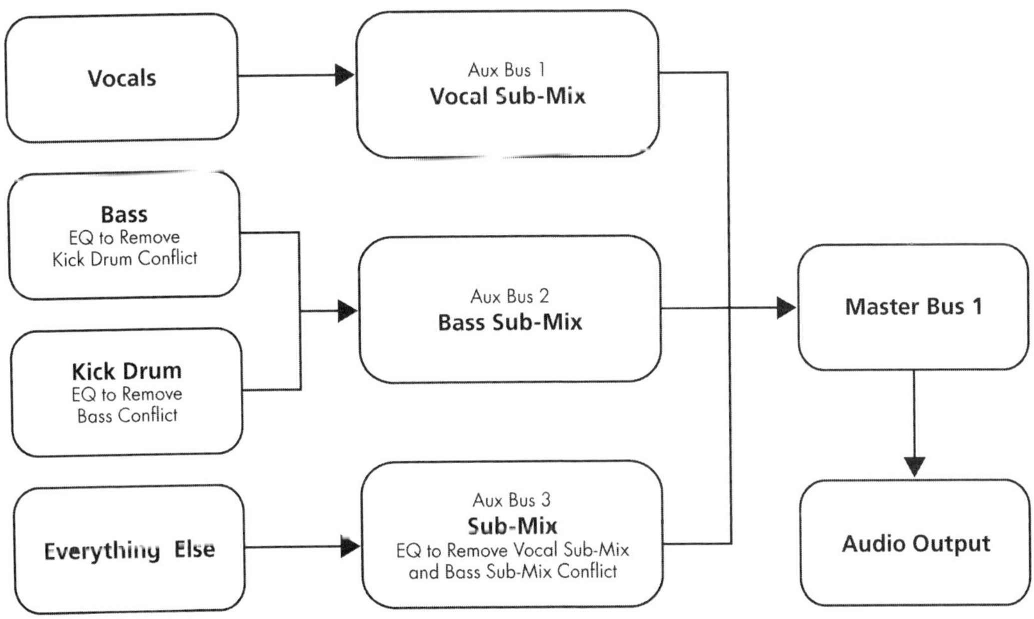

Figure 29.1 Using sub-mixes to create separate parts, which can be individually processed to avoid conflicts.

- The kick drum and bass parts are sub-mixed to Bus 2.
- Everything else is sub-mixed to Bus 3.

Before the kick and bass are sub-mixed, they are EQ'd on their individual Tracks to ensure there is no conflict within the Bus. Aux Bus 3 (the "everything else" Bus) is then heavily EQ'd to remove anything that may conflict with either the kick and bass sub-mix or the vocal sub-mix. With this EQ and routing structure, the Project will be comparatively easy to mix without conflicts.

Check out Tutorial 9 for further details about sub-mixing.

More Flexible Mixing Structure

Project5 has been designed with a fast, intuitive workflow in mind. Ultimately, this may lead to some limitations, depending on how you work. For instance, there are two techniques that I like to use when mixing that can't be achieved with Project5:

- **Bussing a Bus.** In Project5 you can't send an Aux Bus to another Aux Bus. So if you use an Aux Bus to create a sub-mix, you need to add your FX units on that Bus. You can't send the sub-mix to another Aux Bus and so share the FX units with other Tracks.
- **Side-chaining.** There are many uses for side-chaining. The most common is to reduce the level of one part when another is present, so for instance, you could reduce the level of your pad when the vocal part is present.

However, there is an answer: SONAR. I can ReWire Project5 in SONAR (see Tutorial 27) and take advantage of SONAR's more flexible mixing structure. In particular, with SONAR 7, I can send an Aux Bus to another Aux Bus (in fact, you can send any Bus channel to any other Bus channel in SONAR) and side-chain using a compressor.

SONAR is a comparatively expensive piece of kit, especially if you're only contemplating using it for occasional mixing. However, there are cheaper versions of SONAR (for instance, SONAR Studio Edition and SONAR Home Studio) that may allow you to achieve your goal for less expense.

Finalizing the Mix

To actually "mix" a song within Project5, you need to sort everything out so the song plays perfectly. In other words, you need to get the levels right, sort any automation, compress and EQ as necessary, and add any FX units. Once that is sorted, the song is mixed. However, it is still not in a tangible form. For that, you need to export the mixed audio, which I will discuss in Tutorial 30: Exporting Audio.

Mastering in Project5

Mastering is the final process before your song is "finished."

Mastering is the process of polishing the final mix. Before you master your song, you need a finished mix—mastering is not intended to sort any shortcomings in the mix. If the mix is wrong, then the mix should be sorted before the mastering process.

You can apply mastering processing to your mixed Track. Alternatively, you can export your mixed audio, and then re-import this mix to a new Project and apply the mastering in the new Project. The choice is yours and will be driven by workflow and available CPU resources. As a third alternative, you could export your mixed Project and then apply the mastering processing in an external program (such as an audio editor or a specialized mastering program).

But What Is Mastering?!

The mastering process involves many activities, which are dependent on the needs of a particular song and often the intended medium (for instance, CD or DVD). However, most mastering involves one or more of the following processes:

- Compression to tighten up the mix and give a more cohesive sound
- EQ to remove any muddiness and add some bass and presence
- Excitation to add a bit of sheen
- Limiting/maximization to make the song "loud"

The order of these steps may vary depending on the needs of the song; however, the limiting/maximization will always come at the end of the chain. If there is a need for any bit reduction and dithering (which were mentioned earlier in this tutorial), then this will happen after the limiting/maximization.

There is one other common step—ensuring that a number of tracks sound good together. This is particularly important for album releases, but obviously if you're just posting a lone Track on the web, this isn't an issue.

I will now look at the individual steps. As with the mixing part of this tutorial, I will assume you have looked ahead to Chapter 7 and are familiar with these tools.

Compression

What? More compression?

If you've read the earlier part of this tutorial that covered mixing, then you may already have added a lot of compression to your individual Tracks. If this is the case, then you may not need to add much compression to your mix during the mastering process.

However, you may still need compression.

As with applying compression to a Track, you can apply compression at the mastering stage for surgical or creative reasons. The main surgical reason is to make the overall sound louder. The main creative reason is to make the whole mix more cohesive and to give it a subjective "tightness." These processes are not mutually exclusive.

When using a compressor on a mixed song, you are likely to have to adopt a different mindset than when you are compressing individual Tracks. You also need to be highly aware of its effect on the sound of the mix (which is one of the main points of adding compression). You may find that very subtle compression ratios (for instance, 1.2:1) work well, although you may find that you can compress the living daylights out of other mixes.

You may also find that two compressors running in series give better results. You can use the first with a high threshold and a fast attack time to catch the peaks, allowing you to increase the volume. The second compressor might have a lower ratio and a slower attack, but might work at a lower threshold to tighten the sound. This might work for you, but it might not.

In the mixing section, I talked about how to address frequency conflicts, in particular whether to cut one element or boost another. My favored approach—and the approach I recommend—is to cut out the conflicting sound with EQ rather than to boost the sound that is being masked. If you boost the sound that is being masked, you will create frequency humps. In terms of mastering, these are bad because they cause the compressor to be triggered, thereby cutting the volume of the Track. By cutting the conflicting sound you will reduce the peak, meaning that the level of the overall Track can be boosted to a higher volume.

Some people like to use a multi-band compressor at the mastering stage. A multi-band compressor is several compressors strapped together—usually between three and five. Each compressor then works on a different area of the sonic spectrum. The advantage of this approach is that if you get a volume hump in one of the bands, it doesn't affect the whole Track. So, for instance, if you've got a prominent kick drum in your mix, it might cause the whole Track to be compressed each time the kick drum kicks. However, if you are using a multi-band compressor, then only the kick drum's compressor would compress, leaving the rest of the Track unaffected.

EQ

You can put EQ before the compressor, after the compressor, or before and after the compressor. There are good reasons for each approach—for instance, the compressor can change the tone of the sound, so it might be logical to place the EQ after the compressor to compensate for tonal changes. However, the EQ might then reduce the level of the mix, so you might want to compress again. You get the idea.

Mastering equalization is different from Track equalization. It is much less of a surgical process and more of a creative process. It can still be a surgical process, especially when the EQ precedes the compressor in the signal chain, in which case the EQ will determine the extent to which elements of the frequency spectrum will be compressed. Post-compression EQ is much more focused on getting the tone right.

There are often two changes made over a wide frequency range: The midrange is cut to remove any sloppiness in the sound, and the top end is boosted to give the mix more presence. These are subtle changes: Typically only a few dBs are added or taken away. The aim is to improve the sound that is already present and not to radically reshape it.

Once these large changes have been made, then there may also be surgical changes. In this instance, these surgical changes will be narrowly focused tweaks (usually deep cuts) intended to remove unwanted artifacts that cannot be removed in the original mix or that may have been introduced as an unwanted byproduct of mastering—for instance, the compressor may have added a bit too much "sizzle" to a cymbal.

Excitation

Excitation was big in the 1980s and was abused. Listen to music from back then and you can hear a real brittle quality to it. This brittleness was caused by a lot of factors, including early digital synthesizers, early digital recording, and early digital mixdown. This brittleness was exacerbated with nasty excitation.

However, used in moderation, excitation can add a genuine sparkle to sound that cannot be achieved with EQ. It does this without increasing the level to a noticeable extent.

Project5 has an exciter: HF Exciter. This can be used to good effect on mixes. Alternatively, you can excite one or two tracks to bring them out.

Whenever you use an exciter, please take frequent listening breaks. It is very easy to get accustomed to the sound and not notice its effect. This may encourage you to use the effect even more, leading to an aggressively bright sound that becomes quite fatiguing on the ears. Remember the 1980s. No one wants them to happen again.

Limiting/Maximization

Limiting is essentially compression with a high compression ratio. In order to limit, the compressor will need a very fast attack time (otherwise, the limiting effect will not be consistent). To ensure proper limiting, there are a number of specialized limiters on the market that have "look ahead" features. In essence, these devices actually look ahead at the Track data and apply the limiting before the peak level is exceeded and not after it has been exceeded. These tools are great for digital mixing because they ensure that you never get digital distortion.

One example of this type of tool is Cakewalk's Boost 11 (see Figure 29.2), which is available to purchase from Project5.com.

Although you may not get digital distortion, you can still get audio distortion, and you will find that limiters can have a highly detrimental effect on your mix when used to the extreme.

With tools like Boost 11, you can set the output level. Typically, you will set it just below the level of digital distortion, and then the limiter will ensure that all signals

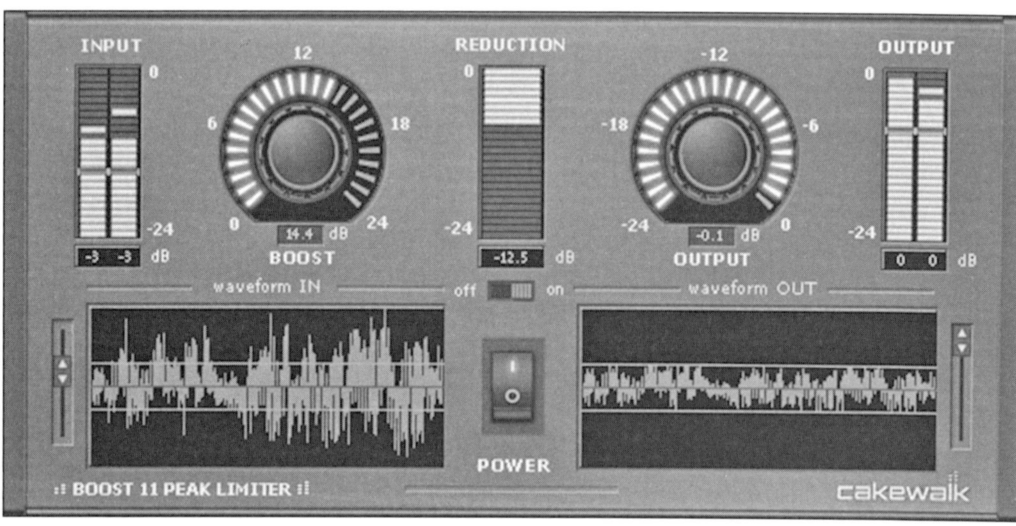

Figure 29.2 Cakewalk's Boost 11 mastering limiter.

are reined in. If you look at Figure 29.2, you can see that the output level has been set to −0.1 dB (where 0 dB is the point of digital distortion).

Once you have set the output level, you can throw all the input level at the limiter that you like. However, you do need to listen to the result because there will come a time when the mix quality is degraded. One other feature of most limiters—and in this respect Boost 11 is no different—is the Boost Control. This is another way to increase the input level.

By increasing the input level, you are not increasing the peak level of the sound—that has already been set and is limited by the Output Control. What you are doing is increasing the density of the sound and so subjectively increasing the loudness of the mix.

Limiter/maximizer tools are some of the main weapons in the "loudness wars" by which everyone tries to make their output sound louder than everyone else's. Used with subtlety, they will add some more kick to your mix. Used to the extreme, the mix will sound fatiguing and will lose all sense of dynamics, and the delicate sonic textures will be lost.

But hey, at the end of the day everyone loves it loud, so go ahead and push up the Boost Knob!

Specialized Mastering Tools

There are a number of specialized mastering tools on the market. I've already mentioned Boost 11, which is a limiter/loudness maximizer. You will find there are other limiters available. In addition, there are tools that do far more than limiting/maximizing and will handle the whole mastering process.

The one I use is Ozone from iZotope (see Figure 29.3). A demo is available, and I recommend you check it out. (Go to www.izotope.com/products/audio/ozone for details.)

Ozone includes a range of mastering tools, including:

- An equalizer
- Mastering reverb
- A multi-band exciter
- Multi-band compression and limiting
- Stereo widening
- Loudness maximization

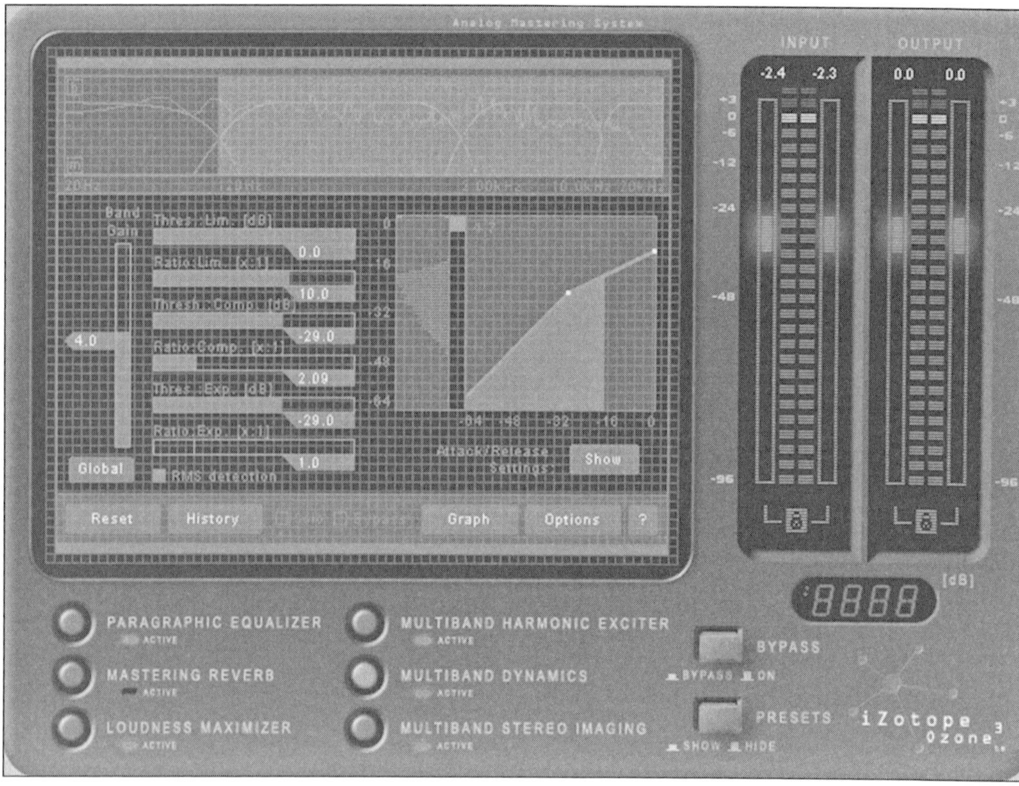

Figure 29.3 Ozone mastering tool.

A Few Closing Words about Mixing and Mastering

You will not become an expert at mixing and mastering just by reading this tutorial. There are many people who dedicate their whole working life to perfecting these skills, and it takes a lot of experience to get truly professional results.

However, Project5 gives you a range of very powerful tools, and with experience your skills will improve. Keep listening and try different things with your mixing and mastering, and you will get truly impressive results.

5 Set the Music Free: Let Other People Hear Your Sounds

Once you've created your masterpiece in Project5, you will want to share it with the rest of the world. You might want to share by creating a CD. Alternatively, you might want to post an MP3 file on the web. Whatever you want to do, Project5 has the tools to get you there.

Tutorial 30: Exporting Audio

The first step in sharing your music is to get it out of Project5 and into one of the commonly recognized audio formats. There are two main audio formats:

- **WAV format.** WAV files are uncompressed, high-quality files that can be played on many audio devices. Sixteen-bit WAV files are CD-quality files.
- **MP3 format.** MP3 is a compressed audio format. While the file size is much smaller than WAV files, the quality is still good. (With a standard MP3 file, your "average" listener will not know whether he or she is listening to a CD or an MP3 file.) The advantage of compression is that you can store a lot of information (so you can get a lot of tracks onto your iPod/MP3 player). The small file size also lends itself to ready distribution over the Internet.

Before you export your audio files, you need to mix your Project. If you haven't read Tutorial 29, then I suggest you check it out before you start to export your files.

Exporting Audio: Choosing WAV or MP3

To export your mixed Project, select File > Export. This will open the Export Audio window (see Figure 30.1).

Toward the bottom of the window there is a Save as Type drop-down menu. This gives you two options:

- WAV files (*.wav)
- MP3 files (*.mp3)

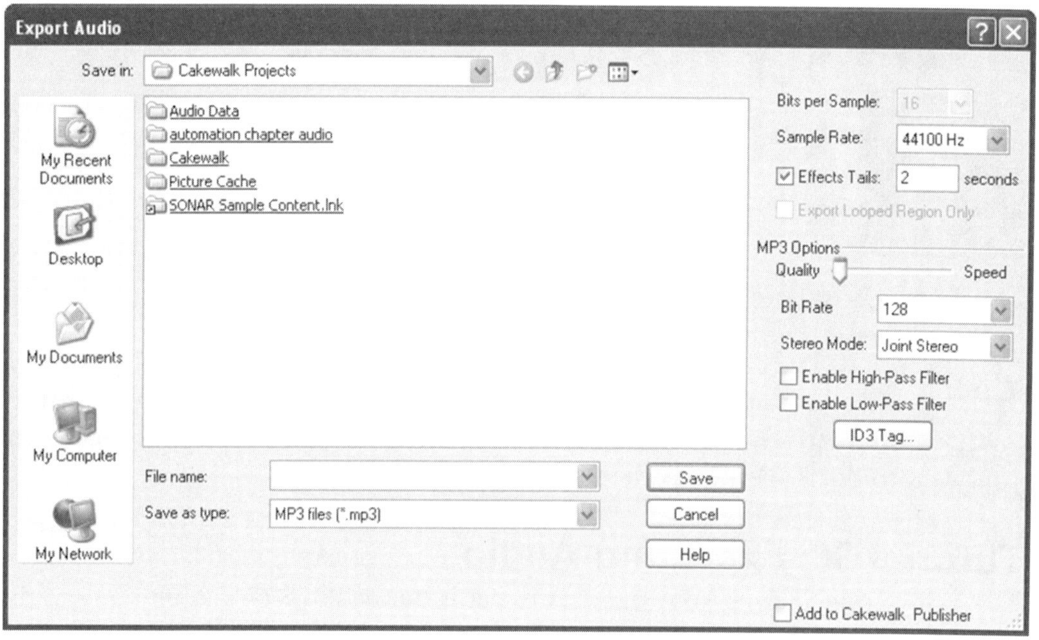

Figure 30.1 The Export Audio window.

Select the appropriate file format, insert the file name in the File Name box, and click Save. Your audio will now be exported. If your mix only uses one Master Bus (or you are using version 2.0 or version 2.01), then Project5 will export a single stereo file. If you are using Project5 version 2.5 or later *and* your mix was directed to more than one Master Bus, then Project5 will export a stereo file for each Master Bus.

By default your exported audio file will be saved in your Cakewalk Projects folder. You can use the standard Windows file manager tools to navigate to any other location where you might want to save the file.

On the right-hand side of the Export Audio window there are two check box options:

- Effects Tails
- Export Looped Region Only

If you select the Effects Tails option, this will allow you to directly enter a value in seconds. This acts very much like the Freeze Tail Duration option discussed in Tutorial 28 and ensures that any sound that continues at the end of the track (such as notes in their release stage or echoes/reverb) will not be prematurely cut off during the export.

The Export Looped Region Only function will only be available if you are trying to export a Project that contains a looped section (using the Loop Selector on the right-hand Main Controls). When this option is checked, only the loop section will be exported.

Exporting WAV Files

WAV files are uncompressed, high-quality files. Since the file format is uncompressed, this may not be the ideal choice if you are going to distribute your songs on the web. However, if you are producing a CD, then you want WAV format.

When you are exporting audio in WAV format, you have two choices. The first choice is the bit rate. The Bits per Sample drop-down menu allows you to choose 16 bit or 24 bit. The choice should be moderately simple:

- If your Project is working in 16 bit, then stay in 16 bit. You won't gain any quality by changing bit rate.
- If you are exporting audio that is going to be used on a CD without further processing, then export at 16 bit.
- If you are exporting audio that is going to be edited again—for instance, you may be sending your songs to a mastering house for final processing, or you are going to re-import the audio into Project5 to apply some mastering—then select 24 bit.

The second choice is sample rate, which is selected from the Sample Rate drop-down. Unless you have a good reason, then it is probably best to stick with the Project's sample rate. However, if you are exporting the audio to be used on a CD without further processing, then select 44,100 Hz (if it is not already selected).

Exporting MP3 Files

MP3 format is perhaps the most widely used audio compression format. Most computers and portable players will recognize the format, and many CD players will also play the format. There are a number of variables in the MP3 format; these allow you to balance file size, audio fidelity, and speed of export. The end result will depend on the combination of these three factors and the material you started with—for instance, you can often get better results when you use smaller files when you are exporting pop music (in all of its many forms) than when you are dealing with acoustic music.

There are no hard-and-fast rules for what works in an MP3 file, so I suggest you take some time to try different settings and find what works best for you. You should also remember that MP3s use a "lossy" form of compression—in other words, audio data is discarded. If you are creating a CD, then you should use the (uncompressed) WAV format, not the (compressed) MP3 format. While you can convert MP3s to WAV files, you will not be able to recover the lost data that was discarded during the conversion to MP3 process.

The MP3 converter that comes with Project5 will only work for a limited period. After that time you will need to purchase a converter from Cakewalk. However, there are other options; for instance, Audacity has a free MP3 converter plug-in. If you are going to use this external conversion route, then you should export your audio as a 24-bit WAV file.

When you export to MP3 you have to set the sample rate. This is the same choice that you have if you are exporting to WAV format. As with a WAV export, I recommend you don't change this setting unless you have a good reason to do so.

There are several other MP3 options in the Export Audio window:

- **Quality/Speed.** This slider allows you to balance the time it takes to create an MP3 file against the quality of the output. Unless you really can't spare a moment or two, I suggest you leave this setting at the maximum Quality and lowest Speed setting.
- **Bit Rate.** The Bit Rate drop-down allows you to select the MP3 bit rate (which is different from the 16/24 bit rate for a WAV file). The higher the bit rate, the higher the quality, and the larger the file size. As a general rule of thumb, 128 is acceptable quality—any rate above that improves the quality but may be harder to detect, and any rate under 128 is likely to give a noticeably degraded sound.
- **Stereo Mode.** The Stereo Mode drop-down gives you four options:
  - **Mono.** The Mono option outputs a mono file. This minimizes the file size.
  - **Stereo.** The Stereo option creates a regular stereo MP3 file.
  - **Joint Stereo.** The Joint Stereo option will achieve a smaller file size than a regular stereo MP3. This reduction is achieved by compromising the stereo separation. You will have to listen to hear whether this reduced stereo effect has a detrimental effect on any particular mix.
  - **Mid/Side Stereo.** The Mid/Side Stereo option maintains the stereo separation, but at a lower quality. You may want to try this option at lower bit rates.

- **Enable High-Pass Filter and Enable Low-Pass Filter.** If you enable either the high-pass or the low-pass filter, the MP3 encoder will remove the top end and the bottom end of the frequency spectrum. By removing this data, you can achieve a smaller file size. You will have to listen to the results to see whether this filtering makes a significant difference to your mix.

If you click on the ID3 Tag button, it will open the MP3 ID3 Tag window (see Figure 30.2).

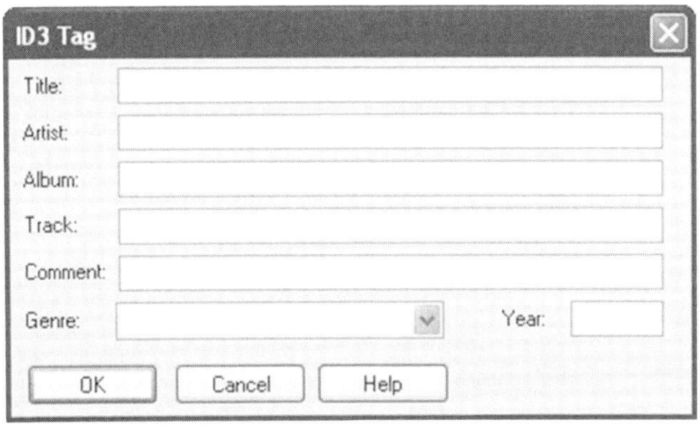

Figure 30.2 The MP3 ID3 Tag window.

This allows you to add metadata to your MP3. *Metadata* is the embedded data that shows up on your MP3 player when a track is played. This is one way that you can mark your work as your own when it passes into the big wide world through the Internet. If you don't add it, nothing shows, and no one knows who created a track. However, please do not regard the addition of metadata as giving you any legal copyright protection under any laws.

There is one further option at the bottom of the Export Audio window: Add to Cakewalk Publisher. This option is available when you are exporting MP3 files and is discussed in Tutorial 32: Making Your Music Available on the Internet.

Tutorial 31: Creating an Audio CD

The audio CD is welcome nearly everywhere and so is a great way of getting your music out there. Project5 includes a separate utility program—the Audio CD Burner; see Figure 31.1—which will create audio CDs for you.

You can run the Audio CD Burner by clicking on Start > Programs > Cakewalk > Project5 Version 2 > Burn Audio CD.

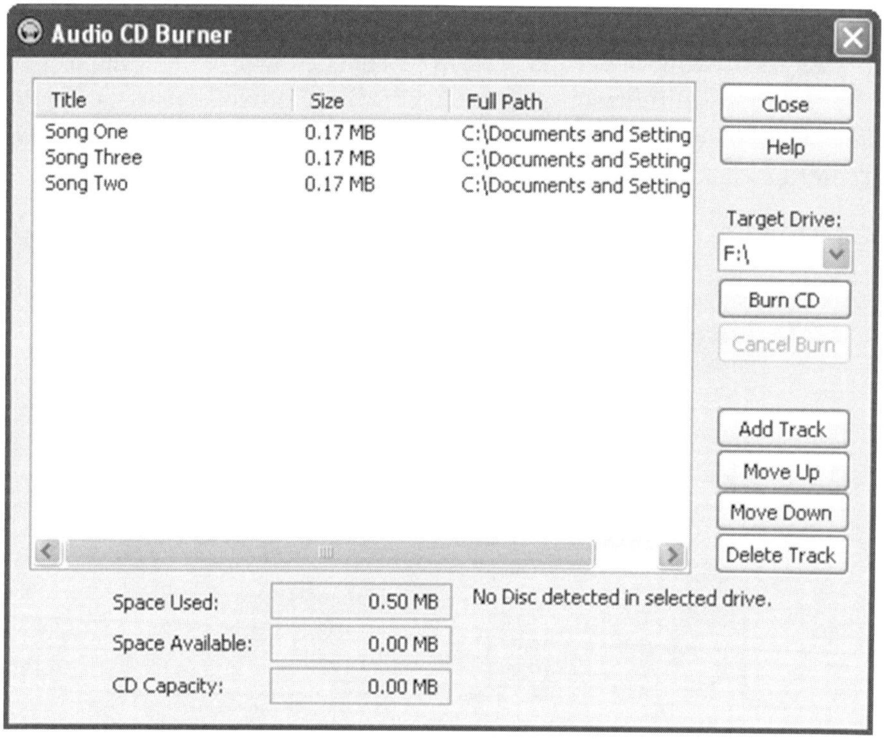

Figure 31.1 The Audio CD Burner utility program.

The Audio CD Burner is a straightforward utility designed to perform one function (to create an audio CD), so don't bother trying to make it do what it was not intended to do. For instance, this isn't a suitable program to back up your files to CD/DVD.

Preparing to Create a CD

You need two things to create a CD:

- Music
- A blank CD-R to burn

I'm making the assumption that you have a CD writer—if you don't, you'll need one of those too.

The music you will need is your mixed-down and mastered audio. This must be in 16-bit/44,100-Hz stereo format. Any other format (such as MP3 or 24 bit), and the Audio CD Burner will refuse to play nicely.

Organizing Your Data

Once you've got your mixed tracks ready and in the right format, you need to get them into Audio CD Burner. To do this, left-click on the Add Track button and select the appropriate Track. Repeat this until you have all of your Tracks loaded.

You will see at the bottom of the Audio CD Burner window there are indicators to show space used, space available, and the CD capacity. I trust these are terms that don't need further explanation.

With the Tracks imported, you can change their playing order—your CD will play the Track at the top of the list first and follow down the list to the last Track. To change the order, left-click on the Track you want to reorder and click on the Move Up or Move Down button as appropriate. Repeat this for each Track you want to reorder.

If you find you have imported a Track you don't want, or if you have too many Tracks to fit on your CD, left-click on the Track you don't want and hit the Delete Track button.

Burning the CD

When you've got the Track loaded and sorted into the right order, then you're ready to burn your CD. To do this:

- Put a blank CD-R into your CD writer.
- Select the CD writer's drive letter from the Target Drive drop-down menu.
- Click on the Burn CD button.

Your CD will be burned. When the process is completed, the CD will be automatically ejected—take it to a CD player, put it in, press play, enjoy. But you knew that. . . .

If you hit the Cancel Burn button while the CD is being burned, you will interrupt the process (although in Windows Vista burning will still continue). After a partial burn you are likely to find that your CD-R will not be usable.

Tutorial 32: Making Your Music Available on the Internet

If you are one of those people for whom CDs are just tragically and irrevocably last century, then you'll be pleased to hear that Project5 also includes another utility—Cakewalk Publisher—that allows you to put your MP3 files onto the web. Not only that, but it allows you to include a player too, so you can post playlists and have your music start immediately whenever your webpage is loaded (if that's what you want to do).

To open Cakewalk Publisher, select Start > Programs > Cakewalk > Project5 Version 2 > Cakewalk Publisher.

Although Cakewalk Publisher is a good way to get your music onto the web, it is not the tool for getting your music heard on iTunes (and this is not the book to discuss that, either).

Preparing to Put Your Music on the Web

Before you get going, there are a few things you'll need:

- Some web space (and details of your web host)
- A bit of HTML
- Music

Web Space

Many Internet service providers will provide free web space, or you can buy some space quite cheaply. If you are going to post your music on the web, then you need some space. You will also need to know the address of this space (if you can't tell people where your music is, then they won't be able to listen to it) and the details for uploading your data (which I'll cover in a moment in the section entitled "Communicating with Your Web Space").

HTML

You are going to need a very small amount of HTML (*Hypertext Markup Language*), which is the computer code in which web pages are written. Cakewalk Publisher gives you the option of embedding a Shockwave player so you can publish playlists and stream music from your site.

Did you notice the term *embed*? The code to control the player has to be embedded into a webpage. This means you need a webpage to drop the code into. The player's code is generated automatically by Cakewalk Publisher—you just have to supply the HTML into which the snippet is dropped. If this makes sense to you, then go to the next section, "Creating Playlists."

If it doesn't make sense, then let me give you a simple way to approach this:

1. Create a new text document. (By default it will be called New Text Document.txt.)

2. Rename the document to have an .htm suffix. (If you don't have any better ideas, I suggest you call the document index.htm.)
3. Open the document, insert the following code, and save the document.

This page then needs to be uploaded to your website. This is a very quick and dirty way of getting things sorted. Although it lacks any form of sophistication, it works. However, I would suggest you learn a bit more about HTML so you can do things such as adding some text to the page.

Here's the code to create your webpage:

```
<html>
<body>
[copy and paste code snippet from Cakewalk Publisher > Configure Player... page]
</body>
</html>
```

The code snippet is discussed in the "Configuring Your Shockwave Player" section, later in this tutorial.

Music

Cakewalk Publisher works with MP3 files, so you need to get your tracks into MP3 format. You can do this by exporting MP3 files as part of the mix process or by converting WAV files to MP3 format.

Publisher is not concerned about the bit rate, quality settings, or size of your MP3 files. However, your listener may be. Well, your listener may be concerned if your files take a long time to download—this will especially be the case if your listener is using a dial-up connection. As a matter of courtesy, I would suggest that any MP3 files that will be made generally available are made as small as possible (while still maintaining reasonable audio fidelity). Check back to Tutorial 30 for some of the options you have for making files smaller.

Creating Playlists

Once you've got your MP3 tracks together, you can create a playlist. The function of the playlist is to put the tracks in the order in which you want them played—that way, you can be really sure that if people only listen to one of your tracks, they will listen to your hottest track first.

If you selected the Add to Cakewalk Publisher option when you exported your MP3 files, then your playlist will be created automatically. If not, then you have to add your files manually. As you would expect, the process is straightforward, and the first step is to open Cakewalk Publisher (see Figure 32.1).

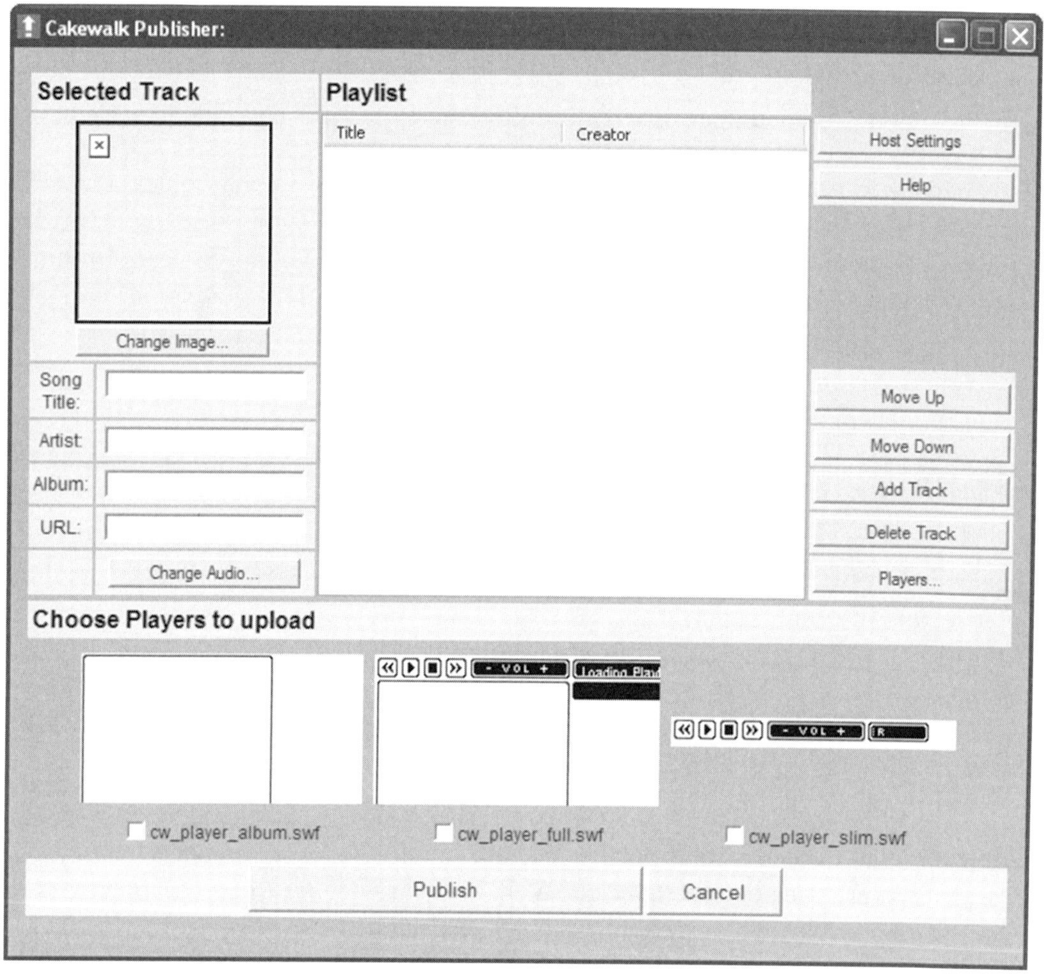

Figure 32.1 Cakewalk Publisher.

Once you're in Publisher:

- Left-click Add Track and navigate to the tracks you want to add.
- If you have a track you want to delete, select it by left-clicking on it and then left-clicking on the Delete button.
- If you want to reorder a track, left-click on it and then left-click on the Move Up or Move Down button as appropriate. Repeat this until your tracks are in order.

When you have loaded your tracks, you can add an image and details about the track with the options on the left-hand side. Click on each track and add that track's details.

Communicating with Your Web Space

Before you can upload your tracks, you need to set up communication with your web host. You can do this by clicking on the Host Settings button, which will bring up the Host Configuration window (see Figure 32.2).

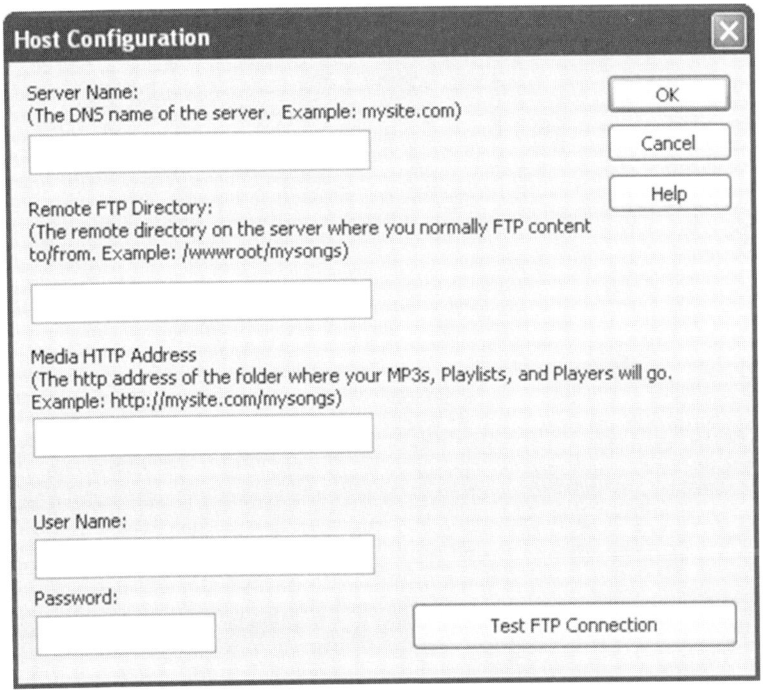

Figure 32.2 The Host Configuration window.

This is the place where you take your web host's details and plug them into the empty boxes and then click on the Test FTP Connection button to make sure everything is working correctly.

You can set up more than one web host profile so you can use Publisher to send files to several websites.

Configuring Your Shockwave Player

When you have got your host configured, you can configure your Shockwave player by clicking on the Players button. This will bring up the Shockwave Players window (see Figure 32.3).

This gives you several self-explanatory choices about your player:

- Always Show This after Publishing calls up this window after you have published a track or tracks.

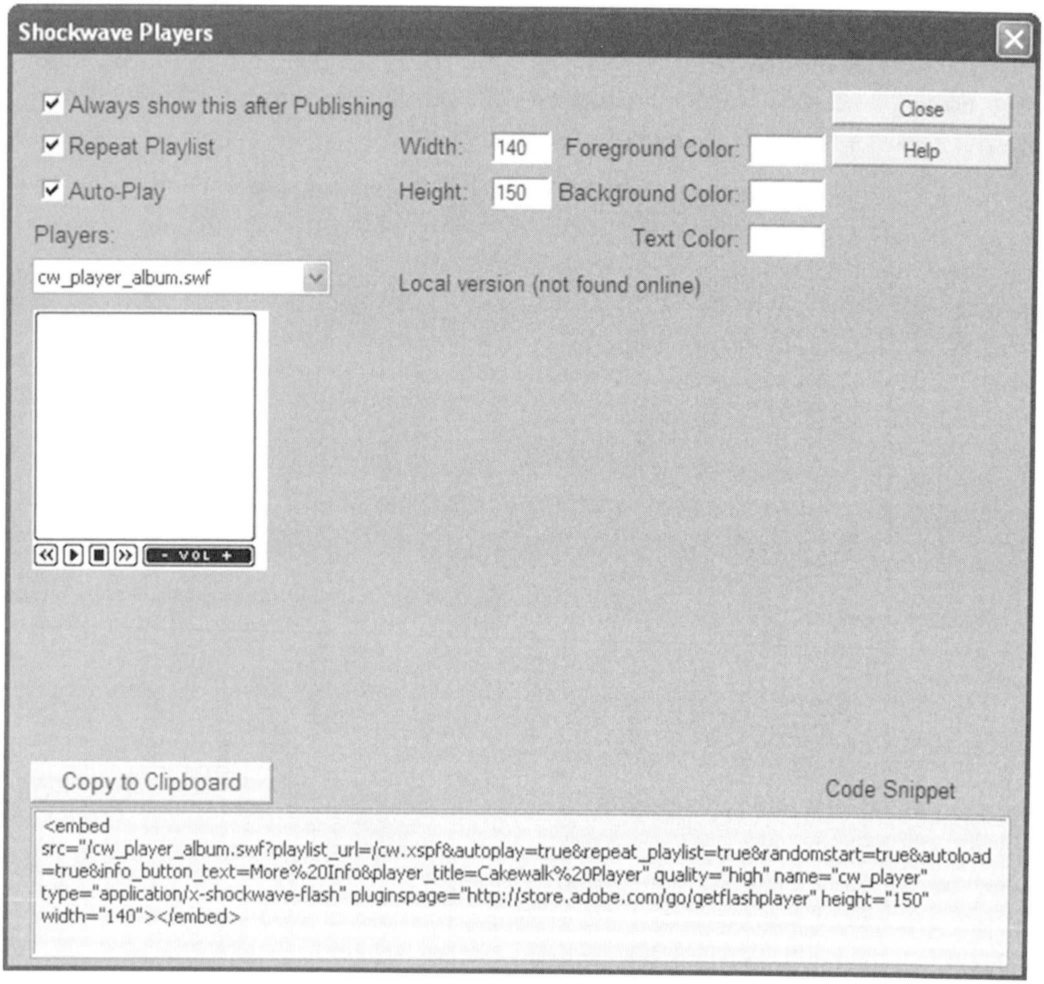

Figure 32.3 The Shockwave Players window.

- Repeat Playlist repeats the playlist.
- Auto-Play sets the Shockwave player to play automatically when your page is loaded.
- Width, Height, Foreground Color, Background Color, and Text Color all set the appearance of the Shockwave player.

The most important button is the Copy to Clipboard button. This copies the code snippet that you need to include on your HTML page in order to embed the Shockwave player in your webpage. All you have to do is click on Copy to Clipboard and then paste the text directly into your webpage.

Publishing Your Music

Once you have set up your playlist, located your host, and configured the Shockwave player, you're ready to publish, so hit the Publish button at the bottom of Cakewalk Publisher. Sit back and wait for your tracks to be uploaded.

Other Ways to Get Your Music on the Web

Personally—and this really is just my personal preference, with which you are quite at liberty to disagree—I don't like Publisher. I find it a nuisance to use, and I don't like the Shockwave player. But as I say, this is just my opinion.

If you're loading songs onto sites such as MySpace, then you don't need the Publisher.

If you're loading songs onto your own site, I think you would be much better served by using a regular file transfer protocol (FTP) program and coding a bit of HTML. (It's *really* not that hard to do the simple stuff such as put a link to an MP3 file.) For instance, you could use a program such as HTMLPad from Blumentals Software (www.blumentals.net). This gives you HTML editing and an FTP package in one.

6 Using Synthesizers in Project5

Project5 comes with a range of synthesizers designed for specific tasks. In addition, you can also open a VSTi- and DXi-compatible synthesizer in Project5, giving you a nearly limitless supply of sound-creating devices.

Depending on whether you have version 2.0 or version 2.5 of Project5, your range of synthesizers will be different. This book covers the synthesizers included with both versions.

It would take more than a chapter to look in detail at the workings of all of the synthesizers that are included with Project5. Luckily, there is a book that contains that level of detail, so if you haven't checked it out already, I suggest you get hold of a copy of *Cakewalk Synthesizers: From Presets to Power User* (Thomson Course Technology PTR, 2006). Full details are available on my website: www.noisesculpture.com/cakewalk.

If you want to know more about synthesizers, then I recommend you get hold of another of my books: *How to Make a Noise* (Coombe Hill Publishing, 2007).

How to Make a Noise is a comprehensive, practical guide to sound design and synthesizer programming using a wide range of techniques. The book is backed with examples using six leading software synthesizers. Details about the book (including a table of contents) are available on my website at www.noisesculpture.com/htman, and you can also find links to Amazon, where you can see extracts from the book by using the Search Inside the Book feature.

Synthesizers are plug-ins, like audio FX units. This means you can use some of the other tools that come with Project5 to manage your synthesizers and arrange your presets. To read more about this, check out:

- Tutorial 7, where you can read more about the Plug-In Manager.
- Tutorial 42: Preset Management Tools, where you can read more about the preset management tools that are available in Project5.

In addition to the preset management tools that are available for every plug-in, as you will read, some of the synthesizers that come with Project5 have their own dedicated preset management systems.

Lastly, before we proceed, you might want to check out Tutorial 23, which covers multi-output instruments (such as Cyclone and VELOCITY).

Tutorial 33: A Bit of Synthesizer Theory

Before we look at the individual synthesizers, I want to look at some of the more common synthesizer tools. For this tutorial I am going to use Triangle II (see Figure 33.1), which is available to download (for free) from Project5.com.

Whichever version of Project5 you have, I suggest you don't skip over this tutorial, since it looks at the main features that are common to many of the synthesizers included with Project5, and many of these features also appear in the audio FX units that we will look at in Chapter 7, "Working with Audio FX Units." If you understand the principles set out in this tutorial, it will make your understanding of the other synthesizers and the audio FX units that much easier.

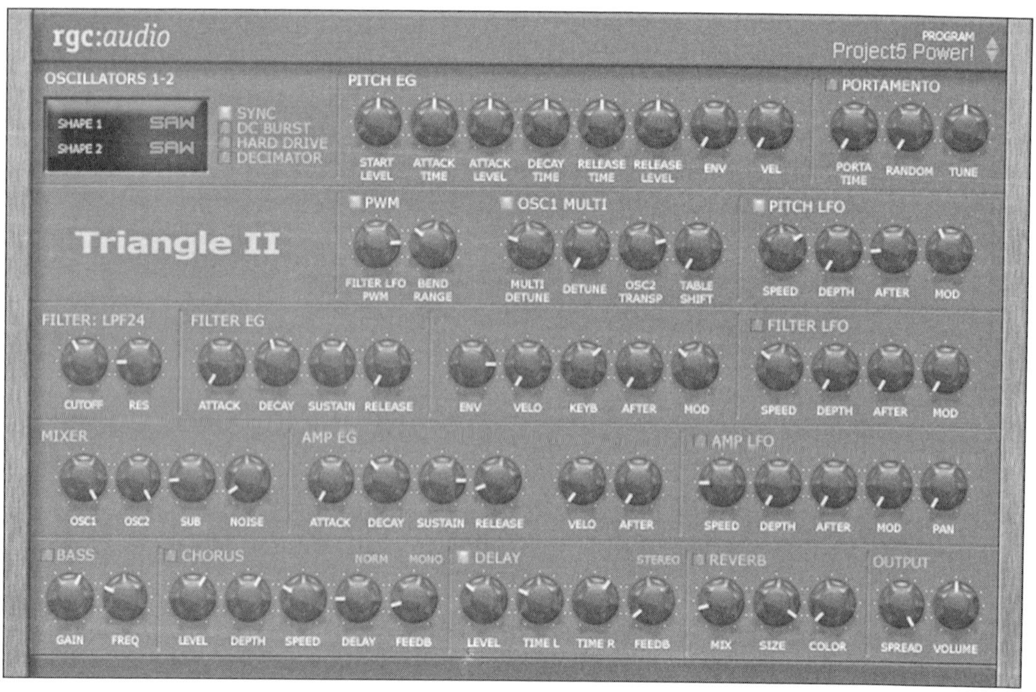

Figure 33.1 Triangle II, which is available for free download from Project5.com.

Synthesizer Architecture

There are many factors in a sound's design, but in essence a sound will usually have three main elements present (see Figure 33.2):

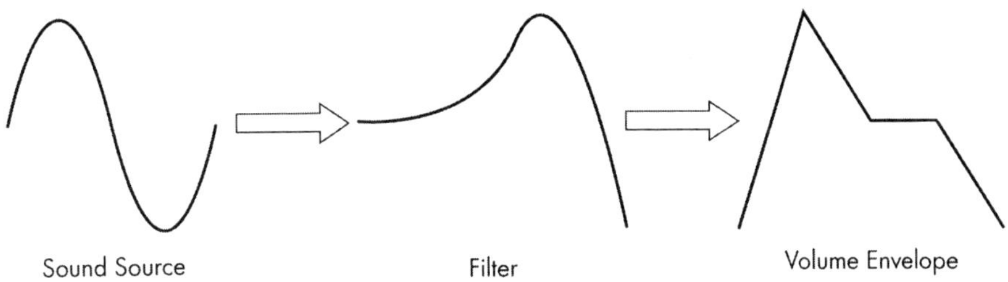

Figure 33.2 The basic signal flow in the sound-creation process.

- The sound generator (usually an oscillator)
- The filter (to shape the tone)
- The Envelope (to control the volume and perhaps the tone, over time)

All synthesized sounds emanate from a sound generator of some sort; this is usually an oscillator. However, the term *oscillator* includes a wide range of sound sources, such as samples. As you will see, many synthesizers use samples as the basis of their sound.

Once the sound has been created, it is then "shaped"—in terms of both the tone and the volume over time—to provide a (hopefully) pleasing tone. It is quite possible that the pitch of the sound may be changed over time too. The control sources that effect these changes may include:

- Envelopes
- Oscillators (often low-frequency oscillators, or LFOs)

The term that is applied when one device controls (or changes) another is *modulation*. So if an LFO controls a filter, perhaps to create a wah-wah type of effect, then we would say that the LFO modulates the filter (or more accurately, the LFO modulates the filter's cutoff frequency).

Envelopes

An Envelope controls a level over time. The most immediate use for Envelopes is controlling volume.

Think of a note played on a piano. When a key is struck, the note goes from silence to the maximum volume instantaneously. From this peak—that is, from the moment of impact when the hammer comes into contact with the string—there is an immediate rapid reduction in the volume, and then the note reaches a level from which it gradually fades to nothing. Now think about a violin note, which slowly fades in, stays at its maximum volume until the note ends, and then gently decays. As you can see, different sounds have different volume Envelope characteristics.

Getting more complicated, as I mentioned, an Envelope changes level over time; its effect will depend on how it is applied. For instance:

- An Envelope could control volume. Depending on the architecture of the synthesizer, the Envelope may control the level of an individual oscillator or the level of a whole program.
- An Envelope may control a filter. If an Envelope does control a filter, it will (generally) control the cutoff frequency and so make the sound brighter over time (or, more often, duller over time—in other words, the sound will start bright and then get duller).
- An Envelope can also modulate pitch. A common use for this would be to give a short (and subtle) pitch wobble at the start of a note to give the sound more emphasis.

The ADSR Envelope

Different synthesizers are designed in different ways. The most common form of Envelope is the ADSR Envelope (see Figure 33.3), which has four main controls:

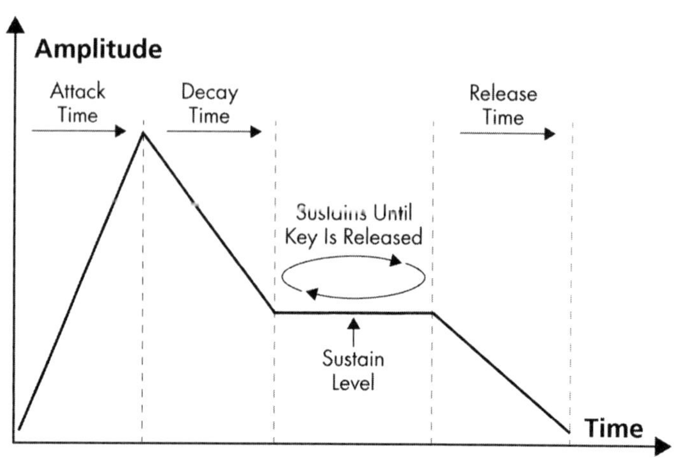

Figure 33.3 The ADSR Envelope.

- **A: Attack time.** This governs the time it takes for the sound to reach its maximum volume after the note is triggered. Using the example of a piano, the attack time would be zero—in other words, it would take no time for the sound to go from nothing to the maximum volume. For a string type sound the attack may be slower.
- **D: Decay time.** This controls how quickly the sound drops (to the sustain level) after it has reached its maximum volume. Again, using the example of the piano, the decay time would be fast, but it would be longer than the attack time.
- **S: Sustain level.** This is the volume of the sound (or the level of the Envelope) while a key is held. This level stays constant until the key is released.
- **R: Release time.** This is the time it takes the sound to decay to zero after a key is released.

Filters

At its most basic, you can think of the filter as being a tone control. A low-pass filter is like the treble control on your stereo—turn it down, and the sound gets "duller." However, a filter can do much more for you.

There are many different types of filters, as discussed in the following subsections.

Low-Pass

The low-pass filter (or, if you prefer, high-cut filter) allows low frequencies to pass through it (see Figure 33.4).

When a low-pass filter is fully open, all frequencies can pass through it. As the filter is closed (in other words, as the cutoff frequency of the filter—which is discussed under the "Filter Parameters" section, later in this tutorial—is lowered), it progressively allows less sound to pass through. You will hear this as the sound becoming

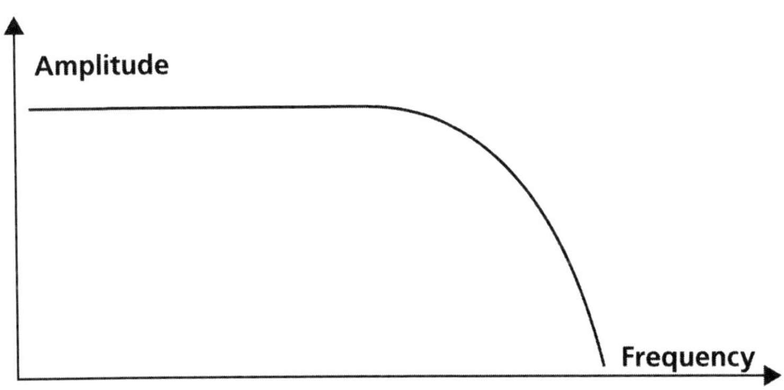

Figure 33.4 A low-pass filter.

duller as the higher-frequency elements of the spectrum are filtered out. When the filter is nearly completely closed, only the very lowest elements of the frequency spectrum can pass.

The effect that the low-pass filter will have on a sound will vary depending on the source waveform you have selected. If you choose a sine wave, then the effect of the filter will be limited. The sine wave comprises only the fundamental frequency; therefore, if the filter cuts this, it cuts the whole sound. However, if you choose a sawtooth wave, which has a lot of high-frequency information, then the low-pass filter will have a much greater perceived effect on the sound.

High-Pass

The high-pass filter (or low-cut filter) is the reverse of the low-pass filter—it allows high frequencies to pass and progressively cuts out the lower frequencies (see Figure 33.5).

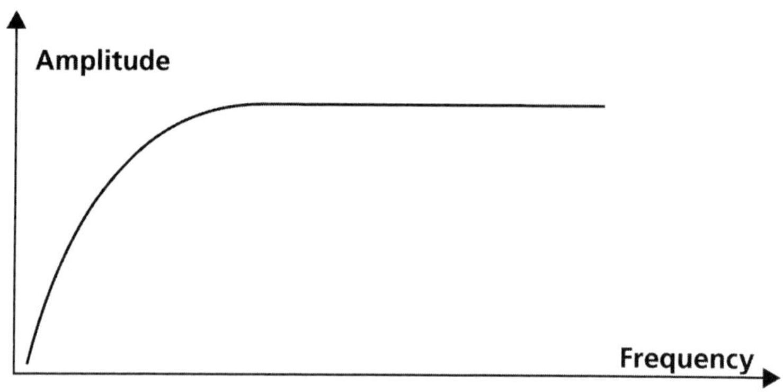

Figure 33.5 A high-pass filter.

As well as sound shaping, high-pass filters have another use: to filter out the junk in the lower end of the mix spectrum. How often have you listened to a track and found it sounds muddy or dull? That could be too much bass. You only get so much dynamic range, and without filtering, you may be filling your low end needlessly. This means that the key elements—your bass and kick—can't shine.

While high-pass filtering may be noticeable if you play a sound on its own, in a mix any change to the tone of a sound is unlikely to be noticeable except with more extreme cuts. However, the net result of the low-end filtering may be to give a cleaner/fuller low end when the bass elements are allowed to come through.

Band-Pass

The band-pass filter acts like a combination of a low-pass filter and a high-pass filter by cutting the frequency spectrum at both ends to only allow a narrow band of sound to pass (see Figure 33.6).

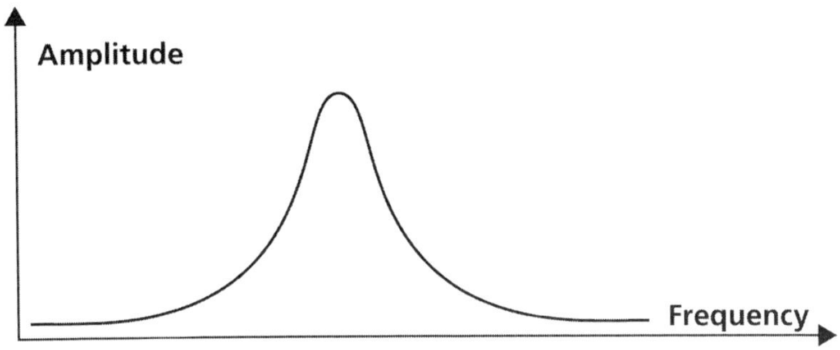

Figure 33.6 A band-pass filter.

The frequency control determines the center frequency where the full signal is allowed to pass—from that point outward, the spectrum of sound is progressively cut. At extremes of frequency, the band-pass filter will sound similar to either a high-pass or a low-pass filter.

Notch

If the band-pass filter is the equivalent of burning the candle at each end, then the notch filter equates to burning it in the middle. The notch filter cuts the frequencies at its current value (see Figure 33.7).

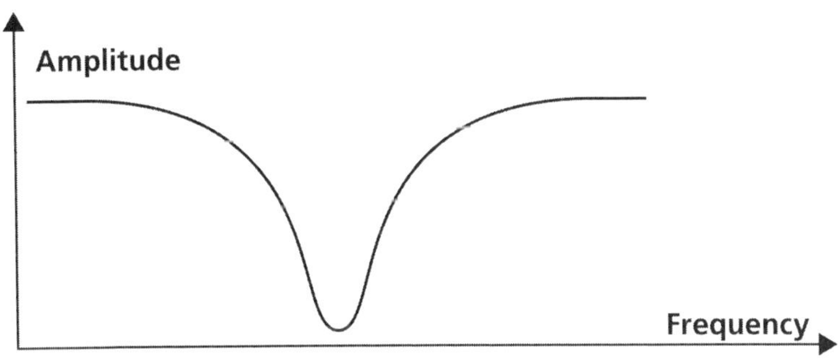

Figure 33.7 A notch filter.

Filter Parameters

All the filters essentially work in the same manner and usually have three controls (once you have selected your filter type).

Cutoff Frequency

The cutoff frequency is the point at which the filter starts to have effect. So if you have a low-pass filter and set the cutoff frequency to 8 kHz, the sound spectrum above 8 kHz will be progressively reduced. However, if you are using a high-pass filter, sounds below the cutoff frequency (8 kHz) will be reduced.

Resonance

Resonance adds some bite to a filter. It works by boosting the sound spectrum around the filter cutoff frequency, as Figure 33.8 illustrates. Used in moderation, the effect is subtle and can make a sound appear brighter and/or slightly thinner (or less fat, if you prefer). When used to the extreme, the effect is noticeable—most dance records use filter sweeps with high levels of resonance.

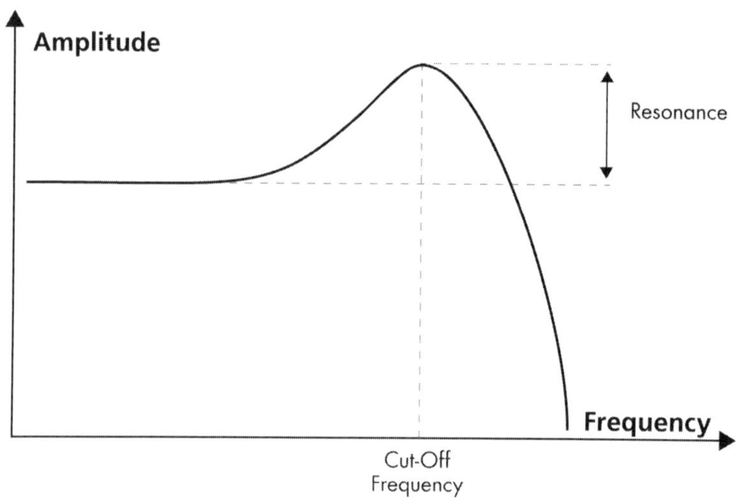

Figure 33.8 A low-pass filter with a resonant peak.

Filter Slopes

A low-pass filter progressively reduces the volume of a sound above the cutoff point. The rate at which the sound wave is reduced above the cutoff frequency is determined by the slope of the filter.

- If you have a 6-dB/octave filter, it will reduce the level of the sound source by 6 dB at one octave above the cutoff point, 12 dB at two octaves above the cutoff frequency, and 18 dB at three octaves above the cutoff. The effect of a 6-dB filter on a sound wave is quite subtle.
- A 12-dB/octave filter (sometimes called a *2-pole filter*) will reduce the level of the sound wave's volume by 12 dB for each octave above the cutoff point.
- A 24-dB/octave filter (sometimes called a *4-pole filter*) will reduce the level of the sound wave's volume by 24 dB for each octave above the cutoff point.

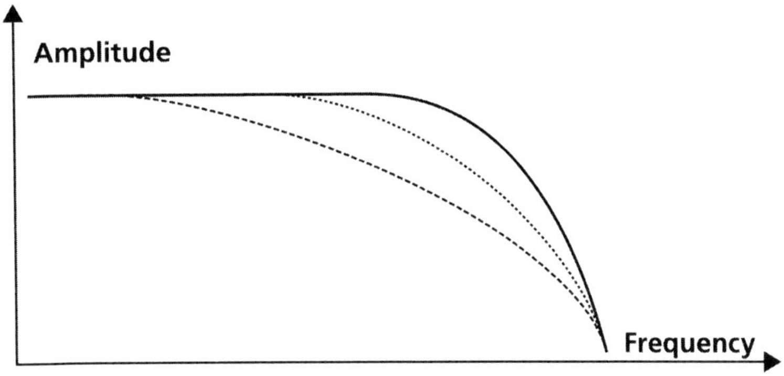

Figure 33.9 Different filter curves. The flatter curves may be gentler, but when these filters are selected, the filter affects a large portion of the sonic spectrum.

You will see some different filter slopes in Figure 33.9. This is an image drawn by hand, and so it is not to scale; however, you can see the differing result of the filter slopes.

Sonic Examples

Here are some sonic examples. All of these have been created with Triangle II:

- As noted earlier, you can download Triangle II from Project5.com. If you run the installer, Triangle II will be available to you in Project5 without any further action.
- There is a bank of sounds to accompany this tutorial, which is available to download from www.noisesculpture.com/p5p (for free). Once you have downloaded the zip file:
    1. Copy the contents of the zip file (a file called Project5 Power! tutorial 33.fxb) to your rgcaudio Triangle II\Presets folder (which will have been created when you installed TII).
    2. Open Project5 and run TII.
    3. Click on the Triangle II logo.
    4. A drop-down menu will appear. Select Program > Load Bank (.fxb).
    5. Click on the file Project5 Power! Tutorial 33.fxb and click on the Open button.

The bank will now be loaded. You can select the appropriate program by:

- Right-clicking on the synthesizer's interface and selecting the program from the pop-up menu.

- Clicking on the up and down nudge buttons next to the name of the currently selected program in the top-right corner of the interface.

This part of the tutorial is intended to give some practical sonic examples of a subtractive synthesizer (in other words, a synthesizer that uses a filter to shape—or "subtract"—the basic oscillator sound to create the end sound. Because Triangle II is not part of Project5, this tutorial will not explain TII in detail—for that, you should check out *Cakewalk Synthesizers: From Presets to Power User.*

Sound Sources

TII has seven waveforms that form the basis of the synthesizer's sound-generating capabilities. These first three programs show three of the waves without any further processing.

- **Saw.** The Saw program features a sawtooth wave, which gives a very bright sound.
- **Square.** The Square program features a square wave, which has a more hollow tone.
- **Harmonic 5.** The Harmonic 5 program features the harmonic 5 waveform, which was created by adding a number of sine waves together to create a bright, almost metallic tone.

If you play any of these programs, you will hear the waveform, which will sustain without variation.

Filters

TII has a number of filters to shape the sound created by the sound sources. These three programs are all based on a sawtooth waveform and demonstrate the effect of two of the filter types.

- **Saw + Low-Pass.** The Saw + Low-Pass program runs a sawtooth wave through a 24-dB/octave low-pass filter. As you can hear, this results in a sound that is considerably duller than the unfiltered sawtooth wave.
- **Saw + Low-Pass + Res.** The Saw + Low-Pass + Res program runs a sawtooth wave through a 24-dB/octave low-pass filter, which then has resonance added. As you can hear, this results in a sound that is duller than the unfiltered sawtooth wave, but it also has more emphasis in the middle of the sound, giving more twang.
- **Saw + Hi-Pass.** The Saw + Hi-Pass Program runs a sawtooth wave through a 24-dB/octave high-pass filter. As you can hear, this results in a much thinner sound.

Like the three previous programs, these three programs sustain without variation.

Envelopes

So far, all of the programs have been static—the notes do not vary as they sustain. These next programs all use Envelopes to introduce some animation. The Envelopes do not make any sound; instead, they work to control other functions.

- **Volume Envelope.** With the Volume Envelope program, the volume of the sound is controlled by the Amp EG (the volume Envelope). If you strike a note it will initially be loud, but as the note sustains, its volume will fall until it reaches the sustain level.
- **Filter Envelope.** With Filter Envelope, a sawtooth wave runs through a low-pass filter, and the cutoff frequency of that filter is then controlled by the Filter EG (the filter Envelope). The Envelope is a bit slow at the start (this is intentional), so you can hear the filter opening and then closing again.
- **Filter Env + Res.** With Filter Env + Res, a sawtooth wave runs through a low-pass filter where resonance has been added. This makes the movement in the filter's cutoff frequency more noticeable and also gives the sound more "squelch."

This is only one example of a modulation being used to control a synthesizer—there are many other modulation sources and many other modulation destinations.

Low-Frequency Oscillators

With the program Vibrato, you will find another example of a modulation source/destination combination. In this case, a low-frequency oscillator modulates the pitch of the sound to create the vibrato effect.

As noted earlier, this part of the tutorial is intended to give some practical sonic examples of a subtractive synthesizer. Triangle II is capable of so much more, as you can read in *Cakewalk Synthesizers: From Presets to Power User.*

Tutorial 34: Introducing Cyclone

Cyclone is a tool that comes with Project5 version 2.0, but it has been dropped from version 2.5. It has also been included with SONAR since version 1.0.

What Is Cyclone and What Does It Do?

Cyclone's prime purpose is to play and manipulate ACIDized loops. You can create sounds by mangling loops, rather than by using filters, LFOs, and Envelopes (since there are no filters, LFOs, or Envelopes).

ACIDized loops are files that contain embedded tempo information and Beat Markers so when the loop is played, its tempo can be changed but the attack transient detail can be maintained, allowing the rhythm to be kept intact. There is a wide range of ACIDized files on the installation DVD, and it is one of the most common formats used by third-party sample providers. In addition, you will find that there are many free ACIDized loops available on the Internet.

Cyclone can also work as a single-shot sample player. However, you are likely to find that VELOCITY may be a better tool if you are playing samples in this manner.

If you are going to play ACIDized loops, then instead of using Cyclone, you could choose to use the Groove Clip Loop Tool. Groove Clips have many advantages over files in Cyclone. However, there are some good reasons to use Cyclone:

- You can change the pitch of whole loops (without changing the tempo of the loop) on the fly.
- You can edit the order of the slices in Cyclone with a simple click-and-drag operation.
- You can create copies of slices by holding down the Ctrl key when you click and drag.
- You can split one loop into several elements (for instance, kick drums, snare drums, hi-hats, and so on). Each element can then be sent to a separate audio output and be treated differently.

Using Cyclone

Let's take a look at Cyclone. Figure 34.1 shows its interface.

Pads

In the top center of Cyclone's interface you will see 16 Pads. On each Pad you can load a loop, trigger it, and tweak it. Take a look at Figure 34.2, which shows the Pad's controls.

As you can see, there are controls to load, trigger, mute, solo, pan, and adjust the volume. In addition, with the Loop button, you can select whether the sample plays once or loops, and with the Sync button, you can decide whether the loop is synchronized to the Project's tempo (which you would normally want to do).

Pad Inspector

Once you have loaded a sample into a Pad, it will show up in the Loop Bin (which is discussed in a moment). You can also tweak the loop in the Pad Inspector. To access

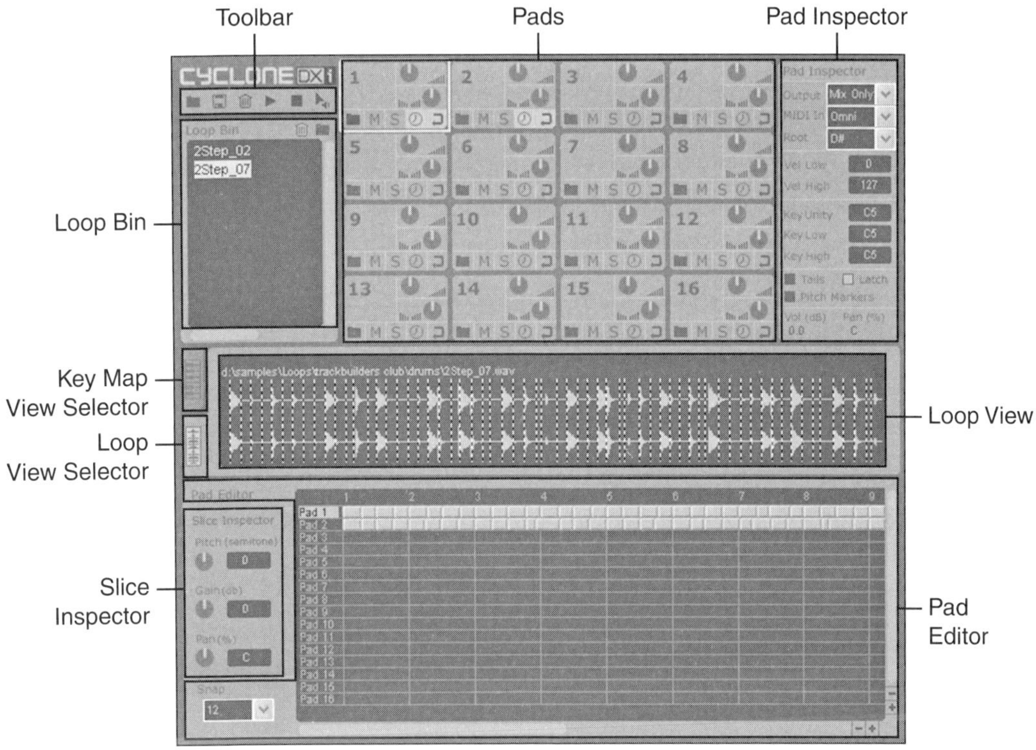

Figure 34.1 Cyclone.

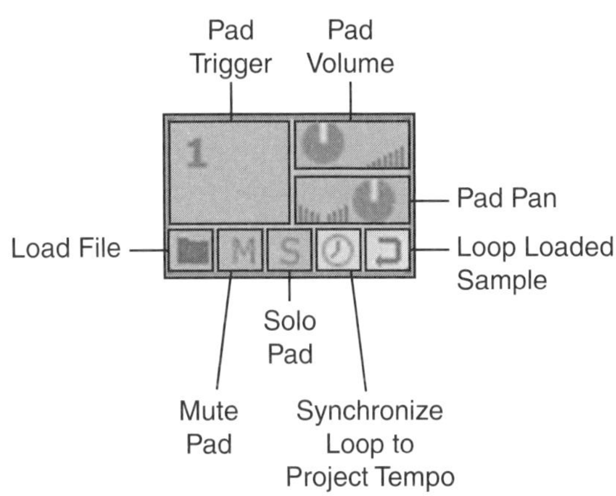

Figure 34.2 A Pad in Cyclone.

the Pad Inspector for a specific Pad, you need to click on the corresponding Pad (much like when you want to access a Track Inspector).

From the Pad Inspector you can select:

- **Output.** Cyclone is a multi-out synthesizer: The audio output channel for each Pad is selected from the Output drop-down menu. If Mix Only is selected, the output is sent to the master output.
- **MIDI In.** MIDI In sets the MIDI channel for the Pad. Each Pad can have a different MIDI channel.
- **Root.** The Root is read from the file when it is loaded. You can adjust this setting from the drop-down menu. The Root setting is used in conjunction with pitch markers (which are explained in a moment).
- **Vel Low and Vel High.** These two controls set the minimum and maximum limits on the MIDI velocity range to which the Pad will respond.
- **Key Unity.** Key Unity selects the MIDI note at which the loop will play without its pitch being changed.
- **Key Low and Key High.** The Key Low and Key High controls select the lowest and highest note to which the Pad will respond. Any pitch transposition is then calculated by reference to the Key Unity setting. You can also adjust the Key Unity, Key Low, and Key High settings on the Key Map (see Figure 34.3).
- **Tails.** The Tails switch increases the length of the slices. When this feature is engaged, you will see that the slices in the Pad Inspector turn from green to blue.
- **Latch.** When the Latch mode is engaged and the Pad is triggered, it will continue to play after the trigger has been released. If the Pad has Loop mode selected, then the Pad will play indefinitely. You can trigger the Pad for a second time to switch off a latched loop.
- **Pitch Markers.** Cyclone recognizes pitch markers embedded in ACIDized files. When the Pitch Markers option is engaged, Cyclone will follow the pitch markers set in SONAR. Unfortunately, this feature is not present in Project5.

Toolbar

From the toolbar (see Figure 34.4), you can:

- Load a .cyc file (a Cyclone bank file).
- Save a .cyc file (a Cyclone bank file). This will save all of the current Pads and their settings.

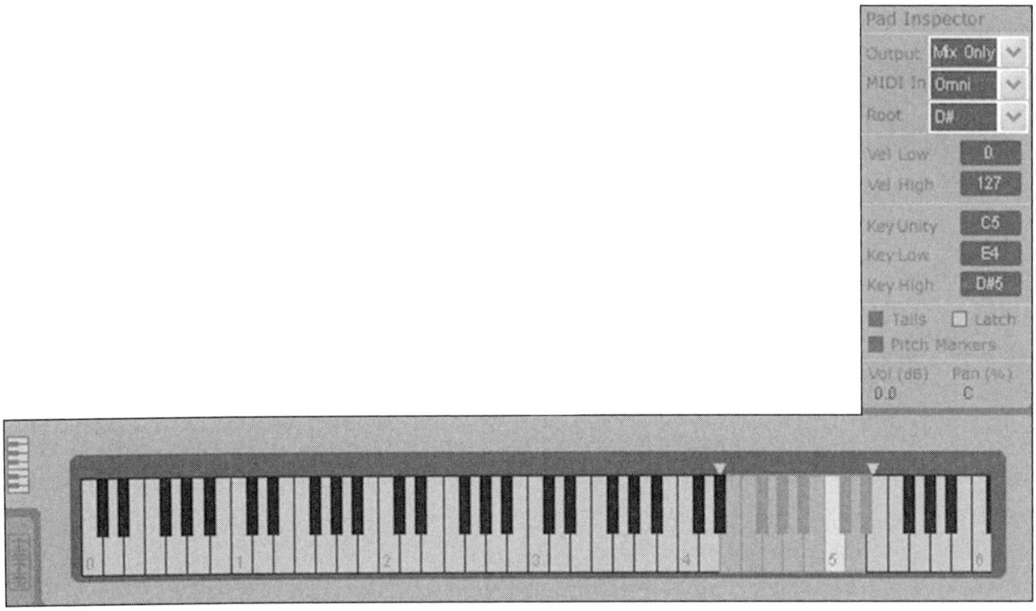

Figure 34.3 The Key Map view shows the Key Unity key (which is highlighted on the keyboard view) and the Key Low and Key High settings, which are indicated by the downward arrowheads above the keyboard.

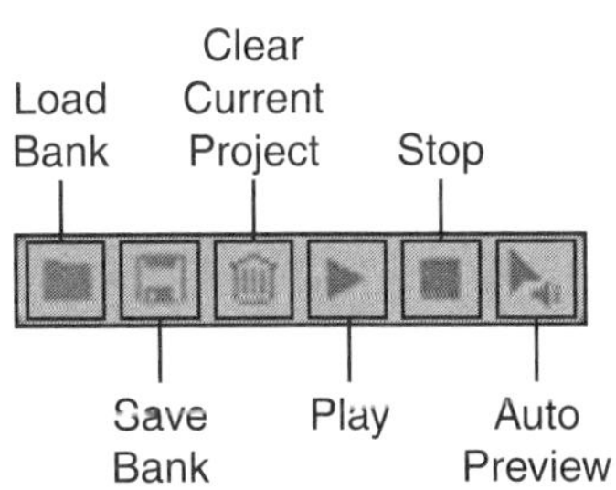

Figure 34.4 The toolbar.

- Clear all of the currently loaded loops and set Cyclone to its default setting.
- Play the currently selected loop in the Loop Bin.
- Stop playback of the currently playing loop in the Loop Bin.
- Select Auto Preview mode. When this mode is selected, you can preview single slices in the Pad Editor by clicking on them.

Loop Bin

The Loop Bin shows all currently loaded loops, whether they were loaded directly into the Loop Bin by clicking on the Load button to the top-right of the Bin or they were loaded directly into a Pad.

If you select a loop by clicking on it and then hit the trashcan to the right of the top bar of the Loop Bin, then that loop will be removed from the Loop Bin. If the loop is currently assigned to a Pad, then the Pad will be reset too.

To assign a loop in the Loop Bin to a Pad (so that you can trigger and manipulate the loop), click on it in the Loop Bin and drag it to the appropriate Pad.

Pad Editor

The Loop view has no function other than displaying the currently selected Pad's waveform and showing the selected slice (if one is selected). To preview a single slice, you must engage Auto Preview mode on the toolbar and then click on individual slices. To preview a whole loop, click on the appropriate Pad (obviously).

The Loop view does have one useful function: You can drag a slice from it to the Pad Editor. You don't have to drag your slice from the Pad's current loop—for instance, you could select a loop in the Loop Bin (which hasn't been assigned to a Pad) and drag a slice from that.

In the Pad Editor, you can:

- Move slices by clicking and dragging them. The Snap Control (to the bottom left) applies quantization to the moving.
- Copy slices by Ctrl+clicking and dragging them. The Snap Control plays its part again.
- Delete slices by selecting them (clicking on them) and hitting the Delete key.

Slice Inspector

When you have selected an individual slice in the Pad Editor, then the Slice Inspector (see Figure 34.5) allows you to transform the slice in three ways:

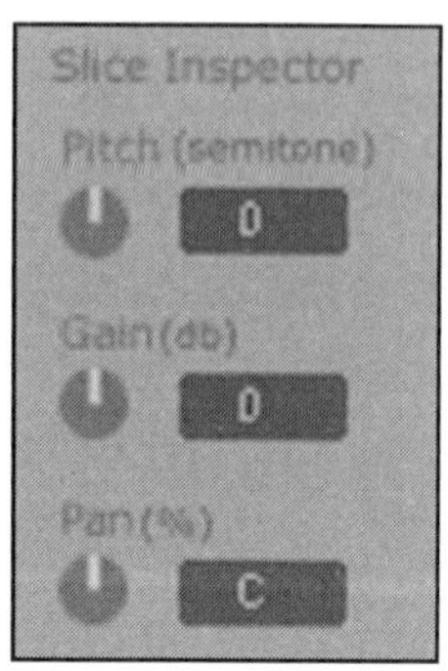

Figure 34.5 The Slice Inspector.

- **Pitch.** The Pitch Knob allows you to adjust the pitch (in semitones) over a range of +/–24 semitones (two octaves).
- **Gain.** The Gain Control allows you to adjust the level of the slice.
- **Pan.** The Pan Control allows you to set the placement of the slice in the stereo spectrum.

Tutorial 35: Introducing Dimension LE

Dimension LE is a new synthesizer that was introduced with Project5 version 2.5. This alone is reason to install the version 2.5 update. Dimension LE is also included with SONAR Home Studio 6XL and SONAR (version 7).

What Is Dimension LE and What Does It Do?

Dimension LE is a four-Element sample-based synthesizer. Each Element can work as a separate synth, which allows you to create complex and detailed sounds. As well as being a highly specified synthesizer, Dimension LE is also a pretty nifty loop-playback device.

Dimension LE is Dimension Pro with a simplified interface and with a cut-down soundset. The simplified interface keeps many of the editing controls—the Envelopes, the LFOs, the EQs, and the Element FX units—hidden. The functions are still available, but they are not directly accessible through the user interface. However, it comes with a large range of presets, making it a very capable sound-creation tool.

Dimension LE is more than just a high-quality playback machine. For instance:

- Dimension LE is built on the same technology as Cakewalk's other flagship synthesizer, Rapture. This same technology (the SFZ Expression Engine) is also used in DropZone, Session Drummer II, and the SFZ player. This means that Dimension LE can load soundsets (in other words, waveforms) from these other synthesizers. Dimension LE can also load any soundest in SFZ format, including SFZ loops.
- Dimension LE can load programs from Dimension and Dimension Pro. Cakewalk has released, and appears to be continuing to release, a wide range of soundsets and programs that can be readily loaded into Dimension LE (although some programs require the full soundsets that are available for Dimension Pro to be available).
- Dimension LE can load REX-format loops (as well as SFZ loops). Both loop formats generate beat information that can be dragged into Project5 and manipulated like other Clips.

- Although the interface doesn't allow you to access all of the controls directly, you can still get at them by using the automation controls and by creating your own SFZ files. You can read more about creating and editing SFZ files in *Cakewalk Synthesizers: From Presets to Power User*.

Using Dimension LE

Figure 35.1 shows Dimension LE.

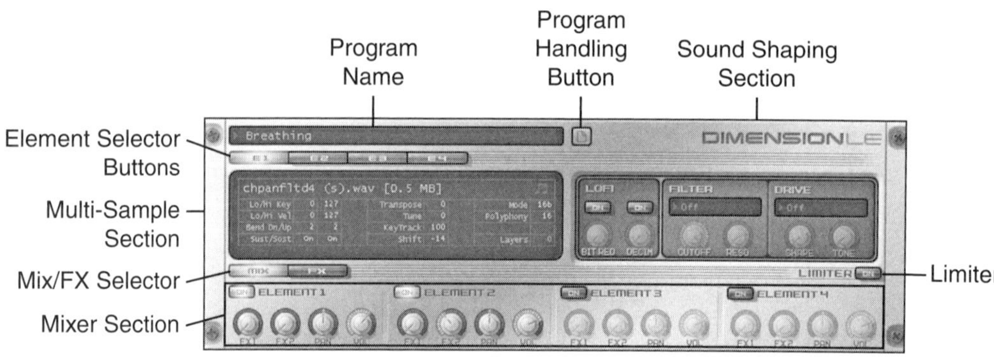

Figure 35.1 Dimension LE.

Adjusting the Controls

Most controls in Dimension LE are fairly straightforward: You can click and drag a knob or value display, or click on a value to step through the options. However, there are a few things that may not be immediately obvious:

- Many options are available from drop-down menus. These are indicated by an arrowhead. Click on the arrowhead to access the drop-down menu.
- You can double-click on a knob/value to reset it.
- When dragging values, Ctrl+drag makes large changes.
- You can adjust the knob or value that has focus (that is, the last edited control) from your computer keyboard (or your mouse wheel). The available controls are:
  - Left/right arrow keys make fine adjustments.
  - Up/down arrow keys (and the mouse wheel) make regular adjustments.
  - Page up/page down keys make large adjustments.

Loading Programs

To load a program, click on the current program name (if there is none loaded, it will show Empty Program). The Program Browser (see Figure 35.2) will then open.

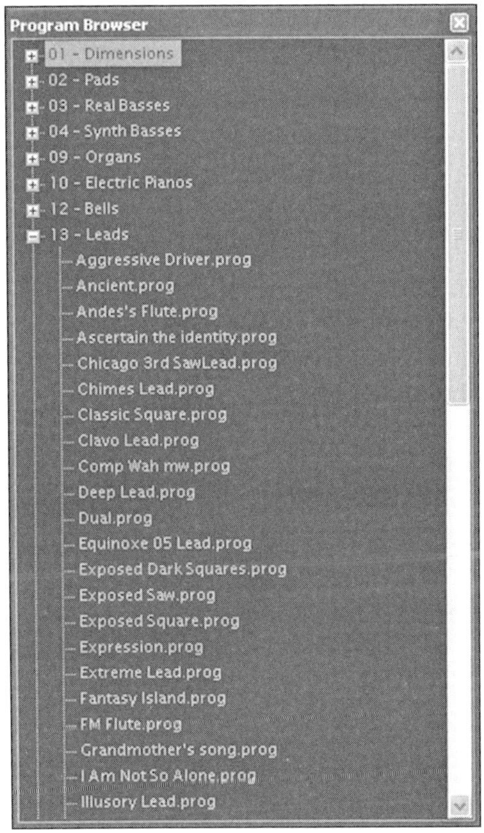

Figure 35.2 The Program Browser in Dimension LE.

You can also click on the recent program's arrowhead (to the left of the program's name) to see a drop-down list of the eight most recently opened programs.

The Program Browser is arranged as an expanding tree with the programs grouped by category. To open a category, click on the plus (+) sign to the left of the category's name. Once the category has expanded to show all of the programs within it, clicking on the plus sign a second time will close the branch.

To load a program, double-click on its name in the Program Browser.

All of your programs are stored in a folder called Programs in your Dimension LE folder. You can reorganize the categories and the categorization of your programs by reordering the content of this folder with Windows Explorer. If you reorganize this folder, open up the Program Browser and hit F5 to refresh its view. The refresh will take a moment or two, but once completed you will see the reorganized files.

To the left of the program's name is an arrowhead. If you click on this, a drop-down menu will appear, showing the eight most recently loaded programs (which you can then select by clicking on them).

Multi-Sample Section

The Multi-Sample section is the sound source in Dimension LE. Most of the controls in the Multi-Sample section are there for display purposes only. If you want to adjust these settings, then you need to access the program through Dimension Pro (or Dimension).

To load a sound, click on the name of the current wave. If no wave is loaded, this will show Empty. When you click on the name, a browser will open, and you can navigate to the WAV you want to load.

Loading SFZ/REX Loops

SFZ and REX loops contain two Elements (although you just load one file):

- The beats, cut into individual slices.
- A MIDI file with the timing information for when the beats should be triggered. When replayed, the MIDI file triggers the individual slices to reconstruct the beat.

The first time in any session with Dimension LE that you load an SFZ/REX loop, you will see a message pop up (see Figure 35.3). This pop-up highlights some musical notes at the end of the waveform's name. You can click and drag these notes into the Arrange Pane, and a MIDI file will be dropped. This MIDI file is a regular Clip that can be edited in the normal way. The purpose of the Clip is to trigger the slices in the loop.

Element Buttons

Each Element works independently within Dimension LE and can be selected by clicking on its corresponding Element Selector button (just under the program's name). If you right-click on an Element Selector button, a pop-up menu will appear (see Figure 35.4).

There are eight options on the menu:

- **Unload Element.** This removes the current Multi-Sample (in other words, the sound source) but leaves all of the other controls unaffected in the Element. If

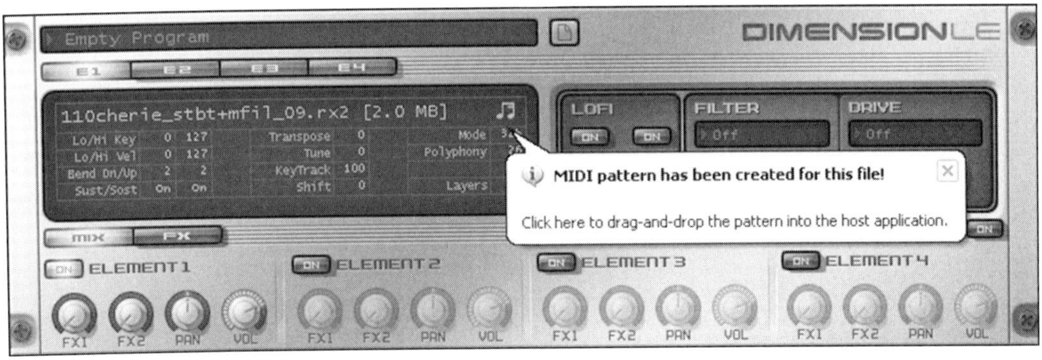

Figure 35.3 When you load an SFZ/REX loop, a MIDI Pattern file is created, which you can drag and drop into Project5.

Figure 35.4 The Element Selector button menu.

you load another Multi-Sample, it will adopt the setting left when the previous Multi-Sample was unloaded. This may be particularly useful in Dimension LE because you cannot readily access the Element settings.

- **Reset Element.** The Reset Element command removes the current Multi-Sample and resets all of the other controls in the Element to their default.
- **Load Element.** Load Element allows you to load a saved Element.
- **Save Element As.** Save Element As allows you to save an Element. This stores all of the Element's settings, such as the filter and bit-reducer settings as well as the Multi-Sample settings. It also stores those Element settings that you cannot readily see on Dimension LE's interface.
- **Copy Element.** Copy Element allows you to copy the Element to the clipboard.
- **Paste Element.** Paste Element allows you to paste a copied Element into another Element.

- **Paste Element FX.** It is not obvious from Dimension LE's interface, but each Element has its own FX unit—these are explained in more detail in the next tutorial, which covers Dimension (where the FX units are exposed). Paste Element FX allows you to paste a copied Element's FX settings into another Element.
- **Chain to Next Element.** Chain to Next Element chains one Element to the next Element. The advantage of this approach is that two Elements can be sent into one FX unit. (The shared FX unit will be the one in the Element to which the first is chained.) Another way to view this arrangement is that one Multi-Sample can have up to four FX units run in series.

Sound Shaping Section

There are three main elements in the Sound Shaping section:

- The LoFi unit
- The Filter section
- The Drive unit

Let's look at them individually.

Bit Red and Decim. In the LoFi unit, the Bit Red and Decim Knobs control the bit rate and sample rate, respectively. When you switch on either of these and push their knobs, the signal is degraded. Check out Tutorial 43: Introducing Alias Factor, which explains the effect of these two transformations in greater detail.

The Filter Section. The Filter section has two main controls:

- **Cutoff.** The Cutoff Knob sets the cutoff frequency of the filter.
- **Reso.** The Reso Knob sets the resonance of the filter (if a resonant filter has been selected).

The third control in the Filter section (above the two knobs) is the Filter Selector drop-down menu, which is accessed by clicking on the arrowhead to the left of the filter's name. You can also left-click and right-click on the filter to cycle forward and back through the filter choices.

The filter choices are:

- **Low-Pass filters:** 1 pole (6-dB/octave) no resonance, 2 pole (12-dB/octave), 4 pole (24-dB/octave), and 6 pole (36-dB/octave).
- **High-Pass filters:** 1 pole (6-dB/octave) no resonance, 2 pole (12-dB/octave), 4 pole (24-dB/octave), and 6 pole (36-dB/octave).

- **Band-Pass filters:** 1 pole (6-dB/octave) no resonance and 2 pole (12-dB/octave).
- **Band-Reject (notch) filters:** 1 pole (6-dB/octave) no resonance and 2 pole (12-dB/octave).
- **All-Pass filter:** 1 pole (6-dB/octave). This filter is most commonly used to introduce sub-sample delays to shift the phase of a waveform.
- **Peak filter:** 2 pole (12-dB/octave). The Peak filter works rather like an EQ unit to boost the signal around the cutoff frequency.
- **Pink:** The Pink filter has the effect of creating a slight darkening of the tone without affecting the sound character too much.
- **Comb:** The Comb filter works by adding a slightly delayed version of a signal to itself, which causes phase cancellations.

The Drive Unit. The Drive unit offers five different drive units.

- Tube
- Soft
- Mid
- Hard
- Asymmetric

These are selectable from a drop-down menu accessed by clicking on the arrowhead to the left of the current unit's name. Alternatively, you can left-click or right-click on the currently selected unit to step up and down through the options.

Each of the five units has a slightly different character. Once you have selected the unit, there are two controls to then shape the sound in the Drive section:

- **Shape.** The Shape Knob controls the amount of distortion. As the knob is turned to the right, the distortion is increased.
- **Tone.** The Tone Knob controls the tone. As it is increased (turned to the right), the tone is cut.

Mixer Section

In the Mixer section, for each Element you can:

- Switch each Element on and off. When the On button is lit orange, then the Element is active.

- Control the level of the Element with its Vol Knob.
- Control the panning of the Element with its Pan Knob. If a stereo soundset has been loaded into the Multi-Sample, then the Pan Knob works as a balance control.
- Control the amount of each Element that is sent to the two Master FX units with the FX1 and FX2 Knobs.

FX Section

There are two Master FX units in Dimension LE. These are both Send FX units (in other words, the signal from each Element only passes through the units to the extent determined by the FX1 and FX2 Knobs in the Mixer section).

To access the FX section, click on the FX button (next to the Mix button). As Figure 35.5 shows, there are two sections in the Master FX section: FX1, the Modulation FX, and FX2, the Reverb.

Figure 35.5 The Master FX section in Dimension LE.

The Modulation FX section offers a choice of four units:

- Chorus
- Symphonic
- Phaser
- Chorus/Phaser

The Modulation FX units all work in a similar manner by adding a dry signal and a delayed signal that has had its pitch modulated by an LFO. The controls in the Modulation FX section are:

- **Freq.** The Freq Knob sets the speed (rate) of the LFO, which modulates the pitch of the delayed signal.
- **Delay.** The Delay Knob sets the delay time of the delayed signal.
- **Depth.** The Depth Knob sets the amount by which the LFO will modulate the pitch of the delayed signal.
- **FeedB.** The Feedback Knob determines the number of echoes introduced by the delay line.

- **Dry/Wet.** The Dry/Wet Knob balances the clean and effected signals.

The Reverb FX section offers seven reverb algorithms:

- Small Room
- Mid Room
- Large Room
- Small Hall
- Mid Hall
- Large Hall
- Chamber

Once the reverberation algorithm has been selected, there are five controls:

- **Pre Delay.** The Pre Delay Control adds an additional delay to the audio signal before it hits the reverberation algorithm. This can give a more distinct and clearer reverberation sound.
- **Size.** The Size Knob controls the room that the reverb unit is modeling and so has an effect on reverberation time. Larger rooms give the impression of more acoustic space. This control should be adjusted taking account of the selection of the reverb algorithm if you are trying to create a realistic sound.
- **Damp.** The Damp Knob controls how quickly the higher-frequency Elements of the reverberation decay and can give more (or less) ring to the reverb.
- **Tone.** The Tone Control adjusts the tone of the reverberated signal.
- **Dry/Wet.** The Dry/Wet Control determines the balance between clean and reverberation signals.

Program Handling

The Program Handling button accesses some of Dimension LE's utility functions. When you click on the button, you access the Program Handling menu, which is shown in Figure 35.6.

The utilities on the menu are:

- **Initialize Program.** The Initialize Program command clears all of the current Multi-Samples and resets all of the controls to their default settings.

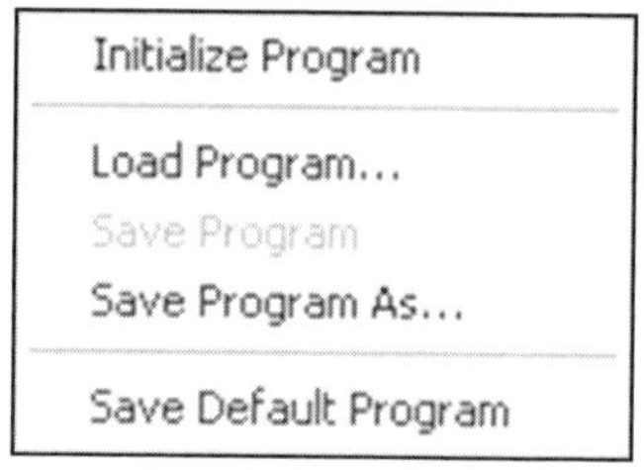

Figure 35.6 The Program Handling menu in Dimension LE.

- **Load Program.** The Load Program command allows you to navigate to a program's location (and load it). This is especially useful if the program is outside of the program's folder and so does not show up in the Program Browser.
- **Save Program.** The Save Program command saves the current program. When this function is invoked, the existing program is overwritten. This function is only available if the current program has been saved. If you are trying to save a program for the first time, you will need to use the Save Program As function.
- **Save Program As.** The Save Program As command allows you to save a new version of the current program. By default, this command will place the new program in your Programs folder; however, you can navigate to any other folder. You can also save a new program within a subfolder in the Programs folder. This subfolder will then become a new category in the Program Browser.
- **Save Default Program.** The Save Default Program command saves the current program as the default program, which will open whenever Dimension Pro is loaded or the Initialize Program function is invoked.

Limiter

The final tool in Dimension LE is the limiter. Switch this on to prevent the audio from exceeding the maximum output level.

Tutorial 36: Introducing Dimension

Dimension was released with Project5 version 2.0. Since then, Dimension LE (with an extended library and additional functionality) and Dimension LE (see Tutorial 35) have both been launched. Dimension is not included with Project5 version 2.5. Like Dimension LE and Dimension Pro, Dimension uses the same technology (the SFZ Expression Engine) that is also used in DropZone, Session Drummer II, and the SFZ player.

What Is Dimension and What Does It Do?

As you can see from Figure 36.1, Dimension has a larger interface and more accessible controls than Dimension LE.

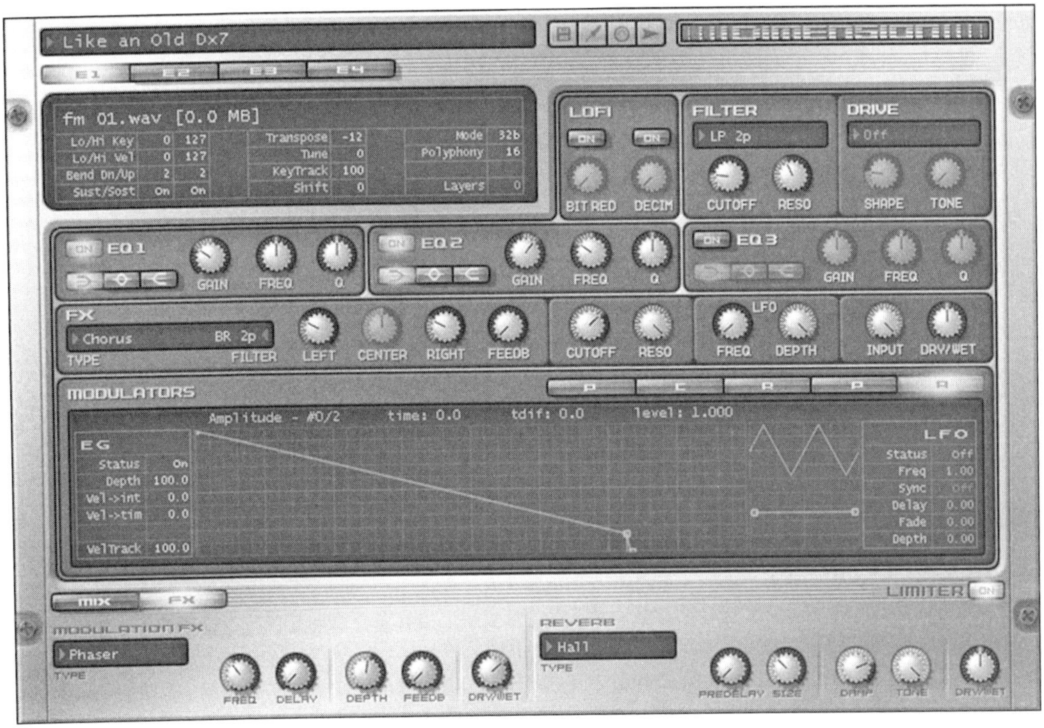

Figure 36.1 Dimension.

Like Dimension LE, Dimension is a four-Element sample-based synthesizer, and each Element can work as a separate synth, allowing you to create complex and detailed sounds. However, there are some key differences between Dimension and Dimension LE beyond a different interface:

- Dimension does not have the facility to load REX and SFZ loops and drag and drop MIDI Clips.
- Dimension gives direct access (on its interface) to all of its controls, such as the Element Multi-Sample section, FX units, EQs, Envelopes, and LFOs.
- Dimension only has two Master Reverb algorithm options: Hall and Room.

One thing to note: Dimension LE will load Dimension and Dimension Pro programs. Dimension will only load Dimension programs and will not load Dimension LE programs or Dimension Pro programs (even if the soundsets are available).

Using Dimension

Since I've already covered Dimension LE, this tutorial will only cover the additional functions that are available in Dimension.

Multi-Sample Section

The Multi-Sample section in Dimension (see Figure 36.2) looks the same as that in Dimension LE. However, there is a key difference: This one actually works. If you click and drag the settings in the Multi-Sample section, you will see that they change. You can, of course, load a waveform in the same way that you would in Dimension LE.

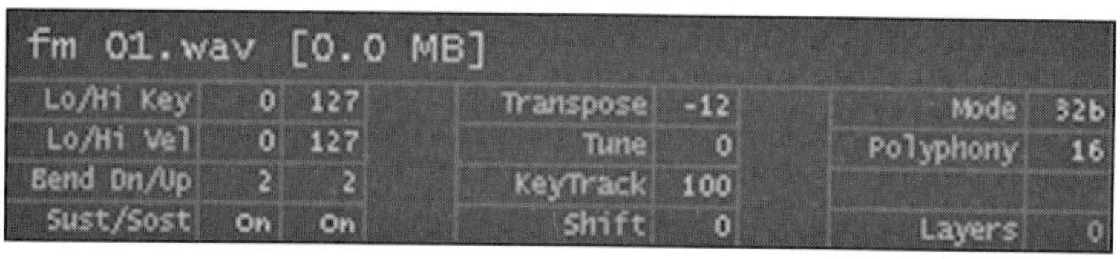

Figure 36.2 The Multi-Sample section in Dimension.

As you can see, the Multi-Sample section gives you a wide range of controls that can be set individually for each Element.

- **Lo/Hi Key.** The Lo/Hi Key Control sets the range over which the Element will respond to incoming MIDI data. Any notes outside of this range will not be recognized and therefore will not sound.
- **Lo/Hi Vel.** The Lo/Hi Vel Control sets the MIDI velocity range over which the Element will respond to incoming MIDI data. Any notes with a MIDI velocity above or below this range will not sound.
- **Bend Dn/Up.** The Bend Dn/Up Control sets the amount (in semitones) by which each Element may have its pitch raised or lowered by the pitch bend wheel.
- **Sust/Sost.** The Sust and Sost Controls are switches that determine whether the Element will respond to MIDI sustain pedal (MIDI CC 64) and MIDI sostenuto pedal (MIDI CC 66) messages.
- **Transpose.** The Transpose Control adjusts the pitch of the Multi-Sample in semitones over a range of +/– 48 semitones (four octaves).
- **Tune.** The Tune Control adjusts the pitch of the Multi-Sample in cents over the range of +/– 100 cents (one semitone).
- **KeyTrack.** The KeyTrack Control determines how the Element responds to MIDI pitch information. When this control is set to zero, the pitch of the

Multi-Sample is controlled by the Transpose and Tune Controls only, regardless of which note is played on the keyboard. When this control is set to 100, each key on the keyboard has a value of 100 cents (in other words, one semitone), so Dimension will respond to the played keys as you would expect.

- **Shift.** The Shift key changes the root key to which the sample is mapped while retaining the key range over which the Multi-Sample is mapped. This retains the tuning but changes the underlying samples and therefore has an effect on the tone. The precise effect is dependent on the source material.
- **Mode.** The Mode Selector determines how the Multi-Sample is loaded into the memory of your computer.
  - When 32b mode is selected, the waves will be converted to 32 bit during loading. This option optimizes performance, but it also uses twice the memory.
  - When 16b mode is selected, the samples are loaded as 16-bit samples. This mode takes half the memory required by 32b mode but increases the CPU overhead as the 16-bit files are converted to 32-bit on playback.
- **Polyphony.** The Polyphony Control sets the number of voices that an Element can play simultaneously. Generally one note equals one layer. However, if you are triggering a Multi-Sample that has several samples mapped to the same key (or keys), you may trigger more than one layer with one note.

  When the Polyphony Control is set to zero, Dimension enters monophonic legato mode. This means that if a key is pressed while an existing key is held, the Envelopes in the program will not be retriggered.
- **Layers.** The Layer display shows how many layers the current Element is playing.

EQ Section

Each Element has a three-band EQ section. Each section within the Element EQ section can be set as:

- A low-shelf EQ, where the signal is cut or boosted below a certain frequency
- A high-shelf EQ, where the signal is cut or boosted above a certain frequency
- A parametric EQ, where a band is cut or boosted at a certain frequency

Parametric EQ is explained in greater detail in Tutorial 49: Introducing Para-Q. Shelf EQ works on a similar principle and has the same controls; however, instead of having a bandwidth, the bandwidth control adjusts the slope.

Figure 36.3 shows the main EQ section controls.

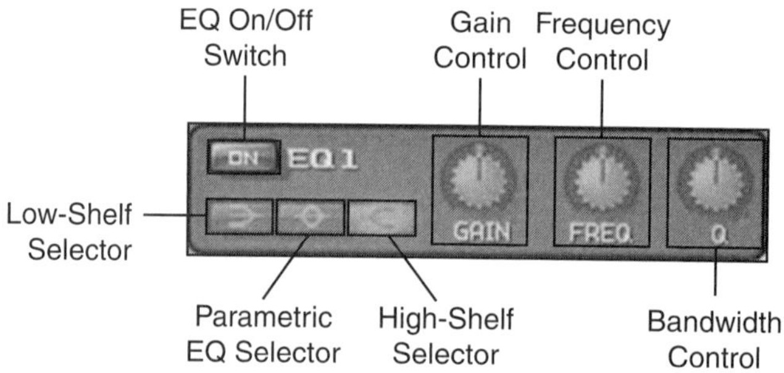

Figure 36.3 The main EQ section controls.

Element FX Section

There are 15 FX units available to each Element in Dimension. These can be selected from the Element drop-down menu in the FX section (see Figure 36.4).

Figure 36.4 The Element FX section drop-down menu.

All of the effects are time-based units. For some units, the delayed signal can have its pitch modulated, and for some units, the tone of the delayed signal can be controlled by a filter. The filter can be selected from the drop-down menu to the right of the FX unit's name—you have the same filter choices as are available in the Filter block. You can read more about time-based effects in Chapter 7.

The controls for all FX units are the same: If a unit does not respond to a specific control, then that knob is grayed out. The controls in the FX section are:

- **Left, Center, and Right.** The Left, Center, and Right Knobs determine the delay time for the left, center, and right audio channels. These delay times are set as a division of the beat of the Project5's tempo.

- **FeedB.** The Feedback Knob controls the number of times the delayed signal is repeated.
- **Cutoff and Reso.** The Cutoff and Reso Knobs set the cutoff frequency and the amount of resonance in a filter, if one of the filters is selected.
- **Freq and Depth.** The Freq Control sets the speed of any low-frequency oscillator (LFO), modulating the pitch of the delayed signal. The Depth Control determines how much the delayed signal is modulated by the LFO.
- **Input.** The Input Control can attenuate the incoming audio signal.
- **Dry/Wet.** The Dry/Wet Control balances the dry signal with the effected signal.

Modulators Section

In the Modulators section (see Figure 36.5), for each Element you will find a dedicated:

- Envelope
- LFO
- Key Tracking Control

for each of the following:

- Pitch
- Filter cutoff frequency

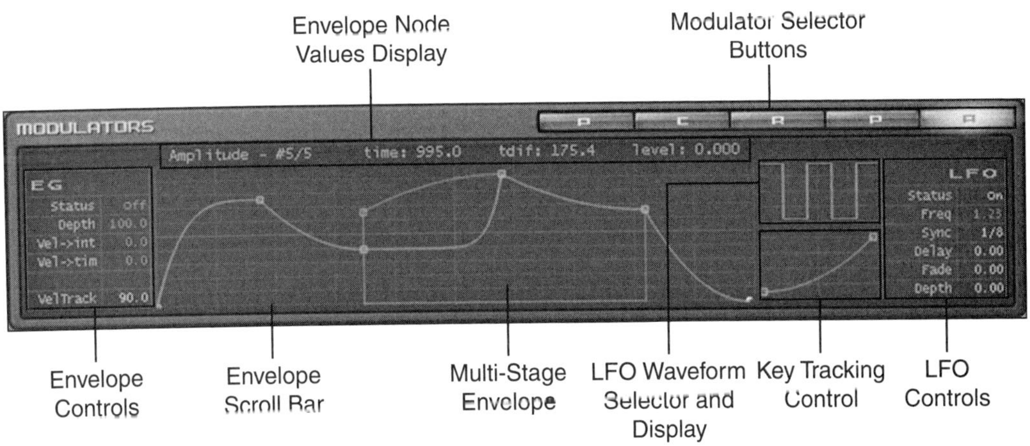

Figure 36.5 The Modulators section in Dimension. The Envelope includes sustain and loop points, which are discussed later in the section headed "Modulators Section: Setting Envelope Loop and Sustain Nodes."

- Filter resonance
- Panning (or balance for stereo Multi-Samples)
- Amplitude (volume)

In other words, there are five modulation sections for each Element.

To use a modulator, select the appropriate destination (from the Modulator Selector button) and then set the appropriate modulator (whether that is an Envelope, LFO, or key tracking).

Modulators Section: Envelopes

Dimension uses multi-stage Envelopes. This means you are not limited to a conventional ADSR (or other) setup.

To create an Envelope, right-click on the Envelope window and add a Node. You can then drag the Node to the appropriate time/level. If you need another Node, repeat the process. If you hold your mouse cursor over a Node, then in the Node Values display, you will see:

- The Node number/the total number of Nodes.
- Time. The time of the Node (in milliseconds). You can shift and drag Nodes to make fine adjustments.
- Tdif. The time elapsed to the current Node since the last Node.
- Level. The relative level of the Node (in percentage terms).

If you want to place a Node outside of the bounds of the Envelope window, then you can drag the Envelope scroll bar (which is the bar underneath the Multi-Stage Envelope display) to reach the areas of the Envelope outside of the main view. You can also use the mouse wheel to zoom in and out of the Modulator window.

When you add a Node, it will be joined to the previous and next Nodes (as appropriate) by a curve (which is usually a fairly straight line). You can change the curve (and therefore change how the level of the Envelope changes over time) by clicking and dragging the curve.

Once you have added the Nodes you need, then you can control how the Envelope behaves with the Envelope Controls section. Before I discuss this, I want to look at some of the additional Envelope features.

Modulators Section: Setting Envelope Loop and Sustain Points

You can set a Node to act as a sustain point. This means that when the Envelope reaches the sustain point, its level will remain constant (at the level of the sustain Node). Any Nodes after the sustain point will act as the release section, so you will hear them play when the key is released.

To set a Node to be a sustain Node:

1. Select the Node by clicking on it (or hovering the mouse pointer over it).
2. Hit the S key on your keyboard.

You will see a vertical orange line under the Node, indicating that it is a sustain Node.

Once you have set a sustain point on your Envelope, you can also set up a loop. The loop will make an Envelope work much like an LFO and keep repeating until you release the key.

To set up a loop:

1. Set a sustain Node in your Envelope by selecting it and hitting the S key.
2. Select the Node at the beginning of the loop (which must come before the sustain point) by clicking on the Node.
3. Hit the L key on your keyboard.

You can have as many or as few Nodes as you want between the loop Node and the sustain Node.

Once you have set your loop Node, an orange box will appear that contains the loop Node and the sustain Node. Whatever level you have set the loop Node to be will be overridden when you set the loop Node to act as a loop Node—the level of the loop Node (from the start of the second loop) will be equal to the sustain Node level (otherwise there would be a level jump on looping). The sustain and loop Nodes were both shown in Figure 36.5.

Modulators Section: Envelope Segment Scaling

Once you have set your Nodes, you can control each segment (in other words, the gaps between the Nodes) so that they play more quickly or more slowly, depending on the pitch of the note that is played (key scaling) or the velocity of the note that is played (velocity scaling).

- To activate key-scaling mode, click on the K key on your keyboard.
- To activate velocity-scaling mode, click on the V key on your keyboard.

When key- or velocity-scaling mode is activated, then you can drag a segment (in the same way that you would drag a curve to change its shape). The scaling is indicated by a bar against the segment. Key scaling is shown by a blue bar, and velocity scaling is denoted by an orange bar. You can set positive or negative scaling so the segment will play faster or slower than is set by the Nodes' spacing. It would have been nice to include an image here, but with the grayscale reproduction, the graphic would not have reproduced clearly. If you go to Dimension, you will see the bars are faint but clear.

Modulators Section: Envelope Controls

The Envelope Controls section is to the left of the Multi-Stage Envelope view. There are five controls in the section:

- **Status.** The Status switch turns the Envelope on and off. When the Envelope is switched off, its settings have no effect.
- **Depth.** The Depth setting controls the extent to which the Envelope affects its destination. The range of Depth settings is dependent on the modulation destination.
    - For the Amp Envelope, the Depth has a scale of +/–100%.
    - For the Pitch Envelope, the Depth has a scale of +/–2,400 cents (in other words, two octaves).
    - For the Cut-Off Envelope, the Depth has a scale of +/–13,700 cents.
    - For the Resonance Envelope, the Depth has a scale of +/–40 dB.
    - For the Pan Envelope, the Depth has a scale of +/–100%.
- **Vel -> Int.** The Vel -> Int Control sets the extent to which MIDI velocity affects the initial level of the Envelope.
- **Vel -> Tim.** The Vel -> Tim setting controls the extent to which velocity affects the time of all Nodes.
- **VelTrack.** The VelTrack setting controls the extent to which MIDI velocity affects the Envelope's output level. When set to zero, the Envelope level will not be affected by velocity. When set to 100, the amplitude of the Envelope is fully controlled by MIDI velocity. This function has effect even when the Envelope Status is set to Off.

Modulators Section: LFOs

In the Modulators section, there is an LFO for each Envelope.

The LFO Waveform Selector and Display shows the currently selected LFO waveform and its phase. You can left-click or right-click on the LFO wave shape display to nudge forward or backward through the LFO waveform choices, or you can use the mouse wheel. You can control the phase of the LFO (in other words, where in its cycle the LFO starts) by Shift-clicking and dragging the waveform.

The LFO Controls section is to the right of the Multi-Stage Envelope view. There are six controls in the section:

- **Status.** The Status switch turns the LFO on and off.
- **Freq.** The Frequency Control sets the speed of the LFO when it is not synchronized to the tempo of the Project. The width of the LFO waveform display will change, depending on the frequency selected.
- **Sync.** The Sync option allows the LFO to be synchronized to the tempo of the Project. You can left-click or right-click on the value displayed to nudge up or down through the options. The tempo sync choices are 16, 8, 4, 2, 1, 1/2, 1/4, and 1/8 beats for each LFO cycle, plus all triplet and dotted values. When set to Off, the LFO frequency is set by the Frequency Control.
- **Delay.** The Delay Control sets the time between the note being struck and the LFO starting its cycle.
- **Fade.** The Fade Control sets the time, after the Delay phase has been completed, over which the LFO fades in. The LFO reaches its full value at the end of the fade time.
- **Depth.** The Depth Control sets the amount of effect that the LFO has on its destination. Like the Envelope Depth Control, the LFO Depth Control can be set over different ranges, depending on the modulation destination.

Modulators Section: Key Tracking

After the Envelope and the LFO, each Modulators section is finished off with the Key Tracking Control. The Key Tracking Control allows the modulation destination to be controlled with pitch information, so, for instance, you can open up the filter when you play higher on the keyboard, mimicking the behavior of real instruments. The Key Tracking Control is not available in the Pitch Modulation section (since the Element responds to pitch information by default).

There are three settings on the Key Tracking Control:

- **Left Node.** The left Node adjusts how lower key ranges affect the destination.
- **Right Node.** The right Node adjusts how higher key ranges affect the destination.
- **Curve.** The Curve Control adjusts the transition between the left and right Nodes.

When a Node is raised above the midpoint, it will have a positive effect on the modulation destination. When a Node is lowered below the midpoint, it will have a negative effect on the destination. By default, the Nodes are set to their midpoint, so the Key Tracking has no effect.

You can adjust both Nodes simultaneously by using the up and down arrows on your keyboard.

Utility Buttons

Next to the program name, there is a row of utility buttons (see Figure 36.6). The functions underlying these buttons will be discussed in the following sections.

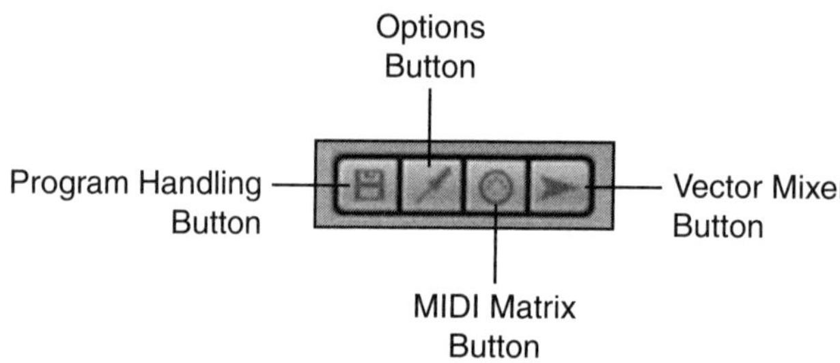

Figure 36.6 The utility buttons in Dimension.

Program Handling Button

The Program Handling button opens up a very similar option to the one in Dimension LE. However, there are two new options:

- Load Element
- Save Element

These options are both available on the Element button's pop-up menu in Dimension LE and have the same function as those options.

Options Window

The Options window (see Figure 36.7) gives you two choices:

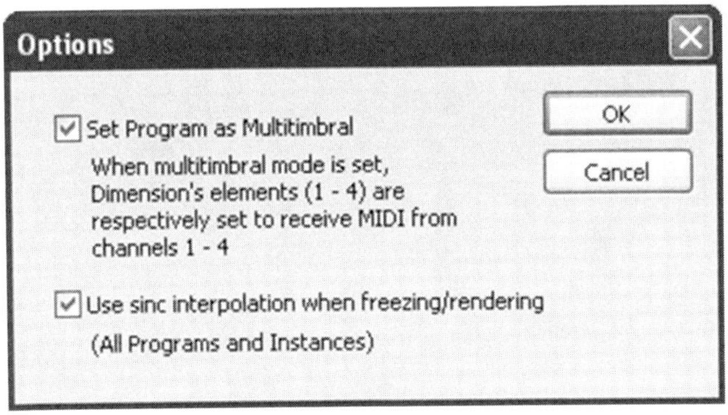

Figure 36.7 The Options window.

- Set Program as Multitimbral
- Use Sinc Interpolation When Freezing/Rendering

When Multitimbral mode is selected:

- Element 1 is addressed by MIDI channel 1.
- Element 2 is addressed by MIDI channel 2.
- Element 3 is addressed by MIDI channel 3.
- Element 4 is addressed by MIDI channel 4.

Check out Tutorial 12 to read more about multi-timbral operation and how to set Project5 to control multi-timbral Instruments.

Sinc interpolation is a special high-quality mode that can be called up when freezing a track or mixing down a whole Project. You should check this option when you want to get the highest-quality sound. Switching on Sinc Interpolation mode does not make any difference to normal playing, but freezing and rendering may take slightly longer due to the additional calculations involved with the higher-quality setting.

Sinc interpolation is a global option and is applied to all programs and all instances of Dimension in the current Project.

MIDI Matrix

If you haven't had enough modulation with the Envelopes, LFOs, and Key Tracking, then open up the MIDI Matrix (see Figure 36.8).

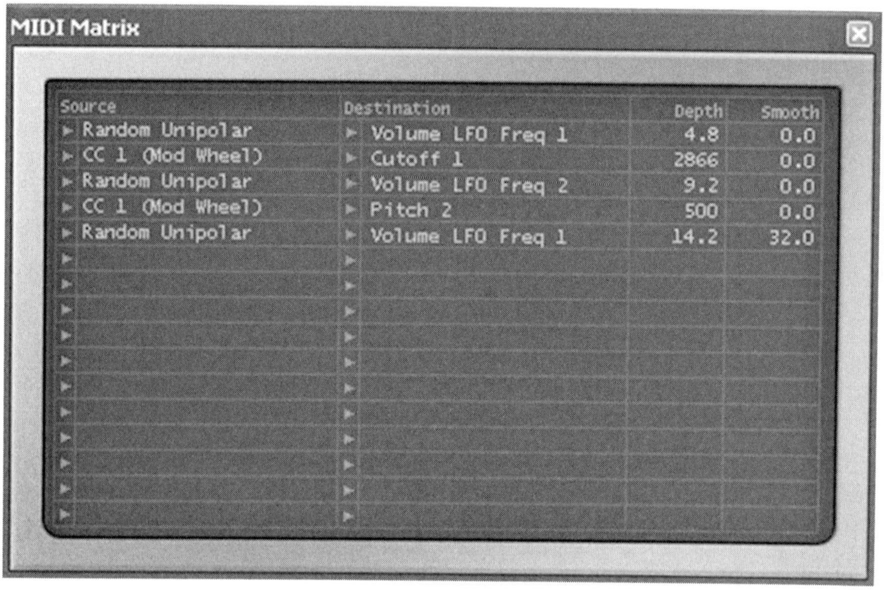

Figure 36.8 The MIDI Matrix.

The MIDI Matrix allows MIDI data to directly control a range of (well, most) modulation destinations. For instance, you could set your modulation wheel to control a filter's cutoff frequency, or you could set a MIDI CC to control the gain on an EQ setting.

The MIDI Matrix has four columns:

- **Source.** From the Source drop-down menu, you select the modulation source (in other words, what you will control, such as a modulation wheel).
- **Destination.** From the Destination drop-down menu, you select the modulation destination (in other words, the control on the synthesizer that will be changed by the modulation source).
- **Depth.** The Depth Control sets the amount by which the source will modulate the destination.
- **Smooth.** The Smooth Control removes some of the spikes when the source controls the destination and slows down the effect of the modulation.

Vector Mixer

The Vector Mixer (see Figure 36.9) allows you to mix the volumes of the four Elements in real time.

Each Element has a corner. When the cursor is in that corner, the Element will be heard at its full volume. As the cursor is dragged away from the corner, the volume

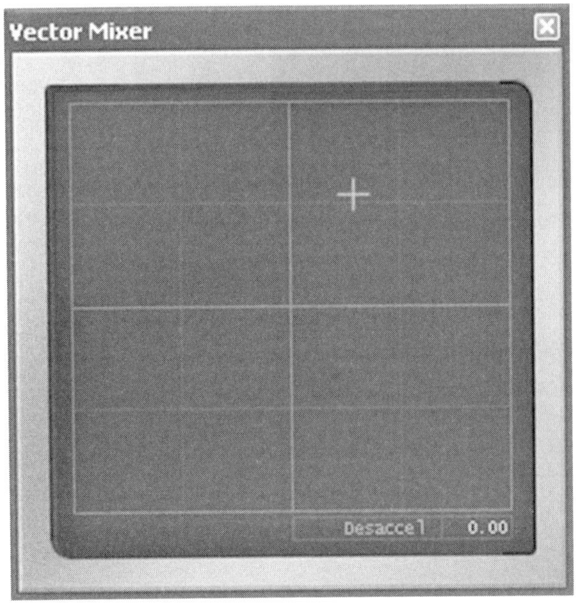

Figure 36.9 The Vector Mixer.

of the Element will fall. When the cursor is in the middle of the Vector Mixer, the volumes of the four Elements are at the level set by each Element's Volume Control in the Mixer section.

The corners assigned to each Element are:

- **Element 1.** The bottom-left corner.
- **Element 2.** The bottom-right corner.
- **Element 3.** The top-left corner.
- **Element 4.** The top-right corner.

You can set the Desaccel field to slow the response of the Vector Mixer. Higher values give a slower response.

Tutorial 37: Introducing DS864

DS864 is a sample-based synthesizer that comes with Project5 version 2.0, but has been dropped from version 2.5.

What Is DS864 and What Does It Do?

DS864 (see Figure 37.1) is a sample-based synthesizer that can load samples in many different formats, including common formats such as Akai S5000 and S6000 formats,

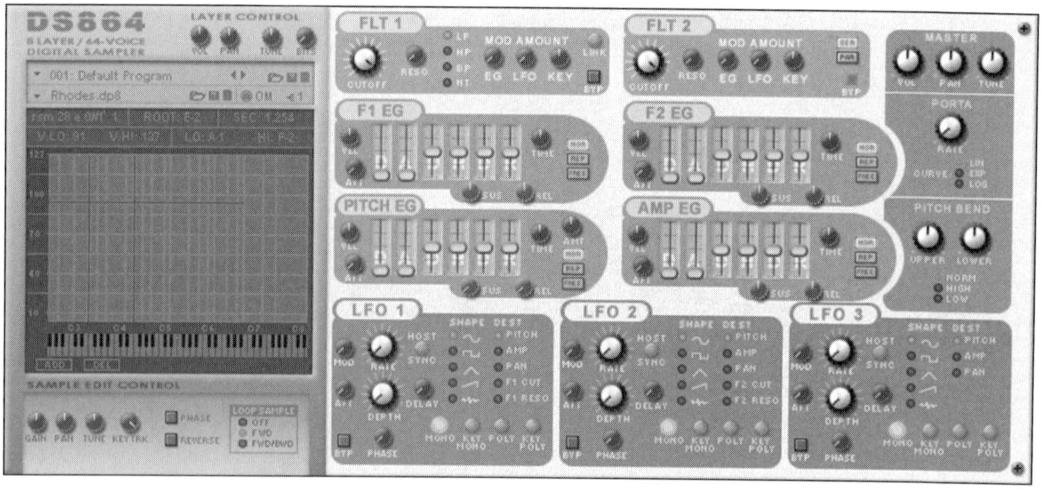

Figure 37.1 DS864 sample-based synthesizer.

SoundFont banks, and WAV and AIFF files. Samples can be mapped (and any preset mappings edited), and then the samples can be processed with a range of synthesis tools, including:

- Two filters (one multi-mode)
- Four dedicated Envelopes (for pitch, volume, and one for each filter)
- Three assignable LFOs

DS864 is also both multi-timbral and multi-output, so you can create very complex programs. Alternatively, you can layer up your sound to create rich and detailed patches.

DS864 comes with a range of sample material that includes:

- Pianos (acoustic and electric) as well as other keyboards
- Choirs
- Basses
- Orchestral sounds
- Synthetic sounds

Using DS864

Let's take a look around DS864.

Loading and Saving Sounds

DS864's included sample material comes in two forms:

- **Sampler Programs (dp8 format files).** Sampler Programs can be loaded into each layer. A multi-sample, its mapping, its MIDI options, and its synthesis settings are stored as a layer. You can load dp8 programs or import other file formats into a layer.
- **Sampler Banks (ds8 format files).** Sampler Banks are collections of programs/layers. A group of layers is called a *program* (which is different from a Sampler Program). A program consists of up to eight layers, and a Sampler Bank can include up to 128 programs.

In DS864 you cannot store programs (remember, programs are groups of layers). You have to store either individual layers (as Sampler Programs) or whole banks (as Sampler Banks).

Figure 37.2 shows the controls to load and save layers, programs, and banks.

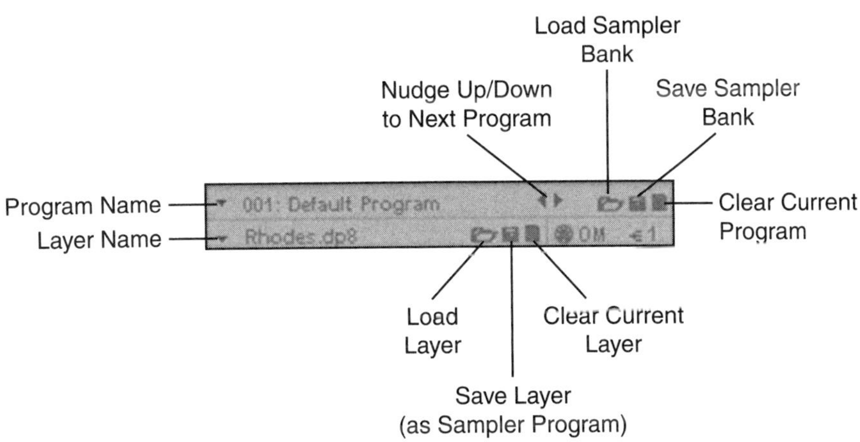

Figure 37.2 The loading and saving controls in DS864.

To change a program's name, double-click on its current name. A window will appear, into which you can insert the new program name.

Layer Controls

You can select a layer by clicking on the drop-down menu next to the layer's name. The Layer drop-down menu will show the eight layer slots. You can control each layer with the Layer Controls (see Figure 37.3), which are above the Load and Save

Figure 37.3 The Layer Controls.

Controls. These controls give you four knobs:

- **Volume.** The Volume Control sets the volume of the layer.
- **Pan.** The Pan Control sets the positioning of the layer in the stereo spectrum.
- **Tune.** The Tune Control adjusts the pitch of all samples in the layer over a range of +/–1,200 cents (one octave).
- **Bits.** The Bits Control reduces the sonic fidelity of the samples in the layer.

Mapping Samples

You are not stuck with the presets in DS864; you can import your own samples (whether these are samples you have created yourself or commercially available samples) and map them over the keyboard to create your own multi-sample soundsets.

The first step to sample mapping is to load a sample. You do this by clicking on the Add button under the Sample Mapper window in DS864 (see Figure 37.4).

Once the sample is loaded, you can drag its sides to set its key range and velocity range. To map its root key, click on the keyboard under the Sample Mapper.

If the graphical Sample Mapper is a bit too tight for you, you can always zoom in by right-clicking on the Mapper and selecting the appropriate zoom (100%, 200%, or 400%).

You will see that underneath the Sample Mapper are the Sample Edit Controls. These controls apply to each individually selected sample. (You can select a sample by clicking on it—it will turn red in the Sample Mapper.) Within the Sample Edit Controls section, you have the following controls:

- **Gain.** The Gain Control adjusts the level of the selected sample.
- **Pan.** The Pan Control sets the position of the sample in the stereo spectrum.
- **Tune.** The Tune Control adjusts the pitch of the sample over a range of +/–1,200 cents (one octave).
- **KeyTrk.** The Key Track Control adjusts the extent to which the pitch of the sample is affected by the pitch of incoming MIDI data. When set to 0 cents/key, the sample's pitch will be fixed. When set to 100 cents/key, the sample will respond to the keyboard normally.

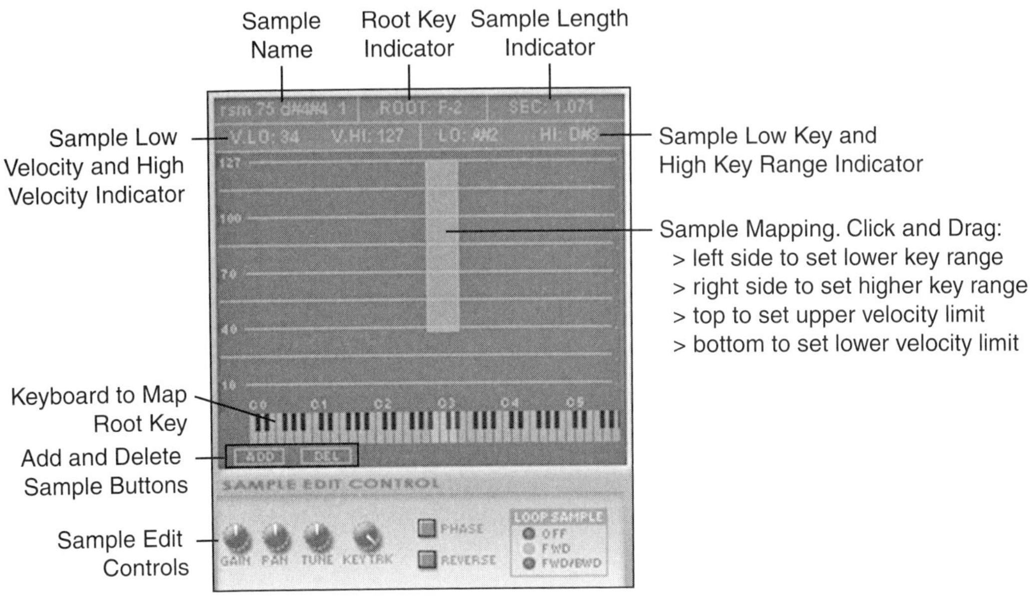

Figure 37.4 The Sample Mapper window in DS864.

- **Phase.** When the Phase switch is engaged (and glows red), the phase of the selected sample will be inverted.
- **Reverse.** When the Reverse switch is engaged (and glows red), the selected sample will play backward.
- **Loop Sample.** There are three options in the Loop Sample box.
  - **Off.** The sample will play once (in other words, as a single shot).
  - **FWD (forward).** The sample loop will play from the beginning of the loop point to the end of the loop point and will then restart from the beginning point.
  - **FWD/BWD (forward/backward).** The sample loop will play from the beginning of the loop point until the end point and will then play in reverse until it reaches the beginning point, where it will start again.

To loop a sample, you need to embed this information into the sample's waveform, which you can do outside of DS864 and Project5 with an audio editor.

Filters

There are two filters in the DS864 Filter block; see Figure 37.5.

Figure 37.5 The Filter block in DS864.

The filters can be arranged in series or in parallel by clicking on the Ser and Par buttons in Filter 2, as appropriate. Each filter can be individually bypassed by clicking on the Byp button.

The filters are similar, but there are some differences:

- Filter 1 is a multi-mode 12-dB/octave filter in which you can select:
  - LP: A low-pass filter
  - HP: A high-pass filter
  - BP: A band-pass filter
  - NT: A notch filter
- Filter 2 is a 24-dB/octave low-pass filter.

Apart from the controls in Filter 1 to select the filter type, the controls are very similar:

- **Cutoff.** The Cutoff Knob controls the filter's cutoff frequency.
- **Reso.** The Resonance Knob controls the amount of resonance in the filter.
- **EG.** EG controls the extent to which the filter's cutoff frequency will be modulated by the filter Envelope. (Filter Envelope 1 controls Filter 1, and Filter Envelope 2 controls Filter 2.)
- **LFO.** LFO controls the extent to which the filter's cutoff frequency or resonance will be controlled by its Envelope. The cutoff or resonance is selected in the filter's LFO: LFO 1 controls Filter 1, and LFO 2 controls Filter 2.
- **Key.** The Key Knob controls the extent to which the filter's cutoff frequency is controlled by the pitch of the incoming MIDI note.

You can link Filter 1 and Filter 2 so that adjustments on one carry through to the other. To do this, click on the Link button to the top-right of Filter 1.

Envelopes

There are four Envelopes in DS864; see Figure 37.6.

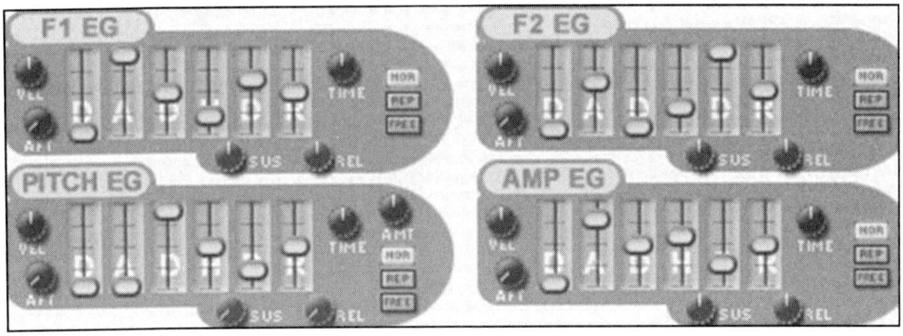

Figure 37.6 The four Envelopes in DS864.

These Envelopes are dedicated to controlling:

- Filter 1 (F1 EG) and Filter 2 (F2 EG)
- Pitch (Pitch EG)
- Volume (Amp EG)

These Envelopes are not conventional ADSR Envelopes, but are multi-stage Envelopes that are best explained with Figure 37.7.

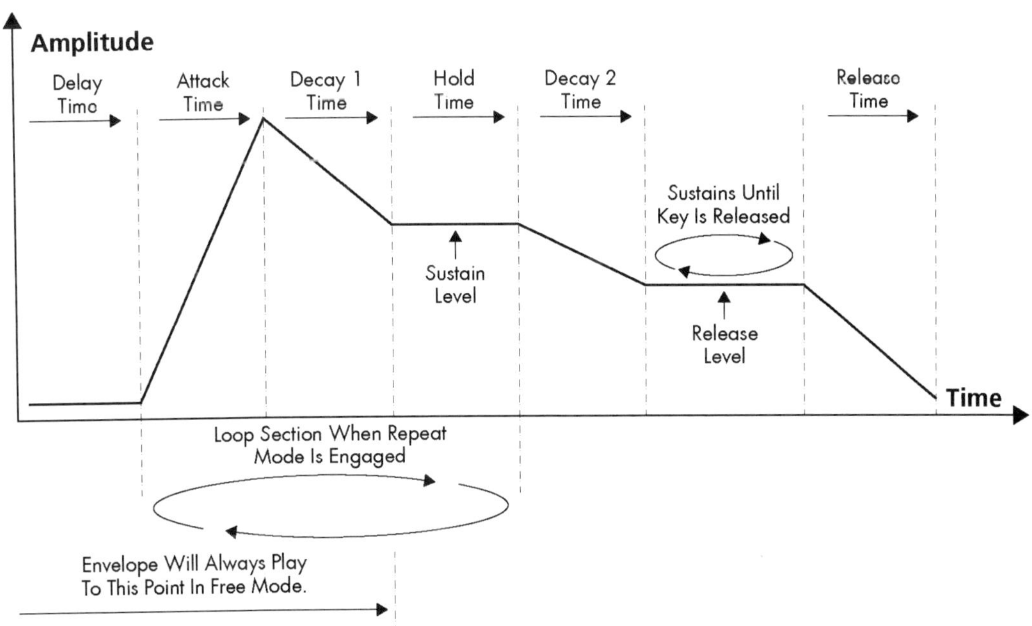

Figure 37.7 The multi-stage Envelopes in DS864 working in practice.

There are three buttons to the right of each Envelope:

- **Norm (Normal).** When Normal mode is selected, the Envelope adopts its normal one-shot behavior. (In other words, it plays from the start to the end.)
- **Rep (Repeat).** In Repeat mode, the Envelope behaves like an LFO. When the Envelope reaches the end of the Decay 2 time, it will restart from the beginning of the Attack time.
- **Free.** In Free mode, the Envelope will always complete the Delay time, Attack time, and Decay 1 time phases, even if the key is released before these three stages have been completed. If the key is held after the Decay 1 time, the Envelope will behave normally.

There are three other knobs in each Envelope section:

- **Vel (Velocity).** The Velocity Knob controls the extent to which MIDI velocity will affect the amplitude of the Envelope.
- **Aft (After Touch).** The After Touch Knob controls the extent to which MIDI after touch information will increase the amplitude of an Envelope.
- **Time.** The Time Knob adjusts the relative time of each stage in the Envelope. Its default value is 50%. If the Time Knob is increased, then each stage will last longer. If it is decreased, then each stage will be shorter.

There is another knob in the Pitch Envelope: Amt (Amount). This determines the maximum depth of the Envelope.

LFOs

There are three LFOs in DS864 (see Figure 37.8). These can be assigned to control:

- Pitch
- Volume (Amp)

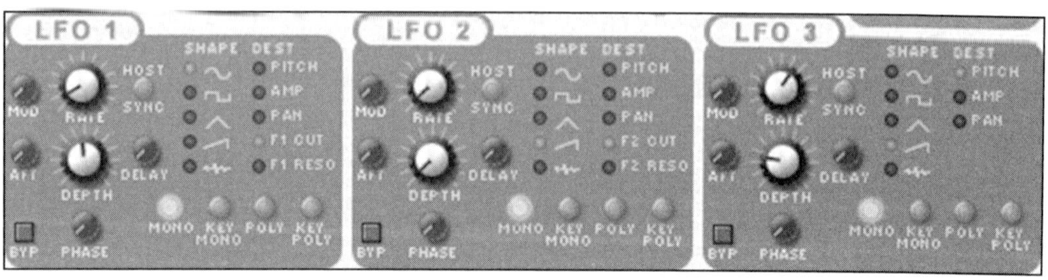

Figure 37.8 The three LFOs in DS864.

- Panning
- Filter cutoff
- Filter resonance

Each LFO has a choice of five waves (in the Shape section):

- Sine
- Square
- Triangle
- Sawtooth (ascending)
- Noise (random)

The LFO destination and the wave shape can be selected by clicking on the appropriate option in the LFO section.

The controls in the LFOs are the same (apart from the switches to assign the LFOs to control the filters):

- **Byp.** The Bypass switch turns the LFOs on or off. When the red bypass light is lit, the LFO will have no effect.
- **Rate.** The Rate Knob sets the frequency of the LFO. If you engage the Host Sync function by clicking on the Host Sync button (which will then turn yellow), the Rate Knob will set the frequency as a division of the beat. The frequency of the LFO, whether as a Hz value or as a division of the beat, will show in a tool tip as you adjust the Rate Knob.
- **Depth.** The Depth Knob sets how much the LFO modulates the destination.
- **Delay.** The Delay Knob sets the time over which the LFO will fade in.
- **Phase.** The Phase Knob controls the phase of the LFO wave over the range of 0 to 360 degrees. The Phase Control works in tandem with the Key Mono and Key Poly Trigger modes.
- **Trigger modes.** There are four Trigger modes that can be selected by clicking on the buttons at the bottom of the LFO. The selected mode will be indicated by an orange light. The four Trigger modes are:
  - **Mono.** There is only one LFO, and that modulates all of the voices simultaneously.

- **Key Mono.** This mode is the same as Mono mode, except whenever a key is pressed, the LFO will restart. The position in its phase from which it will start is determined by the Phase Knob.
- **Poly.** With a polyphonic LFO, each separate voice has its own LFO. This gives a more natural effect when you are adding some subtle vibrato to Pads because each note will have its tuning affected in a slightly different manner.
- **Key Poly.** This mode is the same as Poly, except whenever a key is pressed, the LFO will restart. The position of the LFO's phase from which it starts is determined by the Phase Knob.

There are two further knobs that affect the performance settings of the LFOs:

- **Mod.** The Mod Knob determines the extent to which the modulation wheel (MIDI CC1) controls the depth of the LFO. If the LFO is set to modulate pitch, you could set the Depth Knob to zero and the Mod Knob to the maximum. You would then give the modulation wheel full control over the depth of the vibrato.
- **Aft.** The Aft Knob determines the extent to which MIDI after touch information will control the depth of the LFO modulation.

The Master Section

The Master section (see Figure 37.9) is at the top-right of DS864. It has three controls:

Figure 37.9 The Master section in DS864.

- **Vol.** The Volume Knob controls the overall volume of the Instrument. It affects all layers and all output channels.
- **Pan.** The Pan Control balances the output of the DS864 in the stereo spectrum.
- **Tune.** The Tune Control also affects the whole instrument over a range of +/−1200 cents (that is, +/−1 octave).

Portamento

Portamento is the effect in which one note slides in pitch to the next played note. Typically, this effect works well with monophonic sounds; however, in DS864 you can also slide from one chord to another.

The Rate Knob in the Porta section (see Figure 37.10) controls the time it takes to slide from one note to another. When the knob is set to zero, the portamento effect is disabled. As you increase the value of the knob, the duration of slides between notes increases.

Figure 37.10 The Porta section in DS864.

There are three modes in the Porta section. These are selected by clicking on the appropriate option. The modes are:

- **Lin.** Here, the glide between notes is linear, so the pitch changes from one note to another at a constant rate.
- **Exp.** Here, the change is quicker at first, but slows at the note approaches the destination pitch.
- **Log.** Here, the change is slower at first, but speeds up as the note approaches the destination pitch.

Pitch Bend

The Pitch Bend section (see Figure 37.11) controls how the DS864 reacts to MIDI pitch bend information. The bend range is set by two knobs:

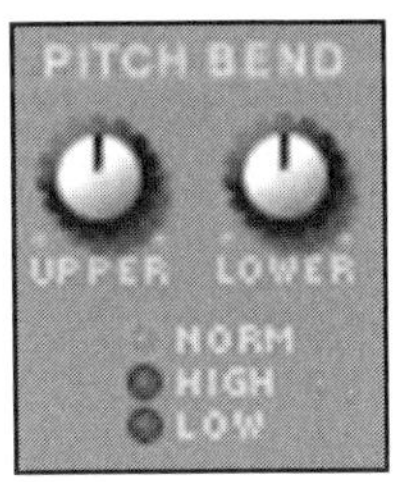

Figure 37.11 The Pitch Bend section in DS864.

- **Upper.** Upper sets the range that the pitch can be bent up.
- **Lower.** Lower sets the range that the pitch can be bent down.

Both knobs allow a maximum bend range of 4800 cents (in other words, four octaves).

There are three bend modes:

- **Norm (normal).** In Normal mode, all notes are bent.
- **High.** In High mode, only the highest held note is bent.
- **Low.** In Low mode, only the lowest held note is bent.

Tutorial 38: Introducing nPULSE

nPULSE (see Figure 38.1) is a drum synthesizer that comes with Project5 version 2.0 and with version 2.5.

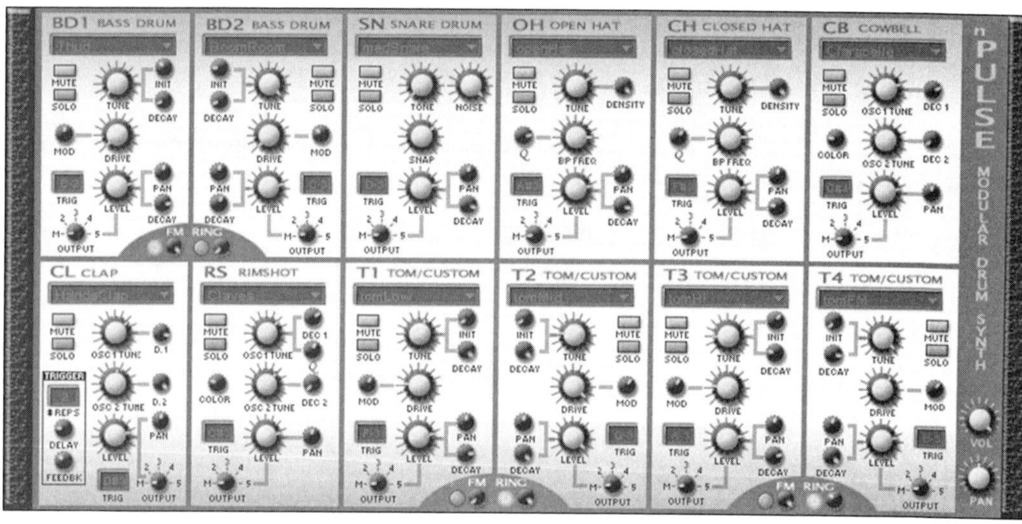

Figure 38.1 nPULSE.

What Is nPULSE and What Does It Do?

nPULSE is a virtual re-creation of an analog drum machine. It is an example of a synthesizer that has been designed with a specific function. It fulfills that function very well and is unlikely to find many other uses outside of those specific functions.

This multi-timbral and multi-output drum synthesizer comes with 12 modules (and hence is called a *modular drum synth*). These modules are all similar, but they do have significant differences that allow for their different characteristic tones.

Each module has a dedicated function, and you will find:

- Two kick (bass) drums
- One snare

- Two hi-hats
- One cowbell
- One clap
- One rim shot
- Four toms/custom modules

The two kick drums and the two pairs of toms/custom modules can work together to create a range of FM and ring-modulated tones.

Using nPULSE

There are no dedicated drum-kit management tools included with nPULSE. You can, however, save kits as presets. (See Tutorial 42: Preset Management Tools for further details.)

Master Section and Common Controls

As it is not burdened with the necessity to provide many utility functions, the Master section in nPULSE has only two controls (see Figure 38.2):

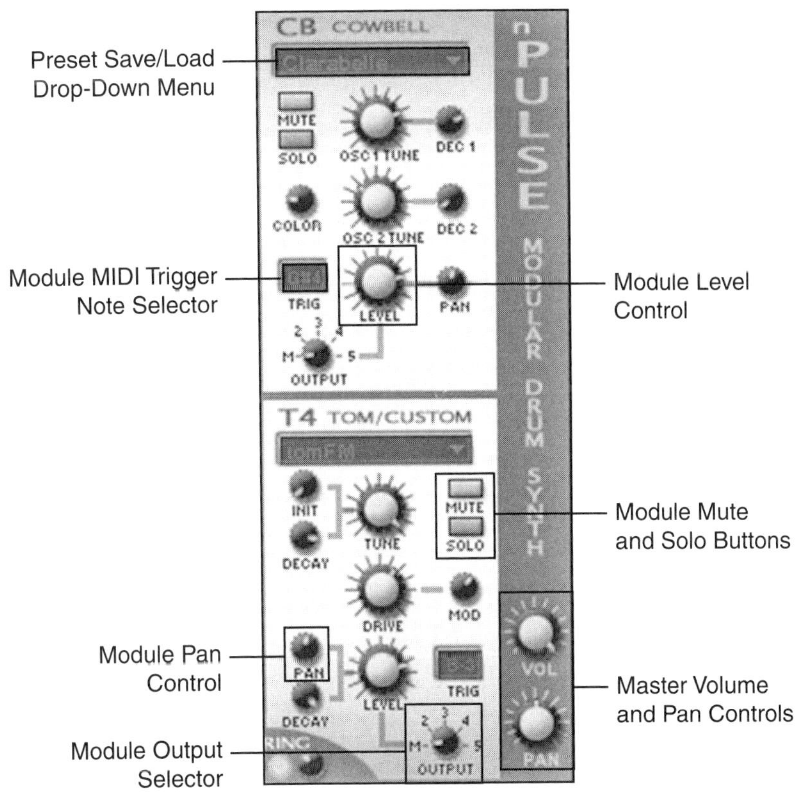

Figure 38.2 The Master Controls and common module controls in nPULSE.

- **Vol.** The Volume Control sets the overall output level for nPULSE.
- **Pan.** The Pan Control balances the outputs of nPULSE in the stereo spectrum.

As you can see from Figure 38.2, each module has a number of common controls:

- **Preset.** From the Preset drop-down menu, you can load a saved module preset. You can also save the current preset (and give it a name) by selecting the Save As option from the drop-down menu.
- **Level.** The Level Control sets the level of the module.
- **Pan.** The Pan Control positions the module's (mono) audio output in the stereo spectrum.
- **Mute and Solo.** The Mute button mutes the specified module, and the Solo button works to mute all non-soloed modules.
- **Output Selector.** The Output Selector determines the audio output to which the module is routed. Check out Tutorial 23 for details of using multi-output Instruments in Project5.
- **MIDI Trigger Note.** The MIDI Trigger Note Selector determines which MIDI note will trigger the specified module.

There is one other thing common to all the modules: You can right-click on them to audition the sound.

Let's have a look at the individual modules.

Bass Drum Modules

The Bass (or Kick) Drum modules (see Figure 38.3) are best suited for creating kick-drum sounds. You can also layer these sounds with kick-drum samples (perhaps in VELOCITY) to create an awesomely deep kick sound.

The Bass Drum modules have the following controls:

- **Tune.** The Tune Knob controls the pitch of the main sound source in this module. The Tune Knob has a significant effect on the weight of the sound. The module's Pitch Envelope also has a major effect on the sound. There are two controls in the module's Pitch Envelope:
  - **Init.** The Init Knob controls the extent to which the pitch of the sound generator is raised by the Pitch Envelope.
  - **Decay.** The Decay Knob controls the decay time of the Pitch Envelope.

Figure 38.3 The Bass (Kick) Drum modules in nPULSE. Note the FM and Ring Controls at the bottom of the modules.

- **Drive.** The Drive Control works in conjunction with the Mod Control. The Drive section creates a distorted/overdriven sound. On its own, the Drive Knob does nothing; however, the Mod Knob controls the depth (positively or negatively) of the effect, and by balancing the Mod and Drive Knobs, you can set the tone.
- **(Level) Decay.** The Decay Knob attached to the Level Control sets the decay time of the Volume Envelope for this module.

In between the two Bass Drum modules, there are two additional controls—FM and Ring. When either option is selected, the appropriate light will show in orange, and the left module will frequency or ring modulate (as appropriate) the right module. The depth of the modulation is controlled by the knob next to the On/Off switch.

The left module is not affected by the FM or Ring modulation effect; however, its controls (in particular the Tune, Init, and Decay Controls) will all have a significant effect on the FM or Ring modulation effect heard from Bass Drum 2.

Snare Drum Module

The Snare Drum module (see Figure 38.4) has two elements to the sound:

- A tuned tone
- Noise

When combined, these create the electronic snare sound.

Figure 38.4 The Snare Drum module in nPULSE.

In the Snare Drum module, you will find the following controls:

- **Tone.** The Tone Knob controls the pitch of the tuned tone element of the sound.
- **Noise.** The Noise Knob controls the volume of the noise element of the sound.
- **Snap.** The Snap Knob controls the decay time of the Noise Volume Envelope.
- **Decay.** The Decay Knob controls the decay time of the overall Volume Envelope.

Hi-Hat Modules (Open Hat and Closed Hat)

The hi-hat modules (see Figure 38.5) are based on a metallic noise source being fed into a band-pass filter.

The controls in these units are different from those in earlier modules:

- **Tune and Density.** The metallic sound in these modules is created by detuning a number of oscillators to create a metallic tone. The Tune Knob determines the detuning (in other words, how metallic/detuned the sound is), and the Density Knob controls the number of additional oscillators (from zero to five).
- **BP Freq and Q.** The cutoff frequency of the band-pass filter in the module is controlled by the BP Freq Knob. The width of the band (which is determined by the filter slopes) is then controlled by the Q Knob. Turning the knob to the right narrows the band and lets fewer frequencies pass.
- **Decay.** The Decay Knob controls the decay time of the overall Volume Envelope.

Figure 38.5 The Open Hat and Closed Hat modules in nPULSE.

Cowbell Module

The Cowbell module (see Figure 38.6) is made up of two oscillators, which then pass through a low-pass filter. The pitches of the oscillators cover slightly different ranges—the difference in the tuning between the two gives the cowbell-like effect.

Figure 38.6 The Cowbell module in nPULSE.

- **Osc 1 Tune and Osc 2 Tune.** The Tune Knobs set the pitch for each of the oscillators.
- **Dec 1 and Dec 2.** The Decay Knobs adjust the decay time in the Volume Envelopes for Oscillator 1 and Oscillator 2, respectively.
- **Color.** The Color Knob controls the cutoff frequency of the low-pass filter.

Clap Module

The Clap module (see Figure 38.7) is built on two filtered noise sources and also includes a delay line to create the effect of many hands clapping.

Figure 38.7 The Clap module in nPULSE.

- **Osc 1 Tune and Osc 2 Tune.** The Tune Knobs set the cutoff frequency for the noise source (Oscillator) 1 and noise source (Oscillator) 2, respectively.
- **D.1 and D.2.** The Decay Knobs set the decay time of the Volume Envelope for noise sources 1 and 2, respectively.
- **Trigger Reps (Repeats).** The Reps Knob adjusts the number of times the sound is repeated in the delay unit.
- **Trigger Delay.** The Trigger Delay adjusts the delay time in the delay unit.
- **Trigger Feedbk (Feedback).** The Trigger Feedback Control adjusts the decay level of successive repeats. When this value is set to the maximum (in other words, turned fully clockwise), the delays have the same volume as the initial hit.

Rimshot Module

The Rimshot module (see Figure 38.8) contains a metallic noise source and a filtered white-noise source.

- **Osc 1 Tune.** The Osc 1 Tune Knob determines the cutoff frequency of the filtered white-noise source.
- **Dec 1.** Dec 1 controls the decay time of Oscillator 1's Volume Envelope.
- **Q.** The Q Knob controls the resonance of the filter (which is controlled by the Osc 1 Tune Knob).

- **Osc 2 Tune.** The Osc 2 Tune Knob controls the pitch of the tone-generating oscillator.
- **Dec 2.** The Dec 2 Knob controls the decay time of Oscillator 2's Volume Envelope.
- **Color.** The Color Knob adjusts the tone and sharpness of the overall sound.

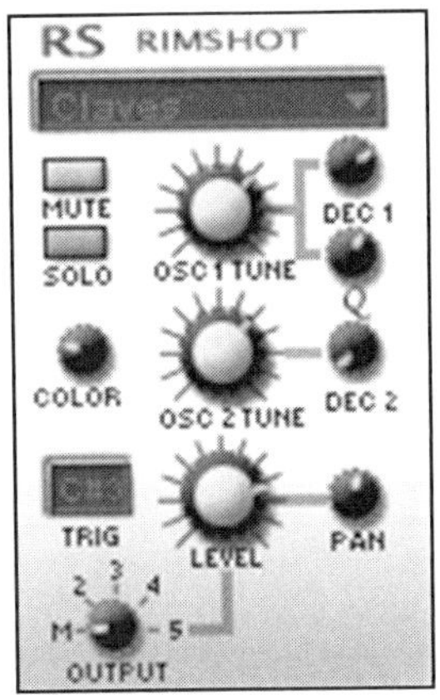

Figure 38.8 The Rimshot module in nPULSE.

Tom/Custom Modules

The Tom/Custom modules (see Figure 38.9) have the same controls and behave in the same manner as the Bass Drum modules noted earlier.

Figure 38.9 The Tom/Custom modules in nPULSE.

Tutorial 39: Introducing PSYN II

PSYN II (see Figure 39.1) is a virtual analog synthesizer that comes with Project5 version 2.0, but it has been dropped from version 2.5.

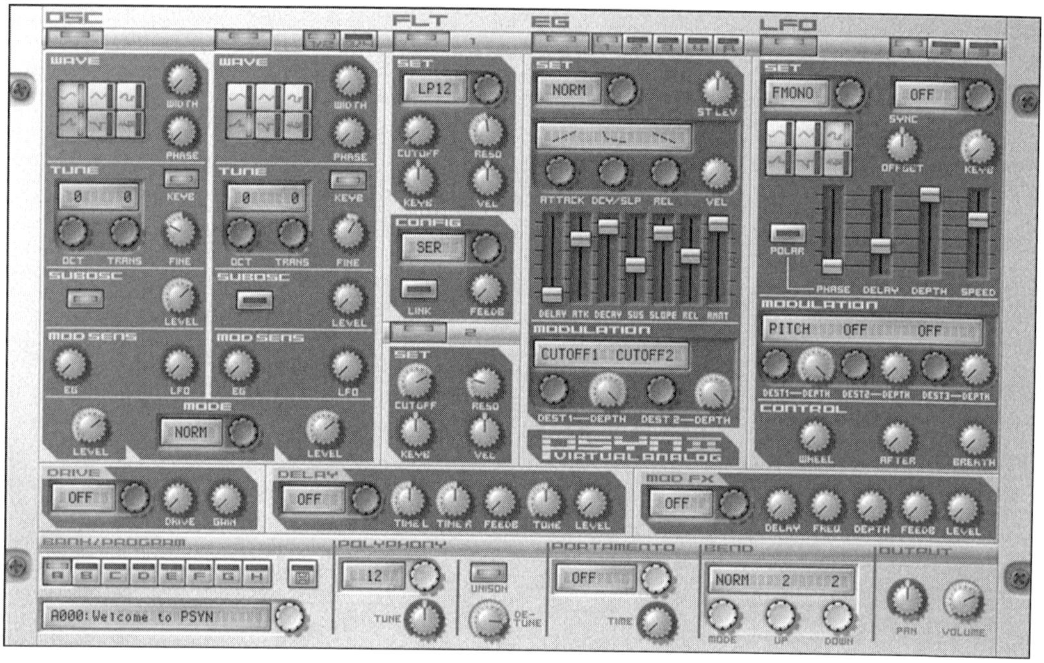

Figure 39.1 PSYN II.

What Is PSYN II and What Does It Do?

PSYN II is a virtual analog synthesizer with:

- Four oscillators
- Two filters
- Five Envelopes
- Three LFOs
- Three FX units

As well as being able to create a wide range of classic "analog" sound, PSYN II can also create frequency-modulated sounds.

Using PSYN II

Let's have a look at PSYN II in a bit more detail.

Oscillators

PSYN has four oscillators (see Figure 39.2) that are engaged by the large button at the top of the oscillator—this lights orange when the oscillator is on. You can see two oscillators at one time. To switch between Oscillators 1/2 and Oscillators 3/4, click on the buttons above Oscillator 2 (or 4). An orange light shows which pair of oscillators you are editing.

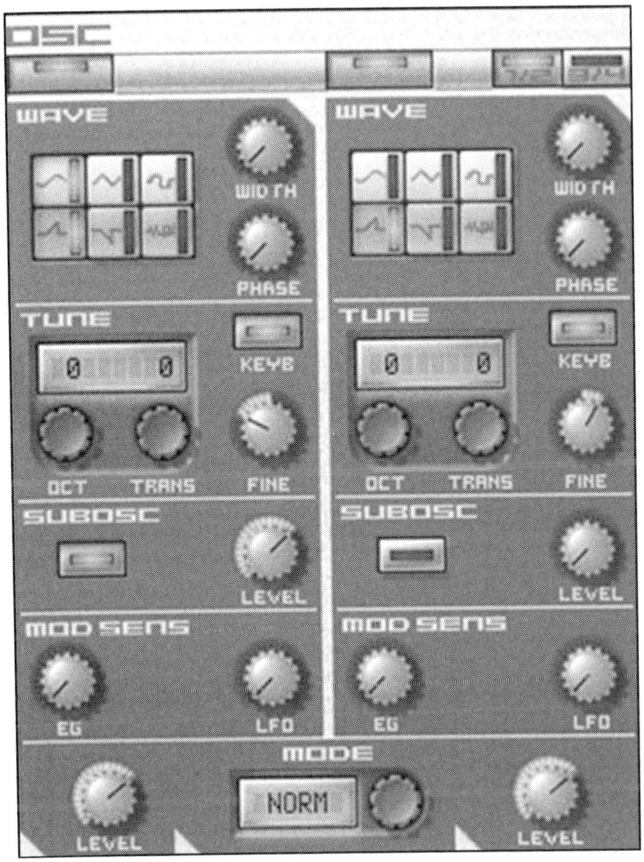

Figure 39.2 The Oscillator block in PSYN.

There are five waveform choices (and you can select more than one waveform at once):

- Sine
- Triangle
- Square

- Saw Up or Saw Down (these options are mutually exclusive because they would cancel each other out if both were used)
- Noise

Each oscillator also has a sub-oscillator that plays the selected wave an octave below the current pitch. The level of the sub-oscillator is controlled by the Level Knob next to the Subosc button (which glows orange when the sub-oscillator is engaged).

You can also thicken the sound by engaging the Unison function by clicking on the Unison button under the Polyphony section in the bottom row. This engages oscillator multi-mode (on a global basis). Instead of having one oscillator, this creates the effect of several oscillators playing together—the Detune Knob controls how much each oscillator is detuned.

Next to the Wave Selector buttons are the Width and Phase Knobs. The Width Knob controls the amount of pulse-width modulation, but only if an Envelope or an LFO has been set to modulate the width.

The initial phase of the waveform is set with the Phase Knob, which can shift an oscillator's phase by up to 180 degrees.

Below the Wave Selector is the Tune section. There are three main knobs:

- **Oct.** The Oct Knob sets the octave for the oscillator (over a range of +/–5 octaves).
- **Transpose.** The Transpose Knob changes the oscillator's pitch in semitones over a range of +/–12 semitones.
- **Fine.** The Fine Knob adjusts the fine tuning of the oscillator over a range of +/–100 cents (100 cents = 1 semitone).

Each oscillator responds to incoming MIDI pitch messages normally when the Keyb button is engaged (the Keyb light is lit). If the Keyb function is switched off (and the light is out), then the oscillator's pitch is fixed (in which case its pitch is controlled solely by the Oct, Trans, and Fine Knobs).

In the modulation sensitivity (Mod Sens) section, you can control the extent to which the pitch of the oscillator is affected by the Envelopes and the LFOs (if those modulation sources have any of the oscillator pitches set as a modulation destination).

Normally each oscillator will work independently. However, the oscillators can be paired using the Mode Selector (in between the two Level Knobs) for special effects.

You can click on the Mode Selector Knob or click on the displayed values (left-click up, right-click down) to change the mode. The modes that are available are:

- **Normal.** When the Mode Selector is set to Norm, the oscillators work independently, as would be expected.
- **Ring.** When the Mode Selector is set to Ring, the oscillators are sent to a ring modulator.
- **Sync.** When the Mode Selector is set to Sync, then Oscillator 1 (or 3) acts as the master and Oscillator 2 (or 4) becomes the slave, restarting its phase each time the master oscillator starts its phase.
- **L-FM and E-FM.** When the Mode Selector is set to L-FM or E-FM (the two FM, or frequency modulation, modes: linear frequency modulation mode and exponential frequency modulation mode), then Oscillator 1 (or 3) will frequency-modulate Oscillator 2 (or 4).

The last knob in the Oscillator section is the Level Knob. This sets the output volume of each oscillator individually.

Filters

PSYN II has two filters (see Figure 39.3):

- Filter 1 is a multi-mode 12-dB/octave filter.
- Filter 2 is a 24-dB/octave low-pass filter.

The filters can be individually switched into the signal path by clicking the On/Off button next to the filter's number and can be arranged:

- In parallel, so the raw oscillator output is fed directly to each filter by selecting Par in the filter Config section (between the two filters).
- In series, by selecting Ser in the Config section.

Filter 1 is a multi-mode filter that offers four possible 12-dB/octave filter types:

- **LP12.** A low-pass filter.
- **HP12.** A high-pass filter.
- **BP12.** A band-pass filter.
- **BR12.** A notch (or band-reject) filter.

Figure 39.3 The Filter block in PSYN.

These are selected by clicking on the display or adjusting the knob next to the display.

Apart from the option to select the different filter types, the controls in both filters are identical:

- **Cutoff.** This sets the filter's cutoff frequency.
- **Resonance.** This controls the resonance of the filter.
- **Keyb.** This controls the key tracking in the filter so the filter opens (or closes if you select negative values) as you play higher notes.
- **Vel.** Velocity controls the extent to which the cutoff frequency is controlled by the MIDI velocity of the incoming note.

There are two other controls in the Config section:

- **Link.** When the controls of the two filters are linked (with this button), you can adjust the parameters on either filter, and they will also be adjusted on the other.

- **Feedback.** Feedback can be used when the filters are running in series to give a harmonically richer sound.

Envelopes

PSYN has five Envelopes (see Figure 39.4), each of which can be used as a modulation source for two possible destinations. The fifth Envelope can be assigned like the other four, but it is also hardwired to control the volume (amplitude) of the whole program.

Figure 39.4 The Envelope section in PSYN.

Under the Envelope Sliders you will find the Modulation section, which allows each Envelope to control two destinations. The destinations are displayed on the screen and can be controlled by either left- or right-clicking on the display or by dragging the black Dest1 and Dest2 Knobs (to set Modulation Destination 1 and Modulation Destination 2, as desired). Once you have set the destination, then the appropriate Depth Knob controls the extent to which the destination is modulated by the Envelope.

Envelopes can modulate the following targets:

- Oscillator level (individual oscillators or all oscillators)
- Oscillator pulse width (individually or all)
- Oscillator pitch (with the individual oscillator sensitivity set on each oscillator)
- Filter cutoff frequency
- Filter resonance

As you can see in Figure 39.5, each Envelope in PSYN has five stages, allowing detailed control over your sound.

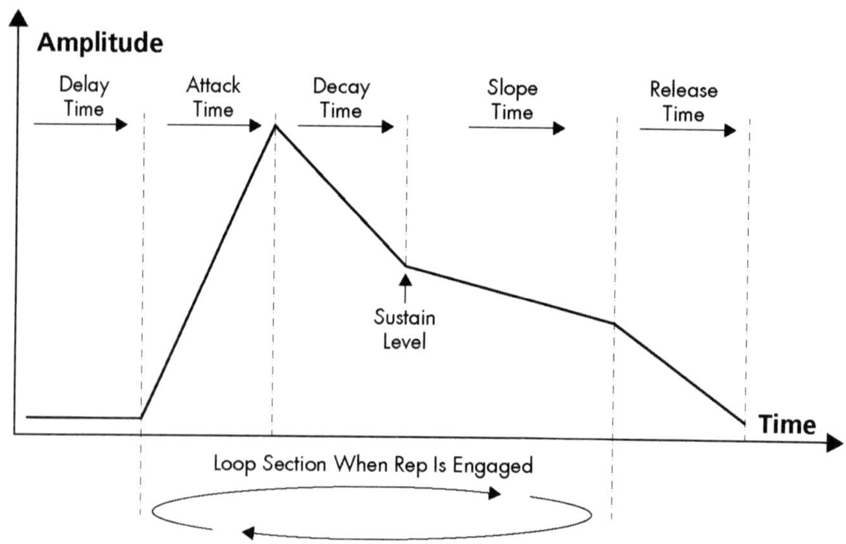

Figure 39.5 PSYN's multi-stage Envelope allows detailed control over your sound.

There is a further slider, Amnt, which determines the maximum depth of the Envelope. By default it is set at 100%. If it is set at zero, the Envelope will have no effect, regardless of the setting of the Depth Control in the Modulation section. If the slider has a negative amount selected, then the Envelope will work inversely, so for instance, instead of opening a filter, the Envelope could close a filter.

PSYN II gives you three options for how a level increases or decreases over time. For the Attack time, Decay and Slope time, and Release time, you can choose:

- Linear change, so the level changes uniformly over time
- Slow, so the change is slow to start but gets more dramatic over time
- Fast, so the level initially changes quickly and gets slower over time

You can adjust these settings with the knobs above the Envelope Sliders—the display will show which curve has been selected. You can also left- or right-click on the curves to change the settings.

Next to the Curve Selector Knobs is the Vel (velocity) Knob. This knob controls how the Envelope reacts to incoming MIDI velocity. When set to zero, velocity has no effect on the output of the Envelope. When set to maximum, the Envelope's output is fully controlled by velocity, so if velocity is low, the output of the Envelope will be low, but if velocity is high, the output will accordingly be high.

At the top-right of the Envelope section, there is a St Level (Start Level) Knob. This can be used when you are using an Envelope to modulate the pitch of an oscillator to control the starting pitch. However, this must be balanced with the Amnt Slider, the Depth Knob in the Modulation section, and the Mod Sens Controls in the modulated oscillator.

The Mode Selector is at the top-left of the Envelope section. With this selector you can make the Envelope behave in one of two ways:

- **Norm.** In Normal mode, the Envelope adopts its normal one-shot behavior (in other words, it plays from the start to the end).
- **Rep.** In Repeat mode, the Attack, Decay, and Slope phases of the Envelope are played in a loop while the note sustains. The Repeat mode is effectively defeated if the Slope Slider is set to its maximum.

LFOs

PSYN II has three low-frequency oscillators (see Figure 39.6), each of which can be used as a modulation source for two possible destinations. Like the Envelope section, each LFO must be switched on (so its orange light is lit) for the LFO to be effective.

LFOs are deployed in a similar manner to Envelopes. Under the LFO Sliders is the Modulation section, which allows each LFO to control up to three destinations. The destinations are displayed on the screen and can be controlled either by clicking on the display or by dragging the black Dest1, Dest2, and Dest3 Knobs (to set Modulation Destination 1, Modulation Destination 2, and Modulation Destination 3). As with the Envelopes, once you have set the destination, then the appropriate Depth Knob controls the extent to which the destination is modulated by the Envelope.

LFOs can modulate the following targets:

- Oscillator level (for individual oscillators or all oscillators)
- Oscillator pulse width (individually or all)
- Oscillator pitch (with the individual oscillator sensitivity set on each oscillator)

Figure 39.6 The LFO block in PSYN.

- Filter cutoff frequency
- Filter resonance

Each LFO's depth can also be controlled by three MIDI controllers:

- **Wheel.** The modulation wheel (MIDI Control Code CC#1).
- **After.** After touch messages.
- **Breath.** MIDI breath control messages (MIDI Control Code CC#2).

The LFOs can work on:

- A monophonic basis (in other words, one LFO is applied to all notes)
- A polyphonic (in other words, one LFO per note) basis

The LFO can also be synchronized, where the phase of the LFO restarts with each note, or free running, where the phase of the LFO is not restarted with each note. These options are chosen with the Mode Selector in the top-left of the LFO block. The options are:

- **FMono.** When FMono is engaged, the LFO works as a free-running, monophonic LFO.
- **SMono.** When SMono is engaged, the LFO is monophonic, and the LFO phase is synchronized to restart with each MIDI note on message.
- **FPoly.** When FPoly is engaged, the LFO works as a free-running, polyphonic LFO.
- **SPoly.** When SPoly is engaged, the LFO is polyphonic, and the LFO phase is synchronized to restart with each MIDI note on message.

Where the LFO phase is synchronized (SMono and SPoly mode), the initial phase can be adjusted with the Phase Slider to set the phase from 0 to 180 degrees.

You can select the LFO waveform by clicking on the appropriate waveform button. Unlike the Oscillator section, you can only choose one waveform. You have a choice of six waveforms:

- Sine
- Triangle
- Square
- Saw up
- Saw down
- Random

The frequency of the LFO is controlled by the Speed Slider, which can adjust the LFO over the range 0 to 20 Hz. The speed of the LFO is also affected by the Keyb Knob (which is above the Speed Slider). The Keyb function adjusts the speed of the LFO depending on the pitch of the note (so, for instance, higher pitches can have higher LFO speeds).

The polarity of the LFO wave is set by the Polar button—the polarity is positive (normal) when the light is off and negative (reversed) when the orange light is lit.

Both of these speed controls are effective if the Sync Control is set to Off. If the Sync function is invoked, the LFO synchronizes its tempo to the tempo of Project5 so that the time it takes the LFO to complete a whole cycle is a subdivision of the Track's tempo. The LFO acts as a monophonic source (even if one of the polyphonic settings has been chosen) if you invoke one of the Sync options. You can select 16, 8, 4, 2, 1, 1/2, 1/4, or 1/8, plus all triplet and dotted values as divisions of the beat.

The amount by which the LFO affects the destination is controlled by the Depth Knob in the Modulation section. This is further controlled by the Depth Slider, which controls the LFO output. The center point of the LFO cycle can also be adjusted with the Offset Knob (above the Delay and Depth Sliders).

Finally, the Delay Slider sets the time (between 0 and 10 seconds) before the LFO starts to have effect after a note has been triggered.

The Drive Unit

The Drive unit (see Figure 39.7) offers four drive options:

- Tube
- Soft
- Mid
- Hard

Figure 39.7 The Drive unit in PSYN II.

These options introduce differing amounts of overdrive/distortion. The difference between the units can be quite subtle, depending on the source material you are using. The amount of drive is then controlled by the Drive Knob, and the level by the Gain Knob. Because this unit is an insert FX unit, if the gain is set to zero, no sound will be heard.

The Delay Unit

The Delay unit (see Figure 39.8) is actually two delay units joined together. This allows for several options:

Figure 39.8 The Delay unit in PSYN II.

- **Ster (Stereo).** When Ster mode is selected, the left and right delay times are set independently. If you adjust both delay times to the same setting, the unit will act as a mono delay line.

- **Cross (Cross Delay).** When Cross mode is selected, each delay line works independently, but the output is then fed into the other delay.
- **Ping (Ping Delay).** When Ping mode is selected, the output of each consecutive delay is fed from one delay line into the other so only the delayed signal is delayed further.
- **LRC (Left-Right-Center Delay).** When LRC mode is selected, the signal bounces from the left, to the right, and to the center.
- **RLC (Right-Left-Center Delay).** When RLC mode is selected, the signal bounces from the right, to the left, and to the center.

The Delay section has five controls:

- **Time L.** The delay of the left channel is linked to the tempo of the Track, being defined as a fraction of the beat. The delay amount is indicated in a tool tip that is visible if you hold your cursor over the Time L Knob.
- **Time R.** The delay of the right channel is also linked to the tempo of the Track, being defined as a fraction of the beat. The delay amount is indicated in a tool tip that is visible if you hold your cursor over the Time R Knob.
- **Feedb (Feedback).** The Feedback Control determines how many times the delay repeats.
- **Tone.** The Tone Control cuts the tone of the delayed signal. When the knob is fully to the left, there is no effect on the tone, whereas when the knob is fully to the right, the tone (of the delayed signal) is very muffled.
- **Level.** The Level Control sets the level of the delayed signals. The Delay unit is a Send FX unit, so the dry signal will always be heard.

The Mod FX Unit

The last FX unit is the Mod FX (see Figure 39.9). This has three options:

- **Chor.** A chorus unit.
- **Symp.** An ensemble-type effect.
- **Phas.** A phaser.

Figure 39.9 The Mod FX unit in PSYN II.

These units are all broadly similar, but have differing tonal variations. They all work in much the same way, with a delayed signal that is modulated by an LFO being mixed with the dry signal. The units all have the same controls:

- **Delay.** The Delay Control sets the delay time of the modulated signal.
- **Freq.** The Frequency Control sets the frequency of the LFO modulating the delayed signal.
- **Depth.** The Depth Control sets the depth of the modulation of the delayed signal by the LFO.
- **Feedb (Feedback).** The Feedback Control sets the number of times the delayed signal repeats.
- **Level.** The Level Control sets the level of the delayed signal. Like the Delay unit, this is a Send FX unit, so the dry signal will always be heard.

Portamento

Portamento (see Figure 39.10) is the effect in which one note slides in pitch to another played note. Typically, this effect works well with monophonic sounds; however, in PSYN II you can also slide from one chord to another. PSYN II has four Portamento modes:

Figure 39.10 The Portamento section in PSYN II.

- **Off.** When the Portamento mode is set to Off, the portamento effect is switched off.
- **NFix (Normal Fixed Time).** In NFix mode, the portamento effect will always be active, and a fixed time will be assigned to each note in the slide range, so longer jumps will take longer than short jumps.
- **FFix (Fingered, Fixed Time).** In FFix mode, the portamento effect will only be active when one note starts before the previous note ends (in other words, legato playing), and a fixed time will be assigned to each note (making long jumps last longer than short jumps).

- **NVar (Normal, Variable Time).** In NVar mode, the portamento effect will always be active, and all jumps last the same amount of time, regardless of the key range they span.

The time of the slide is controlled by the Time Knob.

Polyphony and Tune

You can set the maximum number of notes that PSYN II can play at once in the Polyphony section (see Figure 39.11). You will often get more pleasing results with portamento if the polyphony is set to mono (in other words, one note), especially for certain lead and bass sounds.

Figure 39.11 The Polyphony section in PSYN II.

The Polyphony section also includes the Tune Knob, which controls the pitch of the whole synthesizer. With this control you can raise or lower the pitch by up to an octave.

Bend

The Bend section (see Figure 39.12) determines how the pitch bend wheel affects the program that is currently being played. The range that a note is bent is controlled by the Up Knob (which sets the amount by which the program can be bent upward) and the Down Knob (which sets the amount by which the program can be bent downward). The maximum bend range is 48 semitones (that is, four octaves) up and down.

Figure 39.12 The Bend section in PSYN II.

There are four Bend modes, selected with the Mode Knob (or by left- or right-clicking on the display):

- **Normal.** In Normal mode, all sounding notes are bent.

- **Up.** In Up mode, the bend is only applied to the highest pitched note.
- **Down.** In Down mode, the bend is only applied to the lowest pitched note.
- **Hold.** In Hold mode, only keys that are held are bent. Notes that have been released but still sound will not be bent, nor will notes that are held using a sustain pedal.

Output Section

The Output section is on the bottom-right of PSYN II's interface; see Figure 39.13.

Figure 39.13 The Output section in PSYN.

- **Volume.** The Volume Knob controls the overall output level of PSYN II.
- **Pan.** The Pan Knob balances the left and right outputs of PSYN II to control the position of the output in the stereo panorama.

Program Management

PSYN II can store more than 1,000 programs spread over eight banks. To load a program:

1. Click on the bank in which the program is located (see Figure 39.14).

Figure 39.14 The Bank Selectors in PSYN II.

2a. Right-click on the Bank button. A listing of all the programs in the bank will appear, from which you can select your program.

OR

2b. Scroll through the bank either by using the knob to the right of the program name or by clicking on the program name to browse individually through the programs. (Left-click to nudge up; right-click to nudge down.)

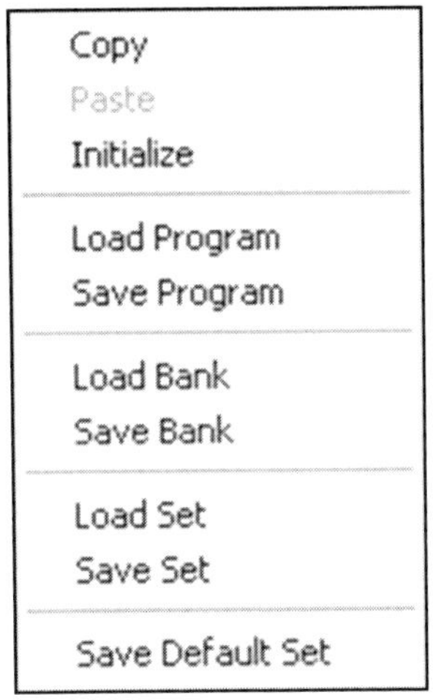

Figure 39.15 The Utilities menu in PSYN.

PSYN II also offers a range of utilities (see Figure 39.15), accessed by clicking on the Disk button to the right of the Bank Selector buttons:

- **Copy.** This command copies the current program.
- **Paste.** This command pastes the copied program to the current location (overwriting the existing program).
- **Initialize.** The Initialize command creates a default blank program.
- **Load Program.** The Load Program command loads a stored program.
- **Save Program.** The Save Program command saves the current program.
- **Load Bank.** The Load Bank command loads a bank of presets (programs) into the currently selected bank.
- **Save Bank.** The Save Bank command saves the currently active bank of presets.
- **Load Set.** The Load Set command loads a set of banks (in other words, banks A to H).
- **Save Set.** The Save Set command saves the current set of banks.
- **Save Default Set.** The Save Default Set command sets the current banks/presets as the default set when PSYN II is loaded.

You can rename a program by Shift-clicking on the program name and entering a new name. When you have finished, either hit the Tab key or click anywhere outside the program name.

Tutorial 40: Introducing Roland GrooveSynth

Roland GrooveSynth is a synthesizer that comes with Project5 version 2.0, but it has been dropped from version 2.5.

What Is the GrooveSynth and What Does It Do?

The Roland GrooveSynth (see Figure 40.1) is a preset machine that you can tweak. It comes loaded with a range of presets, many of which are sampled straight from classic Roland synthesizers and drum boxes. There is also a dedicated rhythm section. All of the sounds can be tweaked with the Filter, Volume Envelope, and EQ Controls.

Figure 40.1 The Roland GrooveSynth.

Using the GrooveSynth

Let's have a look around the GrooveSynth.

Choosing a Preset

You could, of course, use Project5 to select a preset (in the Instrument Track Inspector). However, it is probably easier to click on the name of the current program (in the middle of GrooveSynth's interface) to display a categorized drop-down menu from which you can select your program. If you select a program from the Rhythm Set, then you will invoke the special Rhythm mode. With this mode, the interface turns from blue to yellow, and you have the ability to modify individual drums.

Volume Envelope Section

Once you've loaded a preset, you can start tweaking. The first thing you can adjust is the Volume Envelope section. This has three controls:

- **Attack.** The Attack time—in other words, the time it takes for the Envelope to reach its maximum level after the note is triggered.
- **Decay.** The Decay time—in other words, the time it takes for the level to drop to the sustain level after it has reached its maximum volume at the end of the attack phase. Note that you have no control over the sustain level.

- **Release.** The Release time—the time it takes the level to decay to zero after a key is released.

Vibrato Section and Mod Depth

The Vibrato section is an LFO that has three controls:

- **Rate.** The Rate controls the frequency of the LFO.
- **Depth.** The Depth Knob controls the amount by which the LFO will affect the pitch of the program.
- **Delay.** The Delay setting controls the time before the LFO will have effect.

The Depth Control applies a fixed amount of vibrato. The depth can also be controlled with the modulation wheel. The Mod Depth Knob (located in the top-right corner) sets the maximum modulation depth when the modulation wheel is pushed to the maximum.

Mono

The Mono button (to the left of the program name) selects Monophonic mode so that only one note can be played. When Monophonic mode is invoked, the Mono light will glow orange. All new notes are retriggered when in Monophonic mode. Also, if you hold a note, trigger a new note, and then release the new note while still holding the original note, then the original note will be retriggered.

Filter Section

The filter is a straightforward low-pass filter offering:

- **Cutoff.** The Cutoff Knob controls the cutoff frequency of the filter.
- **Reso.** The Resonance Knob controls the resonance of the filter.

When a Rhythm Set has been selected, the Filter section is on the right side of the interface. In this case it will work in exactly the same manner, and all changes will be applied equally to all sounds.

Character

The Character feature is slightly unusual. It modifies the harmonics of the program to change its tone. The effect of this control differs, depending on the source material that has been selected.

Tone Section

The Tone section is switched on by clicking the button to the right of the Tone label; the button will then glow orange. The tone section has three controls:

- Treble
- Mid
- Bass

These boost or cut the sound in the predefined frequency ranges.

When a Rhythm Set has been selected, the Tone section is on the left side of the interface (see Figure 40.2). In this case, the Tone Controls will work in exactly the same manner and will affect the entire selected Rhythm Set.

Figure 40.2 The GrooveSynth Rhythm Set interface.

Porta

The portamento feature is engaged by switching the button next to the Porta label. This button will then glow orange. The Time Knob sets the glide time—in other words, the time it takes for one note to reach the next played note.

Bend

The Bend section includes the Range Knob, which sets the maximum bend (by the pitch wheel) in the range of zero to 24 semitones (two octaves).

Tuning Section

The Tuning section has two controls:

- **Coarse.** The Coarse Control allows the pitch to be changed over +/−48 semitones (four octaves).
- **Fine.** The Fine Control allows the pitch to be changed over +/−50 cents (one semitone).

Voice Level and Pan

When a Rhythm Set has been selected, the Level and Pan settings are applied individually to each drum. You have two options to select the drum piece you want to edit:

- Click on the drum piece name (under the program name), and a drop-down menu will appear so you can select the appropriate piece.
- Click the nudge up/nudge down buttons to the right of the piece name.

When a Rhythm Set has been selected, the Envelope, vibrato, filter, character, porta, mod depth, and bend features are not available.

Voice Tune Section

The Voice Tune section acts when a Rhythm Set has been selected. The Coarse and Fine settings are applied individually to each drum in the same way that Level and Pan settings are applied to each individual drum.

Master Section

The Master section allows you to set:

- **Level.** The Level Control sets the overall output volume of the preset.
- **Pan.** The Pan Control sets the stereo balance of the synthesizer's output.

Utilities

If you right-click on any knob, you will have the option to change MIDI controllers. In particular, you can use this menu to select the MIDI Learn function (see Figure 40.3).

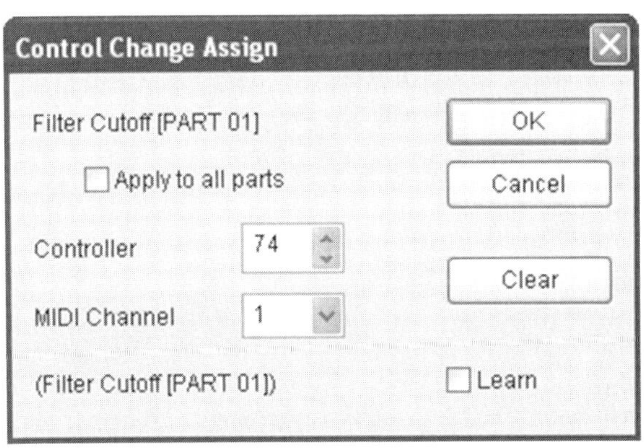

Figure 40.3 The Control Change Assign window, in which you can invoke the MIDI Learn function and change controller assignments.

Tutorial 41: Introducing VELOCITY

VELOCITY (see Figure 41.1) is a drum sampler tool that comes with Project5 version 2.0 and version 2.5.

Figure 41.1 VELOCITY.

What Is VELOCITY and What Does It Do?

VELOCITY is a drum sampler that is fast and easy to use, and it also has a low CPU hit. It is also quite sophisticated, with facility to layer many samples under one drum pad, so that timbre changes can be controlled by MIDI velocity while allowing you to take advantage of its many automatable features. As well as loading samples, VELOCITY allows these sounds to be edited to give character and to create wholly new sounds.

VELOCITY can work as a loop player, but since its strength lies in creating sample sets (including velocity-layered sample sets), its loop tools are rather "old skool," and there are much better loop tools in Project5, I'm going to focus on its more conventional uses in this tutorial.

Using VELOCITY

Let's take a look around VELOCITY.

Main Section

The Main section of VELOCITY (see Figure 41.2) controls some of the more utilitarian functions that affect the whole unit (rather than just individual pads/sounds).

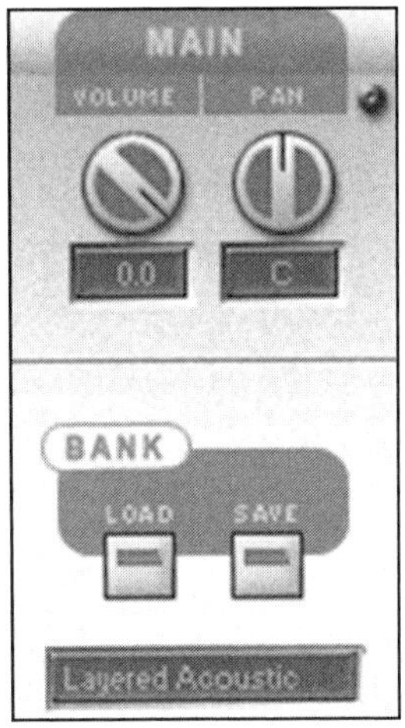

Figure 41.2 The Main section in VELOCITY includes many of the utility functions.

- **Volume.** The Volume Knob controls the overall output level of VELOCITY. Its default position is at the maximum, so its effect is to cut the volume.
- **Pan.** The Pan Control balances the left and right outputs of VELOCITY to control the position of the output in the stereo panorama.
- **Load Bank.** There are two ways you can load up banks (or drum kits, as you are more likely to think of them).
  - The first way is to click on the Load button in the Bank section. Clicking on this button will allow you to navigate to the kit you want to load. With this option you can load a kit in .p5d format (that is, VELOCITY's own kit format) or .txt format.
  - The second way to load banks is by using the Bank Selector. This is below the Load and Save buttons. Click on the selector, and a menu of kits will appear. To load the kit you want, release the mouse button when the cursor is on the kit's name in this menu. By default, these banks are located in the folder C:\Program Files\Cakewalk\Shared Dxi\Velocity\Velocity Banks.
- **Save Bank.** To save a kit (as a bank), click on the Save button. If you save your bank along with your other VELOCITY banks (in the Velocity Banks folder), then your new kit will be accessible through the Bank Selector.

Pad Inspector

The Pad Inspector (see Figure 41.3) allows you to fine-tune your pad and make some utilitarian changes (on a per-pad basis).

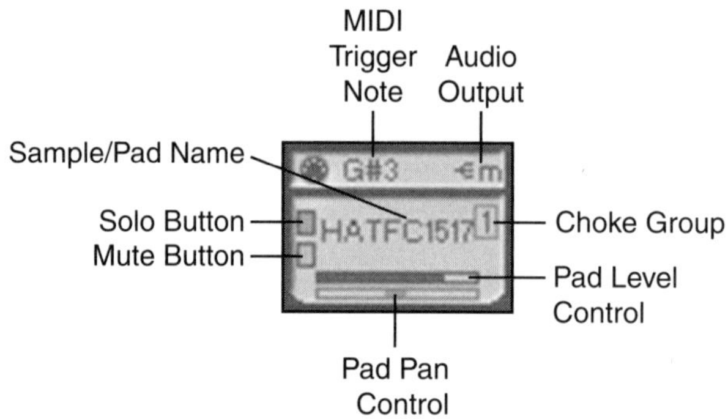

Figure 41.3 The Pad Inspector in VELOCITY.

The Pad Inspector gives you a range of controls and feedback:

- **Pad name.** In the middle of the Pad Inspector, you will see the pad's name. The pad name will show the first sample assigned to that pad. You cannot change the pad name except by changing the name of the first sample before you assign it to the pad.
- **Click on the pad.** If the pad has a sample assigned to it, then when you click on the pad, the sample will play. If no sample has been allocated, then the Load Sample dialog will open when you click on the pad (as if you had clicked on the Add button in the Sample Layers Inspector, which is discussed later in this tutorial).
- **Level Control.** Below the pad name you will see a blue horizontal line. This represents the pad level, which you can adjust by dragging to the left (to reduce the level) or to the right (to increase the level).
- **Pan Control.** Below the level is a very thin orange rectangle. This is the Pan Control, which can be dragged to the left or right to control that pad's position within the stereo panorama.
- **Solo button.** To the left of the pad's name is the green Solo button. When this is pressed, the button turns bright green, and the pad is soloed—in other words, all other non-soloed pads are muted.
- **Mute button.** Below the Solo button is the Mute button. This is yellow and turns bright yellow when engaged. When engaged, any muted pad will be silent when it is triggered.
- **MIDI Trigger Note.** At the top of the Pad Inspector is a note name and its octave (for example, C#4). This is the MIDI note that triggers that pad—it is adjusted

by clicking on the note and dragging up or down. You can assign the same MIDI note to several pads so they can be layered.

- **Audio output.** To the right of the MIDI Trigger Note is a three-pronged fork. To the right of this is either the letter M or a number between 2 and 5. This indicates the audio output to which the pad is assigned. By default, each pad is assigned to M (the main output); however, by clicking and dragging, the output can be changed.
- **Choke group.** To the right of the pad name is a box with either a dash (–) in it or a number between 1 and 4. This indicates the pad's choke group—the dash indicates that the pad has not been allocated to a choke group.

  Choke groups are often used for hi-hats. A real drummer can play with his hi-hat either open or closed—he cannot play both an open and a closed hi-hat at the same time. Within a choke group, only one of the allocated pads can play at once, so if you assign your open hi-hat and your closed hi-hat to the same choke group, then, as with a real drummer, only one can be heard at a time.

Sample Layers Inspector

You can create drum kits in VELOCITY one sample at a time.

- To assign a sample to an empty pad, click on the pad where you want to add the samples, and a dialog box will open, from which you can navigate to the sample you want to load.
- To add another sample layer, click on the Add button in the Sample Layers Inspector (see Figure 41.4), and then navigate to the sample you want to add. Repeat this process for each pad until your kit is built, and then don't forget to save your new creation.

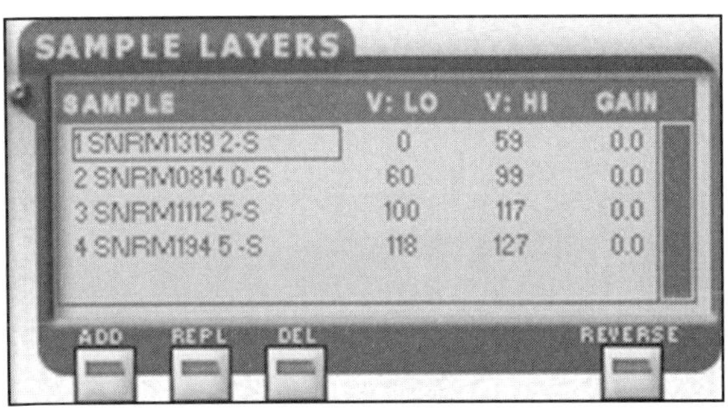

Figure 41.4 The Sample Layers Inspector in VELOCITY.

If you want to edit the sound of an existing kit, then you will need to delete and/or replace the pad/samples in the kit you want to change:

- To delete the contents of a pad, click on the pad you want to edit, then click on the names of the samples you want to delete (in the Sample Layers Inspector) and click the Del (Delete) button. If you have several VELOCITY layers assigned to the pad you are editing, then you will need to delete each layer individually.
- To replace the contents of a pad, click on the pad you want to edit, then click on the names of the samples you want to replace (in the Sample Layers Inspector) and click the Repl (Replace) button. If you have several VELOCITY layers assigned to the pad you are editing, then you will need to replace each layer individually.

Once you have loaded your samples, you set the velocity range over which they will play and adjust their volumes:

- **V:Lo.** The V:Lo Control sets the lower range of the MIDI input velocity to which the sample will respond.
- **V:Hi.** The V:Hi Control sets the upper range of the MIDI input velocity to which the sample will respond.
- **Gain.** The Gain Control adjusts the relative level of the individual samples.

Velocity ranges can overlap if you want to hear more than one sample playing at one time.

Sample Edit Controls

The Sample Edit Controls (see Figure 41.5) are applied to all of the samples assigned to a pad. The Reverse button on the Sample Layers Inspector is applied in the same manner. When this feature is engaged (and the green light is lit), all of the samples relating to the selected pad will be played backward.

Figure 41.5 The Sample Edit Controls in VELOCITY.

The Sample Edit Controls section gives you four controls:

- **Tune.** The Tune Knob increases or decreases the pitch of the sample. As the pitch increases, the sample is played faster, and as the pitch decreases, the playback is slower.
- **Bits.** The Bits Knob allows you to reduce the quality of your samples (non-destructively) to give a more "crunchy" or retro sound.
- **Start and End.** The Start and End Knobs give you control over the start and end of a sample. This allows you to cut either the start or end of a sample, or both.

Synthesis Tools

VELOCITY offers a range of synthesis tools (see Figure 41.6). These are applied on a per-pad basis, so if you load several samples under one pad, then the synthesis tools will be applied to all of those samples equally.

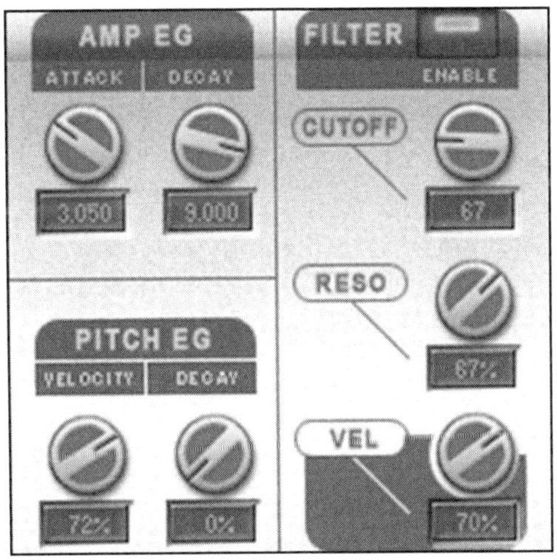

Figure 41.6 The synthesis tools in VELOCITY.

The Amp EG (Volume Envelope) is always switched on. There are two knobs to control the level of a pad over time:

- **Attack.** The Attack Knob sets the time it takes from when the note is struck to when the sample reaches its maximum volume.
- **Decay.** The Decay Knob sets the time it takes for the sample to decay from its maximum volume to zero.

The Pitch EG (Pitch Envelope Generator) controls the pitch of a pad over time.

- The Pitch EG is a one-stage Envelope where the Decay Knob controls the time over which the pitch of the pad falls.
- The other control in this section is the Velocity Knob, which controls the extent to which the pitch of a pad is increased as the MIDI velocity increases.

Both of these controls should be considered in conjunction with the Tune Knob in the Sample Edit section.

The Filter section contains a low-pass filter that can be used to shape the tone of a sample.

There are four controls in the Filter block:

- **Enable.** The Enable button switches the filter on and off.
- **Cutoff.** The Cutoff Knob sets the cutoff frequency for the filter.
- **Reso.** The Reso Control sets the amount of resonance in the filter.
- **Vel.** The Vel Control sets the extent to which the filter's cutoff frequency is controlled by incoming MIDI velocity.

Loops

VELOCITY's Loop section allows you to loop a sample. As I've already said, this is a fairly clunky approach to looping, and you are likely to get more satisfactory results using the other loop tools that are available in Project5. However, this feature may still be useful for creating stuttery effects within a highly "tweaked" drum kit.

- **Enable.** The Enable button switches the loop tool on and off.
- **Count.** The Count Control sets the number of times the loop is repeated—this controls the number of repeats after the loop is first played.
- **Start and End.** The Start Control sets the start point for the loop, and the End Control sets the end point for the loop. These two points set where the loop begins and ends: If you want to cut the front of the sample, you should use the Start Knob and End Knob in the Sample Edit Controls box.

7 Working with Audio FX Units

Project5 includes a range of effects units, and you can also use other VST and DX FX units, including the many freeware units that are available.

There are two main uses for FX: creative and surgical. When you use FX creatively, you create a new or enhanced sound—often the sound you end up with will be unrecognizable compared to the original sound. Used surgically, your FX units can enhance your sounds while remaining invisible to the listener. An example of a surgical use might be if you use an EQ unit to remove some unwanted hiss from a recorded audio track.

Of course, the line between creative and surgical can be quite blurred—for instance, you might use a compressor to tame the peaks on a snare drum but find that the tonal changes this introduces enhance the sound in a way that you like and want to exploit.

One feature that is common to all of the FX units and should be mentioned here is that if you double-click on any knob on the audio FX unit's interface (but not a slider on the Spectral Transformer), you will reset it to its default value.

Tutorial 42: Preset Management Tools

One benefit of the Project5 FX units is that they come with a range of presets, so you can quickly find the sound you are looking for or take inspiration from these presets. As you would expect, you can also save your own presets.

Calling Up a Preset

Calling up a preset is simple: Click on the preset name box (see Figure 42.1). This will give you a drop-down menu from which you can select your desired preset. You can also step through the presets individually by using the nudge up/nudge down buttons to the right of the preset's name.

As Tutorial 6 discussed, you can also call up a preset from the Track Inspector where the audio FX unit has been loaded. Click on the drop-down menu and select a preset.

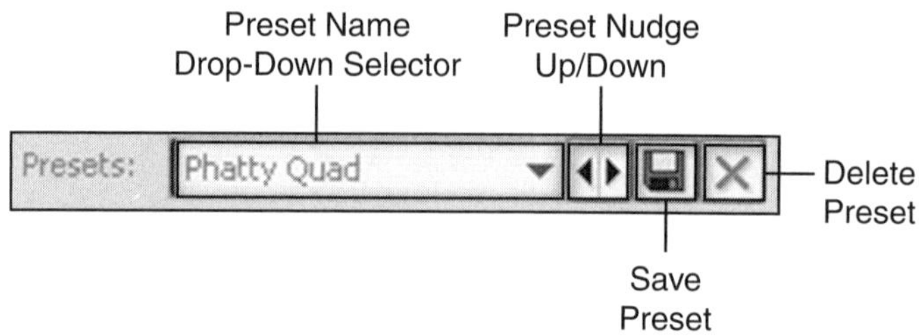

Figure 42.1 The preset management tools available with the FX units.

Saving a Preset

Saving a preset is equally straightforward:

1. Adjust your settings.
2. Type the new preset's name into the preset box.
3. Hit the Save Preset button.

Again, you can save a preset on the Track Inspector.

Deleting a Preset

To delete a preset, click on its name and hit the Delete Preset button. You will be asked to confirm the deletion, which you should do (assuming you want to delete the preset).

Backing Up Presets and Transferring between Computers

You can also back up your presets, transfer them between computers, and perform a range of operations on your presets using the SONAR Plug-In Manager. (Refer to Tutorial 7 for further details.)

Tutorial 43: Introducing Alias Factor

Alias Factor (see Figure 43.1) introduces distortion—not heavy-metal distortion like a cranked up Marshall amplifier, but digital distortion, which is reminiscent of the sound you might get from vintage sampling gear. This FX unit allows you to add and control lo-fi artifacts to shape your sound.

You will probably use Alias Factor for creative purposes, perhaps on an individual instrument or on a Bus sub-mix. You might use it on a whole performance, but in this case you are likely to only use it for a limited portion of your piece of music, so you will need to switch it on and off by automation (refer to Tutorial 25).

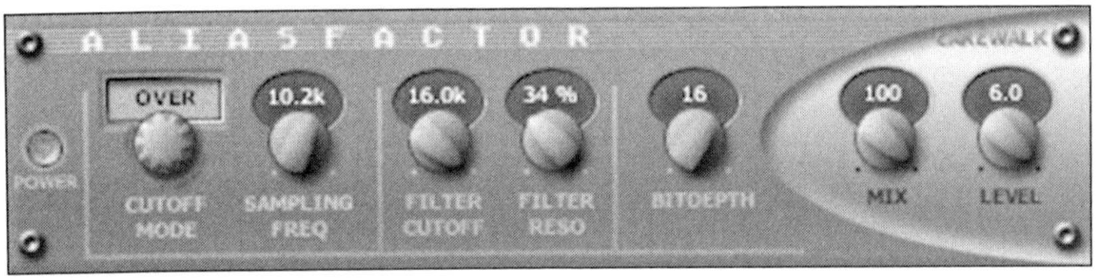

Figure 43.1 Alias Factor.

What Alias Factor Does

To understand what Alias Factor does, you need to understand a bit about digital waveforms, which, in essence, are what all of the sounds in Project5 are.

There are two main factors that affect the quality of digital waveforms: the bit depth and the sampling frequency. The bit depth determines the number of degrees of loudness in a waveform, and the sampling frequency determines how many slices the waveform is cut into (see Figure 43.2). As a rule of thumb, more bits and a higher sampling frequency are good because they give you higher audio fidelity (and therefore a better sound). However, this may not always give the sound that you are after, and hence we have Alias Factor.

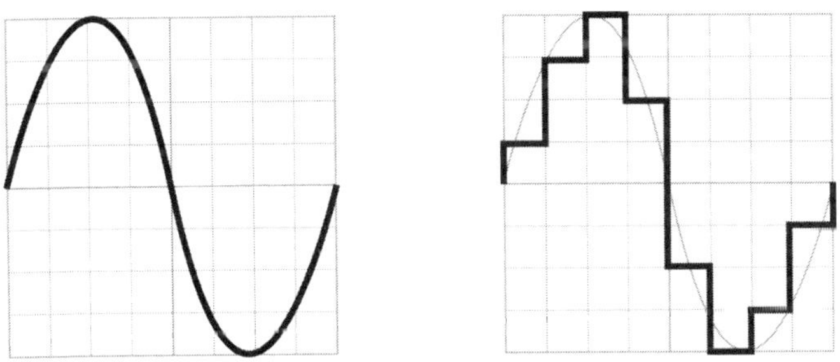

Figure 43.2 If you take a sine wave and restrict its bit depth (vertical axis) and sampling frequency (horizontal axis), then the audio wave will be distorted. As you reduce the bit depth and the sampling frequency, the sound becomes coarser, and more audio artifacts become evident.

Project5 works with 16-bit and 24-bit waves. Older synthesizers used to work with a bit depth of 8 or 12. A bit depth of 16 bit means there are 65,536 (2^16) possible loudness values for any one sample. A bit depth of 24 bit gives 16,777,216 (2^24) possible loudness values for any one sample.

Both 16 bit and 24 bit give high-quality audio playback (16 bit is the CD standard). However, when you start reducing the bit rate (which you can do with Alias Factor), the sound quality can degrade. Initially this degradation will be heard as a rougher, brighter sound, but as the bit depth gets further reduced, the sound becomes noticeably distorted (digitally distorted).

As I have mentioned, sound quality is also affected by sampling frequency. Project5 can work with a wide range of sampling frequencies, the most common being 44,100 Hz, which is the CD standard. This means that each waveform is cut into 44,100 slices per second and results in a high-quality sound. As the number of samples per second is reduced, the quality reduces.

Alias Factor allows you to mess with the bit depth and the sample rate of a sound without having to get a wave editor out. It also has a filter (which acts as a very specialized tone control) to help shape the distorted sound.

Let me bring in one more concept at this stage: the Nyquist point. This is a feature—or if you prefer, unfortunate side effect—of digital sound creation. The Nyquist point is one-half of the sampling frequency, so if the sampling frequency is 11,026 Hz (which is quite a low rate), then the Nyquist point will be at just above 5,000 Hz, which is well within the audio spectrum. Any sound that has its frequency *above* the Nyquist point will lead to digital distortion or aliasing. Alias Factor gives you immense control over the aliasing, allowing you to use quite harsh digital distortion in a very creative manner.

The Controls in Alias Factor

Let's look at the controls in Alias Factor to see how you can use this tool. One thing you will notice is that there is a lot of interaction between the controls. The key to using this tool is subtlety—you only need to make small adjustments to get a big sonic change.

- **Power switch.** The first button in Alias Factor is the Power switch. This turns the effect on and off, so no surprises there.
- **Cutoff mode.** There are four cutoff modes that have an impact on how the filter (which is discussed in a moment) behaves. The modes are:
  - **Free.** The filter cutoff frequency is set by the Filter Cutoff Knob.
  - **Under.** The filter cutoff is automatically adjusted so that it is below the Nyquist point. This means many of the frequencies that would be aliased are filtered out, which results in a much smoother form of aliasing.
  - **At.** The filter cutoff is automatically set at the Nyquist point. This gives a rougher form of aliasing than is usually achieved with the Under option.
  - **Over.** The filter cutoff is automatically set above the Nyquist point. This gives a much rougher form of aliasing. To push the effect further, turn up the resonance. Since the resonant peak is above the Nyquist point, it will boost the frequencies that are affected by the effect and so give a more pronounced sound.

- **Sampling Frequency Knob.** The Sampling Frequency Knob adjusts the internal sampling frequency of Alias Factor in the range from 100 Hz to 32 kHz. This control works to degrade the sound through both:
  - Lowering the sampling frequency, thereby reducing the fidelity of the audio
  - Controlling the Nyquist point to increase or decrease the amount of aliasing
- **Filter Cutoff Knob.** The Filter Cutoff Knob only has effect when the Cutoff mode is set to Free, although the Filter Reso (see below) Control always has effect. The filter in Alias Factor is a low-pass filter, which means that frequencies above the cutoff frequency are attenuated, so you can think about the filter as being a sophisticated tone control.
- **Filter Reso Control.** The filter in Alias Factor is a resonant filter, which means that the audio signal is boosted around the filter cutoff point. This makes the filter effect more pronounced. The Filter Reso Control sets the amount of resonance.
- **BitDepth Knob.** The BitDepth Knob adjusts the internal bit depth of the audio signal. The effect is subtle, giving a "vintage" sampler type of sound; it works best in conjunction with the Sampling Frequency Control.
- **Mix.** The Mix adjusts the mix between the incoming and the effected signals. At 0 you will hear the incoming signal only, and at 100 you will hear the effected signal only. In between these two extremes you get a varying mixture of the input and the effect signals.
- **Level.** The Level Control sets the output level of Alias Factor.

Automating Alias Factor

If you want to automate Alias Factor (and I suggest you do), here's a translation between what the knobs on Alias Factor's interface say and the exposed automation parameters:

- Power = Enabled
- Cutoff Mode = AutoPreFilter
- Sampling Freq = Decim Freq
- Filter Cutoff = PreFilt Freq
- Filter Reso = Resonance
- BitDepth = BitDepth
- Mix = Mix
- Level = Level

Tutorial 44: Introducing the (Multi-Voice) Chorus/Flanger

The (Multi-Voice) Chorus/Flanger (see Figure 44.1) creates many classic sounds. If you flick through some of the presets, you will come across many familiar sounds. By the way, I'm putting the Multi-Voice label (which I will explain shortly) in parentheses because the label is included on the FX Selector but not on the interface itself.

Figure 44.1 The (Multi-Voice) Chorus/Flanger. You will see that the interface does not include the Multi-Voice label.

What the (Multi-Voice) Chorus/Flanger Does

Chorus and flanger units work in a similar manner: They take a clean signal and mix it with a delayed signal, which has also had its pitch modulated by an LFO. You will also find that the (Multi-Voice) Chorus/Flanger offers more than just chorusing and flanging. It offers a range of different chorus and flanger units and offers other delay-based effects in the form of a range of ensemble effects.

There is a certain similarity between the sounds of the three unit types; however, there are differences too. The flanger effects will tend to give the sound more "whoosh," whereas the ensemble will thicken the sound. The chorus can also thicken the sound, but it can add a lot of brightness, too.

The Controls in the (Multi-Voice) Chorus/Flanger

Let's have a look at the controls in the (Multi-Voice) Chorus/Flanger.

Power Section

The first button is the Power switch, which turns the effect on and off.

Chorus Mode Section

The Chorus Mode Selector works by dragging the knurled knob. This allows you to select the processor that will be used. The options you have are:

- **Off.** When Off is selected, the unit will have no effect, although it will still consume CPU resources until the unit is bypassed.

- **Mono Chorus (Mon Ch).** Mono Chorus selects a single-channel chorus unit. If used with a stereo input signal, then the inputs will be summed into a single mono channel before processing.
- **Stereo Chorus (Ste Cho).** With the Stereo Chorus, stereo input signals are processed independently to give full stereo separation.
- **6-Voice Chorus (6 Vo Cho).** The 6-Voice Chorus is similar to the Stereo Chorus in that each channel is processed separately, but there are three chorus units per channel, giving a much richer effect.
- **Ensemble (Ensmbl).** The Ensemble effect is much like a multi-voice chorus, but it tends to give thinner sound.
- **Mono Flanger (Mon Fla).** The Mono Flanger produces a straightforward flanging effect. Stereo input signals are summed for processing.
- **Stereo Flanger (Ste Fla).** The Stereo Flanger operates like the Mono Flanger, but the stereo input signals are processed separately to give a richer effect.

LFO Section

Whichever effect you choose, there will be a delayed signal that has its pitch modulated by an LFO.

- **Waveform.** The Waveform Selector allows you to choose the modulating LFO waveform. There are three choices:
  - Sine
  - Sine^3 (Sine Cubed, which is rather like a "soft" triangle)
  - Triangle
- **Delay.** The Delay Knob sets the delay time of the delayed signal. In practice, this delay is so short that you will not hear it as a separate, distinct delay—instead, you will hear it as part of the chorus/flanging/ensemble effect.
- **Feedback.** The Feedback Knob, which is in the EQ section to the right of the EQ Knobs and to the left of the Mix Control (both are discussed in a moment), determines the number of echoes introduced by the delay line.
- **Speed.** The Speed Knob sets the speed (rate) of the modulating LFO.
- **Depth.** The Depth Knob sets the amount by which the LFO will modulate the pitch of the delayed signal.

EQ Section

The EQ section includes a two-band EQ section. This cuts frequencies from the delayed signal but adds some resonance—sometimes a low amount, sometimes a high amount.

- **EQ Mode Knob.** The EQ Mode Knob allows you to select the EQ mode. Each EQ mode sets the Low and High Knobs to work at different frequencies, introduces different levels of resonance, and varies the bandwidth (the amount of frequency that is cut—narrow bandwidths are more subtle, whereas wide bands may give a more aggressive change). Table 44.1 displays the settings in the various modes.
- **Low Knob.** The Low Knob controls the amount by which the lower band is cut.
- **High Knob.** The High Knob controls the amount by which the higher band is cut.

Table 44.1 The EQ Modes in the (Multi-Voice) Chorus/Flanger

EQ Mode	Band Frequencies	Resonance	Band Width
Off (unit is switched off)	n/a	n/a	n/a
Std	Low: 250, High: 500	Low	Narrow
Wide	Low: 250, High: 1000	Low	Narrow
Hight	Low: 500, High: 1500	Low	Narrow
Res Std	Low: 500, High: 2500	High	Wide
Res Wide	Low: 1000, High: 4000	High	Wide
Res High	Low: 500, High: 8000	High	Wide

Output Section

- **Mix.** The Mix Control sets the balance between the dry signal (knob turned to the left) and the wet (processed) signal (knob turned to the right).
- **Level.** The Level Control sets the output level of the unit.

Automating the (Multi-Voice) Chorus/Flanger

If you are going to automate the (Multi-Voice) Chorus/Flanger, then here's the translation between what the knobs on its interface say and the exposed automation parameters:

- Chorus Mode = Mode
- Waveform = Waveform
- Delay = Delay

- Speed = Speed
- Depth = Depth
- EQ Mode = Eq Mode
- Low = Eq Lo
- High = Eq Hi
- Feedback = Feedback
- Mix = Mix
- Level = Level
- Power = Power

Tutorial 45: Introducing Classic Phaser

The sound of a phaser is probably closest to a flanger, although a phaser will give a more nasal tone, whereas a flanger tends to give a whooshier tone. In either case, over-reliance on the effect can become tiresome.

What the Classic Phaser Does

A phaser is similar to a chorus/flanger and creates its classic sound by adding a delayed signal to the dry signal. Instead of modulating the pitch of the delayed signal, the Classic Phaser (see Figure 45.1) passes its signal through a notch filter to change its tone, which gives the phaser its classic characteristic.

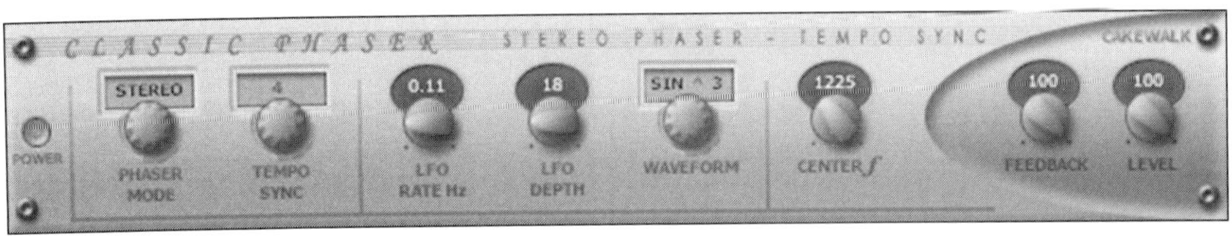

Figure 45.1 The Classic Phaser.

Controls on the Classic Phaser

Let's have a look at the Classic Phaser Controls.

- **Power button.** The Power button switches the unit on and off.
- **Phaser Mode Knob.** The Phaser Mode Knob selects the three Phaser modes. The fourth option is Off. The available Phaser modes are:
  - **Mono.** The Stereo input signals are summed and processed together.
  - **Stereo.** The Stereo input signals are processed separately.

- **Quad.** The Quad option works like the Stereo option, but the polarity of the modulation is reversed.

The delayed signal is sent through a notch filter, which has its cutoff frequency modulated by an LFO.

- **Tempo Sync.** When Tempo Sync is set to Off, then the frequency of the LFO is set by the LFO Rate Knob. At all other settings, the LFO's frequency is locked to the tempo of the Track as a division of the beat. The available beat division options are 16, 8, 4, 2, 1, 1/2, 1/4, 1/8, 1/16, and 1/32. For all beat divisions (apart from 1/16 and 1/32), dotted and triplet values are available.
- **LFO Rate Knob.** The LFO Rate Knob sets the speed of the modulating LFO if the Tempo Sync Knob is set to Off.
- **LFO Depth Knob.** The LFO Depth Knob sets the extent to which the cutoff frequency of the notch filter is modulated by the LFO.
- **Waveform.** The Waveform Selector selects the wave shape for the LFO. There are three choices:
  - Sine
  - Sine^3 (Sine Cubed)
  - Triangle
- **Center.** The Center Control sets the cutoff frequency of the filter before it is modulated by the LFO.
- **Feedback.** The Feedback Control sets the number of times the delayed signal is repeated.
- **Level.** The Level Control sets the output level of the Classic Phaser. The control affects both the dry and the wet signals.

Automating Classic Phaser

If you are going to automate the Classic Phaser, then here's the translation between what the knobs on its interface say and the exposed automation parameters:

- Power = Power
- Phaser Mode = Mode
- LFO Rate = Rate
- LFO Depth = Depth
- Waveform = Waveform

- Center = Center Frequency
- Feedback = Feedback
- Level = Level

There is no provision to automate the Tempo Sync setting.

Tutorial 46: Introducing Compressor/Gate

Some effects are intended to change the sound of an audio source. For instance, you can "hear" a chorus unit working even if you don't know what it is. Other units are often used for surgical purposes. For instance, if you use an EQ unit to remove a snare-drum rattle, then when you listen to the end result you won't be able to hear the effect of the EQ (although if you listen to the before-and-after sounds side by side, you may be able to hear the difference).

A compressor's prime purpose is to tame levels. However, compressors can have an effect on the tone of a sound. The main ways that a compressor can shape a sound (both objectively and subjectively) are:

- By making the sound fatter or smoother
- By enhancing the perceived loudness of a sound (which will always make the sound appear to have more depth/richness and so on)
- By giving it some punch

Gates are intended to stop unwanted noise. Therefore, generally you would use a compressor/gate for surgical purposes. However, there are creative uses to which these tools can be applied.

What the Compressor/Gate Does

Let's look at the operation of the two components separately.

Compressors

It is often difficult to "hear" a compressor because it doesn't make any sound of its own. Indeed, there is a strong argument that a compressor should be sonically neutral. However, compressors are used to a greater or lesser extent in virtually every recording today, and when used inappropriately, a compressor will strangle the life out of an Audio Track.

A compressor is essentially an automatic gain control. It works by controlling how much louder a signal can get after it reaches a predetermined level (called the *threshold*).

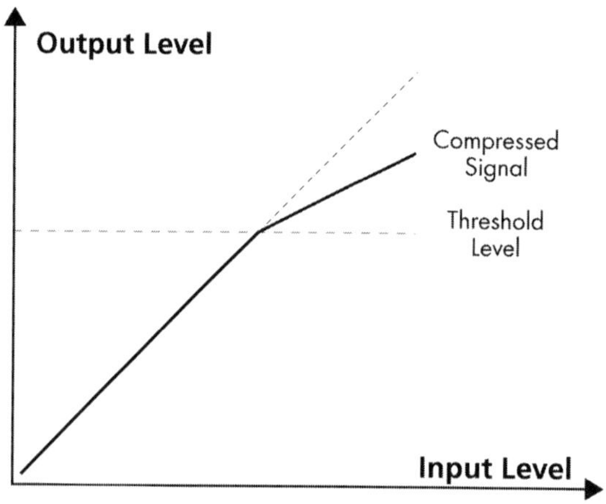

Figure 46.1 A compressor set to control an input signal.

Once a signal level reaches the threshold, then any further output level gains will be in a ratio to the incoming sound (see Figure 46.1). This ratio can be controlled by the user. So, for instance, if a compressor has set its ratio at 4:1, then for every 4 dB that a sound input increases over the threshold level, the output level will only increase by 1 dB.

As the compressor works to reduce the level of a signal, this gives extra headroom, so the compressed signal can then be increased in level. This increases the level of the quieter elements and increases the sound's density. Through using a compressor in this way, you can thicken up a sound considerably. Very often this technique is used to thicken up vocals or as part of the mastering process to make the whole track sound subjectively louder.

Gates

A gate works to cut out noise. It is essentially an on/off switch that is controlled by the incoming audio signal. When the audio signal is above the gate threshold, then the gate will open, and the audio will be heard. When the audio signal is below the gate threshold, then the gate will close, and the audio will not be heard. By closing the gate you can close off any background noise.

Therefore, the trick with a gate is to ensure that its threshold is sufficiently below the background noise level that it closes off the noise, but to ensure that it doesn't affect the signal more than is necessary.

The Controls in the Compressor/Gate

Let's have a look at the controls in the Compressor/Gate (see Figure 46.2).

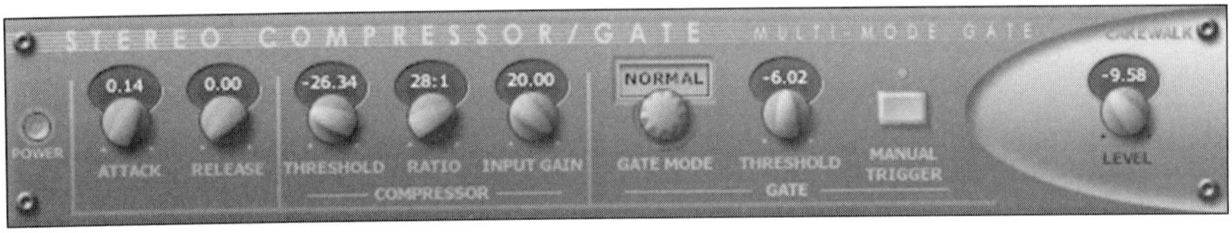

Figure 46.2 The Compressor/Gate.

- **Power switch.** The Power switch turns the effect on and off.
- **Attack Knob.** The Attack Knob controls the attack time. This is the time, after reaching the threshold, over which the compressor will start to have effect, or the gate will open. For the compressor, this can be useful for letting peaks through, and for the gate, this can be useful to ensure that the gate doesn't open when you don't want it to.
- **Release Knob.** The Release Knob controls the release time, which is the time, after falling below the threshold, over which the compressor will cease to have effect, or the gate will close. Generally, you would want to set the shortest release time possible; however, this may give unwanted audio side effects. For instance, you may get "pumping" sounds from the compressor, or the gate may truncate the tail of a note.
- **Level.** At the right end of the unit you will find the Level Control. This sets the output level of the unit and can be very useful for compensating for any level reduction due to compression.

Compressor Section

There are three controls in the Compressor section.

- **Threshold.** The Threshold Control sets the level at which the compressor will start to have effect. If you set this too high, then the compressor will not have sufficient effect. If you set this too low, then all of your sounds will be compressed, which may make your sounds become flat and lifeless.
- **Ratio.** The Ratio Control sets the amount of level reduction above the threshold. A ratio of 1:1 gives no compression. A ratio above 10:1 gives extreme compression, or limiting (in other words, the volume is limited to the threshold).
- **Input Gain.** The Input Gain increases the level of the signal before it hits the threshold, thereby allowing more control over the threshold.

Gate Section

There are three controls in the Gate section.

- **Gate Mode.** The Gate Mode Control sets how the gate will operate. There are three modes:
  - **Off.** The gate is disabled.
  - **Normal.** The gate is controlled by the level of the incoming audio signal.
  - **Manual.** The gate is opened and closed by the Manual Trigger button.
- **Threshold Knob.** The Threshold Knob sets the level at which the gate will open or close.
- **Manual Trigger.** The Manual Trigger will open or close the gate manually when the gate is in Manual mode. When the red light above the button is lit, the gate is closed. When the light is off, then the gate is open. You can automate this parameter to create rhythmic effects.

Automating Compressor/Gate

If you are going to automate the Compressor/Gate, then here's the translation between what the knobs on the interface say and the exposed automation parameters:

- Power = Power
- Attack = Attack
- Release = Release
- (Compressor) Threshold = Compressor Threshold
- Ratio = Compressor Ratio
- Input Gain = Compressor Gain
- Gate Mode = Gate Mode
- (Gate) Threshold = Gate Threshold
- Manual Trigger = Manual Trigger
- Level = Level

Tutorial 47: Introducing HF Exciter

HF Exciter-type devices were overused in the 1980s and are a small part of the reason why many of the records from back then sound so brittle. However, used with some care, these devices can really lift a part of or a whole mix.

What HF Exciter Does

The HF Exciter (see Figure 47.1) will enhance the top end of the audio spectrum, producing a brighter, tighter, clearer sound. In some ways the effect can be thought of as creating a top end that may not be present. The key difference between an exciter and EQ is that the exciter will have little effect on the level of the sound, while the EQ will change the level (which may have implications for the whole mix and the mastering).

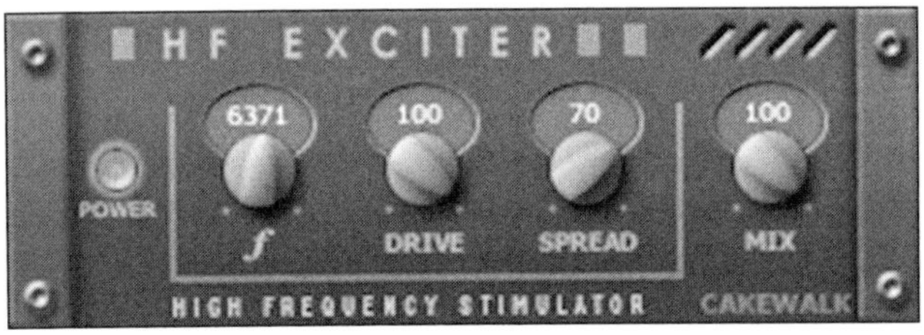

Figure 47.1 The HF Exciter.

The effect of the HF Exciter is very much dependent on the material you feed it. Give it a dull bass sound, and it may not appear to have much effect (even if it does add considerably to the sound). Give it a finished mix that needs a bit of mastering polish, and you may find the HF Exciter becomes a very broad-ranging tool.

The Controls in HF Exciter

There are only a few controls in the HF Exciter, but they need to be used with care if you're keen to ensure you don't burn your Track.

- **Power button.** The Power button switches the unit on and off.
- **F (frequency).** The Frequency Control sets the central frequency that is processed by the HF Exciter.
- **Drive.** The effect works by subtly distorting the high end of the audio spectrum. The Drive Control determines the amount of this high-end energy.
- **Spread.** The Spread Control gives the impression of a broader stereo spread.
- **Mix.** The Mix Control balances the clean and effected signals.

Automating HF Exciter

If you are going to automate HF Exciter, then here's the translation between what the knobs on the interface say and the exposed automation parameters:

- Power = Power
- F (frequency) = Frequency

- Drive = Drive
- Spread = Spread
- Mix = Mix

Tutorial 48: Introducing Mod Filter

As its name suggests, the Mod Filter (see Figure 48.1) is a low-pass filter unit that has some modulation sources bolted on. If you're not sure what a low-pass filter does or what LFOs and Envelopes can do, then check back to Tutorial 33, where these were discussed.

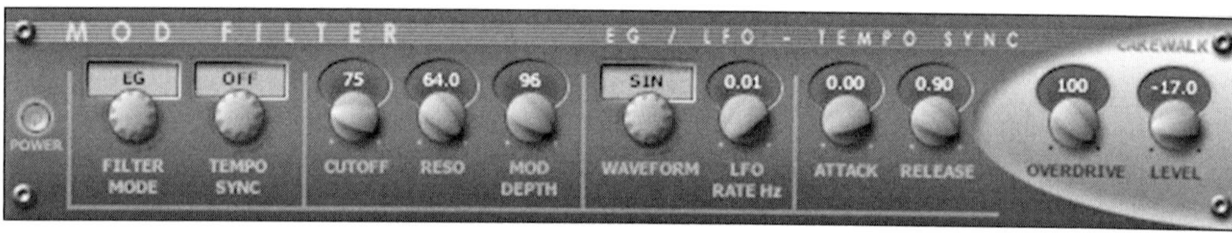

Figure 48.1 The Mod Filter.

What the Mod Filter Does

The Mod Filter can work in four main ways:

- As a simple low-pass filter
- As a low-pass filter that has its cutoff modulated by the internal LFO
- As a low-pass filter that has its cutoff modulated by the internal Envelope
- As a low-pass filter that has its cutoff controlled by Project5's automation

Of course, you can combine several options, so for instance you could control the cutoff with the LFO and automation at the same time (and control all of the other parameters with automation, too).

The Controls in the Mod Filter

Let's have a look at the Mod Filter Controls.

- **Power switch.** The Power switch turns the Mod Filter on and off.
- **Filter Mode.** The Filter Mode selects the modulation source for the filter. There are four options:
  - **Off.** The filter is switched off.
  - **Manual.** The filter is switched on, and its cutoff frequency is set manually. In other words, it is not affected by the Envelope or LFO settings.

- **EG.** The filter's cutoff frequency is controlled by the internal Envelope generator.
- **LFO.** The filter's cutoff frequency is controlled by the internal LFO.

The filter can be externally automated when either Manual, EG, or LFO mode is selected.

- **Tempo Sync.** When Tempo Sync is set to Off, the LFO's speed is set by the LFO Rate Control. At all other settings, the LFO's frequency is locked to the tempo of the track as a division of the beat. The available beat division options are 16, 8, 4, 2, 1, 1/2, 1/4, 1/8, 1/16, and 1/32. For all beat divisions (apart from 1/16 and 1/32), dotted and triplet values are available.
- **Cutoff Knob.** The Cutoff Knob sets the cutoff frequency for the low-pass filter. When the cutoff frequency is modulated by the LFO or the Envelope, this control sets the frequency from which the cutoff is modulated.
- **Reso Knob.** The Reso Knob sets the amount of resonance in the filter.
- **Mod Depth Knob.** The Mod Depth Knob sets the extent by which the filter's cutoff frequency is modulated by either the LFO or the Envelope generator when either EG or LFO mode has been selected.
- **Waveform Knob.** The Waveform Knob selects the LFO's wave shape. There are four choices:
    - **Sin.** A sine wave.
    - **Tri.** A triangle wave.
    - **Sqr.** A square wave.
    - **S&H.** Sample and Hold: a random wave.
- **LFO Rate Knob.** The LFO Rate Knob sets the frequency of the LFO when the Tempo Sync Knob is set to Off.
- **Attack Knob.** The Envelope in the Mod Filter is a simple two-stage Envelope. The Attack Knob sets the attack time of the Envelope.
- **Release Knob.** When the Envelope has completed its attack phase, it begins its release phase. The Release Knob sets the release time.
- **Overdrive Knob.** The Mod Filter has a built-in overdrive function that is set by the Overdrive Knob.
- **Level Knob.** The Level Knob sets the output level of the unit.

Automating the Mod Filter

If you are going to automate the Mod Filter, then here's the translation between what the knobs on its interface say and the exposed automation parameters:

- Power = Power
- Filter Mode = Mode
- Tempo Sync = Sync
- Cutoff = Cutoff
- Reso = Resonance
- Mod Depth = Mod Depth
- Waveform = Waveform
- LFO Rate = Rate
- Attack = Attack
- Release = Release
- Overdrive = Overdrive
- Level = Level

Tutorial 49: Introducing Para-Q

Para-Q (see Figure 49.1) is Project5's EQ effect, and as such, it can be used creatively to sculpt your sound or surgically to correct errors.

Figure 49.1 Para-Q.

EQ can be used either on individual Tracks or on a whole mix. Usually you will use it in both situations. In addition, since Para-Q only has two bands, you can stack several units together for more detailed control of your audio spectrum.

What Para-Q Does

Para-Q combines two parametric EQ units. Two what? Let me explain...

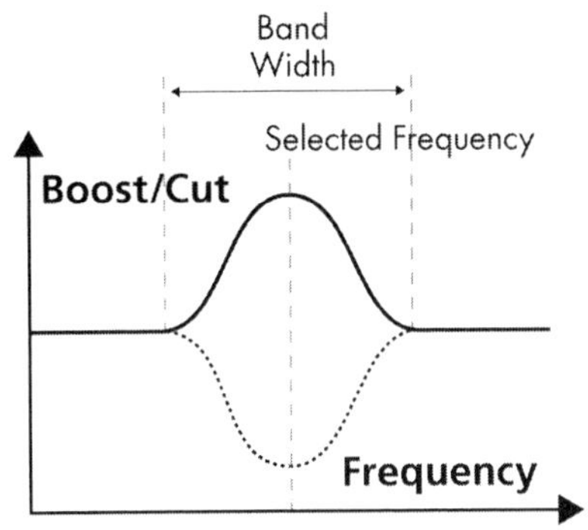

Figure 49.2 A parametric EQ.

Parametric equalizers are tone controls that allow you detailed control over your sound spectrum. They have three controls (see Figure 49.2), which allow you to control:

- The frequency to be cut or boosted.
- The amount of boost or cut.
- The bandwidth of the boost or cut. The bandwidth determines how wide the boost or cut is, much like a constantly variable slope control on a filter.

The Controls in Para-Q

You will notice in Para-Q that the Band 1 EQ and Band 2 EQ Controls are exactly the same. While the controls are duplicated, I see no need to duplicate the explanation.

- **Power switch.** The Power switch turns the effect on and off.
- **F.** The Frequency Control sets the center frequency to be cut or boosted.
- **Gain.** The Gain Control sets the amount of cut or boost.
- **BW.** The Band Width Control determines the bandwidth of the cut or boost.
- **Level.** The Level Control adjusts the output level to compensate for gains or cuts in the signal introduced by the Para-Q. When setting the Para-Q, use the Level Control to keep a constant volume. That way, you will hear the effect of the EQ changes, and you will not be influenced by any level controls (since increases in volume often make things sound "better," while cuts tend to make things sound subjectively "worse").

Automating Para-Q

If you are going to automate Para-Q, then here's the translation between what the knobs on its interface say and the exposed automation parameters:

- Power = Power
- (Band 1) F = Frequency 1
- (Band 1) Gain = Gain 1
- (Band 1) BW = Bandwidth 1
- (Band 2) F = Frequency 2
- (Band 2) Gain = Gain 2
- (Band 2) BW = Bandwidth 2
- Level = Level

Tutorial 50: Introducing Tempo Delay Stereo Delay

Delay lines such as the Stereo Delay (see Figure 50.1) can be used in many ways. The two most common ways are:

- To create an echo effect (which is the major use for a delay line)
- To create a second signal

Figure 50.1 The Tempo Delay Stereo Delay.

When you have two separate audio signals, you can then place the two signals in different parts of the audio spectrum to create stereo effects. If each part is then treated separately—for instance, different EQ settings are applied to each separate audio signal—then the stereo separation effect can be increased. Often, signals are split in this way to make it easier to place a part in the stereo spectrum, since it means that you don't have to leave everything in the center of a mix to keep the sound balanced between the speakers.

By the way, Stereo Delay is another one of those oddly labeled FX units. On the FX Selector menus it is called *Tempo Delay*, while on its face it is called *Stereo Delay*. For consistency, I am calling it Stereo Delay.

What Stereo Delay Does

The Stereo Delay does what you would expect: It delays the audio signal. However, this unit has some more tricks up its sleeve. For instance:

- As a stereo unit, the unit is actually two delay units working together, so separate delays can be applied to the left and right audio channels.
- There is a range of algorithms so that the delays can be bounced around the stereo spectrum.
- The delays can be tempo-synchronized.
- The delays can be EQ'd to further shape the tone.

The Controls in Stereo Delay

Let's have a look at the controls in the Stereo Delay.

- **Power switch.** The Power switch turns the Stereo Delay on and off.
- **Delay Mode.** The Delay Mode Knob selects the delay mode. There are four modes to select from:
  - **Stereo.** With Stereo mode, the left and right channels are processed separately, and the delay time for each channel can be separately set.
  - **Ping.** With Ping mode, the output of each consecutive delay is fed from one delay line into the other so that after the initial impulse, it is only the delayed signal that is getting delayed. With this delay, the delayed signal bounces around in the stereo field.
  - **Cross.** With Cross mode, each delay line works independently, but the output is then fed into the other delay.
  - **LRC.** With LRC (left-right-center) mode, the delayed signal bounces from the left, to the right, to the center, and so on.
- **Tempo Sync.** When Tempo Sync is set to Off, the delay times are set by the Time Left and Time Right Knobs. At all other settings, the delay times are locked to the tempo of the Track as a division of the beat. The available beat division options are 16, 8, 4, 2, 1, 1/2, 1/4, 1/8, 1/16, and 1/32. For all beat divisions (apart from 1/16 and 1/32), dotted and triplet values are available. If one of the Tempo Sync options is selected when the unit is in Stereo mode, then both delays will be the same, giving a mono effect.
- **Time Left and Time Right.** When Tempo Sync is set to Off, the Time Left and Time Right Knobs independently set the delay time for the left audio channel and the right audio channel, respectively. If one of the Tempo Sync delay times has

been set and either the Time Left or the Time Right Knob is moved, then the Tempo Sync Control will be overridden by the moved knob setting. Each channel can have a delay time of up to 2 seconds, with a 1/100th-second resolution in the delay time.

- **EQ mode.** The EQ Mode Knob allows you to select the EQ mode. Each EQ mode sets the Low, Mid, and High Knobs to work at different frequencies, introduces different levels of resonance, and varies the bandwidth (the amount of frequency that is cut—narrow bandwidths are more subtle, whereas wide bands may give a more aggressive change). This allows you to select with a high degree of precision which frequencies from the incoming audio are affected by the plug-in.

  The six EQ modes are:

  - Standard, which has low resonance and narrow bandwidths.
  - Wide, which has low resonance and narrow bandwidths. With this mode, the EQ bands are more widely spaced.
  - High, which has low resonance and narrow bandwidths. With this mode, the EQ bands work at higher frequency ranges.
  - Res Std, which has higher resonance and wide bandwidths.
  - Res Wide, which has higher resonance and wide bandwidths. With this mode, the EQ bands are more widely spaced.
  - Res High, which has higher resonance and wide bandwidths. With this mode, the EQ bands work at higher frequency ranges.
- **Low, Mid, and High.** The Low, Mid, and High Knobs control the amount by which the Low, Mid, and High frequency bands (set by the EQ Mode Selector) are cut.
- **Feedback.** The Feedback Knob controls the number of times a delay will repeat.
- **Mix.** The Mix Control balances the dry signal (knob turned to the left) with the delayed signal (knob turned to the right). If you are using this effect on an Aux Bus, then you will probably want to turn the knob to the right so that you can only hear the delayed signal.
- **Level.** The Level Control sets the overall output level of the unit.

Automating Stereo Delay

If you are going to automate the Stereo Delay, then here's the translation between what the knobs on its interface say and the exposed automation parameters:

- Power switch = Power
- Delay Mode = Mode

- Tempo Sync = Sync
- Time Left = Time Left
- Time Right = Time Right
- EQ Mode = Eq Mode
- Low = Eq Lo
- Mid = Eq Mid
- High = Eq Hi
- Feedback = Feedback
- Mix = Mix
- Level = Level

Tutorial 51: Introducing Spectral Transformer

The Spectral Transformer (see Figure 51.1) is a unique effect (for many different reasons), and it is also an apparently complicated effect. Instead of thinking of it as being one effect, think of it as a wrapper around four effect slots with five LFOs, and you'll be getting the right idea. Into those four slots, you can put one of seven separate Spectral Transformer processing modules. Some of these modules appear straightforward; others may not.

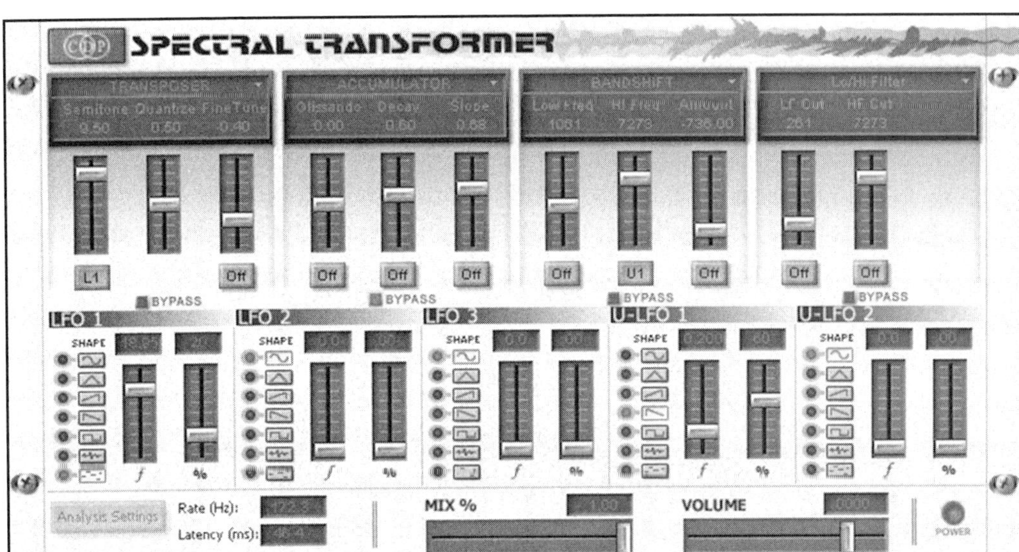

Figure 51.1 The Spectral Transformer with the Transposer, Accumulator, Bandshift, and Lo/Hi Filter modules loaded.

On their own, the modules can give some unique sounds. When you combine the modules and add some LFO modulation, you will find a whole world of new textures.

One thing to note with the Spectral Transformer is that although it can work with stereo signals, its output is mono. Indeed, you will find that the unit converts the whole channel to a mono channel, even if the Power switch is off.

The Controls in Spectral Transformer

Let's have a look at the controls in the Spectral Transformer.

Mix and Volume

Before we go any further, let's look at the Mix and Volume Controls on the bottom row of the Spectral Transformer.

The Mix Control works much as you would expect: It mixes the dry and the effected signals together. When the slider is to the left, the dry signal is heard, and when the slider is to the right, the effected signal is heard.

However, the Volume Control does not necessarily work like you might expect. Most importantly, it does not control the overall volume of the Spectral Transformer. Instead, the Volume Control works to control the internal level that is sent to the effected channel in the Spectral Transformer. This allows you to compensate for some of the effects that rob the audio signal of much of its energy.

Analysis Settings

When the Power switch is turned off (it will be grayed out), then you can access the analysis settings by clicking on the Analysis Settings button on the left-hand side. If the blue Power light is on, then you will need to switch it off to adjust the analysis settings.

Spectral Transformer takes a different approach to that adopted by many other FX plug-ins. Instead of simply processing the incoming audio signal, it addresses (overlapping) chunks of data. The size of these chunks has implications for:

- The amount of CPU required
- The latency introduced by the plug-in

There are three main options in the Analysis Settings window (see Figure 51.2):

- FFT Size
- Overlap
- Window Size

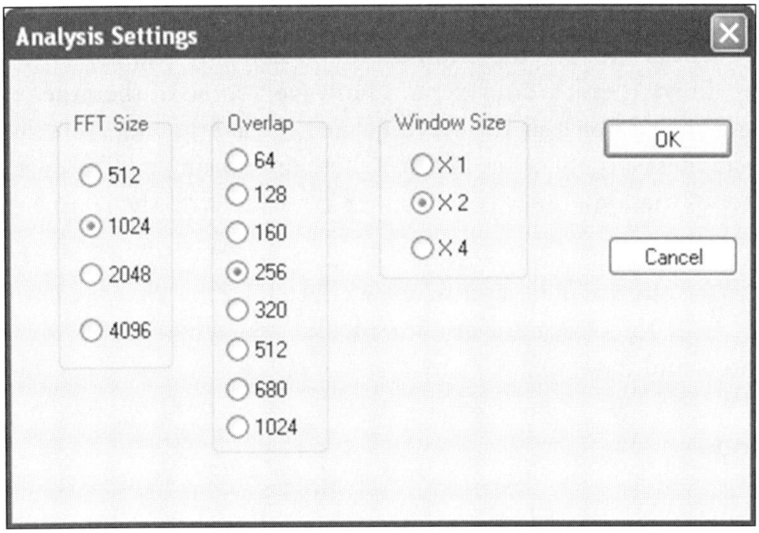

Figure 51.2 The Analysis Settings window.

The FFT Size setting sets the number of samples in the chunk of data analyzed by Spectral Transformer—with larger settings, higher quality can be achieved. The FFT Overlap setting determines the size of the FFT overlap. With lower settings, the CPU consumption will be increased; however, the increased CPU will give a quality improvement, too. The Window Size Control multiplies the FFT setting, so there is a direct correlation with the CPU consumption.

As you get to know the individual units within the Spectral Transformer, play with these analysis settings and listen closely to the results. The change in quality will be quite noticeable. You need to balance the quality (taking into account the sound you are trying to create) against CPU hit and the latency that is introduced.

As well as hearing the latency delay, you will also be able to get an indication of the processing delay from the Latency display on the bottom row of the interface (which indicates the latency in milliseconds). As you adjust the FFT Size and the Window Size settings, you will see that the latency changes significantly.

Above the Latency display, you will see a Rate (Hz) display. This indicates the CPU hit from the analysis settings.

The Effects in Spectral Transformer

There are seven effect modules in the Spectral Transformer. They all transform the sound in unique and different ways. As you will find, this is very much a creative tool and is not one for surgically fixing up your audio! Some of the modules behave largely as you would expect—for instance, the Transposer and the Voice Transposer will generally do what you would expect. However, some of the other modules (for instance, the Exaggerater and the Accumlator) behave in more unexpected ways. This unexpectedness largely arises because there are no similar FX units on the market. The effect of these modules is very much dependent on the source material that you feed into them.

The quality of the effect will be significantly affected by the analysis settings that you have chosen, so if the effect doesn't sound like you would hope, then tweak the analysis settings and try it again.

Loading Modules

There are four module slots in Spectral Transposer. When the slot is empty, the top of the slot will show –Load Effect– with a down arrow to the right. Click on the down arrow and choose the appropriate module from the drop-down menu. The selected module's name will now show.

To change the module, click on the arrow again and select the new module. To empty the slot, select (No Effect) from the drop-down.

Common Controls

Before we look at the modules, let's look at the common controls on each module. There are two:

- **Bypass button.** When this is lit, the module is engaged. Usually this reduces the CPU hit by the module; however, it doesn't always take the module totally out of the chain (so you may still get some hit).
- **LFO Selector.** Under each slider you will see a button that by default is labeled Off. When it shows as off, then that slider destination is not modulated. Click on the button, and you will be able to select one of the five LFOs as a modulation source for that destination.

Transposer

The Transposer (see Figure 51.3) changes the pitch of the incoming note. Unlike when you put a sample into a sampler, this effect will not change the length of the note.

The Transposer (along with the VOC-Transposer) is one of the effects that is particularly sensitive to the analysis settings.

Figure 51.3 The Transposer module in Spectral Transformer.

There are three sliders on the Transposer:

- **Semitone.** The Semitone Slider sets the coarse amount of detuning over a range of +/–12 semitones.
- **Quantize.** The Quantize Slider has five settings: 0.00, 0.25, 0.50, 0.75, and 1.00. These settings determine whether the Semitone Slider will have a constant pitch-shifting effect or whether it will be able to make stepped changes (for instance, changes in quarter-semitones).
- **FineTune.** The Fine Tune Control adjusts the pitch over the range of +/–1 semitone (and is not affected by the Quantize Control).

Like all of the modules, the balance between the dry and transposed audio signals is controlled by the Mix Control on the bottom row of the interface. This is influenced by the volume, which controls the level of the effected signal.

VOC-Transp (Voice Transposer)

The Voice Transposer (see Figure 51.4) is virtually identical to the Transposer; indeed, it has exactly the same controls. However, behind the scenes the two units work differently.

Any sound will have formants. *Formants* are the frequency peaks in a sound's audio spectrum. When you re-pitch a sound, the formants are re-pitched too. This will lead to a change in the sound's character.

With the Voice Transposer, the formants are not re-pitched. This aims to maintain a similar character for a sound after retuning. Sometimes the effect works, sometimes it doesn't.

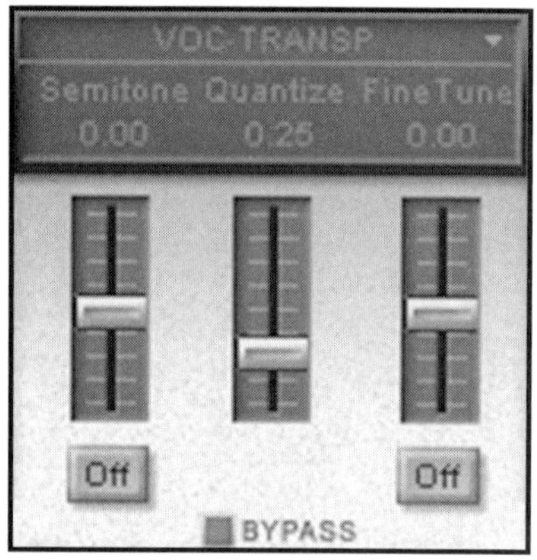

Figure 51.4 The Voice Transposer.

One side effect of the way that this module works is that the formants can be emphasized even more than they already are. If you transpose a sound and the formants are maintained, then they will be increased if some of the sound spectrum is retuned into the formants' region. Therefore, you need to take care with the Voice Transposer to ensure that you don't overload the sound spectrum and introduce distortion (unless that is the effect you are after).

Exaggerator

The Exaggerator, as you can see in Figure 51.5, has one control: Emphasis.

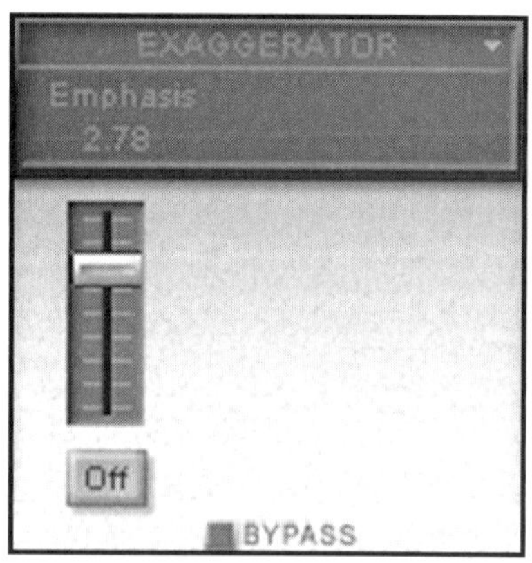

Figure 51.5 The Exaggerator.

When the Emphasis Control is set to 1.00, the Exaggerator has little effect (although, subjectively, it may thin the sound a bit).

When the Emphasis Control is set below 1.00, the sound becomes progressively thinner and brighter. By the time the control is set to 0.00, the sound has disappeared. As the Emphasis Control is set above 1.00, the sound gets muffled, losing any bite.

Accumulator

It's quite hard to describe what the Accumulator (see Figure 51.6) does. Perhaps the best way to describe it is like a reverb unit where the reverb falls or rises in pitch so you can hold a note, and then when you release it, the sound will sustain, but its pitch will rise or fall.

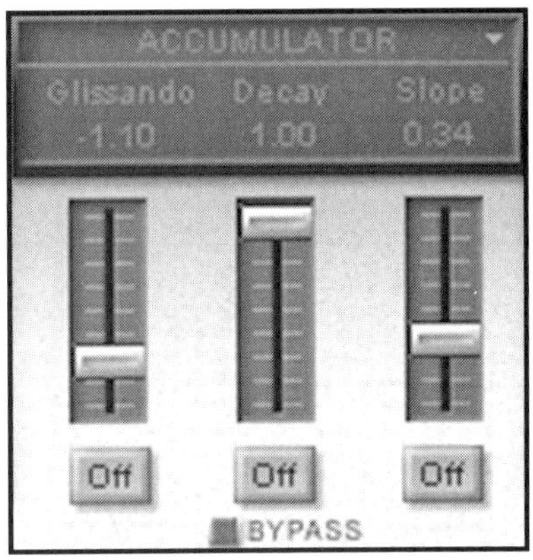

Figure 51.6 The Accumulator.

There are three controls on the Accumulator:

- **Glissando.** The Glissando Control determines the pitch to which the decaying note rises or falls. When set to 0.00, the note will just reverberate. When set above 1.00, the sound will increase in pitch as it reverberates, while if it is set below 1.00, the sound will fall in pitch. At greater settings, the pitch will rise or fall further than at smaller settings.
- **Decay.** The Decay Control sets the time over which the pitch will rise or fall. When set to 0.00, there will be no decay time, so there is no apparent effect. As the Decay Time Slider increases, the time over which the note falls or rises will increase.
- **Slope.** The Slope Control has the effect of increasing the density of the reverberation-type effect. When set to 1.00, the effect is normal. As the slider is reduced, the effect increases, giving a more metallic sound.

Lo/Hi Filter

The Lo/Hi Filter (see Figure 51.7) works somewhat like a band-pass filter, described in Tutorial 33. However, whereas with a band-pass filter you set the center cutoff frequency, with the Lo/Hi Filter you can set each side of the band separately.

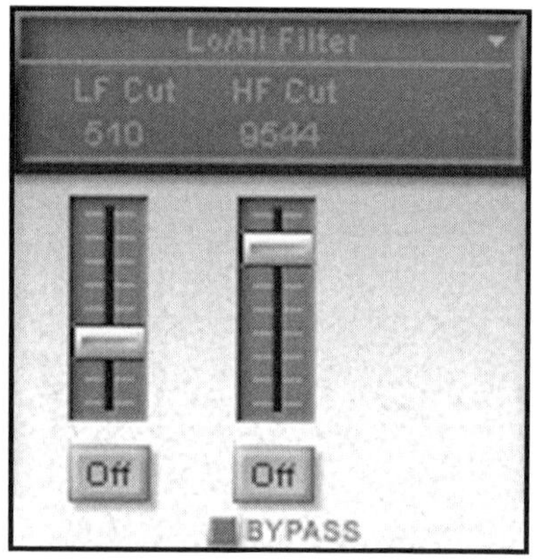

Figure 51.7 The Lo/Hi Filter.

There are two controls on the Lo/Hi Filter module:

- **LF Cut.** The LF Cut Control sets the frequency below which the sound spectrum is cut. (In other words, this control acts like a high-pass filter.)
- **HF Cut.** The HF Cut Control sets the frequency above which the sound spectrum is cut (and so the control behaves like a low-pass filter).

Trace

The Trace module (see Figure 51.8) is another single-slide module.

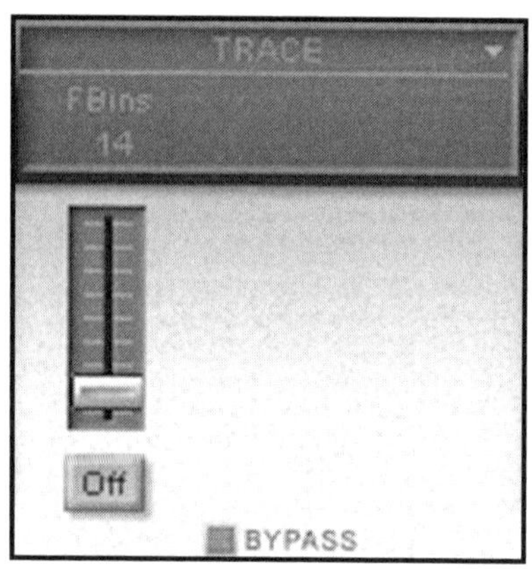

Figure 51.8 The Trace module.

The Trace module looks for the loudest frequency components in a sound and emphasizes them. When the FBins Slider is set to 100, the sound is close to the clean sound (but not exactly the same). As the FBins Slider is increased, the sound becomes brighter, and as it is decreased, the sound becomes duller.

Band Shift

The Band Shift module (see Figure 51.9) shares some features with the Lo/Hi Filter. However, it behaves in a different manner.

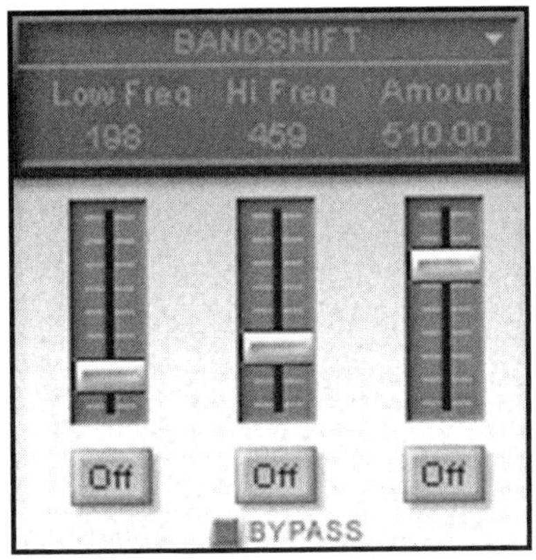

Figure 51.9 The Band Shift module.

There are three controls in the Band Shift module:

- **Low Freq.** The Low Frequency Control sets the frequency of the lower end of the band.
- **Hi Freq.** The High Frequency Control sets the frequency of the higher end of the band.
- **Amount.** The Amount Control determines the extent to which frequencies are added to or subtracted from the frequencies in the band range.

The LFOs

There are two types of LFOs in the Spectral Transformer (see Figure 51.10):

- Three regular LFOs (LFO 1, LFO 2, and LFO 3)
- Two Ultra-LFOs (U-LFO 1 and U-LFO 2)

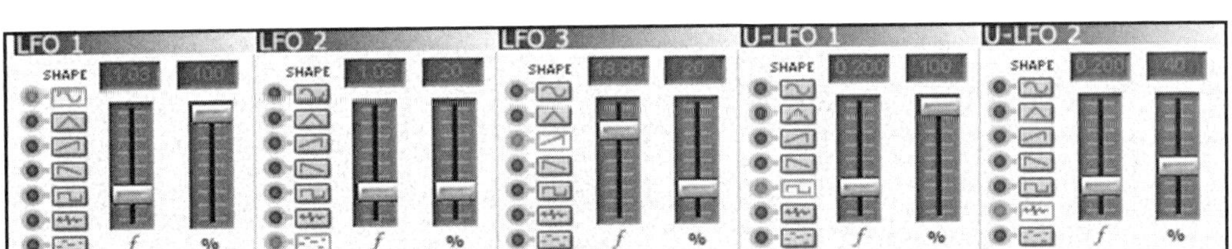

Figure 51.10 The five LFOs in the Spectral Transformer.

The key difference between the two LFO types is the frequency at which the oscillator works. In the regular LFO, the oscillator can work at a higher frequency. In the Ultra-Low Frequency Oscillators, the frequency of the oscillator can be between 0 Hz and 1 Hz.

As already mentioned, an LFO is set to modulate a destination when you click the Off button under the destination's slider and select the appropriate LFO from the drop-down menu.

The five LFOs all have three controls:

- **Wave Shape Selector.** Each LFO allows you to select one of seven wave shapes by clicking on the appropriate wave shape button. The choices of wave shape are:
  - Sine
  - Triangle
  - Rising sawtooth
  - Falling sawtooth
  - Square
  - Random, but where the level slides between successive steps
  - Random, but with each step being a separate step (with no sliding)
- **F.** The frequency of the LFO. For the Ultra-LFOs, the frequency range is set from 0 to 1 Hz. For the three main LFOs, the range is 0 to 50 Hz.
- **%.** The % Slider is the depth control—in other words, the extent to which the LFO modulates its destination.

Automating Spectral Transformer

Like the other audio FX units, Spectral Transformer can be automated. The labeling for the automation controls is slightly more straightforward than on the other units; however, since there are many more permutations of controls that can be automated, you're going to have to look at what you're doing.

The Mix, Volume, and Enable Controls do what you would expect. In addition, the labeling for the LFOs (including the U-LFOs) is clear. However, instead of exposing a labeled control for each module, Spectral Transformer exposes the controls' sliders according to their assigned slots. So you need to load a module before you automate it, and if you change a module's slot, then you will need to change the automation.

That being said, the automation is clear. For Slot 1, there is FX1 Param1, FX1 Param2, and FX1 Param3 for the three possible sliders and FX1 Bypass to bypass the unit. Analogous controls are exposed for the other three module slots.

Tutorial 52: Introducing Studioverb II

Reverb units are intended to perform a comparatively simple task: to create the audio illusion of space. On the face of it this may sound like a comparatively simple task, but in practice it is much harder. Reverberation is essentially a series of very short echoes, and it is quite easy to create a digital echo. However, simply creating a series of digital delays with a very short delay time gives a nasty metallic tone. Instead, it is necessary for the echoes to decay and for their tone to change in order to create something approaching natural reverberation.

What Studioverb Does

Studioverb II (see Figure 52.1) does what you would expect: It provides a reverberation effect. However, it is a highly controllable effect offering a wider range of tone than may be available on many reverb FX units (especially reverb units built into synthesizers). In particular, many of the controls on Studioverb's interface are intended to help create and shape a natural reverberation sound.

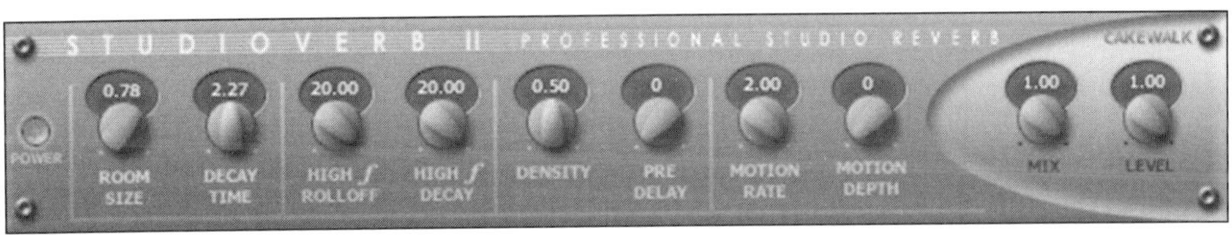

Figure 52.1 Studioverb II.

Studioverb can be set up to work for individual Instruments/Tracks or on Busses. Most typically, reverberation is set up on a Bus. By setting up a reverberation unit in this way, it can be shared between several sources. Not only does this reduce the overall CPU requirements, but it can give a more cohesive sound to the whole song.

You may also find that if you have several synthesizers that are all using their own on-board reverb, you can achieve a lower CPU hit by switching off the individual units and sending them all to a single instance of Studioverb. You may also find that this routing option increases the quality of the reverberation because Studioverb may be of a higher quality than many built-in reverb units.

The Controls in Studioverb

Let's have a look at the controls on the Studioverb.

- **Power switch.** The Power switch turns the unit on and off.
- **Room Size Knob.** The Room Size Knob controls the room that the Studioverb is modeling. Larger rooms give the impression of more acoustic space. However,

this control should be adjusted in conjunction with the other controls if you are trying to create a realistic sound.

- **Decay Time Knob.** The Decay Time Knob controls how long the reverberation sound lasts after the initial impulse. Longer decay times generally work better with larger room sizes; otherwise, you tend to get the effect of being in a tunnel (which may be the effect you are trying to achieve).
- **High F Rolloff Knob.** The High Frequency Rolloff Knob is much like a tone control for the reverberated signal. As you turn it to the left, the reverberation will become duller. Natural reverberation tends to have a duller sound, so you may find the effect becomes more unnatural as you turn the knob to the right.
- **High F Decay Knob.** The High Frequency Decay Knob controls how quickly the high-frequency elements of the reverberation decay, so this control is much like a secondary Decay Time Control. The reason for having a second control is that it allows the sound of the reverberation to be shaped to give a far more natural sound.
- **Density Knob.** The Density Knob controls the extent to which each individual echo is kept separate. By allowing the individual signals to diffuse, a more natural, less metallic reverberation can be created. As you turn the knob up, the echoes become more diffused.
- **Pre Delay.** The Pre Delay Control adds an additional delay to the audio signal before it hits the reverberation algorithm. This can give a more distinct and clearer reverberation sound. Used to extreme, it can also separate the reverb from the dry signal, giving the effect of standing in a very large room.
- **Motion Rate Knob.** Studioverb has the facility to add some spatial motion to its reverb, allowing for a more natural sound. The speed of this motion is controlled by the Motion Rate Knob.
- **Motion Depth Knob.** The extent of the motion (set by the Motion Rate Knob) is controlled by the Motion Depth Knob.
- **Mix.** The Mix Control determines the balance between clean and reverberation signals. If you are using Studioverb on a Bus, then you would want to turn this control fully to the right.
- **Level.** The Level Control sets the overall output level for the Studioverb unit.

Automating Studioverb

If you are going to automate the Studioverb, then here's the translation between what the knobs on its interface say and the exposed automation parameters:

- Power = Power.
- Room Size = Room Size. (Note that if you change this control in real time, you may get some unwanted audio effects.)
- Decay Time = Decay Time.
- High F Rolloff = High Freq Rolloff.
- High F Decay = High Freq Decay.
- Density = Density.
- Pre Delay = Pre-Delay.
- Motion Rate = Motion Rate.
- Motion Depth = Motion Depth.
- Mix = Wet/Dry Mix.
- Level = Output Level.

8 MIDI FX Units

The MIDI FX units are a range of specialized tools that are designed to process MIDI data in real time. You can insert a MIDI FX unit on any MIDI or Instrument Track—it will then process the MIDI data much like the audio FX units process audio data.

You will also see that there are many similarities between the MIDI FX units and the tools that are available from the Process menu. However, there is a key difference between the two: The Process units make destructive (permanent) edits to your MIDI data. By contrast, the MIDI FX units are processing the data in real time, so you can switch them off or change the effect of the transformation.

These MFX units are also available in SONAR. In SONAR, MIDI FX units can be applied at the Track level and at the equivalent of the Clip level. Check out *SONAR 7 Power!* (Thomson Course Technology PTR, 2007) for further details.

Tutorial 53: Common Controls on the MIDI FX Units

You can load a MIDI FX unit by clicking on the Add MFX button in a MIDI Inspector or an Instrument Inspector (see Figure 53.1). You *can* add a MIDI FX unit to an Audio Track, but it will have no effect unless it is controlling an audio FX unit that responds to MIDI generated by the MIDI FX unit.

The operation of MIDI FX units is very similar to that of the audio FX units. In particular, you will see that the preset management tools (in the Inspector and on the MFX interface) are the same as for the audio FX units. Check back to Tutorial 42 for details about how these work in practice. You can also check back to Tutorial 7 for details of how to back up your presets with the Plug-In Manager.

There are two minor differences between the operation of the audio FX and the MIDI FX:

- You can't switch a MIDI FX unit on or off in the Inspector. Instead, you can open the MFX unit's interface and click on the Power button.

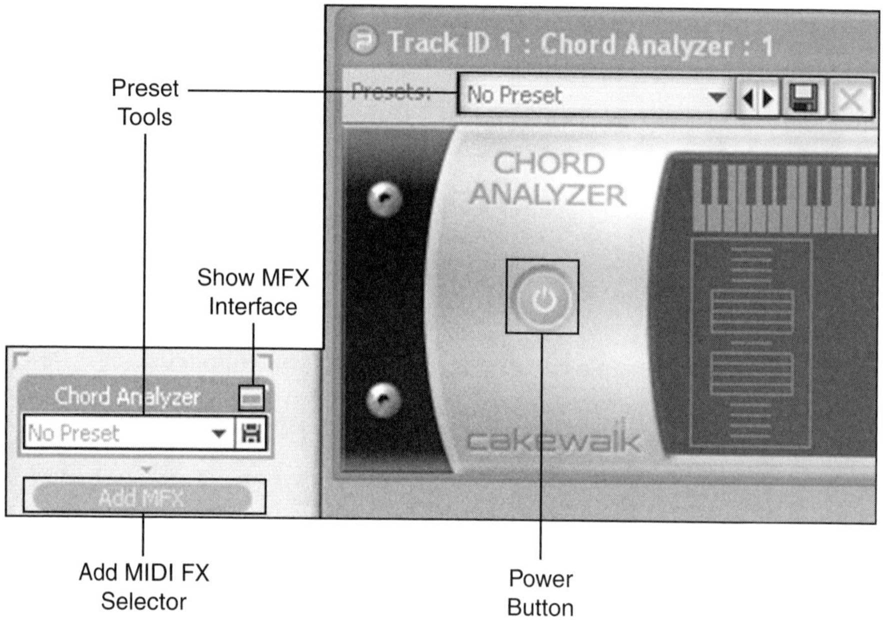

Figure 53.1 The common controls for the MIDI FX units.

- There is no twisty to open up the sliders (and there are no assignable sliders). However, as just mentioned, you can control the MFX units with automation, so this isn't a great loss.

Tutorial 54: Introducing the MFX Arpeggiator

The MFX Arpeggiator (see Figure 54.1) works in a similar manner to the Track Arpeggiator, which was discussed in Tutorial 24.

As you know from the Track Arpeggiator, an arpeggiator takes the notes of a chord and plays them individually in a preset order, thereby converting a plain chord into a rhythmic pattern. In essence, like the Track Arpeggiator, this is what the MFX Arpeggiator does. However, the MFX Arpeggiator has a few other tricks.

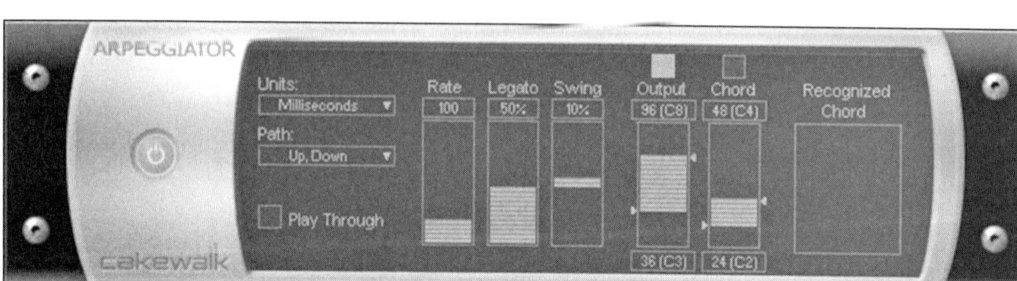

Figure 54.1 The MFX Arpeggiator.

The first box on the MFX Arpeggiator is the Units drop-down menu. From this you can select how the timing of each arpeggiated noted is calculated. The options are:

- **Notes.** When Notes are selected as the units, the speed of the arpeggio will be calculated as a division of the beat (much like a tempo-based delay and the setting on the Track Arpeggiator).
- **MIDI Ticks.** The MIDI Ticks option calculates the speed of the arpeggio in MIDI ticks.
- **Milliseconds.** The Milliseconds option calculates the speed of the arpeggio in milliseconds.

The Rate Slider controls the speed of the arpeggio. Once you have selected the units, the Rate Slider will display the appropriate units.

The Path drop-down menu selects the pattern of the arpeggiator, so for instance, you can choose whether the arpeggio notes are played in ascending order, descending order, ascending and then descending order, and so on.

The Play Through check box allows you to select whether you hear the notes you are playing in addition to the arpeggiated effect.

The Legato and Swing Controls function very much as you would expect. The Legato Control determines the duration of the arpeggiated notes, and the Swing Control introduces an element of swing/shuffle, much like the swing function that is available on a per Clip basis.

When the Output check box is selected, the arpeggiator will function. When the Output check box is not selected, the incoming data will be heard without the arpeggio effect.

When the Chord check box is selected, the Recognized Chord display will show the chord you are holding down. This function is not as sophisticated as the MFX Chord Analyzer.

Under the Output and Chord check boxes, there are two double-ended sliders. You can adjust these by clicking and dragging the top or the bottom of the central displays. Alternatively, double-click on the values shown in the boxes at the top or bottom and manually enter the correct data.

These sliders both control key ranges. The display values at the top and bottom show the top and bottom notes of the key ranges. These values are displayed as note numbers (for instance, 106) and note names (for instance, A#8).

These ranges select:

- The key range from which the notes in the arpeggio will be selected
- The key range over which the notes to be analyzed for the chord recognition function will be considered

Tutorial 55: Introducing the MFX Chord Analyzer

The MFX Chord Analyzer doesn't actually transform MIDI data. Instead, it analyzes the incoming MIDI data and then displays:

- The notes that are being played (both on the stave view to the left of the interface and on the keyboard view across the top of the interface).
- The chord that is present. As you can see from Figure 55.1, the Chord Analyzer gives several possible chord inversions for each chord. You can clear the recognized chord list by clicking on the Clear button.

Figure 55.1 The MFX Chord Analyzer.

To the bottom right of the interface is the Analysis window. You can double-click on the value to set the number of ticks over which the analysis is performed. This can be helpful for analyzing chords over faster or slower pieces.

Tutorial 56: Introducing MFX Echo Delay

The MFX Echo Delay (see Figure 56.1) is a MIDI FX echo unit. It works by echoing MIDI data—the original MIDI data and the echoed MIDI data then trigger the synthesizer to give an echo-like effect.

The delay time for the echo can be calculated in:

- Notes (in other words, as a division of the beat)
- MIDI ticks
- Milliseconds

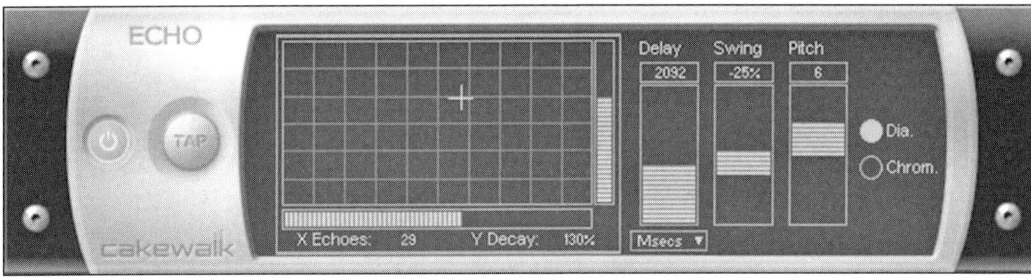

Figure 56.1 The MFX Echo Delay.

The three choices can be selected from the drop-down menu found at the bottom of the Delay Slider. Once the delay time units have been selected, the delay time can be set in two ways:

- With the Delay Slider.
- With the Tap button. You can use the Tap button to set the delay time when the delay time is calculated either in MIDI ticks or in milliseconds. To set the delay time this way, left-click on the Tap Tempo button with a steady rhythm.

Once you have set the delay time, you can set the number of echoes and how these echoes decay (and since you're working in MIDI, you can even set the echoes to increase in volume by setting the Decay Control to over 100%). To set the number of echoes and the decay, go to the grid in the middle of the interface. You will see that there are crosshairs that you can drag around. As you drag the crosshairs, the sliders across the bottom and to the right will change. You can also drag these sliders directly to move the crosshairs in only one direction.

The horizontal axis controls the number of echoes, and the vertical axis controls the decay of those echoes. Drag the crosshairs until you get the right balance of echoes and decay.

The Swing Slider shifts the echoes so that instead of them being evenly spaced, you can introduce an element of shuffle to the echoes.

The final slider is the Pitch Slider. This shifts the pitch of each echo over a range of plus or minus 12 semitones. The Dia (diatonic) and Chrom (chromatic) Selectors determine whether the pitch changes are made diatonic (and so follow a scale) or chromatic (and so each delay increases or decreases by a semitone).

Tutorial 57: Introducing the MFX MIDI Event Filter

The MFX MIDI Event Filter (see Figure 57.1) is intended to filter MIDI data. For a number of different parameters and elements of MIDI data, you can use the filter to specify what information is allowed to pass—all other information will be excluded.

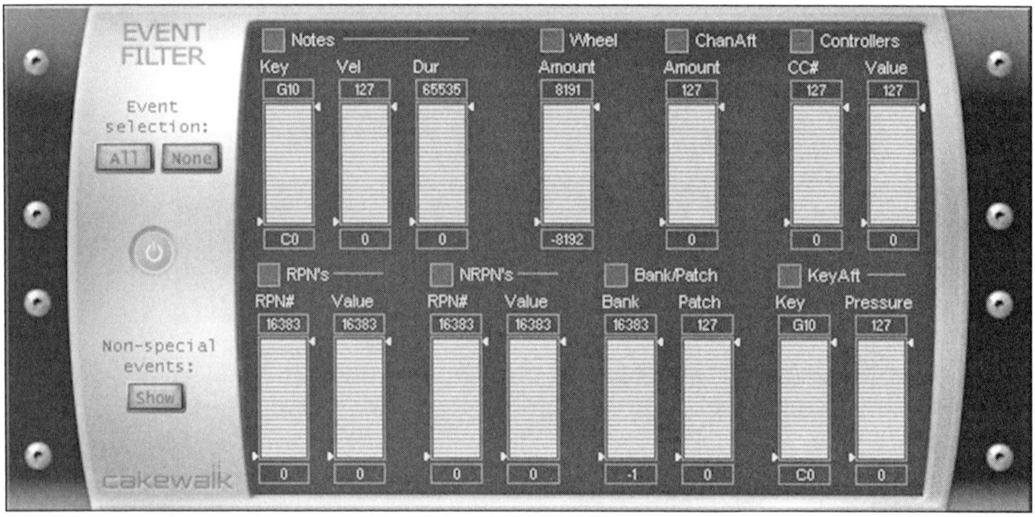

Figure 57.1 The MIDI Event Filter.

This means that if you are using a MIDI Clip that contains information that is causing an unwanted effect, you can filter the data to ensure that you get the right performance.

The MIDI Event Filter can filter eight events (in other words, remove them from your MIDI data stream):

- Notes
- Wheel—pitch-bend wheel data
- ChanAft—channel (monophonic) aftertouch data
- Controllers—MIDI CC (control code) data
- RPNs—registered parameter numbers data
- NRPNs—non registered parameter numbers data
- Bank/Patch—bank and patch information data
- KeyAft—key (polyphonic) aftertouch data

Each of these events can be switched on or off by clicking in the corresponding check box. The filter is active for that event when the yellow box shows in the check box. If the filter is inactive for that event, the check box will show black, and the filter will allow all events of that data type to pass. You can switch all of the filters on or off by using the All and None buttons under the Event Selection heading on the left-hand side.

Each slider has a minimum and a maximum value, which can be set by:

- Dragging the top or the bottom of the slider
- Double-clicking on the value displayed at the top or bottom of the slider and entering a new value

The minimum and maximum settings determine the minimum and maximum data values that the filter will pass. So, for instance, if you switch on the Notes filter and set the Key minimum to C5 and the Key maximum to C6, then only the note between C5 and C6 will be passed to the synthesizer. Any notes outside of that range will not be heard.

If you invert the minimum and maximum settings (so that the minimum is higher than the maximum), then the MFX MIDI Event Filter will pass data outside of the range. In other words, it will remove (rather than pass) data between the two settings.

You can also filter the data by MIDI channel, beat, and tick. To filter one of these three criteria, click on the Show button under the Non-Special Events heading. The Non Special Events window (see Figure 57.2) will appear, from which you can set the filter parameters.

Figure 57.2 The Non Special Events window.

Tutorial 58: Introducing MFX Quantize

MFX Quantize (see Figure 58.1) works very much like the Quantize function under the Process menu and the Input Quantize Tool and shares many similar controls. In essence, it is a "snap to grid after the event" tool. The difference with MFX

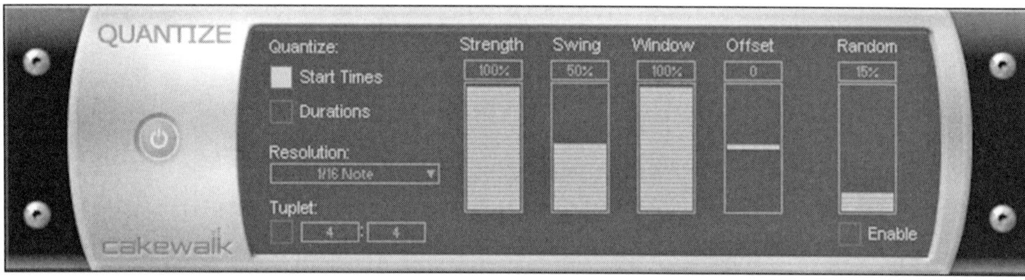

Figure 58.1 The MFX Quantize Tool.

Quantize is that with automation, you can apply different amounts of quantization to different sections of a Track.

Under the Quantize heading, you can determine how the quantize effect applies by selecting one or both of the check boxes.

- **Start Times.** When you quantize start time, you snap a note's start time to the grid selected in the Resolution section.
- **Durations.** When Durations is selected, the length of the note is quantized to the nearest multiple of the Resolution value.

The snap grid is set from the Resolution drop-down.

The Tuplet Controls (engaged by left-clicking in the check box) allow you to define the number of notes and the beats in the tuplet. Double-click on the values to enter the appropriate amounts.

There are five sliders that you can set by left-clicking and dragging the sliders or by double-clicking on the value display and entering an appropriate amount.

- **Strength.** The Strength Control determines how close to the quantization grid (set from the Resolution drop-down) a note is snapped. When this is set to 0%, there is no snapping, and when it is set to 100%, the note snaps precisely to the timing set by the grid.
- **Swing.** The Swing Control swings the beat, giving a shuffle to the quantization. At 50% there is no swing. With Swing values set below 50%, the swing will be ahead of the beat, and with Swing values set above 50%, the swing will be behind the beat.
- **Window.** The Window Control sets the area in which the MFX Quantize looks for notes to quantize. With higher settings, all notes will be quantized. At lower settings, only those notes that are slightly mistimed will be quantized.

- **Offset.** The Offset function works to subtly shift the quantize grid to which the notes are snapped. This allows you to push or pull the beat, giving a slightly more musical result than may be achieved with hard quantization.
- **Random.** The Random Control adds an element of random timing to a note. This allows you to add some humanization once the quantization has sorted the timing problems. To engage the Random Control, you also need to switch it on with the Engage button.

Tutorial 59: Introducing MFX Transpose

Although the MFX Transpose unit performs the same basic function (in other words, it transposes MIDI data), it is far more sophisticated than the Transpose function found under the Process menu.

If you look on the right-hand side of MFX Transpose (see Figure 59.1), you will see a table, headed From and To. This shows how notes are transposed by the unit. You can see the view in terms of pitch or note number by selecting the Pitch and Note options as appropriate. Notes that are slightly inset in the table are sharp.

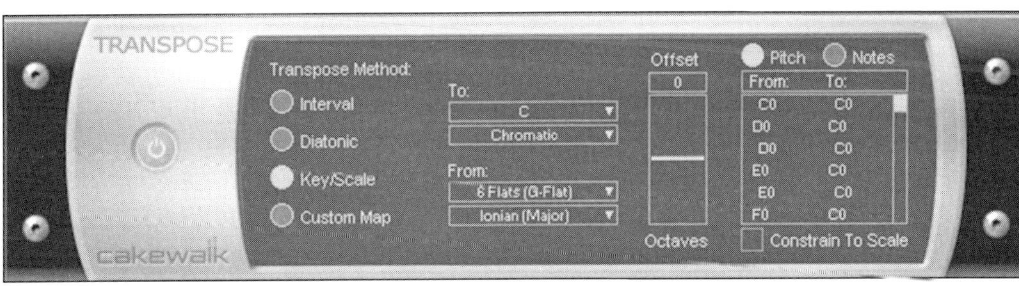

Figure 59.1 The MFX Transpose Tool.

There are four transpose methods, selected by clicking on the circle next to each option.

Interval Transposition

With Interval transposition, the MFX Transpose acts in a straightforward manner: The pitch of the MIDI data is increased or decreased in semitone steps set by the Offset Control.

Diatonic Transposition

With the Diatonic transposition option, there are two controls affecting the transposition:

- The To drop-down menu allows you select the transposition as a key to transpose to.

- The Offset Control increases or decreases the pitch of the MIDI data in scale degree. So if you are in the key of C and you increase the pitch by one scale degree, then a C will rise to a D (one tone), and an E will rise to an F (one semitone).

Key/Scale Transposition

The Key/Scale transposition mode allows you to select both a Key and a Scale mode to transpose from and to. This gives you the possibility, for instance, that you could play a minor triad, but it would sound as a major triad if you keep the same key but choose the appropriate Scale modes.

In this mode the Offset Slider works as an octave control for the transposed notes.

Custom Map

With the Custom Map you can map individual transpositions on a note-by-note basis. This might get a bit tedious, but it does offer ultimate flexibility.

To set up a Custom Map, with Custom Map selected, double-click on the values in the From/To table on the right-hand side and insert the appropriate mappings.

Tutorial 60: Introducing MFX Velocity

As you will have realized, the person who named the components in Project5 had a limited vocabulary, and hence there is VELOCITY (the sample drum tool) and MFX Velocity (the MIDI velocity editing tool, which is shown in Figure 60.1).

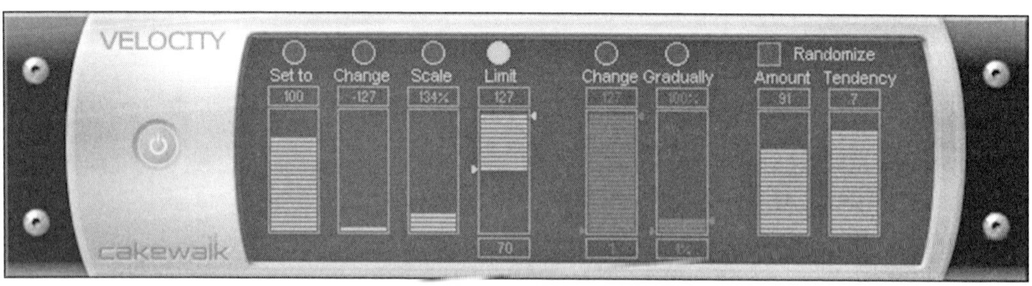

Figure 60.1 The MFX Velocity Tool.

There are four main sliders in the MFX Velocity Tool. Click on the dot above the slider if you want that slider to have effect.

- **Set To.** The Set To Slider sets all velocities to the level set by the slider.
- **Change.** The Change Slider increases or decreases the velocity amount of a note by the amount set by the Change Slider.

- **Scale.** The Scale Slider increases or decreases the velocity of a note by the percentage set by the Scale Slider.
- **Limit.** The Limit Slider sets a minimum and maximum velocity for your MIDI data.

You can also add some randomization to your velocity by clicking on the Randomize check box. When this function is engaged:

- The Amount Slider determines the range of randomization.
- The Tendency Slider determines the likelihood of randomization.

The Change Gradually options look interesting, don't they? However, unfortunately they don't work in Project5! They will work in SONAR when you process the MIDI FX offline.

Tutorial 61: Introducing MFX Synchron 32

Synchron 32 (see Figure 61.1) is the one MIDI FX unit in Project5 that is not available in SONAR, although with SONAR version 7, SONAR now has its own step sequencer. Synchron 32 is also probably the most comprehensively specified of all of the MIDI FX units included with Project5.

Synchron 32 emulates an analog-style sequencer and operates much like the Step Sequencer. However, with its ability to flick between Patterns and its (apparent) limited functionality, it provides a very fast way to make music and try ideas out.

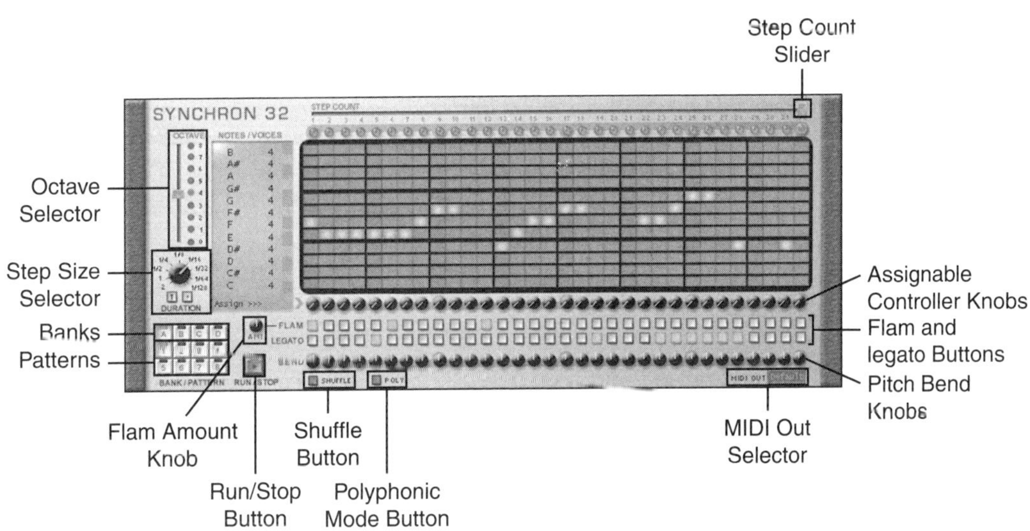

Figure 61.1 Synchron 32.

One downside of the Step Sequencer is that if you change the number of steps, it will change the step length so the notes fit the Pattern, which may have unwanted consequences. This behavior is not present in Synchron 32.

Getting Started with Synchron 32

The first thing you are likely to want to do in Synchron 32 is put in some notes. This is a good place to start; however, make sure that Synchron's MIDI output is being directed somewhere (in other words, make sure an Instrument is loaded on the MIDI Track and has some MIDI hardware attached at the other end).

While we're talking about MIDI Out, you will see that Synchron has a MIDI Out drop-down in the bottom-right corner. Most of the time I would expect you to leave it on its default setting; however, you may want to select an individual MIDI channel if you are working with a multi-timbral Instrument.

Playing Patterns

You can click on the Run/Stop button to play a Pattern. See, Synchron really is straightforward!

A red light (just below the Step Count Slider) will show which step is playing.

Entering Notes

To enter a note, left-click on the grid. To remove a note, left-click on the note you want to remove.

The grid is arranged in steps. The pitch of the note is shown in the Notes/Voices window to the left of the grid. When you enter a note, an LED will light next to the note's octave. You can change the viewed octave by dragging the Octave Selector Slider.

By default Synchron is monophonic, so you can only enter one note at each step. If you enter a note where there is an existing note, then the newly entered note will take precedence (and the old note will be automatically deleted). However, you can enter polyphonic patterns by clicking on the Polyphonic Mode button.

If you right-click on a note, you will get a pop-up menu with three options:

- Soft
- Normal
- Hard

From each of these three options, you can select the MIDI velocity of the note (which becomes the default value for the next note you enter). Notes will show up as different colors, depending on their velocity:

- Soft notes show as a sort of medium-blue color.
- Normal notes show as red.
- Hard notes show as bright/light blue.

Setting the Pattern Length and Note Durations

You can set the length of the Pattern, in terms of the number of steps, with the Step Count Slider. A green light will show above the last step. Any inactive steps will be grayed out.

You can set the step size by clicking and dragging the Step Size Selector Knob. Unlike the Step Sequencer, this has no effect on the number of steps, which is solely determined by the Step Count Slider. You can select a step length between 1/128th notes and 2 measures; in addition, you can select triplet and dotted amounts.

Shuffle

The Shuffle mode is engaged by clicking on the Shuffle button. The button turns red when Shuffle mode is engaged.

When the Shuffle mode is engaged, Synchron will follow the Shuffle setting set in the left-hand Main Controls.

More Advanced Tools

Under the grid there are two knobs and two buttons for each step.

Assignable Controller

Each knob has an assignable controller knob. You can assign one controller to be controlled by the knobs.

To select the control destination, click on the Assign label at the bottom of the Notes/Voices window and select the appropriate MIDI CC (control code).

Flam

The Flam button flams that step. When engaged for a step, the Flam button turns orange. The Flam Amount Knob sets the flam amount for all flammed steps.

Legato

When the Legato button is engaged, it will turn orange. Theoretically, it works to extend the previous step into the current step. In practice, the selected step will sustain slightly longer than would be the case if the button were not engaged.

The Legato effect will vary from synthesizer to synthesizer, depending on the synthesizer's settings. Legato works best on synthesizers with monophonic patches and some portamento.

Bend

The Bend Knob adjusts the bend (up or down) of the current step. The amount of bend is dependent on the synthesizer that is being played.

Patterns and Banks

There are four banks and eight Patterns within each bank. You create Patterns automatically whenever you write a step. You don't have to do anything to store a Pattern (other than save the whole Project). When you create Patterns, these can then be deployed within Project5 in the same way that Clips can be. (See the upcoming "Deploying Patterns through the Arrange Pane" section.)

If you right-click anywhere in the Banks/Pattern button, a pop-up menu will appear with two options:

- Clear Pattern.
- Copy Pattern To. (A list of destinations is selectable from a submenu.)

The commands from this pop-up menu apply to the currently selected Pattern, irrespective of which Bank/Pattern button you right-click on.

Deploying Patterns through the Arrange Pane

Once you have set up your Patterns, you are likely to want to put them in some sort of order. This is a simple task.

In the Arrange Pane, in the Track where Synchron is loaded, right-click to display a pop-up menu. Select Project5 Synchron 32 and choose the appropriate Pattern. A Clip will be inserted, which can be dragged, moved, cut, pasted, rolled out, or deleted. Repeat the procedure for each Synchron Pattern you want to use and arrange as normal.

Index

D

F

G

P

Q

R

S

T

U

V

W

COURSE TECHNOLO
CENGAGE Learning™
Professional • Technical • Refe

INTERACTIVE TRAINING
for serious musicians
Cool School Interactus™ CD-ROMs

If you prefer an interactive, hands-on style of learning,
check out our *CSi Starters* and *CSi Masters* on various topics including:

ACID | Pro Tools | Cubase SX | Nuendo | Digital Performer | Logic
GarageBand | Reason | SONAR | Sound Forge | Audio Plug-Ins | Waves Plug-Ins

Find these CD-ROM tutorials and more at www.courseptr.com/csi.

CSi STARTERS=Beginning to intermediate training ■ CSi MASTERS=Intermediate to advanced training

To order, visit www.courseptr.com or call 1.800.648.7450

COURSE TECHNOLOGY
CENGAGE Learning™
Professional • Technical • Reference

SHARPEN YOUR SKILLS, RELEASE YOUR SOUND
with these learning resources from Course Technology PTR

The Studio Business Book, Third Edition
ISBN: 1-59200-747-3 ■ **$34.99**

Musicianship in the Digital Age
ISBN: 1-59200-983-2 ■ **$39.99**

A Music Producer's Thoughts to Create By
ISBN: 1-59200-985-9 ■ **$29.99**

The Truth About the Music Business:
A Grassroots Business and Legal Guide
ISBN: 1-59200-763-5 ■ **$29.99**

The Art of Mixing:
A Visual Guide to Recording, Engineering, and Production, Second Edition
ISBN: 1-93114-045-6 ■ **$49.99**

Live Sound Reinforcement, Bestseller Edition:
A Comprehensive Guide to P.A. and Music Reinforcement Systems and Technology
ISBN: 1-59200-691-4 ■ **$49.99**

Networking Strategies for the New Music Business
ISBN: 1-59200-753-8 ■ **$24.99**

Course Technology PTR also publishes a complete offering of books, interactive CD-ROMs, and DVDs on music technology applications.

With various levels of instruction on leading software—

Pro Tools ■ SONAR ■ Home Studio ■ Cubase SX/SL ■ Nuendo ■ ACID
Sound Forge ■ Reason ■ Ableton Live ■ Logic ■ Digital Performer
GarageBand ■ Traktor DJ Studio ■ Soundtrack ■ and many more—

you are sure to find what you're looking for.

Visit our Web site for more information and **FREE** sample chapters.

To order, call **1.800.648.7450** or order online at **www.courseptr.com**

COURSE TECHNOLO
CENGAGE Learning
Professional • Technical • Refe

SHARPEN YOUR SKILLS, RELEASE YOUR SOUND with these Music Technology guides!

Reason 4 Ignite!
ISBN: 1-59863-478-X ■ **$24.99**

Reason 4 Power!
ISBN: 1-59863-477-1 ■ **$39.99**

Pro Tools 7 Power!, Second Edition
ISBN: 1-59863-473-9 ■ **$44.99**

Ableton Live 7 Power!
ISBN: 1-59863-522-0 ■ **$39.99**

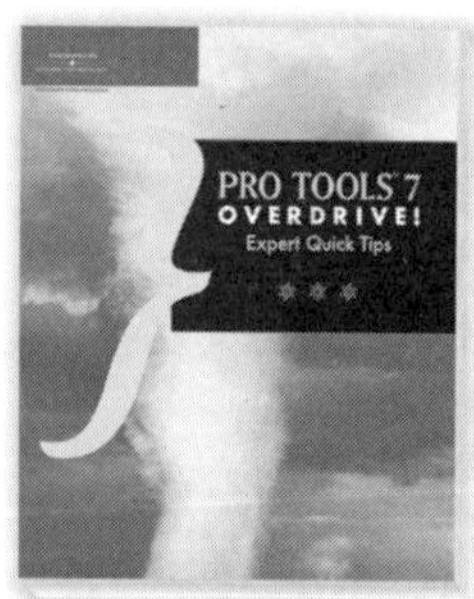

Pro Tools 7 Overdrive!
ISBN: 1-59863-008-3 ■ **$39.99**

Cubase 4 Power!
ISBN: 1-59863-002-4 ■ **$34.99**

SONAR 7 Power!
ISBN: 1-59863-442-9 ■ **$39.99**

Logic Pro 8 Power!
ISBN: 1-59863-369-4 ■ **$36.99**

Acid Pro 6 Power!
The Official Guide to Sony Acid Pro 6 Software
ISBN: 1-59200-977-8 ■ **$35.99**

Visit our Web site for more information and **FREE** sample chapters.

To order, call **1.800.648.7450** or order online at **www.courseptr.com**